Shadow Play

Shadow Play

Shadow Play

The Unsolved Murder of Robert F. Kennedy

WILLIAM KLABER
AND
PHILIP MELANSON

ST. MARTIN'S GRIFFIN

NEW YORK

www.stmartins.com

Designed by Omar Chapa

The Library of Congress Cataloging-in-Publication Data is available upon request.

ISBN 978-1-250-16661-6 (trade paperback)

Our books may be purchased in bulk for promotional, educational, or business use.
Please contact your local bookseller or the Macmillan Corporate and Premium Sales
Department at 1-800-221-7945, extension 5442, or by email at
MacmillanSpecialMarkets@macmillan.com.

First Updated Edition: April 2018

10 9 8 7 6 5 4 3 2 1

Shadow Play is dedicated to the memory of Allard K. Lowenstein and Gregory Stone.

The 2018 edition carries the added dedications to Paul Schrade, who has fought for the truth for fifty years, and to the memory of coauthor Professor Philip Melanson, who created the Robert F. Kennedy Assassination Archives at the University of Massachusetts Dartmouth.

Robert Kennedy's death, like the president's, was mourned as an extension of the evils of senseless violence . . . a whimsical fate inconveniently interfering in the workings of democracy. What is odd is not that some people thought it was all random, but that so many intelligent people refused to believe that it might be anything else. Nothing can measure more graphically how limited was the general understanding of what is possible in America.

—former New York congressman Allard Lowenstein (1977)

Contents

✳ ✳ ✳

Introduction

✳ ✳ ✳

As Robert Kennedy addressed the cheering crowd, Paul Schrade looked on with pride. An hour earlier he had been upstairs at the Ambassador Hotel, working with the senator on the details of his speech. Now he watched as Kennedy declared victory in the California primary and assumed his place as a front-runner for the Democratic presidential nomination.

When he had finished speaking, Robert Kennedy stepped off the stage into a dimly lit hallway en route to another press conference. He spotted Schrade and called out for him to follow. Kennedy then passed through a set of doors into a narrow kitchen area, where he paused to shake hands with several busboys. *Finally,* Schrade thought, *a real president.*

Just then, Paul Schrade experienced what felt like a severe electric shock. His body began to convulse, and as he fell to the floor he was certain he was being electrocuted.

When he regained consciousness a short while later, Paul Schrade felt bruises on his chest, where he had been stepped on. There was a sharper pain in his forehead, where a bullet was lodged. A short distance away Robert Kennedy lay mortally wounded.

Years later, the pain of that awakening still scarred Schrade. Sirhan Bishara Sirhan, to everyone's satisfaction, had been convicted of Robert Kennedy's murder, but Schrade was troubled because the wound in his own head made no sense, given the explanation offered for it by the Los Angeles police. When he tried to find out more, Schrade discovered that the police files were sealed. But why?

In 1974, at the urging of former New York congressman Allard Lowenstein, Paul Schrade joined a small group of citizens trying to open the secret police files. A year later he became a plaintiff in an unsuccessful lawsuit seeking to force disclosure. In the decade that followed, Schrade took the fight to Mayor Thomas Bradley and the Los Angeles Police Commission.

Finally, public pressure prevailed. In 1988 the police files in the Robert Kennedy assassination were made available for inspection by the California State Archives. Schrade and a small group of researchers (including this book's coauthor Philip Melanson) began to slowly sift through the more than fifty thousand pages of released documents.

On April 2, 1992, almost twenty-four years after the assassination, a silver-haired Paul Schrade, accompanied by several colleagues, walked down the polished corridors of the Los Angeles County Courthouse pulling a small wagon carrying five heavy boxes. In the boxes were copies of a "request," a formal petition asking the Los Angeles County Grand Jury to appoint a special prosecutor to investigate the Los Angeles Police Department for "willful and corrupt misconduct" in its investigation of the murder of Robert Kennedy. Accompanying the request were eight hundred pages of exhibits backing up claims of the LAPD's "destruction of evidence, falsification of evidence, and coercion of witnesses."

In addition to that of Schrade, the petition bore the signatures of over fifty prominent citizens, including historian Arthur Schlesinger, Jr., former RFK press secretary Frank Mankiewicz, former Watergate prosecutor Sam Dash, author Norman Mailer, farm workers' leader Cesar Chavez, and Harvard law professor Gary Bellow.

The request was also signed by several men who played a direct role in the events surrounding the assassination. One of these was William Bailey, who on the night of the murder was an agent for the FBI. Bailey inspected the crime scene and interviewed witnesses a few hours after the shooting. Over time he became convinced that the official version of the murder was a fabrication.

William Bailey taught criminal justice at a small college in New Jersey. Each year he put on a mock trial of Sirhan in which the class sat as jury. As Bailey explained, his trial of Sirhan was a tutorial in the suspension of judgment. "I want to show them that in criminal investigations, things are not always what they seem."

Dr. Cyril Wecht also signed the grand jury petition. Wecht is a lawyer, a medical doctor, and a former president of the American Academy of Forensic Sciences. In the days following the death of Robert Kennedy, Wecht worked with Los Angeles County coroner Dr. Thomas Noguchi on the autopsy report. What he discovered alarmed him. To Wecht, the evidence strongly suggested that Sirhan Sirhan was not the source of the bullets that struck Robert Kennedy. "This case has never been as simple as it looked," he would say. "Forensically speaking, it's a puzzle."

But the assassination of Robert Kennedy was not regarded as a puzzle by those who investigated the crime. The case against Sirhan Sirhan in their minds could hardly have been more open and shut. Robert Kennedy was shot and killed, and Sirhan Sirhan, firing a pistol, was apprehended only a few feet away. In time, the accused assassin would admit to the crime, offer a motive, and assert that he acted alone—a prosecutor's dream. Rumors of conspiracy seemed, for once, not only unfounded but easily refuted.

But this seemingly most apparent of political assassinations in the 1960s turns out to be, in many ways, the most complicated; certainly, the most bizarre. For example, while the accused assassin insisted he acted alone, numerous witnesses saw him being led to the crime by a beautiful woman, who shortly thereafter was seen running from the hotel laughing. She then vanished. More disturbing, ballistic evidence collected by the police strongly suggested that a second gun was fired during the murder and that Sirhan Sirhan may not have shot Robert Kennedy at all. Some of the most important pieces of this evidence also vanished. Most strange, despite his admission of guilt, the confessed assassin seemed genuinely to have no memory of the crime. What did this mean? Normally, one would expect a murder trial to sort through these circumstances to separate fact from fiction. Not in this case.

The trial of Sirhan Sirhan was, from the beginning, a self-conscious event. "We are aware that this is not just another criminal matter," said Los Angeles district attorney Evelle Younger. "The whole world is watching." So many newsmen, in fact, attended the trial, that an overflow courtroom had to be outfitted with video monitors, and those in attendance spoke about the trial in reverential terms. "A classic of criminal jurisprudence," intoned *Time* magazine. Anticipating, incorrectly, a parallel proceeding against James Earl Ray, *The New York Times* said, "both will represent trials of the American system of justice as much as trials of the men in the dock."

In the late 1960s, the image of legal authority in America badly needed affirmation. The country, it seemed, was fracturing along racial and generational lines. Each week hundreds of young men died in an unpopular Asian war, riots were increasingly common on university campuses and in the streets of the nation's cities, and political murders were occurring with stunning frequency.

For its part, the government appeared powerless to halt the political violence, and the judicial system seemed unable to deal with these events after the fact. Lee Oswald, the accused assassin of President John Kennedy, forcefully asserted during his brief public moment that he was a patsy. He was then shot to death on TV by a local hoodlum. James Earl Ray, the accused assassin of Dr. Martin Luther King, while suggesting there was more to the story and perhaps in fear for his life, stopped the legal process by entering a plea of guilty. But a week later he petitioned Judge Preston Battle to withdraw that plea and go to trial. Judge Battle was about to rule on Ray's motion when he was found dead at his desk, and James Earl Ray, still asking for a trial, was hustled off the stage.

So it fell to the prosecutors and defenders of Sirhan Sirhan to reassert the authority and integrity of American justice. Those involved understood and accepted this mandate, but in so doing they became careless with the truth. Each act of neglect, each deceit in pursuit of an adjudicated truth, seemed small given the assumed certainty of the defendant's guilt and the greater good of the nation's honor. But the negligence, secrecy, and deceit accumulated and ultimately gave cover to those who were guilty of things more serious than small lies. Destruction of evidence, falsification of evidence, coercion of witnesses—these were criminal acts that struck at the heart of American democracy.

Shadow Play

ONE

The Embassy Room

✳ ✳ ✳

JOHN HOWARD STEPPED through the door of the interrogation room and stared at the man seated in the chair. The prisoner, now showered, looked considerably better than he had before. Still, nobody knew his name.

An hour earlier Howard had told the prisoner, who had not been saying anything, that he had the right to remain silent. The slightly built, dark young man responded politely that he wished to "abide" by that "admonishment." Well, that settled one thing: he could speak English. The deputy district attorney then offered a card with his telephone number: "If you want to talk to someone."

Upon learning that the husky man in a suit was with the Los Angeles County DA's Office, the prisoner brightened and made his first non-perfunctory utterance since being in custody.

"Remember Kirschke?"

"I've known Jack for a long time," answered a surprised Howard. "Why? Why did you ask that?"

"Interested," the young man replied.

When John Howard got word a little later that the prisoner was asking to speak with him, he had forgotten all about Jack Kirschke. But the mysterious young man had not. To Howard's chagrin, that is what he wanted to talk about.

"Yeah, we were talking about Kirschke," said Howard, thinking that if they could get going about one thing it might lead to something else. "How come you followed that?"

"No, I didn't follow it. I was hoping you'd clue me in on it, brief me on it, you might say."

"It was a tough lawsuit. You'd have to know Jack. He was a deputy. I worked with him."

"No, I mean—I mean the substance of the case."

Jack Kirschke, like Howard, had been a deputy district attorney in Los Angeles. Several years earlier, he had been charged with the bedroom murder of his wife and her lover. The story made headlines for months.

"The substance," Howard found himself saying, "actually was whether or not he was the guy that—there is no question his wife and a friend of hers got shot. There is no question about that. The question was who did it."

But the prisoner wanted to talk about things more subtle than guilt or innocence: Had Jack Kirschke sown the seeds of his own destruction? In prosecuting others, did he feel he was above the law?

Suddenly the absurdity of the situation overwhelmed John Howard. Only hours before, the unidentified man in front of him had gunned down a United States senator, a presidential candidate. Now the two of them were having a friendly philosophical discussion. Either this guy was one cool customer or something was wrong. Howard's instincts took over.

"Do you know where we are now?" he asked. "I've told you you've been booked."

"I don't know," replied the prisoner.

"You are in custody. You've been booked. You understand what I've been—"

"I have been before a magistrate, have I or have I not?"

"No, you have not. You will be taken before a magistrate as soon as possible . . . You're downtown Los Angeles in the central jail. Now, when I say this, if you know, you know—I'm not saying this because *I* don't know. We're not communicating very well up to now, but you are downtown Los Angeles, okay? This is the main jail for the L.A. Police Department. You'll be booked into a cell. . . . Do you understand that? Do you understand where you are?"[1]

Like the prisoner, John Howard had not had any sleep that night. Normally on a Tuesday he would have been home in bed early, but this was primary night in California. Howard had been out at the Plush Horse Inn in Redondo Beach, campaign headquarters for his friend Lynne Frantz, who was running, unsuccessfully, for Congress in the Seventeenth District.

Political gatherings were happening all over Los Angeles. There were three in the Ambassador Hotel alone, the largest of these in support of the presidential campaign of Robert Kennedy.

June 4, 1968, was arguably the most important day in the political career of the young senator from New York. A week earlier, in losing the Oregon presidential primary to Senator Eugene McCarthy, he became the first Kennedy to be defeated in an election of any kind. California, however, was the big test. The winner would take its 174 delegates into the Chicago Democratic convention, now only weeks away.

Even with a victory in California, Robert Kennedy would still trail Vice President Hubert Humphrey in the crucial delegate count. But the momentum gained would be impressive, and there were many who thought

Kennedy would swoop down upon the Humphrey delegates like a cattle rustler. Kennedy was a proven master at managing a convention floor, and there were still favors owed to the family that could be called in. In addition, Kennedy could leverage the feeling within the party that he was the man best suited to defeat Richard Nixon in the general election, as his brother had eight years before. But for any of this to happen, Robert Kennedy had to win in California.

As the first results of the evening came in, Senator McCarthy took the lead. But the vote from Los Angeles County, where Kennedy expected to do well, was locked up in an electronic purgatory—something had gone wrong with the new computer vote-counting system. Eager for a resolution, CBS projected a win for Kennedy just after 9 P.M. A little later, NBC did the same. But the vote from Los Angeles was still not in, and McCarthy, despite the network predictions, was leading in the vote that was.

In the Royal Suite on the fifth floor of the Ambassador, Robert Kennedy huddled with what amounted to his shadow cabinet. Pierre Salinger, Richard Goodwin, Ted Sorensen, Fred Dutton, Frank Mankiewicz, Larry O'Brien—all these men had worked closely with President Kennedy. Also nearby were supporters such as United Farm Workers leader Dolores Huerta, pro-football lineman Roosevelt Grier, Olympic decathlon champion Rafer Johnson, and labor activist Paul Schrade. These were friends the senator had made on his own and, in a sense, they represented the new energy that was igniting the campaign.

Downstairs in the Embassy Room more than eighteen hundred jubilant campaign workers and admirers filled the hall beyond capacity. The Secret Service, however, was not there: they would protect presidential candidates only after the events of this night. Also absent were the Los Angeles police, even though three political functions were going on with thousands of participants. Safety and order depended on less than a score of hotel security personnel and hired guards from the Ace Guard Service.

By 11:30 a Kennedy victory seemed certain. Aides begged the candidate to move quickly to salvage some small portion of the national TV audience that could have been his only two hours earlier. As Kennedy prepared to go downstairs, he paced back and forth rehearsing his remarks and the list of people he would thank. On a nearby couch his wife, Ethel, rested, three months pregnant with their eleventh child. Kennedy asked if she was ready. Ethel rose from the couch, and the two of them headed toward the service elevator that would take them to the kitchen on the second floor. Once there, Kennedy flagged down a waiter, popped an olive into his mouth, and then made a triumphant entrance onto the ballroom stage.

The night before, in San Diego, Robert Kennedy had nearly collapsed while making his final speech. The campaign had left him physically and emotionally drained. Now, in victory before his followers, he seemed refreshed. He thanked by name many of those who had helped him in California. Then, feeling a little giddy, he also thanked his dog Freckles, "who has been maligned"; jokingly attacked his brother-in-law Stephen Smith for being "ruthless"; and, to great applause, invoked Don Drysdale's sixth straight shutout as though he had been watching the Los Angeles Dodger pitch that evening. When the cheering died down, Kennedy spoke about healing a divided country.

"What I think is quite clear is that we can work together [to overcome] the division, the violence, the disenchantment with our society, the division . . . between black and white, between the poor and the more affluent or between age groups or over the war in Vietnam. . . . We are a great country, an unselfish country and a compassionate country. And I intend to make that my basis for running. . . ."

Kennedy's words were engulfed by cheers. After a long wait, his supporters were finally getting satisfaction.

"What I think all of the primaries have indicated," he continued, ". . . [is that] the people in the United States want a change. . . . The country wants to move in a different direction. We want to deal with our own problems within our own country and we want peace in Vietnam."

In ending his remarks Kennedy made a playful swipe at an old political enemy. "Mayor Yorty has just sent me a message that we've been here too long already. So my thanks to all of you and on to Chicago and let's win there."

Once again, the room erupted. "We want Bobby! We want Bobby!"

As Kennedy stepped away from the podium he seemed to be heading toward the campaign workers who had formed an escort phalanx off the right front of the stage. "This way, Senator," said someone in his entourage, and Kennedy moved instead to the back of the stage and toward the food-preparation area, which has become known as the pantry—the route that would take him to a scheduled press conference in the Colonial Room. It was 12:15 A.M.

Bill Barry, the ex-FBI man who functioned as Kennedy's bodyguard, attempted to help Ethel down from the stage.

"I'm all right," she said. "Stay with the senator."

Barry left her and tried to catch up. He pushed his way through the crowd, but he was too late to assume his usual position in front of Kennedy, who was being led down the narrow hallway behind the stage by hotel maître d' Karl Uecker.

As Kennedy passed through the doorway that led into the pantry, he was joined by twenty-six-year-old security guard Thane Eugene Cesar. Cesar wore the uniform of Ace Guard Service and had a holstered revolver on his hip. He took hold of the senator's right arm at the elbow and moved along with him.

The room was crowded and a bit chaotic as Kennedy and his entourage made their way through. The splicing of events filmed before the shooting and the chaos captured afterward has led many people to believe that they saw the murder replayed on television, but all the television cameras were shut down as they passed from the dramatic speech to the upcoming press conference.

By official count there were seventy-seven persons in the pantry when Robert Kennedy was shot. But it was not as though the senator were onstage with a roomful of people looking on. It would be more useful to imagine seventy-seven people stuffed into a subway car. Taller people see more than shorter people, but even their views are obstructed. One of the tallest men in the pantry was Jesse Unruh, the powerful speaker of the California legislature. When asked if he had seen Kennedy fall, Unruh said, "I would not say he was in my view, but I could tell approximately where he was. There were several larger people behind him, including Paul Schrade. I saw glimpses of him."[2]

The sound in the room was also a confusing montage. There were greetings and cheers, balloons popping, some pushing, more cheers, some more popping sounds, a few screams, cheers, cursing, some shoving, people falling down, screams, more shoving, and then general chaos. Most people in the room saw only bits and pieces of things that happened right around them. What we know of the event is a mosaic, derived from their accounts and the physical evidence.

As Kennedy made his way through the pantry, he stopped to shake hands with Jesus Perez and Juan Romero, busboys at the hotel. Karl Uecker, the maître d', who had been leading the procession, was eager to keep moving. "Let's go, Senator," he said in his thick German accent. He took the senator's arm and began to lead him forward again.

Lisa Urso, a San Diego high school student, stood near the pantry exit. As Kennedy moved toward her, she was shoved from behind. A young man considerably shorter than she stepped in front of her and moved to her right.

"I thought it was gonna be a waiter and it looked like he was trying to get in there and shake the senator's hand," she recalled.[3] But then the young man's arm made an odd movement across his body, and Urso sensed something was wrong. Vincent DiPierro, a waiter at the Ambassador, saw the short dark man push past Urso and advance on Kennedy. The man had a strange smile on his face. TV producer Richard Lubic thought he heard the man say, "You son of a bitch!" Lisa Urso saw a flash from the gun. She saw Paul Schrade fall, then Robert Kennedy.

Karl Uecker also saw the gun. He felt it fire very close to his face—twice.

After the second shot, Uecker said he grabbed the man's gun hand and slammed it onto the steam table—leftward and downward, away from Kennedy. Several men, including Roosevelt Grier and Rafer Johnson, joined the struggle for the weapon, but after a short pause it began firing again. Down went seventeen-year-old Irwin Stroll, shot in the leg. Down went TV director William Weisel, hit in the stomach. Several more shots. Reporter Ira Goldstein was wounded in the hip, and artist Elizabeth Evans was struck in the head.

Radio reporter Andrew West turned on his tape recorder and began to narrate over the screams and the sound of gunfire:

"Senator Kennedy has been shot. Is that possible? It is possible, ladies and gentlemen. It is possible. He has. Not only Senator Kennedy but . . . Oh, my God! Senator Kennedy has been shot and another man, a Kennedy campaign manager, and possibly shot in the head."

The struggle for the gun went on and on.

"Rafer Johnson has ahold of the man who apparently fired the shot. . . . He has fired the shot. He still has the gun. . . . Be careful! Get the gun! Get the gun! Get the gun! Get away from the barrel. Get away from the barrel, man. Look out for the gun!"

As soon as he heard shots fired, writer George Plimpton joined the struggle. Just inches from the assailant's face, Plimpton noticed something odd. The man with the gun had "enormously peaceful eyes," an almost beatific expression on his face. "In the middle of a hurricane of sound and feeling," Plimpton recalled, "he seemed peaceful."[4]

Peaceful or not, the small man had great strength. It took over forty seconds to separate him from the gun. Once disarmed, the man began to feel the kicks and punches of angry onlookers. "Keep people away from him!" yelled Andrew West. "We don't want another Oswald."

Jesse Unruh tried to stop people from attacking the gunman. The physically imposing politician started pulling people away. Finally he jumped up onto a steam table to try and calm the situation. "We don't want another Dallas," he shouted. "If the system works at all, we're going to try this one."

Robert Kennedy lay on his back, limbs spread, bleeding from behind the ear. Juan Romero knelt down beside the fallen senator. "Come on, Mr. Kennedy," he said. "You can make it." Young Daniel Curtin took rosary beads from his pocket and handed them to Romero. The busboy wrapped them in Kennedy's left hand.

"Is everybody all right?" Kennedy asked in a barely audible voice.

Dr. Stanley Abo, a Los Angeles radiologist, was the first medical doctor to reach Robert Kennedy. He put his ear to the senator's chest and heard very shallow breathing. He took a pulse. Abo then stuck a finger into Kennedy's head wound to relieve the pressure that had built up. The wound bled profusely. "You're doing good," the doctor told Kennedy. "The ambulance is on the way."

Ethel Kennedy arrived. She begged, with little effect, for the crowd and newsmen to move away. Then she began to comfort her husband. Robert Kennedy was aware of her presence.

"Oh, Ethel, Ethel," he said softly.

Police Sergeant Paul Sharaga had just stopped to buy cigarettes. As he climbed back into his patrol car he heard a radio call about a shooting at 3400 Wilshire. Sharaga knew that was the Ambassador; he was a block away. He swung his car around and drove quickly to the rear of the hotel.

As Sharaga moved through the parking lot he encountered a couple in visible anguish. The woman, in her late fifties, told him that they had been near the exit stairs when a young woman and man ran past shouting gleefully, "We shot him! We shot him!" In response to the question "Who did you shoot?" the woman, who was wearing a polka-dot dress, replied, "Senator Kennedy. We shot him! We killed him!" The young woman and her companion then disappeared into the parking lot, laughing as they went.

Sharaga immediately went back to his car and put out an all-points bulletin on the two reported suspects.

While Sergeant Sharaga was in the parking lot behind the Ambassador, LAPD patrolmen Travis White and Arthur Placencia arrived at the hotel's front entrance. Both were rookies. White had been active on the force for about a year, Placencia for two weeks. The officers jumped out of their squad car and followed the motions of various bystanders who were shouting, "He's up here. He's up here."

White and Placencia entered the hotel pantry and saw a pile of bodies at the far end of the room. Several large men had a small man pinned to a table and were warding off people who were trying to get at him. "Kill the bastard! Kill him!" Placencia heard someone shout.

Another police officer who had just rushed in, Randolph Adair, noticed something odd about the man being held. "The guy was real confused," recalled Adair. "He had a blank, glassed-over look on his face—like he wasn't in complete control of his mind."[5]

The officers then began to peel people away, trying to take the man into custody. They had to pry the man away from Jesse Unruh. "I charge you with responsibility for this man," Unruh ordered. Neither White nor Placencia recognized Unruh, but they handcuffed the prisoner and then, with Unruh escorting them, made their way out into the lobby and then down to the first floor, where the patrol car was waiting. The crowd was ugly and threatening.

When they got to the car, Placencia stuffed the prisoner into the back seat, then sat next to him. Unruh jumped into the front seat with Officer White. Normally, any unauthorized person would have been ejected immediately, but there wasn't time. People were pounding on the vehicle. White turned on the siren and gunned the engine. The crowd stepped back and the police car pulled away.

Officer Placencia took out his handbook. "You have a right to remain silent," he said, reading with his flashlight, "and if you give up the right, anything you say can and will be used against you." Placencia asked the dazed-looking prisoner if he understood. No reply. The officer read the prisoner his rights a second time, then again asked the suspect his name. No reply.

Placencia then turned his attention to the man in the front of the car. "Who are you?"

"Jesse Unruh."

"Oh," said Placencia, wondering why one of the most powerful men in California was riding in his patrol car. "Who'd he shoot?"

"Bobby Kennedy."

As Officers White and Placencia were escorting their prisoner from the hotel, two medical attendants arrived in the pantry. They lifted Robert Kennedy onto a stretcher and rolled him outside and into an ambulance. Ethel Kennedy and several close aides rode with the wounded senator, and the ambulance quickly covered the twenty-some blocks to the Central Receiving Hospital, where treatment room 2 was being prepared.

According to Dr. Faustin Bazilauskas, Robert Kennedy arrived "lifeless"—no blood pressure, no pulse. Bazilauskas forcefully massaged Kennedy's heart by pressing on his chest while Nurse Supervisor Bette Eby readied a heart-lung machine. In three minutes Kennedy was hooked up. He was then given a shot of Adrenalin, and the senator's breathing and heartbeat began again.

Once his condition was stabilized, Nurse Eby inspected the senator. Behind the ear she saw a gunshot wound with powder burns around it. It was obvious the wound was severe, and the nurse suggested an immediate transfer to nearby Good Samaritan Hospital, where Kennedy could receive the attention of a neurosurgeon. Calls were made and the transfer took place quickly.

When Robert Kennedy was wheeled into Good Samaritan at 1 A.M., he came under the care of Dr. Henry Cuneo, an experienced brain surgeon. Cuneo examined the senator and found two gunshot wounds to the armpit area and another to the back of the head behind the ear. As the other attending doctors continued to prepare Kennedy for the expected surgery, Dr. Cuneo walked over to Ethel Kennedy.

"Extremely critical," he told her bluntly. Then to give her what little good news there was, he added, "His blood pressure has gone down, his heart is beating strongly, and his color is good."

Despite the doctor's attempt to brighten the news, Ethel Kennedy understood exactly what he had said. She almost fainted and then got ahold of herself. She was offered a sedative. "No, thank you," she replied.

A little before three in the morning Robert Kennedy's press secretary, Frank Mankiewicz, held a news conference from the hood of a police car in front of Good Samaritan. Mankiewicz told reporters that Robert Kennedy was about to undergo surgery for a bullet lodged in his brain. "His breathing is good; his heart is good," said Mankiewicz. "He's unconscious and the doctors describe his condition as very critical."

Officer Frank Foster sat in Parker Center interrogation room 1, facing the prisoner. The two men were alone, and the similarity in their ages seemed to create a small bond of trust. The prisoner asked Foster if he had children.

"I have two," Foster replied, "a little girl and a little boy. . . . The little girl, she's three; she was three in February. The boy, he'll be—let's see—eight months old the ninth of this month. He crawls around a lot, gets into everything. He sure wants to move about."

"You know," said the prisoner, "it—it happens about that time, you know—you know, that—that age."

"I think—I think in another month he'll probably—"

"Start," offered the prisoner.

"Yeah."

"Creeping."

"Of course, he's pretty big for his age," Foster continued. "He's kind of heavy, but he gets around pretty good."

"How much did he weigh when he was born?" the prisoner inquired.

"Well, let's see. I think it was eight pounds something . . . but afterward he grew like a little weed—he'd gained and gained, and now his hands—fantastic. They're big and strong. He gets ahold of something, you can hardly pull him off, you know—"

"About eight months or so," agreed the prisoner, "he will still be wanting to try to walk, but as soon as maybe the third month, he—his hands,
you know, the grip."

"Yeah, fantastic," said Foster.

"Wonderful, little kids," replied the prisoner.[6]

Down the hall in room 318, Sergeants Frank Patchett and Adolph Melendres were interviewing Vincent DiPierro. DiPierro was a college student
employed part-time as a waiter at the Ambassador, where his father,
Angelo, was one of the maître d's. DiPierro told the police that he had
entered the hotel pantry closely behind Senator Kennedy. As Kennedy
stopped to shake hands with busboys Perez and Romero, DiPierro's eye
had been caught by a young man hanging on to a tray stand. He watched
as the young man moved toward Kennedy as if to shake his hand. Then
he saw the man pull a revolver and fire; blood spattered DiPierro's eye-
glasses, and Kennedy aide Paul Schrade fell against him.

Because his account of the murder was clear and detailed, and because
he was watching the assailant before the shooting began, Vincent DiPierro
was perhaps the best eyewitness the police now had. There was only one
problem: DiPierro had seen the assailant with an attractive woman. Sergeant Patchett asked the young man what made him think that the girl
was with Sirhan.

"Well, she was following him," answered DiPierro. ". . . She was holding on to the other end of the tray table and she—like—it looked like she
was almost holding him."

"Did you see him get off the tray stand?"

"Yes, I did."

"And then he walked toward the senator?"

"Yes."

"This girl—"

"She stayed there."

"At the tray stand?"

"Right. I glanced over once in a while. She was good-looking, so I
looked at her."

Patchett, perhaps not entirely convinced that DiPierro understood the
seriousness of what he was saying, asked once again, "What is in your mind
that makes you think they were together?"

At that point deputy district attorney John Howard, who had just come
in from interviewing the assailant, broke into the conversation. "Did you
see him speak to her?"

"He turned as though he did say something."

"Did she move her mouth like she was speaking to him?"

"No, she just smiled."

"And would it seem to you that she smiled at something that had been said?"

"Yeah."

DiPierro was again asked to describe the girl. She was "very good-looking," he said almost apologetically. She "wore a white dress with black or purple polka dots"; her hair was brown, and she had a "pudgy" nose.

"Okay," said Patchett, looking to conclude. "Just to sum this up, what's the thing that sticks out in your mind?"

"The stupid smile on his face."

"Smile on his face?"

"It was kind of like an envious smile, like, ah, you know, villainous. I don't know how to describe it."[7]

Back over at Rampart Station the police were interviewing another witness, who, like DiPierro, reported the movements of a mysterious woman.

Sandra Serrano was a twenty-year-old keypunch operator who had cochaired the Youth for Kennedy Committee in the Pasadena-Altadena area. She had come to the Ambassador Hotel with several of her friends. While waiting for the final election results, she sought relief from the crowded ballroom and went outside to sit on an exit stairway. At about 12:15, according to Serrano, a man and a woman came running down the stairs. The woman seemed exuberant, and she and Serrano had a bizarre exchange of words.

"We shot him! We shot him!" the woman exclaimed.

"Who did you shoot?" asked Serrano.

"Senator Kennedy," answered the woman, who then ran off laughing.

In shock, Serrano went inside, but everyone seemed jubilant and relaxed. But then word began to spread. Soon Serrano found herself being interviewed by NBC correspondent Sander Vanocur on national television. A stunned, bleary-eyed audience heard a dramatic account given by a shaken but coherent young woman:

"This girl came running down the stairs in the back, came running down the stairs and said, 'We shot him. We shot him.' And I said, 'Who did you shoot?' and she said, 'We shot Senator Kennedy.' . . . She was Caucasian. She had on a white dress with polka dots. She was light-skinned, dark hair. She had on black shoes, and she had a funny nose."

At about 4 A.M. Officer Foster was relieved by George Murphy of the DA's office and Sergeant Bill Jordan of the Los Angeles Police Department. The prisoner still had not revealed his identity, nor had there been any talk about what had happened earlier that night. The conversations that did occur were the kind one might have in a bus-terminal waiting room. The officers asked the prisoner if he had an extensive education.

"No," he replied. "I read a lot."

"I gathered that," said Jordan. "You like to read?"

"I enjoy it."

"What do you like to read?" asked Murphy.

The prisoner tried to engage the officers in a discussion of *To Kill a Mockingbird,* Harper Lee's depression-era novel about a white attorney in rural Alabama who defends a black man unjustly accused of rape. The novel won a Pulitzer Prize in 1961 and touched the conscience of the nation. Now, in the basement of police headquarters, it was being offered as a topic of conversation by the captured assailant of a United States senator. Neither Murphy nor Jordan, however, had read the book.

The men found common ground for conversation when the prisoner confessed that he didn't understand the stock market and asked the officers what they knew about it.

"A lot of money changes hands on stocks," said Jordan. "It's kind of a legalized gambling, is about what it boils down to."

"If you wanted to buy stock, you'd do it just the same way I would," said Murphy.

"How?" asked the prisoner.

"Call up a broker and say, 'I'd like to buy some stock.'"

"But, hell," the prisoner replied, "if you want to gamble, you can call up any old bookie and say, 'Play such and such a bet.'"

"No," answered Jordan, "it's accepted, no stigma attached to it; even in church they accept the stock market."

"I never had any money to fool around with stocks," Murphy added. "Policemen don't make that much money."

"I wish I had," replied the prisoner. "I wish I had some. Really, that would be a good adventure to—to experiment with."

From money the conversation got philosophical once again.

"What is justice?" asked the prisoner.

"Fair play," replied Murphy.

"What is fair play?" asked the prisoner.

"Well," said Murphy, "fair play is only that you don't take advantage of anybody."

"Right," agreed the prisoner. "Treat others as you would want them to treat you—that's what Jesus said. Beautiful thing."

"Do you go along with that?" Murphy asked the man who had just shot and wounded six people he had never met.

"Very much so, sir. Very much."[8]

In the middle of the night Robert Kennedy was moved to the ninth floor of Good Samaritan. There he was operated upon by Dr. Cuneo, Dr. Maxwell Andler, and Dr. Nat Downs Reid. The doctors opened the back of the senator's head, removed a large blood clot that had formed, and then retrieved as many small fragments of metal and bone as they could. The operation took three hours.

At sunrise Frank Mankiewicz informed the press that the operation was over and Robert Kennedy had been returned to intensive care. He reported some small improvement: the senator could now breathe unassisted. But Mankiewicz also told the reporters that Robert Kennedy may have suffered an impairment of blood to the midbrain. "The next twelve to thirty-six hours," said the press secretary, "will be a very critical period."

As the new day began, the Los Angeles police still didn't know the identity of the man they had in custody. They had his fingerprints, which were being sent around the country. They had a key that was now being tried in every car door anywhere near the Ambassador Hotel. They also had the pistol from the scene of the shooting. Using the weapon's serial number, the police discovered that the gun had been originally purchased by one Albert L. Hertz in 1965. It had changed hands several times since then, and detectives were tracking the line of possession.

When young Munir Sirhan reported early for work at Nash's Department Store, he saw a knot of coworkers gathered around a television set. Robert Kennedy had been shot. Munir watched as the image of the unidentified gunman was put on the screen. It was his brother Sirhan whose first and last name were the same. Munir was stunned. The Sirhan family had come to the United States from war-torn Palestine in 1956 when both Munir and Sirhan had been boys. Things had not been easy, but for the most part the family had lived a peaceful, honest life, led by their mother, Mary, who was a devout Christian. Now his brother Sirhan was in custody for shooting a United States senator. Munir drove home to wake his older brother Adel and tell him the awful news. He then drove Adel to the police station in downtown Pasadena.

At around 9:30 Adel entered the station alone, carrying a newspaper with a photograph of Robert Kennedy's assailant. "I think this is my brother," he said softly to the desk sergeant as he held up the paper.

Soon he was upstairs talking to a collection of men from the LAPD and the FBI.

After convincing investigators that he was not part of any conspiracy, Adel returned home with a contingent of police led by Sergeant William Brandt. Several hundred people were already in front of the Sirhan home, sent there, in effect, by Los Angeles mayor Sam Yorty, who had just gone on television and announced that the attacker of Robert Kennedy was one Sirhan Sirhan of 696 East Howard Street.

"Can we come in, or do you have something to hide?" asked Brandt.

"No," said Adel, looking at the crowd, "you can come in."[9]

Once inside, the police were shown to Sirhan's room. There they found literature pertaining to a mystic group called the Rosicrucians as well as other books on the occult. They also found two spiral notebooks filled with odd repetitive writing, including several passages that seemed to target Robert Kennedy for murder. Sergeant Brandt filled several boxes with material from Sirhan's room and returned to Rampart Station.

That evening President Lyndon Johnson went on television to speak to the nation:

> "Tonight this nation faces once again the consequences of lawlessness, hatred, and unreason in its midst. It would be wrong, it would be self-deceptive, to ignore the connection between that lawlessness and hatred and this act of violence."

Johnson continued, now playing the other side of the court:

> "It would be just as wrong, and just as self-deceptive, to conclude from this act that our country itself is sick, that it has lost its balance, that it has lost its sense of direction, even its common decency.
>
> "Two hundred million Americans did not strike down Robert Kennedy last night any more than they struck down President John F. Kennedy in 1963 or Dr. Martin Luther King in April of this year.
>
> "But those awful events give us ample warning that in a climate of extremism, of disrespect for law, of contempt for the rights of others, violence may bring down the very best among us."[10]

Johnson told the nation that he was appointing a special presidential commission. Serving on the commission would be Archbishop Terrence Cooke, Senators Roman Hruska and Philip Hart, university president Milton Eisenhower, attorney Albert Jenner, law professor Patricia Harris, workingman philosopher Eric Hoffer, district judge Leon Higginbotham, and Representatives William McCulloch and Hale Boggs. The purpose of this new commission, Johnson declared, would be to discover "what in the nature of our people and the environment of our society makes possible such murder and such violence" and to propose ways to prevent it in the future.

California governor Ronald Reagan was also quick to go on national television to ease the conscience of the nation. "Two hundred million Americans did not do this," he said. "One young man did it, and for not even an American reason."

A little later Reagan had more to say at a press conference in Sacramento. He attributed the shooting of Robert Kennedy to a growing permissiveness in society and the attitude

"that says a man can choose the laws he must obey, that he can take the law into his own hands for a cause, that crime does not necessarily mean punishment. This attitude has been spurred by demagogic and irresponsible words of so-called leaders in and out of public office, and it has been helped along by some in places of authority who are fearful of the wrong but timid about standing up for what is right. In so doing they have thrown our nation into chaos and confusion and have bred a climate that permits this ultimate tragedy."[11]

Governor Reagan, whose presidential ambitions were already public knowledge, left the press conference without taking any questions from the stunned newsmen. Robert Kennedy was in the hospital fighting for his life, and Reagan had pointed a finger at some number of "so-called leaders." Who were these men the governor was attacking, the reporters asked Reagan's communications director, Lyn Nofziger?

"We're just not going to get into a position," said Nofziger, "of calling names or making accusations against certain people in this country."

"You've already done that," called out one reporter.

"All right, then, we'll stand on the statement."

Another newsman asked if the governor's statement wasn't pointed at Senator Kennedy himself.

"You'll have to draw your own conclusions," replied Nofziger, speaking as though he were defending a moral principle, "because the statement is there and we do not intend to go beyond it."[12]

The record for public pronouncements on June 5 belonged to Los Angeles mayor Sam Yorty. He seemed to be everywhere. Shortly after Sirhan Sirhan's identity became known, Yorty was in front of network television cameras. With chief of police Thomas Reddin at his side, Yorty revealed that the police had "learned his car was seen outside meetings where Communist organizations or Communist front organizations were in session. From that circumstance we probably can deduce he was in contact with Communists."[13]

The so-called front organization that Yorty was referring to was the W.E.B. Du Bois Club on Hollywood Boulevard, a left-wing political group named after the black American civil rights leader. What Yorty failed to mention was that the car belonged to Sirhan's brother Adel, who frequently played music at an Arab nightclub a few doors away.

Yorty's next stop for the day was Rampart Station, which was serving as the police command post for the Kennedy investigation. The police had scheduled a press conference for a little after noon. Once at the station Mayor Yorty began to paw through the box of belongings the detectives had just brought in from their search of Sirhan's home. He examined the two spiral notebooks. A little while later, as the police press conference in the basement was ending, Mayor Yorty just happened to wander in.

"What can you tell us about Sirhan Sirhan?" asked Robert Blair Kaiser, then a reporter stringing for *Life* magazine.

"Well," said the mayor, "he was a member of numerous Communist organizations, including the Rosicrucians."

"The Rosicrucians aren't a Communist organization," said the reporter.

Yorty ignored Kaiser and waited for the others to set their mikes and position their cameras.

"It appears," he said, "that Sirhan Sirhan was sort of a loner who harbored Communist inclinations, favored Communists of all types. He said the U.S. must fall. Indicated that RFK must be assassinated before June 5, 1968. It was a May 18 notation in a ringed notebook."[14]

Yorty was hardly done for the day. There would be an interview by Radio News International and another session with the press in front of television cameras. Yorty was now thumping Sirhan's notebooks like they were the Old Testament, warning the congregation that an "evil Communist organization has played a part in inflaming the assassination of President [*sic*] Kennedy."

Yorty's behavior, to almost everyone's dismay, was a gross breach of legal ethics and procedure. The evidence he was touting on television had been secured from Sirhan's home without a warrant. It had yet to be determined if the notebooks were Sirhan's, or whether he had done the writing in them. They had not yet been ruled admissible in a court of law, and the mayor's antics were increasing greatly the possibility that they would be barred as evidence.

State attorney general Thomas C. Lynch telephoned the mayor to express his concern. So did U.S. attorney general Ramsey Clark and Los Angeles district attorney Evelle Younger, who appealed to Yorty to end his posturing. The mayor was unmoved. "If they haven't got enough evidence to convict this man," he said, "then we need to get someone else to prosecute."[15]

The next day, during arraignment proceedings, superior court judge Arthur Alarcon issued an order banning public officials and all persons connected with the case from engaging in indiscreet talk that might prejudice a fair trial. The order promised "contempt-of-court action" for violators. Just to make sure it was understood to whom it applied, a copy of Judge Alarcon's order was personally served upon the mayor of Los Angeles.

As Robert Kennedy lay unconscious in the intensive-care ward of Good Samaritan, Dr. James Poppen of Boston's Lahey Clinic arrived in Los Angeles, brought there by a U.S. Air Force transport. Poppen was a skilled neurosurgeon who had attended to President John Kennedy at various times and to Senator Edward Kennedy when he had been severely injured in a plane crash. At about 10 A.M. Poppen examined Robert Kennedy and knew right away that the outlook was near hopeless. Kennedy's life depended upon the abatement of the swelling and bleeding in his head. If the trauma continued, the blood circulation to the brain would be cut off.

At about noon, the doctors hooked Robert Kennedy up to an electroencephalograph, a device that monitored the senator's brain waves. Initially the readings were good. "Just slightly below normal," noted Dr. Cuneo. But by late afternoon the signals began to diminish. The damage in Robert Kennedy's head was now compounding. The senator's heart, however, still beat strongly.

Outside Good Samaritan Hospital hundreds of people, many of them young, waited together. They had been there all day, and they would stay the night. Some held signs saying PRAY FOR BOBBY. Except for a brief statement at 5:30 in the evening, which said that Robert Kennedy's condition continued to be "extremely critical," there had been no official word since the operation.

Then at 2 A.M. Frank Mankiewicz walked slowly down the emergency ramp of the hospital. He crossed the street to an auditorium that was now serving as press headquarters. Mankiewicz stood before the newsmen, bit his lip, then began to speak.

"Senator Robert Francis Kennedy died at 1:44 A.M. today. With the senator at the time of his death was his wife, Ethel, his sisters Mrs. Patricia Lawford and Mrs. Stephen Smith, and his sister-in-law Mrs. John F. Kennedy. He was forty-two years old."

Robert Kennedy's death initiated a week of national mourning. In New York, schools closed, taxis displayed black ribbons, and WPIX-TV broadcast the single word "SHAME" for two and a half hours. Hundreds of thousands of people lined the railway tracks from New York to Washington, an unofficial honor guard for Kennedy's funeral train. In a week Ethel Kennedy received more than 325,000 letters of sympathy.

Newspaper columns and commencement addresses were common forums for dismay. "There is something in the air of the modern world," said James Reston in *The New York Times*. "The fantasy violence of American literature, television and the movies provides a contemporary gallery of dark and ghastly crime, which undoubtedly adds to the atmosphere in which weak and deranged minds flourish."[16]

There were many variations on this theme: Robert Kennedy was murdered because the violence America was perpetrating abroad in places such as Vietnam was finally coming home; or Robert Kennedy was murdered because disrespect for law (fostered by those opposing the war) had become epidemic.

In a ceremony at Tufts University, Harvard professor and Kennedy family friend John Kenneth Galbraith expressed his disgust at this repeated analysis. He noted that all across the country, "men of well-padded intellect with a genius for platitude have been warning against violence." Galbraith had even greater contempt for the commission just appointed by President Johnson, citing "the effort to sweep problems under the rug by asking elderly men of great repute and inertia to study them."[17]

And there were a few people of note who gave voice to the unthinkable. On NBC's *Tonight Show*, Truman Capote, author of *In Cold Blood*, suggested that the murders of President Kennedy, Dr. Martin Luther King, Jr., and Senator Kennedy were part of one large conspiracy. Capote said that the paradigm for the murders might be found in Richard Condon's *The Manchurian Candidate*, a novel (and then movie) in which the president of the United States is to be killed by a hypno-programmed assassin.

In *The New York Times*, columnist Jack Gould labeled what occurred on *The Tonight Show* as "not within the acceptable province of entertainment television shows." Gould reprimanded Johnny Carson for his interview, and scorched Capote for indulging in "an orgy of rampant conjecture."[18]

The *Times*, however, took a less judgmental position when it reported the reaction of Yevgeny Yevtushenko, whose perception of the crime was not very different from Capote's. The Soviet poet had met Robert Kennedy in 1966, felt a fondness for him, and, following the murder, he wrote a long poem titled "Freedom to Kill." The *Times* printed it in full.

In the poem Yevtushenko pictured the United States as a nation going "dangerously insane," a place where "ears of grain filled with bullets wave in the fields of Texas," and "murderers attend funerals dressed in mourning." The poem begins:

The color of the Statue of Liberty
Grows ever more deathly pale
As, loving freedom with bullets
You shoot at yourself, America.[19]

The prisoner, nursing a sprained knee and sitting in a wheelchair, was rolled into the prison chapel, now devoid of religious insignia, as it had been converted into a makeshift courtroom for security reasons. Clad in blue dungarees and a white shirt with the sleeves rolled up, the accused was lifted in his chair by four deputy sheriffs to a raised platform, where he faced superior court judge Arthur Alarcon at the altar. Robert Kennedy had been dead a day.

Earlier, the Los Angeles County Grand Jury had convened in the chapel to hear twenty-three witnesses before handing down an indictment for murder. Now the prisoner was to be arraigned. The proceeding took about half an hour. The prisoner's court-appointed lawyers, Richard Buckley and Wilbur Littlefield, did most of the talking. Could they postpone the plea until psychiatric tests could be completed? The judge agreed.

During the proceedings Judge Alarcon pronounced the defendant's name "SEER-han Bishara SEER-han." The defendant, who two days before would not reveal his identity to anyone, now made his first public statement: "It's not SEER-han," he said in a voice heard throughout the room. "It's pronounced Sir-han."

TWO

Summer of '68

✳ ✳ ✳

AT THE JUNE 7 chapel arraignment there was, in addition to the public defenders, another attorney looking after the defendant's interests. This was Abraham Lincoln Wirin, chief counsel of the local office of the American Civil Liberties Union. Wirin, who was formally known by his initials "A. L." but was called "Al" by almost everyone, was introduced during the proceedings when Judge Alarcon announced that the civil liberties lawyer had been invited by the court to observe "the manner in which the constitutional and procedural rights of the defendant have been obeyed and preserved."

Actually, Wirin had been invited into the case earlier by the defendant, the morning after the shooting. Sirhan, while still the anonymous assailant, requested to see an attorney from the ACLU. Wirin, who had been attempting to get in to see the prisoner, was immediately available. When the two met under heavy security, the prisoner whispered his name into Wirin's ear. Then, with the imperfect knowledge that the ACLU sometimes championed the rights of minorities, Sirhan asked if Wirin would represent him. The attorney responded that he could not: the ACLU only took cases with constitutional issues at stake. But he was interested in seeing that the accused received a fair trial, and toward that end Wirin offered to help Sirhan find suitable representation.

The Los Angeles County Public Defender's Office, which provided Sirhan with Buckley and Littlefield, was perhaps the best operation of its kind in the country. It was well funded and had 208 full-time attorneys on staff. Still, the prevailing opinion was that a case of this importance required an experienced, respected, private defense attorney.

Although it would not be a pleasant job to defend, without compensation, the man who allegedly shot Robert Kennedy, Wirin thought he might be able to find a qualified lawyer to volunteer. Indeed, inquiries soon came in from nationally known criminal attorneys F. Lee Bailey and Melvin Belli. But Wirin was focusing on local talent. He commissioned journalist Robert Blair Kaiser, who had contacted him in hopes of getting an interview with Sirhan, to approach the well-known criminal attorney Grant Cooper. When Wirin returned to Sirhan with a list of possible attorneys, Sirhan recognized Cooper's name and selected him as his first choice. At about the same time, after talking to Kaiser, Cooper made up his mind to offer his services to Sirhan.

Grant Cooper had practiced law since 1927. He earned a reputation as a tough prosecutor while serving in the Los Angeles County DA's Office from 1929 to 1935. He returned to that office in 1940 for a two-year tour as chief deputy district attorney. During that time, Cooper played a key role in the successful fight against the powerful crime and gambling interests that had corrupted the mayor's office and large segments of the police force. Mayor Frank Shaw was forced to step down, a commission was empowered to oversee the police, and the gambling interests looked to the desert of Nevada for a new home.

After he left the prosecutor's office, Grant Cooper devoted himself full-time to criminal defense. His most famous case was that of Dr. Bernard Finch and his girlfriend, Carole Tregoff, who were accused of murdering Finch's wife. Cooper defended Finch and Tregoff twice and came away with two hung juries. The pair were convicted in 1961, defended a third time by another lawyer.

By 1968 Grant Cooper was at the top of his profession. The sixty-five-year-old attorney had recently served as president of the Los Angeles County Bar Association. He had also been president of the American College of Trial Lawyers and vice president of the State Bar of California. Colleagues often spoke of Cooper's "unquestioned integrity." For Wirin and the penniless Sirhan, securing the services of such an attorney was an enormous coup. There was just one hitch: Cooper was already engaged.

Earlier in the year, Maurice Friedman, a Las Vegas developer, retained Cooper to defend him in federal court. Friedman, along with four others, was charged with rigging gin-rummy games at the Beverly Hills Friars Club. The defendants had installed several "peekholes" in the ceiling over the game tables, and information had been relayed to certain players by way of electronic signals. The scam reportedly cost several businessmen over four hundred thousand dollars in losses, and celebrities Phil Silvers, Tony Martin, and Zeppo Marx had also been cheated out of substantial sums. The case had been given great attention in the media, and the start of the trial was only days away.

Thus Cooper's ability to represent Sirhan was complicated. He could head the Sirhan defense only if another attorney could be found to handle the initial phases of the case, and only if his future participation could be kept secret so as not to prejudice a jury against his present client. When his first two choices declined to serve, Cooper suggested an experienced California appeals lawyer named Russell Parsons.

On June 19, at 6 A.M., Al Wirin telephoned Russell Parsons in his room at the Elks Club, the place Parsons called home. The two met for breakfast, and Wirin proposed that Parsons handle the Sirhan case while Cooper was occupied. Parsons accepted, and by noontime he was with Sirhan, who seemed delighted to finally have an attorney. Parsons's feisty talkative style appeared to put the young prisoner at ease.

Immediately after the visit Parsons held a press conference. He told the collected newsmen that he would represent Sirhan without fee. "There's a poor devil in trouble," said Parsons, finessing the fact that this particular poor devil was also notorious, "and that's enough for me."

Parsons also said that he would be joined by another attorney: "He's a prominent lawyer who has tried many cases. But he is now representing a client who has paid him a large fee to represent him. If it is known that he plans to be Sirhan's lawyer, it might damage the case of the client he is now representing. For that reason if it is even hinted that he might be planning to represent Sirhan . . . he will withdraw from the Sirhan case."[1]

As he would on other occasions, Parsons had said more than he needed to say. If only a hint would ruin the deal, why hint? Grant Cooper was prominent indeed. So prominent that he had been featured on the front page of the Los Angeles Times only the day before. Cooper, the paper reported, had been playing gin rummy while federal court was in session. Actually, the defense attorney had agreed to play a hand of rummy with card expert Oswald Jacoby to demonstrate to the Friars Club jury how the game is played. Cooper beat Jacoby by fifty-nine points and then announced, "I'll quit while I'm ahead."

Astute observers didn't need more clues. They soon focused their suspicions upon Cooper. A week later the beleaguered defense attorney was forced to answer the rising speculation about his assuming the Sirhan defense by saying, "Definitely, positively, unequivocally no." If that didn't convince everyone, those who knew better stayed politely silent.

Russell Parsons had been practicing law since 1917. When asked his age at the initial press conference, the seventy-five-year-old attorney replied, "In the late sixties, that good enough? Who are you going to tell? Some girl?" The Los Angeles Times dutifully reported Parsons's age as sixty-nine.[2]

Like Cooper, Parsons had worked in the Los Angeles County DA's Office as a prosecutor in the late 1930s. Before that he had gained some notoriety defending one "Rattlesnake" James, a villain who murdered his wife by forcing her foot into a box of poison snakes. By filing numerous appeals, Parsons managed to keep the convicted James alive for seven years, at a time when appeals were not easily strung together.

In the modern era, Parsons was best known for his appeal on behalf of Charles Cahan, a convicted bookmaker who was tried on evidence secured by placing hidden microphones in his home without a search warrant. In 1955, the California Supreme Court overturned Cahan's conviction, saying that such evidence was illegally seized. Six years later, in Mapp v. Ohio, the U.S. Supreme Court made this prohibition against unreasonable search and seizure applicable in all states. "It used to be a question of 'Have you got the evidence?'" Parsons told reporters eager for some color; "now it's 'How did you get the evidence?'"

The *Los Angeles Times* described Parsons as "peppery." Most everyone else referred to him as "the well-known California appeals lawyer." But not all the reviews were favorable. Journalist Robert Kaiser, who himself would join the defense team, characterized Parsons to the authors as "garrulous, funny, senile, and a fool." "Cooper wanted an attorney that wasn't going to take over the case," he said, "somebody who would do what he was told, and not be a problem later on. So he got harmless old Russell Parsons, way over the hill Russell Parsons. And Parsons enjoyed his few months basking in the publicity and giving interviews to the *Toronto Sun,* and the *Bombay News,* all of this, seeing his face on television and enjoying it. Until Cooper came into the case and then he was decidedly a fifth wheel."[3]

As the team to defend Sirhan was being assembled, District Attorney Evelle Younger was deciding who would present the state's evidence. On June 14, Younger announced that the prosecution would be led by chief deputy DA Lynn D. "Buck" Compton.

Compton had been born in Southern California in 1921. He attended UCLA, and in his senior year he played guard for the Bruins in the 1943 Rose Bowl. Two years later, as an infantry platoon leader in the 101st Airborne, Compton took part in the desperate defense of the Belgian town of Bastogne. For heroic service Compton received a Silver Star, a Bronze Star, and a Purple Heart.

Upon returning from Europe, Compton joined the LAPD. While a police detective he attended Loyola University Law School at night, passing his bar exam in 1949. Two years later he joined the district attorney's office. He was elevated to the position of chief deputy DA in 1966. Upon being chosen to lead the Sirhan prosecution, Compton informed the press that one of the purposes of the trial would be to "restore public faith in law enforcement."

Joining Compton on the prosecution team were deputy DA John Howard and deputy DA David Fitts. Howard was chief of the DA's Special Investigations Division and had presented the case at the Sirhan grand jury hearing. He had been with the district attorney's office for sixteen years, having, like Compton, studied law at Loyola University. David Fitts was considered one of Evelle Younger's most able prosecutors. He had been a deputy DA for fourteen years, having joined the prosecutor's office upon completing his law studies at Stanford University.

On June 28, Russell Parsons appeared in the temporary courtroom set up in the prison chapel. Presiding was Judge Richard Schauer. Unlike his previous appearance, when he had entered in a wheelchair, this time Sirhan, dressed in dark slacks and a blue shirt, strode briskly into the courtroom and stood when addressed by the judge. Parsons told Judge Schauer that he would not be able to enter a plea for the defendant until he received a report from the court-appointed psychiatrist, Dr. Eric Marcus. Schauer consented.

After the seven-minute court session Parsons told the attending press that he had "strong doubts" that his client was in full possession of his faculties when he shot Senator Kennedy, hinting heavily that the defense for Sirhan would be psychiatric. The DA's office had already come to that conclusion. In a front-row seat that day, observing Sirhan, was Dr. Seymour Pollack, an experienced psychiatrist who had been brought in to advise the prosecutors.

On July 19, preliminary trial proceedings were moved to a sheriff's briefing room on the thirteenth floor of the Hall of Justice, a downtown edifice that held a strange mix of courtrooms, county offices, and jail facilities. Sirhan was placed in a room on the same floor, a windowless cell that would be his home for the next nine months. Security was tight. New shades on the improvised courtroom's windows were made of quarter-inch steel plate. Overhead, a sheriff's helicopter kept watch.

As the first order of business, Judge Schauer consented to Russell Parsons's request for another two weeks to enter a plea. Then District Attorney Evelle Younger entered a motion to vacate Judge Alarcon's order limiting public discussion of the case. Judge Schauer set the hearing date on the motion for August 2. On that date Sirhan Sirhan would plead not guilty. This provided the following day's headlines, but it was a minor moment in the day's proceedings: expected and without much meaning. "Not guilty" left open the most options, and it could be changed.

The real action of the day centered around Evelle Younger's motion to override Judge Alarcon's order. Younger himself argued the motion before Judge Schauer, citing "the fundamental concept that appears throughout our Constitution and our entire system of government, where, if possible, you let the people know as much as possible about the way your government is performing."

In this forum, Younger argued heartily for the free flow of information in a democratic society. This would stand in stark contrast to Younger's performance after the trial, when the district attorney would change lyrics. Then, the people's right to know didn't count for much, as Younger and the LAPD decided that the police files in the Robert Kennedy murder would be kept secret indefinitely.

Younger probably had personal reasons for wanting Judge Alarcon's order lifted. It was no secret that he coveted higher office. Just days earlier he had been appointed by Richard Nixon to head the presidential candidate's Advisory Council on Crime and Law Enforcement, a symbolic post. Now, in Sirhan's trial, Younger had the perfect vehicle to enhance his reputation, yet Judge Alarcon's order stood in the way of any public statements that could give him additional recognition.

"We certainly don't want any prejudicial material to disseminate," argued Younger, "but we are not for one minute agreeing that you can determine prejudice by measuring the amount of space given to a matter."

"I hesitate to interrupt," said Schauer. ". . . Who is to judge whether a certain comment is prejudicial?"

"I think you, at the moment," answered Younger; "ultimately there may be others."

"But under the position that you are asserting," responded Schauer, "I would make that judgment after the statement was made."

Evelle Younger went on to hypothesize certain questions in which it would be in the public interest to have comments from involved authorities. "Was there a conspiracy to assassinate Senator Kennedy? Is there any foreign government involved? . . . Is there any evidence that more than one gun was fired? . . . I think those are important issues where not only the public interest but also the defendant's interest requires that we be able to answer the question."

Younger was trying hard to conjure threats to the public well-being, but at the time conspiracy was not being seriously considered by the media or anyone else. The newspapers had printed some details about the woman in the polka-dot dress, after witness Vincent DiPierro described her to the grand jury on June 7. But when on June 21 the LAPD canceled their "wanted-for-questioning" bulletin concerning this woman, there was no public outcry. There also was no serious speculation about the involvement of foreign governments. Perhaps most significant, Younger's statement was the very first to raise the issue of a second gun in the pantry. The first public speculation on the matter would not occur until the following year, when Sirhan's trial was already over.

Judge Schauer was not moved by Younger's argument, and he denied the motion. But Evelle Younger wasn't finished. He brought his case to the Second District Court of Appeal. When he lost there, he went to the Supreme Court of California, which also affirmed the right of Judge Alarcon to restrict public statements about the Sirhan trial.

Accompanying Russell Parsons into the case was a private detective in his mid-thirties named Michael McCowan. McCowan had worked for the LAPD for ten years while putting himself through law school. His ambition to be an attorney, however, came to an end when he became involved in what police termed "a land swindle scheme." According to police documents, McCowan "resigned from LAPD in 1965 in lieu of disciplinary action after being arrested for theft and tampering with the United States mail."[4]

During his legal difficulties McCowan had retained Russell Parsons to represent him. Later, when McCowan set himself up as a private detective, Parsons availed himself of his services, using McCowan primarily as a process server and routine investigator. When Parsons returned to his office after having visited Sirhan in jail, the news of his entry into the case had already spread. McCowan was inside the office waiting. "I'm here to help," he said to Parsons. "I'll drop everything I'm doing."[5]

Another investigator would come into the case by a more circuitous route. In the weeks following the murder of Robert Kennedy, journalist Robert Blair Kaiser followed events closely. He had initially contacted Al Wirin requesting an interview with Sirhan. Although Wirin was in no position to grant such a request, he reported back that Sirhan seemed open to the idea. Next, under Wirin's direction, the journalist had played a pivotal role in bringing Grant Cooper into the case. Kaiser sensed that he had created an inside track to a very big story.

Robert Kaiser had begun his career in journalism in the late 1950s as a reporter for *The Arizona Republic,* after having spent ten years studying for the Jesuit priesthood. In 1961 he went to work for *Time* magazine, where in 1963 he won the Overseas Press Club's award for the best magazine reporting on foreign affairs for his reports from Rome. In that same year he wrote *Pope, Council, and World,* a best-selling book on Pope John XXIII's effort to modernize the Catholic Church.

By 1968 Kaiser was freelance writing in Los Angeles. Although he had written successfully on a variety of subjects, his high-profile work in Rome had given him a reputation as a reporter of religious news. Now the journalist saw an opportunity to demonstrate the full range of his skills. Kaiser proposed to Cooper that in exchange for exclusive rights to the Sirhan story, he would contribute a percentage of his take to the defense effort. Cooper and Parsons were donating their time, but money was still badly needed to meet the many expenses of litigation.

Cooper agreed to Kaiser's idea but told the journalist that the mechanics would have to be worked out. After all, how could they conveniently gain access to Sirhan for the writer? What assurance did they have that Kaiser wouldn't write something that would damage the defense? How could they be sure that Kaiser wouldn't end up as a witness for the prosecution?

Cooper's idea was that Kaiser could sign on as a defense investigator. This would give the writer access to the defendant. At the same time he would be prohibited from writing about the substance of the case before trial, and he would be out of reach of the prosecution.

In early August, using his new status as defense investigator, Robert Kaiser first gained access to Sirhan. Kaiser had two projects in mind. The first would be a background story on Sirhan for a national magazine; the second would be a book on the case. Both projects would bring much-needed money into the defense effort, but there was another benefit. In doing his research the writer quickly gained a familiarity with the case beyond that held by the defense attorneys themselves. Thus equipped, Robert Kaiser became a valued member of the Sirhan defense team.

On August 8, six days after Sirhan pleaded not guilty, Richard Nixon was nominated in Miami Beach to be the Republican Party's presidential candidate. Nixon promised the cheering GOP delegates that he would "bring an honorable end to the war in Vietnam." He also promised "a militant crusade against crime," saying, "the right to be free from domestic violence has become the forgotten civil right."

Three weeks later startling images of such violence would be featured on the nightly news as the Democratic Party gathered in Chicago to nominate its candidate for president. During the week preceding the nomination, confrontations between protestors and police had escalated. Initially the disturbances were confined to Lincoln and Grant Parks, but by nomination night the violence had engulfed several miles of downtown Chicago.

With Hubert Humphrey's nomination assured by the murder of Robert Kennedy, debate over the party's Vietnam policy plank became the chief dramatic focus. Party regulars put forward a plank supporting the present administration's policies in Vietnam. A minority plank called for a swift end to American participation in the war. When former JFK press secretary Pierre Salinger addressed the delegates he declared, "If Robert Kennedy were alive today, he would be on the platform speaking for the minority plank." The majority position carried by a margin of 3 to 2.[6]

Outside the convention center a horrific scene was unfolding. In front of reporters and delegate spouses looking out the windows of the Conrad Hilton Hotel, police seemed to be attacking everyone in sight, focusing particular violence upon newsmen and their equipment. One account, printed on the front page of *The New York Times,* told how the police, without warning, attacked onlookers standing quietly behind a police barrier in front of the hotel. According to reporter Anthony Lukas, the police pushed the screaming bystanders, including middle-aged women and children, through a plate-glass window of a street-level restaurant and then ran into the restaurant to beat and arrest the bleeding victims.

A few months later President Johnson's Commission on Violence, brought into being by the murder of Robert Kennedy, issued a report describing what happened in the streets of Chicago as a "police riot." Not everyone saw it that way. But whether one saw irresponsible youths desecrating the political process or a police apparatus gone berserk, the televised images from Chicago were profoundly disturbing.

On October 4, Judge Schauer announced that he was assigning the Sirhan trial to Judge Herbert V. Walker. It was an obvious choice. Walker was at the end of a distinguished career and was well thought of by those in the legal profession. In 1964 the Criminal Courts Bar Association, an organization of criminal defense attorneys, gave him an award that praised his standards of fairness and justice. The *Los Angeles Times* applauded Walker as "the dean of the criminal court judges."

Herbert Walker was born in 1899. He spent most of his childhood in central California. By age fourteen he was alone, his father dead and his mother in a mental institution. At the first opportunity Walker joined the U.S. Navy and served two years on the battleship *Kentucky* during the First World War. Following the war Walker worked various jobs in the Louisiana oil fields and got bit parts in silent films after he moved back to California.

Walker graduated from the USC Law School in 1928. Fifteen years later he would succeed Grant Cooper as chief deputy district attorney for Los Angeles County. Thus, the chief prosecutor (Lynn Compton), the lead defense attorney, and the judge had all held the same high position of chief deputy of the Los Angeles district attorney's office.

In 1953 Herbert Walker was appointed judge of the state superior court by then governor Earl Warren. During his sixteen years on the bench, Walker had sentenced nineteen men to die in the gas chamber. Only one was ever executed: Walker's most famous defendant, Caryl Chessman, convicted of robbery and rape in 1948.

Herbert Walker lived in a modest house in the suburbs. He was a registered Republican, a practicing Episcopalian, and he wore a Stetson hat when he wasn't indoors. He was considered "old school" by his peers, one of whom described him as "a period piece." Another colleague reported, "He has a very good, strong code of morality and believes in a fair trial. But he believes in the dry words of the law and doesn't consider the courtroom an appropriate place for the humanities."[7]

This last assessment might have given Sirhan's attorneys some pause, for the defense of Sirhan was to be constructed on a foundation of new ideas. Yet neither Parsons nor Cooper was concerned. Walker's reputation was "firm, but fair." And so long as he was fair, it would be the jury and not the judge who would make the important decisions.

Herbert Walker brought the Sirhan court to order for the first time on October 14. "This is a petition of Sirhan Bishara Sirhan for an order of discovery," the judge announced as the session began.

Under California law the defense was entitled to petition the prosecution to reveal certain evidence they might have that would shed light on the case. "Any orders I make are directed to the district attorney only," cautioned Walker, making sure everyone understood the limits of discovery, "and can only affect those documents and other things that he, the district attorney, has in his possession."

The motion for discovery had been primarily drawn up by investigators Michael McCowan and Robert Kaiser. There were thirty-seven groups of requested materials. At one point prosecutor David Fitts approached the defense table and dropped upon it a large pile of papers representing witness interviews, transcripts, and summaries for sixty-seven witnesses who had been in the Ambassador Hotel the night of the murder. Then Fitts deposited another pile representing fifteen witnesses who had seen Sirhan at a local gun range.

In remarks to the court, deputy DA Compton characterized the surrendered witness interviews as "negative" in regard to the question of a possible conspiracy. Russell Parsons would parrot those words later in the afternoon when he talked to reporters. "We have seen," said Parsons, who had not yet had time to review the material gained in discovery, "no evidence of conspiracy." The following morning the *Los Angeles Times* ran with the large-type, front-page headline BOTH SIDES AGREE SIRHAN WAS ALONE.

The same day Judge Walker was overseeing the mechanics of discovery, the Summer Olympic Games were getting under way in Mexico City. There would be several stunning performances by U.S. athletes. Bob Beamon would leap over 29 feet to break the world long-jump record by nearly an astounding 2 feet. High jumper Dick Fosbury would win a gold medal by employing the "Fosbury Flop," a previously unknown technique of jumping over the crossbar backward.

The most lasting image from the games, however, came when American sprinters Tommie Smith and John Carlos rose to accept their gold and bronze medals in the 200-meter dash. As the American national anthem played, Smith and Carlos raised gloved fists in black-power salutes protesting the treatment of blacks in the United States. The two were suspended from the games and expelled from the Olympic Village for misusing the Olympic forum.

On October 22, Judge Walker once again called court into session. This time the issue to be decided was whether or not the notebooks taken from Sirhan's bedroom the morning of the murder had been obtained legally by the police.

"Are you ready to proceed?" asked Judge Walker.

"Yes, Your Honor," replied David Fitts. "Sergeant William Brandt."

Under Fitts's direction Brandt told the story of how he came to interview Adel Sirhan the morning of the murder on the second floor of the Pasadena Police Department, and how he and several other officers accompanied Adel back to the family home on Howard Street. Fitts asked if the police had asked for permission to enter and search the home.

"I asked him if we could search the home," Brandt replied. "He said as far as he was concerned we could; however, it was his mother's house."

When Sirhan's older brother Adel took the witness stand, he told a similar story. When Fitts asked if he had consented to a search, Adel replied, "I said, 'I have nothing to hide, but the house isn't mine, I do not own the house.'"

Other witnesses were introduced, including Sirhan's mother, Mary, and brother Munir, but the facts remained stable. Judge Walker asked for final arguments. Russell Parsons rose and said he did not think the search was "reasonable." When it was his turn, Lynn Compton said that he thought the police officers were entitled to rely on "ostensible rather than actual" authority to search the house. Judge Walker agreed with Compton and ruled the search legal.

Two days later it was revealed that District Attorney Evelle J. Younger had petitioned the Supreme Court of the United States to overturn the Supreme Court of California and do away with Judge Alarcon's order restricting public comment on the Sirhan trial. "The only feasible way to meet the danger of false charges and rumors," said Younger in Washington, "is to allow responsible public officials to indicate on occasion, why certain witnesses have not been used, or how certain leads have proven false or irrelevant."[8] It would be several months before the U.S. Supreme Court would be able to consider Younger's petition, but there would be time: the set date for the start of the Sirhan trial kept receding.

When Grant Cooper agreed to assume direction of Sirhan's defense, he believed the Friars Club affair would be over by September. In that expectation Russell Parsons had gotten a November 1 trial date. When the card-cheating trial dragged on, Parsons asked for another continuance, and the trial was put off until December 9.

On November 5, Richard Nixon defeated Hubert Humphrey to become the thirty-seventh president of the United States. Nixon won a comfortable victory in the electoral college, but his margin in the popular vote was only .5 percent. The televised street violence during the Chicago convention had clearly injured Humphrey's chances, and early political forecasts had him losing to Nixon by 30 percentage points. In the final weeks of the campaign, however, Humphrey steadily closed the gap, only to lose the election in a near dead heat.

On December 2, the Friars Club verdict came in. All five defendants were found guilty. That same day Grant Cooper announced that he was going to head the Sirhan defense team. A few days later Cooper made his first appearance in court.

Cooper told the court that he had met Sirhan for the first time a few days earlier for a short get-acquainted visit. "I am now familiar with the facts in a general way, have read about them in the press and discussed them generally with Mr. Parsons, but I have not had an opportunity to do the type of preparation that is so essential." He then asked that the trial be put off for another month, and Judge Walker set January 7 as the new date. Cooper then announced that in January an attorney from New York would be joining the defense team.

Emile Zola Berman had been born in New York to Russian Jewish immigrants. He was named after the famous French author whose letter "J'Accuse . . . !" had excoriated the French military for bringing false charges of treason against Captain Alfred Dreyfus. Zola had helped Berman's mother emigrate from Russia and looked out for her while she was in Paris.

Emile Berman grew up on New York's Lower East Side, where he acquired the nickname "Zuke," a name that would carry over into in his future professional life. In 1925 Berman graduated from NYU Law School. He then practiced law in New York. During the Second World War, Berman flew bombers in the China-Burma theater for the Army Air Corps and was discharged as a lieutenant colonel with a Distinguished Flying Cross, an Air Medal, and a Bronze Star.

After the war Berman worked primarily as a negligence lawyer, with some criminal work mixed in. He was highly thought of in New York legal circles. On several occasions he was appointed by the state appellate division to conduct investigations of attorneys suspected of misconduct. In 1962 Berman ran and lost as the Democratic candidate for district attorney of Nassau County.

Although Berman's skills in criminal law had been amply demonstrated, it was his experience in negligence litigation that most interested Grant Cooper. Berman was an acknowledged expert in handling medical witnesses; he lectured on the subject at various universities. Since it was already decided that Sirhan's defense was going to be psychiatric, Cooper wanted a man on the team who was skilled in presenting medical evidence. Moreover, Berman was a Jew, and Cooper thought that might help in defending an Arab in a case with political overtones.

On December 9, the U.S. Supreme Court refused to hear District Attorney Evelle Younger's third and final appeal, leaving in place Judge Alarcon's order forbidding public comment on the Sirhan trial. The following day Grant Cooper visited the offices of the district attorney to meet with Deputy DA John Howard and Deputy DA David Fitts. Cooper wanted to obtain the results of tests done upon blood reportedly taken from Sirhan the night of the murder. (The test results would come back negative for syphilis, but, remarkably, according to the police, no tests were conducted to detect the presence of drugs or alcohol in Sirhan's system.) Cooper was also eager to view photocopies of pages from Sirhan's notebooks, which until this time had not been provided to the defense.

The prosecutors were looking for something as well. According to a memorandum by David Fitts:

> Mr. Cooper was asked whether his client might consent to the administration of a lie detector test to be performed by an acknowledged and totally impartial expert with a view to determining whether Sirhan acted alone or in concert with others. Mr. Cooper was advised that the results of such tests would be for their ultimate historical significance and would not be available to the parties. Mr. Cooper was receptive in principle, but with this proviso: In the event that something beneficial to the defendant was developed in the course of the test, [he would be allowed] to make use of it after a final judgment was obtained in the case, presumably at an executive clemency hearing.[9]

The proposal offered by Howard and Fitts is remarkable for several reasons. It appears to transgress the proper boundary between the prosecution and the defense. One might wonder why the results of the examination were to be kept secret, and why, if something exculpatory were found, it would not be used until after the case had been decided. Most strange is the prosecution's desire to probe Sirhan's affiliations for their "ultimate historical significance." The question of whether Sirhan acted alone or in concert with others should have been of interest to the district attorney as a prosecutorial matter, not a historical one. That the prosecutors were speaking in these terms indicates that the answer to the polygraph exam was presupposed.

The opening of the Sirhan trial was still weeks away, but the prosecutors were already seeking to make peace with history, and, toward this end, looking to enlist the aid of the chief defense attorney. They met with some success. Although a polygraph session with the defendant did not take place, there would be other joint-venture examinations of Sirhan, to be described, to which Cooper would consent—examinations that would violate the normal boundaries of accepted criminal procedure.

Grant Cooper's first extensive interview with Sirhan had occurred just days before his meeting with Fitts and Howard. The session, which took place in Sirhan's windowless cell in the Hall of Justice, had been Cooper's introduction into the complexities of what he had thought was a tragic but simple case. Prior to this, as Cooper had admitted, what he knew of the murder he had learned from the newspapers, a few brief meetings with Russell Parsons, and a summary report written by Michael McCowan.

To Cooper's pleasant surprise, he found his client to be cooperative, intelligent, and well-spoken. But the attorney was positively baffled by a number of Sirhan's statements. "I just can't figure this kid out," Cooper would confess to Robert Kaiser.[10]

The chief defense counsel wouldn't have a lot of time to apply himself to this problem. His focus was about to be split again. On January 3, just four days before the Sirhan trial was scheduled to begin, Grant Cooper was called to testify before a closed-door session of a federal grand jury on a matter unrelated to Robert Kennedy's death. Cooper was in front of the grand jury for over three hours. At the end of the day rumors began to circulate that the well-respected attorney was about to be on the receiving end of a criminal indictment.

THREE

The Friars Club

✳ ✳ ✳

THE TRIAL OF Sirhan Sirhan began on January 7, 1969, in a
small seventy-five-seat courtroom on the eighth floor of the Hall of Justice. Only a dozen members of the general public and less than a third of
the more than one hundred credentialed newsmen were given seats in the
courtroom. Journalists who didn't work for a major news outlet were sent
to an auxiliary courtroom several floors below, where for three months
they would watch the proceedings on closed-circuit TV.

Guarding the eighth-floor corridor was a set of newly installed armored
doors, through which entrance was gained by display of the proper color-
coded plastic badge. Beyond the doors, newsmen, witnesses, and court officers were searched and then scanned by a handheld metal detector before
being allowed to pass another line of police officers in front of the courtroom itself. Inside, sheriff's deputies, both in and out of uniform, were
strategically placed around the room. Heavy beige curtains hid steel plates
covering the windows, and the remote TV camera was concealed in an
air-conditioning unit in an attempt to maintain a normal courtroom
atmosphere.

Five floors above, Sirhan Sirhan was led from his six-by-eight-foot
windowless cell, where he had spent most of the last six months. He was
taken by elevator to the ninth floor and then down a secured staircase and
into the courtroom. The defendant was dressed in a crisp gray suit. He
appeared nervous and kept touching his mouth with his fingers as the
proceedings began. On occasion his gaze would stray to his mother and
his younger brother Munir, who were seated in the back of the room.

The mood in court was expectant. The day before, in a front-page
article, *New York Times* reporter Douglas Kneeland spoke of the historical
importance of the trial by recounting the murder of Robert Kennedy.
"With his death," Kneeland said of the fallen senator, ". . . politics lost its
bright edge for countless thousands of Americans." In *Newsday,* reporter
Bob Greene predicted that the Sirhan trial would become "one of the most
celebrated in American judicial history."

But there was little to celebrate this day. As soon as Judge Walker called
the court to order, Sirhan's attorney, Grant Cooper, approached the bench

and, to the audible disappointment of those in attendance, requested that the proceedings be adjourned to the privacy of Judge Walker's chambers. Once all were assembled inside, Cooper addressed the judge.

"If Your Honor please, the defendant moves the Court for a continuance of at least thirty days for the reason that there has been certain adverse publicity that will materially affect the defendant's right to a fair trial at this time, publicity . . . with respect to the personal problems of Grant Cooper."

Sirhan's chief attorney was indeed having problems. On December 3, the very day it was reported that Cooper would represent Sirhan, another article about the defense attorney appeared on the front page of the *Los Angeles Times*. This story reported that Cooper was the object of a federal investigation concerning irregularities in the Friars Club trial.

The difficulties for Cooper had begun some months before when on July 24 assistant U.S. attorney David R. Nissen spotted a transcript of a secret grand jury proceeding on the defense attorney's table. It was a document the Friars Club lawyers were not entitled to possess. Nissen immediately called for a conference in Judge William P. Gray's chambers, where he asked how the secret transcript came to be in Grant Cooper's possession.

"The only documents I have are the ones I got from you," said Cooper.

"Well, Mr. Cooper," replied Nissen, "that document did not come from me."

After a brief recess during which the defense attorney was given the opportunity to examine the document, Judge Gray asked Cooper if he had ever seen it before.

"I have it," Cooper said. "I had it in my file, Your Honor."

"You don't know how you got it?" Judge Gray asked.

"I didn't get it from any other source," answered Cooper, implying once again that the document had come from the prosecution.

Two days later U.S. attorney Matthew Byrne again asked Cooper in Judge Gray's chambers how he came to possess the transcript.

"I found it on the table in the courtroom," replied Cooper, now contradicting his earlier statement.[1]

A subsequent investigation by the U.S. attorney revealed that the transcript on Cooper's desk had been secured by bribing a clerk at the office that photocopied the documents for the grand jury. In addition, it was discovered that other transcripts had been obtained in the same manner and that Cooper and several other attorneys in the case were aware of this repeated illegal violation of the grand jury process. Action against the suspected offenders, who were still litigating for their clients, was delayed until the Friars Club trial was concluded.

With the verdict now in, Grant Cooper was being called upon by the U.S. attorney to account for his actions. He had not only participated, to some degree, in illegally obtaining secret grand jury transcripts, he had lied on two occasions to a federal judge. The Friars Club card-cheating scandal had now become the Friars Club bribery and perjury scandal.

The question of who was behind the stolen transcripts was never publicly resolved, although by most indications it was Friars Club defendant Johnny Roselli, who was represented by attorney James P. Cantillon. Indeed, one of the questions put to Grant Cooper during the bribery probe was "Did your numerous phone calls to Mr. Cantillon . . . pertain to the then and continuing possession of the illegally obtained federal grand jury transcripts?"[2] Cooper refused to answer this question.

Johnny Roselli described himself as a businessman, but the *Los Angeles Times* made note of Roselli's long-term relationship with the Chicago mob, labeling him a "one-time lieutenant of Chicago gangster Al Capone." In 1944 Roselli had been convicted of attempting to extort millions from motion picture companies by manipulating their unions. After serving three years of a ten-year sentence, he was paroled in 1948.[3] In more recent years it was said that Roselli had looked after the West Coast interests of Chicago crime boss Sam Giancana.

Johnny Roselli had not dreamed up the Friars Club scam, nor had he participated in the card cheating itself. Several years after the operation was up and running, Roselli found out about it, and because he was Johnny Roselli, he demanded and received a cut. Along with the others he was implicated when the FBI closed in.

There may have been moments when the authorities wished they hadn't bagged Roselli. His very presence as a defendant created difficulties. Out of apparent fear, two of the alleged peekhole operators, Edwin Gebhard and Albert Snyder, both of whom the FBI was courting as potential witnesses, refused to cooperate with the investigation, even though they were offered immunity from prosecution. Later, assistant U.S. attorney David Nissen said that certain witnesses "pleaded to the point of tears that they not be required to testify against [Roselli] for fear they would be killed."[4]

Gebhard and Snyder's fear of retribution was apparently well-founded, and Grant Cooper came close to being unwittingly involved in something more serious than bribery. With Gebhard and Snyder absent, the government's card-cheating case rested primarily upon one witness, George Seach. Seach had put in time as a peekhole operator at the Friars Club and then moved on. When he got into trouble elsewhere he became an informant for the FBI and triggered the Friars Club investigation.

When the Friars Club indictments were handed down, Roselli met with his friend Jimmy (the Weasel) Fratianno. According to Fratianno (in a detailed confession published in Ovid Demaris's book *The Last Mafioso*),

Roselli proposed that Fratianno murder Seach. Roselli then handed Fratianno an envelope with several thousand dollars "for expenses." According to Fratianno, the cash had come from Grant Cooper's client and Roselli's friend, Maurice H. Friedman. As the story goes, Fratianno and several cohorts then went out to Las Vegas, where Seach was living, but before the hit could be made the FBI put the witness under federal protection.[5] Thus, Seach testified, and all the defendants were convicted.

At court on January 3, Grant Cooper attempted to satisfy the grand jury's bribery investigation by making a limited confession.

> COOPER: Well, to begin with I knew that transcripts of the federal grand jury were not available to defense counsel. That I knew. And I also knew that at some place in the chain of events somebody had to come in possession of these illegally; that I knew as a lawyer. . . .
>
> QUESTION: So at the time . . . you were aware that if a federal grand jury's transcripts were available, they had been obtained illegally?
>
> COOPER: I assumed that somewhere at some time they had been obtained in some improper fashion, that is right.
>
> QUESTION: An illegal fashion?
>
> COOPER: Yes, I would say that is true.[6]

Cooper's antiseptic mea culpa did not end the matter. It only suggested more questions—forty-six of them. These were drawn up by presiding U.S. district judge Francis C. Whelan, who posed them for Cooper to answer. Realizing that there would be no satisfactory end to the probe if he continued to blindly cooperate, Cooper changed strategy. Invoking the right of attorney-client privilege, he refused to answer any further questions. Whelan threatened to hold Cooper in contempt and send him to jail if he did not answer, but Cooper responded that he was willing to go to jail and fight the issue of attorney-client privilege in court.

On January 7, the set starting date of the Sirhan trial, Grant Cooper would be photographed at nine in the morning walking down the corridors of the Hall of Justice with Emile Berman, his cocounsel in the defense of the alleged murderer of Robert F. Kennedy. At one in the afternoon the same day, Cooper would be photographed walking down the corridors of the Federal Court Building across the street with Herman F. Selvin, the criminal defense attorney representing him in the grand jury probe of the Friars Club bribery allegations. For six months Cooper had delayed public knowledge that he would represent Sirhan so as not to prejudice a jury against his client in the Friars Club trial. Now it was the Friars Club trial that was threatening to prejudice a jury against Sirhan.

This is what Cooper argued on January 7, when he petitioned Judge Walker for another thirty-day "cooling off" postponement. But Judge

Walker was in no mood for another delay. He denied the motion for a post-ponement but ruled that the defense could submit for the record whatever evidence they had concerning potentially prejudicial press reports. Court was then adjourned so that attorney Cooper could attend his own inquest in federal court.

As the day's session had illustrated, the grand jury proceedings against Grant Cooper and the trial of Sirhan Sirhan were on a collision course. The U.S. attorney had evidence on Cooper, but Cooper was doing the entire legal establishment a tremendous favor by representing Sirhan Sirhan. Cooper certainly could not defend Sirhan while he was in jail, and further discrediting the attorney seemed counterproductive. Something had to give way, and the trial of Sirhan Sirhan was clearly the more important of the two. The grand jury proceeding against Grant Cooper was put off to some future time when the attorney could again be held accountable for his participation in the bribery scandal.*

Despite the stated fears of the defense attorneys, the most damaging effect of the new Friars investigation was not its propensity to prejudice a jury against Sirhan Sirhan or compromise Grant Cooper, but its consumption of so much of the chief defense attorney's time and attention. When he spoke to the court in early December, Cooper had admitted that a month was not enough time to familiarize himself with the case and prepare for trial. Now a great deal of that precious month had been spent contemplating not Sirhan's legal defense, but his own.

The remainder of the first week of Sirhan's trial was spent dealing with various motions put forward by the defense. To the dismay of the assembled reporters, much of this took place in Judge Walker's chambers. Cooper's most ambitious motion was one to quash the indictment against Sirhan because, as he asserted, the grand jury handing down the indictment had been improperly constituted. Under the system in place, each judge in the Los Angeles County Superior Court nominated two prospective jurors,

---

*Eight months later the matter was concluded when Cooper pled guilty to two counts of contempt and was fined one thousand dollars. That Grant Cooper was under criminal investigation while he was representing Sirhan Sirhan is open to the interpretation that, in some way, he was on a leash—unable or unwilling to investigate aggressively those who were about to investigate him. The authors have heard this theory advanced. As will be demonstrated, the authors believe that Grant Cooper's conduct toward the prosecution throughout the trial was overly cooperative and conciliatory, and this relaxed posture contributed to Cooper's misunderstanding of important evidentiary issues to the severe detriment of his client. That said, the authors are aware of nothing in Grant Cooper's words or actions that would indicate that his conduct sprang from anything other than his judgment as to the best interests of his client, however wrong he may have been.

the final panel then being selected at random from this list of nominees. Cooper contended that this process resulted in "blue ribbonism," that minority groups and the economically disadvantaged were not properly represented. He asked Judge Walker for a thirty-day continuance while the defense readied its challenge. Walker denied Cooper's motion for a delay but agreed that the challenge could take place after the jury had been selected.

On the following Monday, twenty-five candidate jurors were escorted into the courtroom. After they took an oath of truth, Judge Walker spoke:

> "Under our system of jurisprudence, it is the function of the jury to determine the issues of fact. . . . Now you also understand under the law of this state a person charged with a crime is presumed to be innocent, and that presumption remains with the defendant until the People by good and sufficient evidence have proved him guilty beyond a reasonable doubt."

Walker informed the jurors that they would be questioned about their qualifications to serve on the jury, an examination process known as voir dire, derived from the French "to speak the truth." He told them that the trial might last several months and that those who served would be sequestered in a hotel with conjugal visits by "spouses of record" permitted on weekends.

The first prospective juror to undergo voir dire was Mr. George Doudle. After a few perfunctory questions about Mr. Doudle's occupation and prior jury experience, Grant Cooper went for the heart of the matter as he saw it.

"Now at the outset," he said in a voice loud enough so all the candidate jurors could hear, "there will be no denial of the fact that our client, Sirhan Sirhan, fired the shot that killed Senator Kennedy." Cooper also wanted the jurors to understand that for a killing to be a murder, in addition to an act, there had to be a requisite state of mind: an intent or premeditation. What Cooper wanted to find out in return was whether the knowledge that the defendant pulled the trigger would so influence the juror that he could not fairly decide the issue of the assailant's state of mind.

"Now you have been told," Cooper said to Mr. Doudle, "that this defendant will admit committing the act, the shooting, and would that cause you to be prejudiced against him so you couldn't try the issue of intent?"

"Yes, I believe so," answered Doudle.

"It would cause you to be prejudiced?" Cooper said, a little surprised.

"Yes."

"All right. I will challenge the juror for cause."

Any potential juror who voiced prejudice during voir dire could be excluded from service "for cause" by way of a challenge from attorneys on either side. There is no limit in number to such challenges, though each must be approved by the judge. Later, from the pool of already-questioned "unprejudiced" candidates, each side could eliminate up to twenty candidate jurors with peremptory challenges, which require no rationale other than an attorney's belief that a juror would not look favorably upon his client.

Besides culling the unsuitable and the unwanted, voir dire also eliminated any prospective juror who simply did not care to serve. A candidate juror could always claim, usually with justification, that a prolonged jury service would cause economic hardship. And if that didn't work, an unwilling candidate could then excuse himself by saying that he harbored prejudice. The practical result of these procedures was that all the candidate jurors meriting consideration *wanted* to serve on the jury and were inclined to provide the "correct" responses to questions they were being asked.

Since the jurors were interviewed in one another's presence, the right answers quickly became known. Thus, over and over, the attorneys questioned potential jurors who, yes, had heard that Robert Kennedy had been murdered but really hadn't thought much about it or discussed it with their friends and certainly had no feelings at all about what kind of punishment should be delivered to his assailant if convicted, and so forth. The attorneys expected this, so the questions they asked were geared not so much to elicit information as to impart a certain mind-set about the juror's duties that the attorney wanted to reinforce. This process became apparent the first day during the questioning of Rosa Molina.

Cooper asked Mrs. Molina whether she had any objections to the death penalty. Molina said she did not. Cooper asked if his asking this very question made her think his client was guilty of murder in the first degree. She said it did not. So far she had given the "right" answers. Cooper then asked whether, if a verdict of first-degree murder was rendered, Molina would favor a sentence of life or death.

"I would, according to the law and the evidence," responded Molina, trying to give the appropriate answer. "I would follow according to what the law is."

"Well, the law doesn't tell you," Cooper responded.

"The law doesn't tell me," repeated Molina, searching for some direction.

"The law doesn't favor one punishment over the other," said Cooper. "That is something you have to search your conscience for; there are no guidelines."

"You want me to tell you just what?" asked Molina.

"Do you favor one punishment over the other?"

"I have no prejudice of any kind now," said Molina, seeking the magic words.

Satisfied, Cooper went on. He explained briefly the defense of diminished capacity, whereby a defendant without the requisite premeditation might be found guilty of a lesser crime. Did Mrs. Molina have a prejudice against such a defense? She did not. Cooper explained that the defense might be presenting the testimony of a number of psychiatrists. Some people, Cooper said, called psychiatrists "headshrinkers" and thought they were "crazy." Did Mrs. Molina have any such feelings? She did not. Some of these doctors, Cooper said, employ certain psychological tests, such as inkblots, which some people regard as "silly." Did Mrs. Molina feel this way about those tests? She did not. Was Mrs. Molina the kind of person who believes there are two sides to every story? She was.

When it was his turn to question Molina, prosecutor David Fitts had his own set of questions. Just because a witness had a professional title that ended in "-iatry" or "-ology," would the juror still feel free to make up her own mind about what was being discussed? Molina said she would. Just because the issue at stake is something difficult to prove, like a state of mind, would the juror let that in itself constitute reasonable doubt? Molina said she wouldn't.

Fitts was also interested in countering the most dramatic moment of the day. He referred to Cooper's concession that Sirhan Sirhan fired the shot that killed Senator Kennedy as a "strategy" to win credibility points with the jury.

"Your Honor, please," interrupted Cooper. "I would strike 'strategy' from the question. It isn't a question of strategy."

"Well, let us not be so naive," answered Fitts.

Judge Walker upheld Cooper's objection, and Fitts had to rephrase.

"Merely by virtue of the concession which Mr. Cooper suggested to you," said Fitts carefully, "are you at this time disposed to believe that whatever defense the defendant may offer in this case must necessarily be worthy of credence?"

"What?" responded Molina. "Worthy of what?"

"Credence. Belief," said Fitts.

"Counsel," interrupted Judge Walker. "Get into the habit of using certain words that are normally understood by everybody in the community. I suggest that you eliminate words such as 'credence.'"

"Well," answered Fitts, "if the Court please, one of the things I like to find out is whether a juror understands the word 'credence.'" A short while later Fitts would use the word "vicissitudes," peevishly adding, "if I may use the expression."

Fitts had a final warning to Mrs. Molina. He asked if she ever watched courtroom dramas on TV like *Perry Mason*. Molina said she did.

"These dramatizations," cautioned Fitts, "are generally speaking for the purpose of entertaining you and promoting a product. They may or may not show just what happens in court. You understand we probably won't be as entertaining as the courtroom dramas on TV, but that isn't going to disappoint you too much, is it?" Mrs. Molina said it wouldn't.

By the end of the first day Rosa Molina was the only candidate to have made it onto the panel from which the trial jury would be selected. Two had been challenged for cause, two had claimed hardship, and two had been sent to speak to their employers to see if they would still have a job after a three-month absence. By the end of the second day Molina had been joined by only two others, and it began to appear that jury selection, as some had predicted, would consume an entire month.

On January 17, *Life* magazine published a portrait of Sirhan Sirhan written by defense investigator Robert Blair Kaiser, who by this time had a contract with the publishing firm E. P. Dutton to write a book about Senator Kennedy's assassination.

As someone connected to the case, Kaiser could not discuss anything that might become a legal issue in the trial. As a result, the article was a personality profile, nothing more. Still, for many Americans, it was the first look at the alleged assassin of Robert Kennedy. They learned that Sirhan read books on logic and philosophy and wore forty-nine-cent plastic Japanese sandals. They learned that his chest was hairy, his teeth white, and his handshake firm. They also learned that Sirhan was interested in public affairs. Recently, however, he had stopped ordering the *Los Angeles Times*. Sirhan was becoming depressed by world events.

"It's all violence, chaos, unrest," Sirhan told Kaiser. "Whatever happened to the good old days, peace and quiet?"

Kaiser described Sirhan's reaction to an article in *Esquire* in which William F. Buckley, Jr., said that Sirhan was not an American, but someone whose "loyalties were clearly to Jordan."

"What does he mean?" Sirhan protested to Kaiser. "Not American. I *feel* like an American. If I went back to Jordan I would be a foreigner."

But Sirhan recognized that he would not be looked upon as American by those who did not know him. "My name! My name!" he cried to Kaiser. "As soon as anyone heard it, everything else stopped."

Kaiser portrayed Sirhan's mother Mary as a very religious woman who read her Bible daily and prayed that her son would somehow be exonerated. He described the coffee table in the living room of her modest house, where there were several magazines that featured stories on Robert Kennedy.

"She picks up the magazines now and then," Kaiser wrote, "and talks to the face of Robert Kennedy on the *Time* cover, telling him how sorry she is. Kennedy, moreover, talks to her. 'It's O.K., Mary,' she says he says. 'I forgive you, it's O.K.'"[7]

Judge Alarcon's order to limit pretrial discussion was designed to protect the defendant's right to an unprejudiced trial. Its coincident effect was to limit public understanding of any lurking complexities. Thus, although Robert Kaiser was aware of a number of important unresolved issues, one would never know by reading his article that there were any unanswered questions in the case, much less ones bearing on the guilt or innocence of the alleged murderer.

On January 24, after the questioning of fifty-nine candidates, a jury was selected to try the case against Sirhan Sirhan. Agreement came early Friday afternoon, the last day of the third week of the trial. The prosecution had used only seven of its peremptory challenges; the defense, five. The jury contained eight men and four women. They would not be sworn in for another two weeks, as there were additional motions to be heard and alternate jurors to be selected. In the intervening time, they would be sent home with Judge Walker's admonition not to discuss the case with anyone and to avoid friends and others who "might try to advise you." Walker then recessed court until the following Wednesday, when the attorneys were to have their final arguments ready regarding Grant Cooper's motion to quash the indictment against Sirhan Sirhan.

The mood in the hallway after the day's proceedings was upbeat. Both sides appeared to be satisfied.

"I think we've got people from all walks of life," said Grant Cooper, ". . . and that's America. I just don't know what kind of juror I would have looked for in this particular case, but I think we got a good conglomeration."[8]

"They are nice people," said fifty-five-year-old Mary Sirhan hopefully. "They stand up and say they are sure of themselves. To consider taking a life you have to be sure of yourself. It's up to their conscience. They are nice people. I am satisfied."

Mrs. Sirhan was then asked if her feelings toward the jury would make the trial easier to endure. "Through this, we learn," she said, answering the question with a homily: "Before everything else we get our power from God above. I get my power from Him daily."[9]

On February 3, the defendants in the Friars Club card-cheating case were sentenced by U.S. district judge William P. Gray. Grant Cooper's client, Maurice H. Friedman, received the stiffest penalty: six years and a hundred-thousand-dollar fine. Johnny Roselli was sentenced to five years and a fifty-five thousand-dollar fine.

Judge Gray castigated Friedman for the "cynical cheating of people—many of whom were your friends." Gray made note of Johnny Roselli's long criminal record but also credited him for not manufacturing a defense, "at least not on the stand," as Roselli had not testified at the trial. "I'm not sure what you did otherwise," said the judge, apparently suspicious of Roselli's extracurricular activities.

The Friars Club defendants had protested U.S. attorney Matthew Byrne's presentencing memorandum, which had not spoken favorably of any of them. They had demanded that the judge withdraw from the case. Judge Gray denied the motion but did allow the defendants to submit their own affidavits in opposition to the government memo. Attorney James P. Cantillon then announced that Johnny Roselli's affidavit would have to be kept secret because it "involves national security."*

As jury selection continued for the Palestinian immigrant accused of murdering an American presidential candidate, tensions were once again on the rise in the Middle East.

On January 26 in Iraq, fourteen men, including nine Jews, were hung by the neck for alleged espionage. Shops, offices, and schools were ordered closed for the day, and an estimated three hundred thousand Iraqis gathered in Baghdad's Liberation Square. There they were encouraged by government officials to sing and dance while the bodies of those executed were on display.

On February 2 in Israel, club-wielding government security forces sent ninety-three Palestinian schoolgirls to the hospital with injuries as the forces broke up a demonstration in Gaza by some four thousand girls ages eleven to eighteen. Three young women were jailed on charges of spying and aiding guerrillas.

Two days later in Egypt, which at the time did not have diplomatic relations with the United States, Mohammed Yasser Arafat was elected chairman of the Palestine Liberation Organization. Immediately upon taking office, Arafat promised to escalate "armed struggle" in all parts of "occupied Palestine."[10]

---

*Johnny Roselli had apparently been involved in the CIA-sponsored assassination plots against Cuban premier Fidel Castro in the early sixties. He was presumably trying to use that fact in his sentencing affidavit to put some of his present troubles at bay. In 1976 Roselli would be called before the Senate Intelligence Committee to testify in secret about the joint mob-CIA activities. He was due to appear again when his dismembered body was discovered floating in a barrel off the coast of Florida in July of that year.

Closer to home, riots and disturbances on California's college campuses were making daily headlines. On January 23, 380 students were arrested at a rally at San Francisco State College. A week later the California Highway Patrol had to be called in to restore order at the University of California Berkeley. In speaking out against the growing unrest, Governor Ronald Reagan declared that the dissenters were engaging in "guerrilla warfare," the purpose of which was "to create launching pads for insurrection against the social order."[11]

Grant Cooper's motion to quash the indictment of Sirhan Sirhan was a major undertaking. Cooper not only intended to argue his case but planned to present elaborate evidence to demonstrate that the grand jury selection process was inherently prejudicial.

On Tuesday, January 28, the attorneys for both sides gathered in Judge Walker's chambers. There Cooper revealed that he intended to subpoena all 130 judges of the Los Angeles County Superior Court to have them testify about their nominations for the grand jury. At the time, each judge was entitled to nominate two candidates, although not every judge did so. In 1968 this resulted in 170 nominees, from which the 23 grand jurors were selected by chance.

So that the judges would not have to suspend their own court calendars, Cooper proposed enclosing with the subpoena a questionnaire that the judges could fill out and return in lieu of appearing in court. On the form the judges were to be asked about the age and the racial, educational, and economic status of their nominees and whether they had made any affirmative efforts to nominate individuals from groups who were traditionally underrepresented.

"Our position," contended Grant Cooper, when it was time to argue the motion, "is that the very system itself, as it has existed over the past ten years, has the result of being discriminatory." Cooper wasn't exactly blaming the judges. "They tried to get persons of outstanding ability," he said, "persons of outstanding integrity, but they made no effort to get persons from the lower economic groups or from younger persons in the community. . . . I don't believe there were any poor persons, and a very high percentage—I have been given over seventy percent—were college graduates."

Lynn Compton argued that Grant Cooper's entire contention, even if proved, was irrelevant. The grand jury, he said, did not decide the issue of guilt or innocence, only the question of whether there was sufficient evidence to warrant a trial. The defense, Compton pointed out, had already conceded in court on numerous occasions that the defendant was the one who fired the shot that killed Senator Kennedy.

"So it seems to me," said Compton, "that the defense must, as a primary condition precedent, make some allegation that had the grand jury been differently constituted, that there was some different result that might have occurred."

Judge Walker was in sympathy with Compton's arguments. Nevertheless, perhaps out of caution, he ruled that Grant Cooper could present the evidence on his motion to quash the indictment. The frantic process of printing and serving subpoenas and questionnaires began.

Three of the subpoenaed judges chose to testify in person rather than submit a questionnaire. One was Judge Arthur Alarcon, in whose court the legal proceedings against Sirhan had begun seven months before. When Alarcon assumed the witness stand, Grant Cooper asked the judge whether he had attempted to find grand jury nominees from minority groups. Alarcon, who was of Mexican-American heritage, said that he had tried but that sometimes these efforts were frustrated because persons in lower economic groups were unable to make the financial sacrifice necessary to serve on the grand jury.

Judge Edward R. Brand was next to take the stand. He was noticeably unsympathetic to Cooper's questions.

"Judge Brand," asked Grant Cooper, "in determining whom you were going to approach or solicit as a grand jury nominee, did you attach any importance whatsoever to the racial, ethnic, geographic, economic, or age groupings?"

"Well," replied Judge Brand, "that's one of those questions like, 'Have you stopped beating your wife?' . . . I have never concerned myself, Mr. Cooper, with hyphenated Americans. I only know one kind of American and I am not concerned with whether their ancestors were Polish or Japanese or Scandinavian or what."

Judge Brand wanted it understood that the grand jury did more than just hand down criminal indictments. "You see, Mr. Cooper, as you know, the function of the grand jury is multiple . . . to act as watchdog over many departments of the county; over the budget, which, by the way, is approximately one-point-five-billion dollars, and to examine many penal facilities, juvenile facilities, hospital facilities, facilities for the elderly, to determine whether they are properly operated."

Judge Brand's point was that the duties of the grand jury required an intelligent and educated person, and that its heavy work schedule and ten-dollars-a-day compensation were not attractive to everyone. That grand jurors tended to be people retired from professions from which they brought insight and expertise was simply an efficient use of society's human resources.

By the following week Cooper had received over one hundred questionnaires back from the superior court judges. He then brought to the witness stand Raymond G. Schultz, a professor of business administration at California State College. Using the information from the questionnaires, Schultz had analyzed the grand jury nominees by race, occupation, economic status, and age. The conclusion: the 1968 Los Angeles Grand Jury was older, whiter, more affluent, and better educated than the population at large.

Cooper's marquee witness in the motion to quash was the defendant, Sirhan Sirhan. Other than a few monosyllabic words uttered in previous hearings, this would be Sirhan's first public performance. Though it had been made clear that the defendant would testify only as to his financial situation, the press, with little else to do, played it up. SIRHAN TO TESTIFY, the headlines ran.

When he was called, the defendant strode confidently up to the witness stand. Then, as court clerk Alice Nishikawa administered the oath, Sirhan raised his right arm over his head, fist clenched, mimicking the black-power salute given by sprinters Carlos and Smith at the Olympics several months earlier. This gesture was not likely to please many people in the courtroom, and it overshadowed his uneventful eight-minute testimony, during which it was established that for the five previous years he had an income that averaged about eleven hundred dollars per year.

It was February 4 before Grant Cooper was done making his presentation on the motion to quash. Judge Walker then ruled that the entire matter was irrelevant and deficient on its merits. A week had been consumed in preparing and arguing this motion. It was a colossal waste of time and energy by a defense team that still lacked a full understanding of the physical evidence.

Did Grant Cooper really think that Judge Walker would throw out the murder indictment against Sirhan while simultaneously consigning the entire grand jury process to constitutional limbo? It wasn't going to happen. Cooper had to know that. So why did he do it? Perhaps he was trying to establish grounds for appeal, but most likely he was indulging his desire to be seen arguing constitutional issues. New law is rarely made in high-profile cases, and Cooper's arguments, as Compton and Judge Brand had demonstrated, were seriously flawed.

The effort to quash the indictment was, simply stated, bad law. It was also bad politics. The shortcut interpretation of Cooper's motion was that the defendant should not be held accountable for murdering another man because he was young and poor. This was not an idea that was going to warm many hearts. Its most likely effect would be to inspire emotions against the defendant. The jury was not sequestered during this time, and while they were instructed not to read about the case, it would be the unusual juror who would not discover why the trial was being delayed.

The person most noticeably humiliated by Grant Cooper's motion was Mary Sirhan, who followed her son on the witness stand. Under Cooper's direction Mrs. Sirhan testified that since 1966 she had worked in a church nursery school making a yearly income of between fifteen hundred and eighteen hundred dollars. She also revealed that she was paying off a mortgage on a house she had bought for twelve thousand dollars.

Mary Sirhan had not wanted to testify, not about how poor she was. But she did what was expected of her. Even so, her commonsense revulsion for the point being made was evident. When Judge Walker told Mrs. Sirhan she could step down from the witness stand, the diminutive woman rose from her chair and spoke: "I thank God that He gave me the strength," she said in her thickly accented voice, "and I also thank the United States, that I never got hungry and I have a roof over my head."

Later she would explain herself to newsmen in the hallway.

"I have God's blessing," she said. "They say I make little money. That is not what is poor."[12]

After Judge Alarcon and Judge Brand had testified on Cooper's motion, the attorneys for both sides and the defendant entered Judge Walker's chambers for a private session. David Fitts spoke first.

"I want to go into the subject of the sodium Pentothal or sodium Amytal interview of this defendant," he said.

"I thought it was Pentothal,"* replied Judge Walker.

"Amytal is what they have in mind, Judge," Fitts answered

Fitts explained to Judge Walker that both he and defense attorney Grant Cooper had spoken to prosecution psychiatrist Dr. Seymour Pollack and defense psychiatrist Dr. Bernard Diamond, and that both doctors had requested examinations using the drug.

"There has been some disappointment in the result of the interview[s] under hypnosis," added Fitts, "and the general feeling of the psychiatrists in now requesting this sort of sodium Amytal interview is that which they failed to discover under the hypnotic examination might well be brought out."

"If I might interrupt," said Cooper. "I've talked to my client and he is willing to undergo an examination under sodium Amytal or sodium Pentothal, and that is correct, is it not?"

"Yes, sir," replied Sirhan.

In the preceding weeks, either on days when the court was not in ses-

---

*Note: Sodium pentothal (like amytal) is a drug that can be injected into a subject, producing a hypnotic effect and lowering inhibitions. It is sometimes referred to as "truth serum."

sion or sometimes after court was over, Sirhan Sirhan had been undergoing a series of extraordinary interviews with Drs. Diamond and Pollack. In several of these sessions Sirhan had been put under hypnosis. Judge Walker was told by prosecutor David Fitts that the defendant "was a susceptible subject and did actually fall into a deep hypnotic state."

All of this was unusual in the extreme. Why was anybody hypnotizing Sirhan in his cell? What were they looking for? What was the thing they "failed to discover" under hypnosis? Why did they now need a truth serum?

It had not been spoken about in open court; it had only been alluded to in Judge Walker's chambers. It had not been written about in any newspapers or magazines. But in the winter of 1969 the best-kept secret in America was that Grant Cooper's client, Sirhan Sirhan, apparently and with many reasons to believe his representations, had no recollection of murdering Robert Kennedy. Equally baffling was that, although he had been cooperating in his interrogations (submitting to hypnosis and agreeing to be drugged), during his seven months in custody the defendant had been hard-pressed to come up with a coherent explanation as to why he would commit such a crime.

FOUR

The Secret Deal

✳ ✳ ✳

On the morning of February 13, an atmosphere of anticipation filled the Hall of Justice. This was the day each side was to make its opening arguments, welcome news for those who had suffered through five tedious weeks of defense motions and jury selection. The mood quickly dissipated, however, as defense and prosecution attorneys disappeared, once again, into the chambers of Judge Walker.

Waiting newsmen and spectators milled about; some read the morning paper. ISRAEL DOWNS SYRIAN MIG read the front page of the *Los Angeles Times*. In other stories: elements of the First Air Cavalry were involved in a sharp engagement along the Cambodian border; nine hundred National Guard troops were deployed to quell disturbances at the University of Wisconsin; and in New York, the residents of Queens jeered Mayor John Lindsay as he inspected the borough still paralyzed three days after a snowstorm that would come to bear his name. But it was a story in the previous day's *Los Angeles Times* that would drive the day's events. The article by *Times* staff writer Dave Smith bore the headline SIRHAN CHANGE OF PLEA SEEN LIKELY. In the story, Smith asserted that according to sources, Sirhan Sirhan would "probably" plead guilty to first-degree murder in exchange for a maximum penalty of life in prison.

In the judge's chambers Grant Cooper was upset, claiming that Sirhan could not now get a fair trial. What juror would consider a lesser verdict once he or she had learned that the defendant had been willing to plead guilty to murder in the first degree?

Judge Walker shared Cooper's concern. "Everybody knows," he said. "It's been in the newspapers, certainly in the *Times* yesterday morning."

"The front page," said defense attorney Berman.

"Front page, right-hand column," replied Walker.

"Big headline," added Berman.

Deputy district attorney Lynn Compton suggested that Smith's story was merely "surmise" or "speculation." Judge Walker disagreed. There was too much detail in the article for it not to have had a source. But who? At different moments, each party took a turn at declaring innocence.

"I'm sure none of my staff told it," said Judge Walker. "I'm sure of it."

"None of the information contained in this article was given to Mr. Smith," said Grant Cooper. "I mean none by the defense."

"Nothing in that *Times* article came from anybody in the district attorney's office," said Mr. Compton.

"That remains to be seen," said Judge Walker, responding to Compton. "If it becomes important we'll find out where all the information came from, but . . . someone, someway . . . has revealed everything that went on in these chambers, in spite of the fact that I sealed the records."

The story in the *Los Angeles Times* was correct in almost every detail, except one: Sirhan was not going to plead guilty. But the past week had seen furious negotiations between the judge, the prosecution, and the defense. These negotiations ultimately failed, but they provide a unique window into the thoughts and motivations of all the parties involved.

Very early in the case, Grant Cooper had decided upon a psychiatric defense for Sirhan. To lead the team of doctors in support of this defense, he had engaged Dr. Bernard Diamond of the University of California, a man who had extensive experience in the field of legal psychiatry. Cooper had served with Dr. Diamond on a special California commission appointed by Governor Edmund Brown to modernize California's insanity laws.

Realizing the direction Sirhan's lawyers were going, the prosecution hired its own psychiatrist, Dr. Seymour Pollack of the University of Southern California. Under California law, the prosecution psychiatrist would normally not be allowed to examine the defendant in person but could only observe him in court and comment on the defense psychiatrist's presentations.

But Grant Cooper had another idea. Believing his client to be unquestionably ill, he decided to allow the prosecution psychiatrist access to Sirhan. It was a gamble. If Pollack did not agree that Sirhan was mentally impaired, he could greatly damage Cooper's case by being able to speak with authority from the witness stand based upon his own tests and observations. But if the prosecution doctor held that Sirhan was ill, then some sort of deal with the district attorney would seem unavoidable.

Dr. Pollack made full use of this offer. Between January 19 and February 1 he visited Sirhan eight times, spending a total of twenty-three hours with the prisoner. On two of these occasions he put Sirhan under hypnosis and attempted to probe his mind. Grant Cooper, understandably, was eager to see some profit from this investment. In another unprecedented move, Cooper decided that all the doctors should gather at his office to compare notes to see if some sort of consensus on Sirhan's state of mind could be reached.

On February 2, Dr. Orville Richardson, Dr. Eric Marcus, Dr. Martin

Schorr, and Dr. Bernard Diamond sat down with the prosecution adviser, Dr. Seymour Pollack, in the library of Grant Cooper's office.[1] Cooper and Berman would join the group later. A roundtable discussion of Sirhan's mental state ensued, with each doctor sharing with the others his diagnosis of the defendant. But the crucial opinion belonged to Dr. Pollack, and to everyone's dismay he was evasive.

"I don't have any firm opinions," he told the group. An increasingly vexed Dr. Diamond pressed Dr. Pollack to take some position on the case. "I haven't decided yet," Pollack said at one point, still retreating. "I have raised questions—"

"Seymour," interrupted Diamond. "To hear you say 'questions are raised' communicates no information to me that I didn't already have. I'm thoroughly familiar with the questions."

Diamond was angry. Pollack had been given extended access to Sirhan and was now saying he didn't have a professional opinion about the defendant. "I do not feel, Seymour, that you have played fair. I think you have sat and listened to each one of us give an opinion, but whenever it comes to expressing your opinion, you have quibbled, you have evaded, but not in one significant detail did you make any kind of commitment. Now, either this means that this conference was held prematurely, or you are misusing this conference."

"I told you honestly," Pollack pleaded, "I don't have—and I can't disclose what I don't have."

"You do not have any opinions?"

"I haven't any firm opinions."[2]

Diamond left the meeting early, and what followed was an elaborate presentation on Sirhan's mental state by Dr. Schorr. Whether it was Schorr's diagrams and chrome-plated pointer or the delayed effect of Dr. Diamond's disdain, by the end of the session Pollack was making noises to the effect that he saw Sirhan as "more disturbed than less." When he left the meeting, Pollack phoned the district attorney's office and told them that he thought Sirhan was psychotic.

Only three days after Pollack had represented to the defense doctors that he held no firm opinions, the prosecution psychiatrist would submit to District Attorney Evelle Younger a seventeen-page memorandum packed with opinions. Pollack's memo was wordy and seemed to argue all sides of the case, but in the end he stated, "I have no doubt that substantial mental illness was present and still exists in Sirhan and merits consideration in this case."[3] Cooper's gamble had paid off, or so it appeared, for now there seemed nothing in the way of a deal with the prosecution.

On the afternoon of February 4, chief deputy DA Compton entered Judge Walker's chambers and informed the judge that the prosecution and defense had come to an agreement: Sirhan would plead guilty to first-degree murder in exchange for a life sentence. Normally in a situation where both the prosecution and the defense agree on the disposition of a case, that disposition is accepted by the presiding judge. Not here. To the surprise of everyone, Judge Walker declined to accept the deal.

Since a plea bargain scuttled by a judge was outside the experience of both the prosecution and the defense, each side scrambled to examine the options. District Attorney Evelle Younger flew to Washington. Six months earlier Younger had been appointed head of Richard Nixon's Advisory Council on Crime and Law Enforcement. Now, apparently, it was he who was seeking the advice, but who he saw and what they said has never been revealed. Younger, however, did allude to this trip upon his return when he made reference to the "international implications" of the case. "I have made it convenient for appropriate persons in the government to express an opinion to me. They declined and made no comment or recommendation."[4]

While it is hard to believe that Younger went all the way to Washington to receive no comment at all from the Nixon Justice Department, it was certainly the politic thing to say. The federal government had no right to make any comments or recommendations in a case prosecuted under the laws of California. Whatever was or wasn't discussed in Washington, when Younger returned, it was agreed that the next step would be another, more forceful attempt to get Judge Walker's cooperation. This attempt featured the presence of the district attorney himself, his first such appearance at the trial.

A little after nine on the morning of Monday, February 10, the district attorney, his deputies, and the defense attorneys entered the chambers of Judge Walker. Younger opened the proceedings. "I understand that the defendant is prepared to plead guilty and accept a life sentence," he declared, asking Grant Cooper to confirm this to the judge. Then Younger delivered a remarkable speech.

"We favor it, Judge," he said, alluding to the plea bargain, "and the law requires your approval. . . . Now that we have gotten our psychiatrist's report, a man whom we have great confidence in, we are in a position where we can't conscientiously urge the death penalty.

"It appears that the result is a foregone conclusion. Our psychiatrist, in effect, says that the defendant is psychotic, and his report would support the position of the defense because of diminished capacity and the death penalty wouldn't be imposed. So . . . are we justified in going through the motions of a trial, a very traumatic and expensive trial, when we can't conscientiously ask for the death penalty anyway? We don't think we are."

Judge Walker then turned to Grant Cooper, who said that he believed the psychiatrists' reports would merit no more than a verdict of guilty to second-degree murder. But that, conceded Cooper, would mean little to the defendant. The chief difference between the two in terms of punishment (excluding the death sentence) was the length of the minimum sentence. In this case, Cooper reasoned, "by virtue of the prominence of the deceased . . . the minimum would mean nothing . . . so we have concluded that the wise thing to do would be to enter a plea of guilty to first-degree murder with life imprisonment."

Evelle Younger tried to reassure Walker by promising that "whatever is done not only be the just and proper thing to do, but appear to be the just and proper thing, too. Your Honor, I am sure, doesn't want anybody to think that there was any hanky-panky going on if we do this."

Younger had a proposal: between the time when the plea bargain would be accepted and the sentence imposed, the defense, the prosecution, and the police would work out the mechanics by which they could "put into the record all pertinent materials including statements of witnesses and that sort of thing and the psychiatrists' reports, so that the second-guessers, and they will be legion, who write books and magazines, serials and so forth, wondering why it was done or why this wasn't done, we will at least have it in the record."

Judge Walker shook his head. "I have given this a great deal of thought. I appreciate the cost. I appreciate the sensation, but I am sure it would just be opening us up to a lot of criticism. . . . [T]here are a lot of ramifications. And they continually point to the Oswald matter, and they have us wonder what is going on because the fellow wasn't tried."

Lynn Compton had an idea of his own. "If the defendant were to plead guilty to first-degree murder, there wouldn't be any evidence to put on, we simply would offer no evidence on the penalty and there would be no trial." Compton's idea seemed to be a subtle warning to Walker. If the judge wanted to keep making up new rules, the prosecution could, in essence, take the ball and go home.

Grant Cooper had a different thought. "Another way it could be done, is if we had first-degree [plea], we could put on a very skeleton outline of the case at the time of plea instead of submitting reports, and we could put witnesses on to testify."

"Well, then, they would say that it was all fixed, it was greased," replied Walker, more determined, "so we will go through with the trial. . . . I am not going to argue it any further, gentlemen."

Cooper's suggestion of a "skeleton outline" of a trial seemed at the time to be a spontaneous idea, yet it revealed something deeper in the chief defense counsel's outlook, and ultimately his entire handling of the case. Something approaching that thought had been on his mind from the beginning. In early January, in a meeting with defense investigator

Robert Kaiser and Dr. Bernard Diamond, Cooper revealed that he envisioned a contest in which many of the punches would be pulled. "I'd let them stage anything they want," said Cooper.

"When would you make the plea?" asked Diamond.

"When the evidence was in," Cooper responded. "We'd have a conference with the judge. But it would all be worked out ahead of time."

"You wouldn't need a jury then."

"Well, I wouldn't say that. . . . The verdict—of first-degree murder with life imprisonment—would just be predetermined, that's all."[5]

Cooper's mind-set disturbed Kaiser. A week or two later he would hand the chief defense counsel a memorandum expressing

profound reservations about some kind of prearrangement between you and the DA whereby you would agree in advance to the penalty, and then *stage* [emphasis Kaiser's] some kind of trial. I don't know enough about the ways of the law here, but as a layman . . . either you have your client plead guilty, or you engage in a genuine, if friendly, adversary proceeding, where the truth is given a good test according to the rules of evidence as evolved through centuries of good Anglo-Saxon jurisprudence. I don't see how you can combine the two.[6]

Kaiser's memo appears not to have greatly influenced Cooper, but it hardly mattered, since Cooper was not the person making the key decisions. Judge Walker was, and his pronouncement on the plea bargain seemed final. Yet the prosecution and the defense were still in the mood to make a deal. After Judge Walker had turned them away, Cooper, Parsons, and Berman, accompanied by Lynn Compton, hurried over to the district attorney's office, where yet another alternative was proposed. In this variation Sirhan would plead guilty to first-degree murder and then let the jury decide the issue of penalty. In return, the prosecution would make a positive recommendation of life in prison. After lunch, the attorneys were back in front of Judge Walker asking for a delay in the trial so that they might explore this option.

Walker was worried. "Here's another very practical thing you fellows have to be thinking about, and maybe you have—the district attorney shows up this morning and everybody outside is saying, 'Why was the district attorney up there?' . . . I said he came to show me his respect, but they know that isn't the truth. If we start dragging our feet, I think it could damage the case tremendously. . . . So let's move. You've got two days."

In the two days he was given, Cooper and his cocounsel would meet with Sirhan twice. Cooper had these meetings recorded. On February 13, he would try to have them entered into the court record, justifying his attempt with this explanation: "We had a full and frank discussion with the defendant in the presence of his mother; and the presence of his brother; and his three counsel. . . . We taped the interview so there would be no question as to the advice that we gave him." During these meetings, however, Cooper was almost alone in his inclination to accept the prosecution offer of a positive recommendation of life in prison in exchange for a guilty plea. In the meeting of February 11, Mary Sirhan expressed the seemingly unrealistic hope that the trial might still result in Sirhan's acquittal. Sirhan's brother Munir was also opposed to the deal. Munir, who had recently spent a short time in jail on a vagrancy charge, announced that he'd rather die than spend even ten years in prison. Sirhan asked for a day to think about it.

The next day's deliberations, however, would be complicated by the plea-bargain story on the front page of the *Los Angeles Times*. It made Cooper all the more sure that a verdict of first-degree murder was unavoidable, and he wanted to grab what they could get from the prosecution while offers were still being made.

But he was the only one. Emile Berman was adamant. "If we plead this kid guilty," he said, "we're destroying his right to a fair trial, and he'll never have the possibility of an appeal."[7] Russell Parsons concurred. He told Cooper that he was in favor of a full trial and would make that recommendation to Sirhan. Dr. Bernard Diamond called Cooper as soon as he saw the reports about the plea in the news. As Cooper would report to the others, Diamond was upset by the news. He thought that Sirhan definitely had diminished capacity, and it should be nothing worse than second degree, and he didn't want to compromise his principles in testifying on the penalty phase.

Because of the story in the morning paper, it was difficult for the attorneys to confer with Sirhan unnoticed. A considerable group of reporters waited for them at the foot of the marble stairs leading to the Hall of Justice. Cooper and Parsons had to wade through, repeating the words "No comment."

Once inside, Cooper sat down with Parsons, Berman, Kaiser, and Sirhan. Also at the meeting was a young lawyer named Abdeen Jabara. Jabara represented a group of moneyed Arab Americans from Detroit. The group had been horrified at the murder of Robert Kennedy and its public relations consequences for the Arab American community. But they had also seen in the trial of Sirhan Sirhan a way to tell the Arab side of the Arab-Israeli conflict.

In October of 1968, Jabara had held a confidential meeting in Chicago with Russell Parsons and defense investigator Mike McCowan. At that meeting Jabara reportedly promised monetary support for the defense of Sirhan. In exchange he requested a role in presenting at the trial the historical context of the war with the Jews in Palestine. Parsons saw no problem with this and agreed. Jabara then became what was called a "defense consultant." Being an Arab, he quickly gained the confidence of the defendant and his family, something that Grant Cooper had only done in a tenuous way. Thus when the lawyers met with Sirhan to discuss the plea bargain, Jabara was there, and his opinion carried weight.

Cooper began the meeting by informing Sirhan of Dr. Diamond's sentiments opposing a plea bargain. Berman and Parsons then counseled against making the plea. Abdeen Jabara weighed in with them, pointing out that the story in the *Los Angeles Times* would be "beautiful grounds" for reversible error. He thought Sirhan had an excellent chance of getting second degree on the merits, and he thought that a full-blown trial might help focus world attention on the plight of the Palestinians.[8]

Jabara also knew that the Arab American community was becoming impatient with Sirhan's representation. In the *Los Angeles Times,* Dr. M. T. Mehdi, chairman of the Action Committee on American-Arab Relations, had already commented on the report that Sirhan might plead guilty. The defense attorneys, Mehdi said, "failed to understand that the Sirhan case is an historic political event and not an ordinary legal problem."[9]

Alone in his position, Cooper would argue his case. "You can't overlook the fact that the man that was shot and killed was a candidate for the office of president and was a U.S. senator and a very popular individual. Second degree would be an empty victory. We as lawyers would be big heroes, but what's it going to help Sirhan? It's still life imprisonment. The minimum doesn't mean a damn thing."

Sirhan had his own ideas of what a deal should look like. "I would [plead] to the first degree," he told the group, "with a guarantee of life and having a chance to tell my story on the witness stand, plus another guarantee of parole after seven years. I absolutely want a guarantee of that."

"The parole board," said Berman, a little upset, "has nothing to do with the deal here."

"Well, hell," said Sirhan when all the arguments were heard, "I might as well fight it out."[10]

In chambers the next day Cooper explained Sirhan's position to Judge Walker. "Following a full discussion of the matter, the defendant agreed with his counsel that he would plead guilty to first-degree murder to the Court, with the assurance that he would get life . . . but that he definitely would not plead guilty and submit the matter to the jury."

What followed was yet another effort by both sides to get the judge to accept the original deal, including hints of judicial reversal if Walker didn't comply. "The statute which requires the Court's approval in that particular instance," said Compton, "envisions more the Court's analysis of the proposal from the light of whether it does essential justice to both sides of the case and that the question of the format or the public exposure of the evidence is really not relevant. . . . It is our analysis of the case that this plea would do essential justice to both sides of the case."

But Walker would not be moved. "As far as I'm concerned, this matter of a plea of first degree with life imprisonment has been disposed of. You had ample opportunity the other day to make all the arguments you wanted to. . . . As I said before, I think the jury should determine the penalty. That's my decision. Let's go ahead and try the lawsuit."

When court was finally brought to order on February 13, Grant Cooper, with the jury absent, stood and made his motion for a mistrial, based upon the front-page story appearing in the *Los Angeles Times* the day before, a story that he claimed would irreversibly prejudice a jury against his client. But Judge Walker was in no mood to start over. "As I see it," Walker said, "the mistrial hangs solely on what they have heard and beyond that whatever consideration they have given to it." Walker proposed questioning each juror about the story.

Cooper was skeptical. "Frankly, I don't think it's going to do any good," he said, "because I don't believe that any juror, with the admonition that Your Honor has properly given [about avoiding trial publicity], is going to admit that he is in contempt of court. . . . I don't believe any of them would be willing to admit that they violated Your Honor's order."

Cooper was wrong. In the questioning of jurors that followed, almost all of them admitted to having heard or read some version of the Sirhan plea-bargain story. The real question, which Cooper didn't articulate, was, Would a juror who had heard the news admit to being prejudiced by it? Prejudice, by its nature, is difficult to see in oneself and easy to deny. At this point the jurors present were there because they wanted to be. Only one juror, Ronald Evans, admitted under Cooper's questioning that it would be difficult to bring in a verdict of second-degree murder or manslaughter under the circumstances. But even this did not move Judge Walker. After recess he decided that the jury had not been compromised, and he overruled Cooper's motion. The trial would begin immediately.

On February 20, after the trial had been under way for a few days, another front-page story on Sirhan's plea bargain appeared in the *Los Angeles Times*. It became the focus of another discussion in Judge Walker's chambers. Cooper was the first to speak: "If it please the Court, what I'm about to say is said without rancor . . . [but] I must now quarrel that an article appeared in the Thursday morning, February 20, issue of the *Los Angeles Times* which I now offer in evidence only in part, only in support of the original motion for a mistrial and, second, I move for a mistrial again on this ground."

Cooper was angry about the article's content. "It reflects quite accurately everything that was said in chambers," he said. Cooper then pointed an accusing eye at the prosecution table. "I have had the greatest cooperation from the office of the district attorney and these particular deputies here throughout the trial, but, notwithstanding . . ."

Judge Walker jumped in. "Well, let me say that I gave some of that information out myself. . . . I called Mr. Ron Einstoss and gave him that story and that is how it got out. . . . It was my feeling that if they got the other part, the whole story should be out."

Cooper said that he thought such action was "misconduct" on the part of the judge. Walker responded that he already checked with the bailiff and that the jury had had no access to this story.

Prosecutor Lynn Compton then spoke: "There was an inference made," he said, "that these *Times* articles came from the district attorney's office. I am not sure upon what it was predicated, unless it was the simple fact that the *Times* newspaper has a staff reporter that occupies a pressroom in the district attorney's office."

Compton then went on the offensive, reminding those present, "There's an outfit called *Newsday* in the East which broke the story about the plea and with a lot of details that are in the *Times* article before the *Times* ever ran it . . . and we resent the implication that the *Times* article had to originate with the DA's office when it didn't."

"I will say very frankly," Cooper replied, "that I did believe from a reading of the article that I thought that it emanated from the DA's office, and my impression from a reading of the article was that it came from Evelle Younger himself." Indeed, earlier in the week, Younger had demonstrated incaution by stating on television that Sirhan's trial could take "three months or three days."

Judge Walker then weighed in with a rumor of his own. "The story was given to me that your man, your investigator-writer, was the one that did it."

"Kaiser?" said Cooper incredulously.

But it wasn't Kaiser. As one who was working on a book about the trial, Kaiser had the least incentive to leak anything to anyone. After the trial a friend of the Sirhan family, Rose Lynn Mangan, approached Cooper to ask if Kaiser had really been the one to leak the story. "No," Cooper said with disgust, "it was Berman!"

That Emile Berman had been talking off the record to the press was evident a week before the plea-bargain story broke when, in another *Newsday* article, Bob Greene cited the concern of "defense sources" that Sirhan's "pose of a would-be nationalist hero" would interfere with his defense of diminished capacity. This was Berman's primary worry, and he was most certainly Greene's source.

Berman had quickly become disenchanted with defense strategy, particularly with the political overtones that were beginning to creep in. "He stayed on with great reluctance," Robert Kaiser told the authors. "He was there in name and body only."

According to Kaiser, it was this disenchantment that led to the leaks to the press. "He wasn't in town very long before he started drinking heavily, and the worse things got, the more he drank. And the reporters quickly learned that they could ply him with drinks and then pump him. They were all staying at the Ambassador."

The chain of accusations and denials had now come full circle. Everyone had denied leaking information to the press, yet everyone had done so. Judge Walker, by his own admission, had provided the impetus for the most recent story. The district attorney's office had clearly provided some material to the *Los Angeles Times*. And one of Sirhan's own lawyers was the source of the original leak.

The failed plea-bargain negotiations offer a unique window onto the interior landscape of the trial of Sirhan Sirhan. From the conversations in the judge's chambers, the underlying suppositions and motivations of the various participants can be considered.

For example, why did Judge Walker so adamantly refuse to allow the plea bargain? Was it, as he claimed, because of the historical significance of the case? Walker was sensitive to what was being said about the trial and how he was being perceived, as his leaking the plea bargain story demonstrates. Could it be that a desire to end a distinguished career presiding over a trial of great importance played a major role in Walker's rulings?

Judge Walker's motivation probably derived from an amalgam of sentiments—a strong personal desire to preside at the trial, coupled with a belief that the case shouldn't be put in a box too neatly and tucked away. From a historical point of view, Walker's insistence on a trial was laudable. Still, if his motivation was heavily colored by his own personal desires, then Walker's obstinacy came very close to costing Sirhan his life.

And what of Grant Cooper? From his conversations, it is evident that Cooper, although baffled by his client, believed that Sirhan was a sick man, innocent of the charge of first-degree murder. But, as Cooper saw it, the only differences between first-degree murder and second-degree were the possibility of the death sentence for the more serious crime and a shorter minimum sentence for the lesser. Cooper reasoned that since Sirhan was not likely to be paroled quickly for murdering a presidential candidate even if he was found guilty of second-degree murder, why not grab the sure thing, life in prison, and eliminate the risk of being sentenced to death?

But although Cooper appeared to hold his client's interests at heart (and his calculations in the equation of justice would prove correct), the plea-bargain negotiations exposed the defense attorney's chief flaw: he saw the trial of Sirhan as a staged event with a foregone conclusion. Perhaps he believed Evelle Younger's words when Younger said, "We can't conscientiously urge the death penalty." Perhaps he relied on Compton's idea of the prosecution recommending a life sentence during the penalty phase of the trial in return for a guilty plea. Even though Cooper could not deliver the guilty plea from Sirhan, he seemed to go out of his way to cause the prosecution no grief. By his words and actions it appears that Cooper believed he had forged some sort of gentleman's agreement: if he helped move things along, the prosecution would reciprocate when it came to deciding the penalty. Since Cooper saw no serious evidentiary conflicts, he was betraying no one.

But Grant Cooper would come to feel betrayed. Several years after the trial, he would tell journalist Betsy Langman that the prosecution "reneged" on their promise not to ask for the death penalty.[11] Thus, perhaps believing that he had such a promise, Cooper, during the trial, would journey off into a landscape of psychological constructions and political rationalizations that bore little relation to Sirhan and ultimately rang false to the jury.

It is, however, the prosecution's actions that are the most difficult to understand. Why were the prosecutors so eager for a plea bargain? Are we to believe they cared so ferociously about the taxpayers' money? Was District Attorney Younger's professed conscience their driving force? If we accept the stated reason that as a matter of conscience they couldn't seek a sentence of death, why, when the trial was over, did the prosecutors aggressively ask for that very penalty?

And why did Younger go to Washington? Whom did he see? Did they really offer no comment or recommendation? Or did they decide that the country needed no further reminders of political murder and that another assassin hustled off the stage would be the safest, and therefore the wisest, course to take?

A more shadowed view of the prosecution's zeal in pursuing a plea bargain would be that within the DA's office, and certainly within the Los Angeles Police Department, there were some few men who were aware that there were severe problems with the physical evidence, a nasty little secret kept from the defense attorneys and the public at large. Although Grant Cooper had already chosen a psychiatric defense for his client—a defense that shouldn't have exposed any of the difficulties in the eyewitness accounts, the ballistics, or the autopsy—there was no guarantee that these anomalies would not surface at the trial. What if Cooper just stumbled over something that caused him to view the murder from a different perspective? What if he felt cornered and came out fighting—demanding that the prosecution prove the most basic elements of the crime, such as whether the bullets that struck Robert Kennedy really came from Sirhan's gun?

FIVE

Doorframes and Dish Trays

※ ※ ※

T HE PEOPLE OF the State of California versus Sirhan Bishara Sirhan."
Court clerk Alice Nishikawa, with the jury present, opened the trial's
formal proceedings on Thursday, February 13, 1969, by reading the
articles of indictment. The primary article charged that "on or about the
5th day of June 1968 . . . , the said defendant, Sirhan Bishara Sirhan, did
willfully, unlawfully, feloniously and with malice aforethought murder
Robert Francis Kennedy, a human being."

Judge Walker told the jury that they were not to accept as evidence anything said by either side in an opening statement. He then nodded to
David Fitts, who stood and stepped to the lectern.

Though he was not the man in charge, it was generally agreed that
deputy district attorney Fitts was the class act of the prosecutor's office. In
contrast to his burly, crew-cut associates, the Stanford-educated Fitts was
slim, erect, with a full head of graying hair. He had been compared in the
press to the late screen actor Montgomery Clift—the idealized image of
the thoughtful American man.

Fitts opened the case against Sirhan Sirhan by offering a recapitulation of
the crime. The prosecutor described the line of possession of the alleged
murder weapon, then Sirhan's movements in the week preceding the shooting. After that, he reviewed the movements of Robert Kennedy on primary
night, culminating in his entrance into the hotel pantry.

According to David Fitts, Sirhan Sirhan approached Robert Kennedy
in the pantry and "brought his right hand with the .22 caliber revolver
in it to the very vicinity of the Senator's head and at point blank range in
rapid succession fired eight shots." Fitts promised to demonstrate "that
these shots that were recovered from [victims] Goldstein and from Weisel
and the one recovered from the body of the Senator were all fired by
the same gun, that is the gun recovered by Roosevelt Grier and Rafer
Johnson."

The prosecutor then spoke to an issue that was not being adjudicated,
but was on the agenda nonetheless. "The evidence in this case will show,"
he said in conclusion, "that defendant Sirhan Sirhan was alone responsible
for the tragic incidents at the Ambassador Hotel in the early morning hours

of the 5th of June; that he acted alone and without the concert of others. I thank you very much."

The next morning Emile Berman rose for the defense. As expected, he avoided a direct challenge to the prosecution. "One thing I'd like to fasten down with you," he said, "is that the evidence in this case will disclose that this defendant, Sirhan, is immature, emotionally disturbed, and mentally ill." Berman then recounted a list of gruesome atrocities Sirhan was said to have witnessed as a small boy in war-torn Palestine—his home "bombed," a man torn apart by an explosion, and "a little girl's leg blown off by a bomb, and the blood spurting from below her knee as though from a faucet." These stories represented the awkward marriage of the psychiatric defense to the political motive, something Berman didn't have to make sense of right then and wouldn't be able to do later.

"There is no doubt," Berman told the jury, ". . . that he did in fact fire the shot that killed Senator Kennedy. The killing was unplanned and undeliberate, impulsive and without premeditation or malice, totally a product of a sick, obsessed mind and personality. . . . [Sirhan] was out of contact with reality, in a trance in which he had no voluntary control over his will, his judgment, his feelings or his actions. I do not expect . . . you to accept my statement. . . . [W]e will prove them through great men in the fields of psychiatry and psychology.

"We ask you to listen to the evidence," he concluded, "to adopt what science has to offer, and to consult with your conscience. . . . [W]e ask you to let justice be done."

During the following recess, Berman told reporters out in the corridor that Sirhan had probably not liked his opening statement. "Sirhan was saying to himself, 'That S.O.B. Berman, speaking of me like that, the dirty so and so'—but it's the truth. I tell it just like it was. This is a fantasy kid who went overboard on mysticism and went crazy with power when he saw himself in a mirror. Strictly unbalanced. In short, a nut."[1]

After recess the prosecution began to call witnesses. Many of these were people who had been in the pantry and who could relate some portion of what happened when Robert Kennedy was shot. On the second day, Arthur Placencia, the young police officer who took Sirhan into custody, was called to testify. Under John Howard's direction Placencia recounted how he came upon the defendant, read him his rights in the squad car, and delivered him to detectives at Rampart Station. The only unexpected testimony occurred when Howard inquired about a statement Sirhan was said to have made in the patrol car, something that had been widely reported in the newspapers.

"Did you hear Mr. Sirhan say, 'I did it for my country?'"

"No, sir."

"You didn't hear that?"

"No, sir."

When Grant Cooper began the cross-examination, he asked Officer Placencia whether he had inspected the prisoner's eyes while they were in the squad car. Placencia conceded that he had done so with a flashlight. Cooper asked why.

"Pupil reaction," replied the officer, "to see if anybody you have in custody might be under the influence of a drug or alcohol."

"And how did his pupils react?" asked Cooper.

"I can't recall, sir."

"You can't recall?"

"No, sir."

Grant Cooper then pulled out and began to read a transcript of an inquiry Placencia had undergone in early September.

> Q: Did you check him to determine if he was under the influence of anything such as drugs?
> A: Oh, yes. I checked his pupils.
> Q: How did you check his pupils?
> A: With the flashlight. Put it up to his face and sort of looked to see if his pupils react.
> Q: How did they react?
> A: They didn't.
> Q: They didn't react to light at all?
> A: No. His pupils were real wide.

Grant Cooper put his question again, "Now, did his pupils react to the light?"

"Yes, sir, according to the report. That's what I said."

"In other words, his pupils did not react to the light, did they?"

"No, sir."

"Now what did that mean to you as an officer?"

"That he was under the influence of something."

Had Officer Placencia really forgotten what had happened when he flashed the light in Sirhan's eyes? The memory had certainly been clear only several months earlier. Perhaps the young policeman had been made to understand by his superiors that this testimony might help a murderer escape punishment, and that, as a patrolman with only two weeks' experience, he was poorly qualified to make such a test.

Placencia's loss of memory was a small example of how evidence over time begins to bend to the purposes of those presenting it. Grant Cooper's use of a previous statement to impeach a witness, or in this case, refresh his memory, was an elementary tactic of cross-examination. Unfortunately, this minor skirmish with Officer Placencia very early in the proceedings would represent Cooper's brightest moment of the entire trial. Had he used the same skepticism toward the state's physical evidence, the trial transcript might be quite different.

A month earlier, as the defense was making preparations for jury selection, Grant Cooper received a telephone call from William Harper, a respected criminalist who had been a consultant in over three hundred homicide cases during a thirty-five-year career, Harper had called Cooper to give some advice. "Beware of Wolfer," he said, speaking of the LAPD's criminalist assigned to the RFK investigation; "he gives them what they want." Harper had come up against the police investigator's forensic work on several occasions, work Harper regarded as unscientific and self-serving. "Wolfer's not competent," Harper cautioned. "He will do what's expected of him."[2]

Cooper expressed his appreciation to Harper for the notice, but he told the criminalist that he was not concerned. After all, Cooper reasoned, there was no question about what had happened. Harper was less certain of this than Cooper, but the criminalist had delivered his message, and he let the matter drop—for the time being. Cooper, however, had been warned.

In June of 1968 DeWayne Wolfer was a criminalist assigned to the crime laboratory of the LAPD's Scientific Investigation Division (SID). He had been on the force for fifteen years. Within two hours of the shooting Wolfer was at the Ambassador Hotel directing the collection of evidence, the taking of photographs, and conducting bullet flight-path analysis. In a 1971 deposition he described his work that night:

> I went to the scene of the crime and I explored the trajectory of all the holes in the wall and the walls of victims [sic]. . . . I was there immediately after the death of the Senator. I retrieved and was in charge of the crime scene and I recovered the bullets that were re-covered.[3]

In the deposition, Wolfer speaks of exploring the trajectory of "holes in the wall" and of recovering "the bullets that were recovered." This may have been some sort of mental hiccup, for at other times Wolfer would hold to the official police assertion that there were no bullet holes in the walls and that no bullets were recovered from the crime scene. The sharp conflict between the police assertions and the surviving evidence forms one of the central mysteries of the murder of Robert Kennedy. As will be explained, if there were bullet holes in the walls or bullets recovered in the pantry, then a second gun was fired during the murder. The police assert that there were no bullets or bullet holes. The evidence says otherwise.

There are, for example, a number of photographs (see photo insert) that appear to contradict the police criminalist. In one of these Wolfer himself is posing in front of the pantry doorway, pointing to an apparent bullet mark. In another, the chief medical examiner for Los Angeles County, Dr. Thomas Noguchi, is also pointing at the doorframes. Later, when asked to describe how the photograph came about, Noguchi said that he asked DeWayne Wolfer for the location of any bullet holes. "He pointed, as I recall . . . to several holes in the doorframes of the swinging doors leading into the pantry."[4]

Los Angeles police officers Robert Rozzi and Charles Wright were also shown, in an Associated Press photo, kneeling by a doorway, pointing to a hole and illuminating it with a flashlight. The caption reads, "Police technician inspects a bullet hole discovered in a door frame. . . . Bullet is still in the wood." In 1975, Rozzi elaborated:

Sometime during the evening when we were looking for evidence, someone discovered what appeared to be a bullet a foot and a half or so from the bottom of the floor [*sic*] in a doorjamb on the door behind the stage. I also personally observed . . . a hole in the doorjamb, and the base of what appeared to be a small-caliber bullet was lodged in the hole.[5]

Rozzi's partner, patrolman Charles Wright, confirmed the observation twenty years after the murder, when he was asked by journalist Dan Moldea how certain he was, on a scale of one to ten, that it was a bullet he observed in the hole. "I would say," responded Wright, "it would be as close to a ten as I'd ever want to go without pulling it out."[6]

On the morning of June 5, only hours after the murder, two amateur photographers, John Shirley and John R. Clemente, took pictures of the pantry and the doorframes. In March 1969, Shirley provided a statement to Lillian Castellano of the Kennedy Assassination Truth Committee, a small group of citizens seeking answers to the questions and conflicts in the official account of the murder. Shirley wrote:

In the wooden jamb of the center divider were two bullet holes surrounded by inked circles which contained some numbers and letters. I remember a manager pointing out those particular marked bullet holes to another person who appeared to be a press photographer.

It appeared that an attempt had been made to dig the bullets out from the surface. However, the center divider jamb was loose, and it appeared to have been removed from the framework so that the bullets might be extracted from behind.[7]

The man who helped authorities remove the wood was Dale Poore, a carpenter employed by the hotel. In a 1975 interview conducted by the DA's office, Poore described what he saw. "It looked like the bullet had went [sic] in at sort of an angle as it was traveling this way. So it made a bit of an oblong hole and the fiber of the board had closed in some after it went in."[8]

Shortly after Poore did his work, a veteran crime reporter for the *Chicago Tribune,* Robert Wiedrich, entered the hotel pantry. Wiedrich spoke to several police officers, who pointed out maître d' Karl Uecker as a crime-scene witness. Wiedrich interviewed Uecker and filed his story, "Felt Him Fire His Gun, Hotel Worker Says." The article contained the following:

> On a low table lay an 8-foot strip of molding, torn by police from the center post of the double doors leading from the ballroom. These were the doors through which Sen. Kennedy had walked, smiling in his moment of victory.
>
> Now the molding bore the scars of a crime laboratory technician's probe as it had removed two .22-caliber bullets that had gone wild.[9]

When Philip Melanson contacted Wiedrich in 1988, the reporter still remembered the name of the police officer he had spoken to that night as Detective Sergeant J. R. MacArthur. He remembered MacArthur because he had been "amazingly cooperative." Regarding the two bullets referred to in his article, Wiedrich did not witness the actual removal, but he stated, "The molding had obviously been removed from the wall. They had recovered two slugs."

Apparent bullet holes in the hotel pantry were also observed by crime-scene witnesses Lisa Urso, Martin Patrusky, Vincent DiPierro, Angelo DiPierro, and Karl Uecker. All of them testified at the trial of Sirhan. None of them were asked about the bullet holes by the prosecution or the defense.

It could be argued that these witnesses were not qualified to identify a bullet hole, but such could not be said about William Bailey. An agent with the FBI stationed in Los Angeles, Bailey was in the pantry within hours of the shooting, inspecting the crime scene in preparation for witness interviews. In 1993 Bailey described to the authors what he saw that night:

> As I toured the pantry area I noticed in a wood doorframe, a center divider between the two swinging doors, two bullet holes. I've inspected quite a few crime scenes in my day. These were clearly bul-

let holes; the wood around them was freshly broken away and I could see the base of a bullet in each one.[10]

On the night of the murder the holes in the doorframes were regarded as prized evidence, as demonstrated by the photographs taken of DeWayne Wolfer and others pointing to them—our LAPD crime solvers hard at work. What Wolfer and the others didn't know until the next day was that five bullets would be recovered from the five wounded bystanders, and that Kennedy had been wounded three times, two bullets remaining within him and a third, by police accounts, passing through his shoulder and penetrating the ceiling. A fourth bullet passed harmlessly through Kennedy's suit jacket.

The arithmetic here is devastatingly simple: the gun taken from Sirhan Sirhan held a maximum of eight bullets, thus, with at least eight bullets already accounted for, there could be no bullets in the walls or doorframe if only one gun was fired. Any bullets or bullet holes in the walls would be irrefutable proof of a second gun.

With the recovery of the bullets from the wounded victims, the apparent bullet holes by the door, which had been trophies the night before, now became unwelcome evidence. The doorframes were quickly removed by the police. Under the heading "Work Requested," the police property report for the frames called for "trajectory analysis." The two pieces of wood molding were never seen again by anyone on the outside, including any member of the Sirhan defense team.

Coming, as he did, late into the case, Grant Cooper had no understanding of the physical evidence. Police secrecy regarding the doorframes abetted his ignorance. At no point in the trial was the issue of extra bullets, in the doorframes or elsewhere, ever mentioned.

It is not clear from the accounts of William Harper's cautionary conversation with Cooper whether or not the criminalist was calling to offer his services. Greater interest by Cooper might have been the entrée Harper was looking for before volunteering. The defense was top-heavy with psychiatrists and psychologists, but they had no forensic expertise. No one was focusing on ballistics.

In not inviting Harper to join the defense, Cooper was most likely playing it safe. In his own mind he was certain of the facts and probably saw no advantage to making trouble for the prosecution, even if it could be demonstrated that DeWayne Wolfer's work was flawed. In addition, the defense lawyer had little incentive to look in the direction of extra bullets.

Evidence of a second gun, in any usual circumstance, would not exonerate gunman number one and would settle conclusively, and adversely for the defendant, the issue of premeditation. The circumstances under which this would not be so would have to be bizarre: for example, gunman number one acting without awareness or volition. But in his opening statement, Emile Berman had maintained that his client "was out of contact with reality, in a trance in which he had no voluntary control over his will." If this was the case, then the defense attorneys should have been more vigilant in their examination of the physical evidence.

The first public notice of any problems with the bullet count occurred on May 23, 1969, a full month after Sirhan's trial had concluded. An article by Lillian Castellano and Floyd Nelson titled "Ten Shots from an Eight-Shot Revolver" appeared in the *Los Angeles Free Press.* Basing their analysis on the Shirley/Clemente photograph of the two bullet holes in the center divider and the AP photo of Officers Rozzi and Wright, Castellano and Nelson made a prima facie case that at least ten bullets had been fired during the murder. "This means," the authors concluded, "that the police have not told us the truth—the District Attorney has not told us the truth—the news media have not reported the truth. . . . It is a very frightening thought."

The Castellano/Nelson article received little attention, though the LAPD was certainly aware of the allegations. The following Wednesday, perhaps in an effort to forestall concern raised by the article, District Attorney Evelle Younger made a false promise to release the case files held by the police, saying, "the interests of the public and law enforcement are best served by full disclosure." Younger made no mention of the issue of extra bullets, but just three weeks later, the doorframes and the ceiling tiles would be destroyed by the police.

Even after the publication of the Castellano/Nelson story, most people who had seen the bullet holes continued to have no idea that what they saw represented any problem to the case. It is a tribute to how well the bullet-count secret was kept that years would go by, many years in some cases, before the significance of witness and police observation would be understood.

In the mid-1970s Los Angeles attorney (and former Charles Manson prosecutor) Vincent Bugliosi gathered affidavits from witnesses (including law enforcement investigators Rozzi, Wright, and Bailey) who had not been questioned on this point by the police or trial lawyers. In the 1980s RFK researchers Gregory Stone and Philip Melanson tracked down witnesses (including Urso, DiPierro, and Wiedrich) who had unrecorded bullet-count information.

In the spring of 1990, investigative journalist Dan Moldea conducted an extensive probe into the question of extra bullets. He interviewed scores of LAPD officers and sheriff's deputies who had been involved in the case. His May 13, 1990, article in *The Washington Post,* "RFK's Murder: A Second Gun?" and his subsequent book *The Killing of Robert F. Kennedy* provided strong new evidence of extra bullets:

—Patrolman Al Lamoreaux recalled "seeing one or two holes in the door. . . . It was just obvious. Just being a dumb cop, you look and see where the bullets went."

—Sergeant Raymond Rolon told Moldea, "One of the investigators pointed to a hole in the door frame and said, 'We just pulled a bullet out of here.'"

—LAPD photographer Charles Collier, upon being asked whether he was sure that he took pictures of bullet holes, said: "A bullet hole looks like a bullet hole—if you've photographed enough of them."

—Detective Sergeant J. R. MacArthur, the senior police detective at the crime scene, said he had seen "quite a few" bullet holes.

—Deputy Sheriff Thomas Beringer, when asked if the hole he saw might have had a nail in it instead of a bullet he replied, "It wasn't a nail. It was a definite bullet hole."[11]

LAPD property reports confirm that ceiling tiles and wood from the doorframe were removed from the crime scene. This evidence remained in police possession until June 27, 1969, one month following the publication of the Castellano/Nelson article that raised the issue of extra bullets. On this date police records indicate that the doorframes and the ceiling tiles were destroyed, this while Sirhan's case was still under appeal.

And no one was told. The destruction of the doorframes and ceiling tiles in 1969 was not revealed until 1975, during hearings conducted by the Los Angeles City Council. "There was no place to keep them," asserted an attorney representing the police. "You can't fit ceiling panels into a card file."[12] This raises the question of whether the LAPD also trashed all of the assorted rifles, bales of marijuana, or vehicles that constituted bulky evidence in all of its cases on appeal in 1969, or was there some special reason they wished this particular evidence to disappear?

The LAPD's subsequent position, articulated by then assistant chief Daryl Gates, was that the destruction didn't matter: the artifacts contained no bullet holes, so they were not evidence. One would expect that any department whose publicly and privately pronounced goal was to avoid "another Dallas" should have been eager to preserve and release evidence that would refute critics.

But Gates's explanation made no sense for another reason. The destroyed artifacts included the ceiling tiles, which the LAPD admitted had contained bullet holes—critical evidence if one were trying to substantiate the rather tortured trajectories of the bullets put forth by DeWayne Wolfer. So critical, in fact, that in 1975, California attorney general Evelle Younger, Sirhan's former prosecutor, used the police-ordered destruction as an argument in front of superior court judge Robert A. Wenke, to forestall an investigation into the question of extra bullets through flight-path analysis.

He then went on to offer a nonsense explanation for why this evidence never saw the light of day at Sirhan's trial:

> The Court has already been informed in this proceeding that the crucial ceiling panels and door jambs from the pantry have been destroyed in a routine manner by the Los Angeles Police Department. Without these items, it will be impossible to compute angles of flight for a number of bullets.
>
> One reason this evidence probably was never introduced at trial when it was a subject of speculation [was] because there is no empirical evidence that bullet flight paths can ever be accurately reproduced.[13]

According to the official bullet count as constructed by DeWayne Wolfer, one bullet penetrated a ceiling tile and became lost in the ceiling after having passed through Senator Kennedy's shoulder. Another bullet was said to have penetrated the ceiling, bounced off the cement underflooring, and reentered the pantry through a ceiling tile "and then struck victim Evans in the head."[14] This scenario seems less likely after an inspection of Mrs. Elizabeth Evans's medical report, which describes the bullet as entering "just below the hairline" and traveling "upward."[15] A closer inspection of the ceiling tiles in police custody could have substantiated whether this ricochet scenario was based in fact or was just a convenient way for the LAPD to account for more bullet holes in the ceiling than they knew what to do with. The destruction of the tiles ended any possibility of examination.

Another avenue of inquiry closed off by the quick disposal of evidence relates to the two bullets allegedly discovered on the front seat of Sirhan's car (parked near the crime scene). In 1975 an independent panel of court-appointed firearms experts discovered traces of wood on the base and tip of both bullets. Did Sirhan fire them into wood, dig them out, and then drive around with them on the front seat? Were they really found in his car? Could they have come from wood in the hotel pantry? Without the doorframes, a microscopic comparison of wood from those frames with the wood tracings on the bullets was not possible.

In the official audit of bullets, the item most in conflict with common sense and Newtonian physics was Wolfer's explanation of the bullet that struck Paul Schrade. With four bullets in Evans, Stroll, Weisel, and Goldstein, two bullets in Robert Kennedy, and one lost in the ceiling, Wolfer now had only one bullet left to account for Schrade's wound. This was the bullet that penetrated Kennedy's suit jacket. Wolfer's report said that this bullet "passed through the right shoulder pad of Senator Kennedy's suit coat (never entered his body) and traveled upward striking victim Schrade in the middle of the forehead."[16]

This analysis sounds plausible until one inspects the senator's suit jacket and police reconstructions (see photo insert), which reveal that this bullet was traveling upward at an 80-degree angle (almost vertical) and was moving slightly back to front and, thus, away from Paul Schrade, who was reliably placed by witnesses four to five feet behind Robert Kennedy. When he testified at the trial, Schrade was unaware that the bullet that struck him represented any problem to the police account of the murder. Seventeen years later he was no longer being polite about the matter. "I want you to explain to me," he shouted at a stone-faced Daryl Gates at a police commission hearing, "how a bullet traveling up and away from me can make a ninety-degree turn and end up in my head?"[17]

The doorframes and the ceiling tiles were not the only evidence of extra bullets to disappear. Police logs of work performed describe tests done on the doorframes and ceiling tiles. According to these logs, chemical, microscopic, X-ray, and fluoroscopic tests were conducted. None of the results of these examinations are anywhere to be found in police files. Yet such results were certainly small enough to fit in a filing cabinet, and evidence that there was no second gun involved would presumably be valued currency in an investigation that knew it would eventually face scrutiny.

Other evidence relating to the doorframes appears to be missing or altered. The police files released in 1988 contained detailed personal statements by LAPD officers describing what they did the night of the shooting: gathering evidence, crowd control, finding witnesses, etc. The statements of the officers seen in photos pointing to the holes in the doorframe are silent about this. They are also the only statements not written in the first person. The removal of the ceiling tiles and the doorframes, or their probing, do not show up in any of the officers' statements—as if these activities never occurred.

And someone else's activities were not reported. Once Clemente/Shirley photos of the doorframes emerged, it could be seen that around one of the apparent bullet holes a circle was drawn. Inside the circle was scrawled, "723 LASO, W. Tew." This seemed to indicate that Los Angeles Sheriff's Office (LASO) deputy Walter Tew, badge number 723, had examined this hole. But Deputy Tew would also disappear into the LAPD's evidentiary black hole, as there is not one mention of his name in any document, roster, or log.

In his interviews with LAPD personnel, Dan Moldea talked to several men who had a direct relationship with DeWayne Wolfer. One was Lieutenant Donald W. Mann, who was the LAPD's chief criminalist and Wolfer's direct superior.

"[Wolfer] was hard to supervise," Mann reported to Moldea. "He would go off by himself, and sometimes he would get himself in trouble, and us too."

Moldea then asked Mann if he had signed off on any reports concerning bullets recovered from the crime scene. Mann replied that he would only "hear talk" and that it was "secret stuff." "It was just kind of taken out of my hands."[18]

When Moldea interviewed Wolfer's subordinate, Officer David Butler, he asked who might have removed bullets from the wall the night of the shooting.

"DeWayne Wolfer took two bullets out of the wall," Butler answered.

"Were you there when he took those bullets out?"

"Yes."

Moldea then asked how the bullets were removed from the center divider.

"Tear it out," responded Butler. "We had to disassemble it to find the bullets."[19]

In a subsequent interview with Moldea, Butler would qualify his story only after he realized that it was a potential embarrassment to the police and his mentor, DeWayne Wolfer. Then his rather vivid account of extracting bullets from the doorframes faded into a story of him having seen what he thought were bullets in small evidence packages labeled "bullet evidence" or "firearms evidence." Since any bullets recovered at the crime scene would point to a second gun, Butler's second story is as damaging as his first. Moreover, Butler's second story, coming as it did after the officer realized that his first account was a potential embarrassment, makes it seem likely that the first account was the more reliable.

That Butler, as well as other police officers, could have had knowledge of crime-scene bullets without understanding their significance as proof of a second gun is a measure of how insulated and compartmentalized the LAPD's murder investigation became. Butler's initial story would seem to confirm the crime-scene photographs and the numerous civilian and police accounts of bullets recovered from the pantry doorframes. It stands in direct contrast to DeWayne Wolfer's somewhat less-than-scientific explanation for the holes given in a 1971 deposition:

I found no bullet holes in the doorframe. I found many holes, but none containing or caused by bullets. . . . They were caused by some object poking the wood—a ramrod, a tray, a dish tray. There was [sic] many of those portable carts and that had a round area on it. That could have certainly caused it [the holes].[20]

DeWayne Wolfer could make such a statement in 1971 without the threat of contradiction: the doorframes no longer existed, most witnesses who could challenge him were unaware of the controversy, and the most compromising photographs would remain locked away in police files for another seventeen years. Even so, the dish-tray analysis stands naked.

Compare Wolfer's explanation with the account of maître d' Karl Uecker. After being interviewed by police the morning of June 5, Uecker returned to the crime scene. He noticed two holes in the center divider that he is positive were not there prior to the shooting. Uecker pointed the holes out to a man in plain clothes whom he took to be a detective. The man responded that everything would be checked out. "These holes were never there before," Uecker said steadfastly many years later, "and I knew where the shots were going to. I saw him [Sirhan] shooting, and I know it must have been this way."[21]

In 1975 there was an unexpected confirmation of Uecker's observation and a stunning refutation of Wolfer's casual hypothesis. In response to a Freedom of Information Act initiative by Washington attorney Bernard Fensterwald, the FBI released certain documents from its files on the RFK murder. Fensterwald and his colleagues were startled by what they received. Among the bureau documents was a series of photographs of the pantry interior, including several close-ups of the missing doorframes. Four of these photographs showed what were labeled as "bullet holes." Photograph "E-3" was labeled "Close up view of two bullet holes which is [*sic*] located in the center door frame inside kitchen serving area and looking towards direction of back of stage." Thus, the holes in the doorframes, which were identified by the LAPD's forensic expert as being caused by portable dish trays, were sufficiently sinister in appearance to attract the attention of not only numerous police officers and hotel employees, but also crime-scene photographers from the FBI.

In 1971 Los Angeles County district attorney Joseph Busch wrote a report on the various allegations of impropriety then surfacing about the police handling of the Robert Kennedy murder. One of Busch's targets was Lillian Castellano and her allegation about a second gun.

> Mrs. Castellano suggests that there is evidence that there were more than eight bullets recovered after the shooting. Sirhan's gun was an eight-shot revolver. Her evidence consists of an Associated Press photograph of two police officers pointing to a hole in a door frame, a caption under the picture that says, "bullet still in the wood" and a photograph of two holes in a wooden doorjamb. These holes were circled and had numbers and letters around them. When added to the eight bullets accounted for in Mr. Wolfer's ballistic report, there are supposedly eleven bullets in the pantry. However, no support is

given to the caption or photographs by anyone who actually saw bullets in the holes, or removed bullets from the holes. Mrs. Castellano has no responsible evidence to show that more than eight shots were fired in the Ambassador Hotel on June 5, 1968.[22]

District Attorney Busch cites a lack of supporting evidence in attempting to refute Castellano's claims of extra bullets. As has been demonstrated, this corroborating evidence in the form of pantry witnesses, hotel employees, police officers, FBI agents, and crime-scene photographs was within easy reach of the district attorney. Where the lack of responsibility occurred, and most likely a serious crime committed, was in destroying the doorframes and the tests done upon them, and then offering a highly unlikely explanation for the holes observed in them.

Unaware of a bullet-count problem or a second-gun possibility, Grant Cooper moved without suspicion into the ballistics phase of the trial. William Harper's words had been forgotten, and the chief defense attorney was concerned with being as cooperative as possible. Several days before the prosecution was to summon DeWayne Wolfer, Cooper had a conversation with deputy DA Fitts.

"It is our intention to call DeWayne Wolfer to testify with respect to his ballistics comparison," said Fitts. ". . . It is our understanding that there will be a stipulation that these objects came from the persons whom I say they came from. Is that right?"

"So long as you make that avowal," answered Cooper, "there will be no question about that."

"Fine," replied Fitts. "We have discussed the matter with Mr. Wolfer as to those envelopes containing those bullets and bullet fragments; he knows where they came from."

SIX

The Criminalist

✳ ✳ ✳

DeWAYNE WOLFER STRODE easily to the witness stand. His hair
was slicked back to frame a full forty-three-year-old face. He was dressed
in a business suit, his working attire.

"Your occupation, sir?" asked David Fitts for the prosecution.

"Police officer for the City of Los Angeles," replied Wolfer, "assigned
to the Scientific Investigation Division, Crime Laboratory, where I act as
a criminalist and as a ballistics expert."

"What education and experience have you had to prepare yourself for
this particular field?"

"I have my bachelor's degree from the University of Southern California,
where I was a premed student with a background in the field of chemistry,
physics and different types of laboratory technique courses, photography
and the like."★

Wolfer's primary purpose for the prosecution was to connect the gun
taken from Sirhan Sirhan to the bullets removed from the shooting victims. David Fitts held up envelopes that contained several spent bullets.

"I now ask you to examine the contents of the envelopes which are
before you in evidence. Would you tell me if you have examined them
before?"

"I will stipulate he has seen them all before," said Grant Cooper, interrupting. "Pardon me. Maybe I shouldn't have done that."

"I think the stipulation in this instance might save a little time," said Fitts.

In addition to the bullets, the prosecution was intent on introducing
into evidence several photographs of Robert Kennedy's wounded head.
The photographs would help establish, by way of the "tattooing" in the
vicinity of the fatal wound, a muzzle distance of one to three inches at
the moment the shots were fired.

★At the time of the trial, there was no specific major or grade-point average required for the
position of LAPD criminalist, and Wolfer's studies at USC seemed to relate tangentially at best
to his chosen profession. As a zoology major he received more C's than all other grades combined, and he received five D's, including one in his major and two in chemistry.

Grant Cooper opposed the introduction of the head-wound photographs, believing they would illustrate the horror of the crime and make the jury less inclined to look leniently upon Sirhan. He thought if he would agree to what the prosecution was trying to prove, he might get the photos excluded.

"These photographs are highly inflammatory," he said to Judge Walker. "We will stipulate that there was powder tattooing on the ear of Senator Kennedy, and that the gun was held as close as the witness wants to testify that it was held."

"Your Honor," replied Fitts, "you have heard Karl Uecker and any number of witnesses who described what happened; one witness has put the revolver some three or four feet from the senator's head, others have had it at varying range. The only way we can clear up the ambiguity is by the testimony of this witness."

Judge Walker agreed with Fitts. "I think the prosecution has a right to present its case."

A concession, as Fitts had just made, that the scientific evidence did not match the witness accounts, might ordinarily signal a problem for the prosecution. Not here. Grant Cooper had no intention of exploiting this conflict. He was only dimly aware of it. But the contradictions were more serious than Fitts's casual allusion would indicate. As medical examiner Dr. Thomas Noguchi described in his 1983 memoir *Coroner,* "Not a single witness in that crowded kitchen had seen him [Sirhan] fire behind Kennedy's ear at point-blank range."[1]

As Fitts had conceded, the powder-burn distance of one to three inches did not agree with the account of the prosecution's "star witness" (as they called him), Karl Uecker, who described to the court the week before how he had blocked the assailant from getting point-blank access to Kennedy. But when he took the stand, Uecker wasn't asked about the gun's distance from Kennedy's head. Not by the prosecution, not by the defense.

Uecker, however, was emphatic about the problem in a statement made six years later:

I have told the police and testified [to the grand jury] that there was a distance of at least one and one-half feet between the muzzle of Sirhan's gun and Senator Kennedy's head. The revolver was directly in front of my nose. After Sirhan's second shot, I pushed his hand that held the revolver down, and pushed him onto the steam table. There is no way that the shots described in the autopsy could have come from Sirhan's gun. . . . Sirhan never got close enough for a point-blank shot, never.[2]

However certain he might be, if Uecker alone had made this observation about the firing distance, one might justifiably assume he was mistaken. But Uecker was not alone.

Frank Burns had worked for the Robert Kennedy campaign in 1968 and was a successful Los Angeles attorney. Burns was within several feet of Kennedy when the shots were fired. In a 1987 interview with Phil Melanson, he was adamant that Sirhan's gun was never anywhere near contact with Kennedy's head. "We're talking several, several feet," he asserted. The crime was reenacted in his spacious office using chairs as stand-ins for the principals. Burns positioned the gun three to four feet from Kennedy's head, and he was confident that this was accurate.

Waiter Martin Patrusky was standing near Kennedy. He asserted that the gun never got closer than three feet. Busboy Juan Romero told authorities the weapon was "approximately one yard from the senator's head." Newspaper reporter Pete Hamill placed the gun at least two feet from the senator. Kennedy volunteer Valerie Schulte said it was six feet away. Assistant maître d' Edward Minasian placed it three feet from Kennedy. Lisa Urso told the authors that the gun was "three to six feet" from Kennedy.

TV producer Richard Lubic was walking behind and to the right of Uecker. "Sirhan's gun was two to three feet from Kennedy's head," Lubic insisted in a 1975 interview. "It is nonsense to say that he fired bullets into Senator Kennedy from a distance of one to two inches, since his gun was never anywhere that near to Senator Kennedy."[3]

The fundamental conflict between the eyewitness accounts and the physical evidence was not addressed at the Sirhan grand jury proceeding or the trial. Los Angeles officials would later try to make it disappear by misrepresenting the eyewitness evidence to an unsuspecting public, which had no access to the case files. In December of 1974, Los Angeles district attorney Joseph P. Busch was interviewed by Tom Snyder on NBC-TV's *Tomorrow* show, along with former congressman Allard K. Lowenstein:

SNYDER: The eyewitness testimony does not seem to match up with the coroner's report that the gun that fired the shot was an inch or maybe two inches away from Kennedy's head but no eyewitness can place it closer than eighteen. How would you account for that seeming discrepancy?

BUSCH: Well, that's not true. It was point-blank, right into the right ear of the senator. The gun was right there. The bullet that killed him entered right there, and we can show it.

LOWENSTEIN: Now who has said that they saw it? Just name one witness that said they saw a gun, point-blank, fired into Senator Kennedy's ear? Tell us one.

Busch: Would you like Mr. Uecker, the man that grabbed his arm? Would you like any of the fifty-five witnesses?

Lowenstein: Yes, Mr. Busch, I would, because Mr. Uecker swears that it was two feet.

Busch: Oh, come on, Mr. Lowenstein.

District Attorney Busch was not being truthful about Karl Uecker and the other fifty-five witnesses, but he was right about one thing: the fatal shots were fired from an inch or two away. But Lowenstein wasn't contesting that. His point was that according to the people who were there, Karl Uecker included, Sirhan's gun was never in position to inflict those wounds. And, of course, it didn't need to be a one-or-the-other situation. The conflict is easily resolved when one posits a second gun.

A year after Sirhan's trial, criminalist William Harper, on behalf of the Sirhan appeals lawyers, made his own review of the ballistic evidence. After examining the evidence—bullets, the autopsy report, and the police trajectory diagrams—Harper swore to an affidavit containing his conclusions. Harper's principal finding was that Robert Kennedy "was fired upon from two distinct firing positions":

> Firing Position A, the position of Sirhan, was located directly in front of the Senator, with Sirhan face to face with the Senator. This position is established by more than a dozen eyewitnesses. A second firing position, Firing Position B, is clearly established by the autopsy report. It was located in close proximity to the Senator, immediately to his right and rear. It was from this position that 4 (four) shots were fired, three of which entered the Senator's body. . . . It is extremely unlikely that any of the bullets fired by Sirhan's gun ever struck the body of Robert Kennedy.[4]

The body orientation of Robert Kennedy in relation to Sirhan at the time of the shooting is not as certain as either the police or their critics would like. The autopsy revealed that Robert Kennedy was wounded in the right back. According to the witnesses Kennedy was either walking toward Sirhan when he was shot or was turned leftward shaking hands when the shooting began. The police maintain that Kennedy turned more than 90 degrees when he stopped to shake hands, and was thus presenting his back to Sirhan. Many witnesses disagree with this positioning. One clear description is contained in a 1975 statement by Martin Patrusky, who was only feet away from Kennedy when he was shot: "I saw the man, who turned out to be Sirhan, firing at Kennedy. Kennedy's back was not facing Sirhan. Sirhan was slightly to the right front of Kennedy."[5] If the witnesses who place Kennedy facing Sirhan are correct, then a significant front/back difficulty compounds the already described distance riddle. There are other problems.

According to the autopsy, all the wound tracks were upward: the Kennedy head wound was at a mild 15 degrees off the horizontal, but the three back shots were described as at steep 59, 67, and 80 degrees, as though a gun had been pressed to the senator's back and pointed up so as not to protrude. In contrast, Sirhan was said to have fired with his gun parallel to the floor.

But it is the sequence of shots that poses the most difficult problem to the official account of the wounds in Robert Kennedy. Recall that Kennedy was wounded three times from behind, with a fourth bullet passing through his jacket—all of these shots from the back at very close range. Yet Uecker told the grand jury that he grabbed Sirhan's gun hand after the second shot and deflected it away from Senator Kennedy. This was corroborated by Edward Minasian's grand jury testimony. He described how Uecker had slammed Sirhan's hand down onto the steam table after the second shot. Asked if the shots that were fired after Sirhan's arm was deflected were in the same general direction of the senator, Minasian replied, "I doubt it, because . . . [w]e had him and his arm was somewhere on this steam table here. And I doubt if it was in the same direction as the first two shots."

Even if the distance, front/back, and angle problems are magically solved or ignored, if Sirhan's gun were deflected away from Robert Kennedy after the second shot, then the weapon could not have inflicted four "point-blank" hits on the senator from behind. Is it possible that Uecker and Minasian are mistaken about the shot sequence? Consider the testimony at Sirhan's trial by the crime-scene witnesses:

JACK GALLIVAN: I heard a series of shots, maybe two, then a pause and the rest. . . .

MARTIN PATRUSKY: All of a sudden there was like a firecracker going off; then there was another; then there was a pause. Then all of a sudden there was rapid fire.

RAFER JOHNSON: I thought it was a balloon going off, two *poppings,* and then I looked in that direction and I heard some other popping. . . .

ANGELO DiPIERRO: I heard the shot . . . I thought it was a prank or something . . . then a volley of shots. . . .

VINCENT DiPIERRO: [to the grand jury] . . . the moment the first two shots were fired.

JUAN ROMERO: He [Sirhan] put his arm like that and he shot two shots. . . .

IRWIN STROLL: The procession stopped and then there was one *pop.* . . .

IRA GOLDSTEIN: There were about two of them at first. . . .

BORIS YARO [to the FBI]: I heard what I thought were two explosions.

The collective testimony of the crime-scene witnesses stood in stark contrast to prosecutor Fitts's opening statement, that Sirhan had put a gun "to the very vicinity of the senator's head and at point blank range in rapid succession fired eight shots." But Fitts wasn't interested in arguing with the witnesses, who would be nothing more than historical oddities if Fitts could prove that the bullets that struck Robert Kennedy came from Sirhan's gun. And with Wolfer on the witness stand, that's what he intended to do.

"I direct your attention to this envelope, which is People's 55," said Fitts, "and it bears certain writing, perhaps from your hand. What does it contain?"

"It contains three of the test shots that I took from People's 6, the weapon," replied Wolfer, "and this was from the water recovery tank, and that would be three test shots I used for comparison purposes. . . . Looking at the scratches under the comparison microscope and the lands and grooves of this test bullet, I can say that they were fired from this gun and no other gun, and that is what I attempted to do with each of the exhibits."

"In other words," said Fitts, "it is somewhat analogous to fingerprints. No individual or two individuals have identical fingerprints, no two guns leave the same striations on the projectiles that are being expelled by them."

"That is correct."

Fitts's analogy is a good first step in understanding bullet-striation analysis, but striations differ from fingerprints in that they are not quite so unique. They are also difficult to read, even with a comparison microscope, as Sir Gerald Burrard contends in his book, *The Identification of Firearms and Forensic Ballistics*. Burrard warns his readers not to trust unsupported ballistic comparison testimony:

> Mere assertions by some investigator, no matter how great his reputation, should be regarded with extreme caution. . . . The most ridiculous claims have been put forward on behalf of the comparison microscope, and there is a danger that the mere fact of its possession may endow a witness with all sorts of imaginary skill and knowledge, at least in the eyes of the jury and public. . . . If the evidence is unsupported by photographs which clearly tell their own story, that evidence should be regarded with suspicion.[6]

At Sirhan's trial DeWayne Wolfer claimed that he made a match between all the victim's bullets and those test-fired from Sirhan's gun. Wolfer's testimony, however, was conspicuously lacking in any supporting documentation. According to Burrard, this should have kindled suspicion in the defense attorneys. It did not. The lack of supporting evidence did attract the notice of independent firearms expert Lowell Bradford, who, a few years later in a court petition, would attack Wolfer for his naked presentation at Sirhan's trial. Bradford charged that Wolfer offered "no examiner's notes, no pretrial discovery, no demonstrative exhibits, no explanation of examination methodology, no statement of the basis for the opinions rendered."[7]

Uncontested at the trial, Wolfer's testimony would close the case against Sirhan, as far as any doubt about who fired the bullets that struck Robert Kennedy. But Wolfer's analysis would be challenged in a series of hearings and official investigations that would occur during the next decade.

In 1971, two years after his testimony at the Sirhan trial, DeWayne Wolfer became a candidate for appointment as chief forensic chemist of the Los Angeles Police Department, the director of the entire crime laboratory. Los Angeles attorney Barbara Warner Blehr filed a civil-service action to block Wolfer's appointment, on the grounds that he was "completely unqualified for the position."

Blehr's suit not only faulted Wolfer's work on the Sirhan case but cited two other cases as well, relying on evidence developed by William Harper and other criminalists (including a former head of the LAPD crime laboratory). Listing a number of basic precepts of firearms identification, Blehr then documented instances in which Wolfer had not adhered to them, concluding that "these violations were made in response to an overzealous desire to help the cause of the prosecution."[8]

In Board of Inquiry hearings that followed Blehr's challenge, Wolfer angrily defended himself. "I have never in my life been approached to change opinions or go for the prosecution," he said. "I call them as I see them."[9] Chief of police Ed Davis agreed with the besieged criminalist, calling Blehr's charges a "vendetta." "In my estimation," said Davis, "Mr. Wolfer is the top expert in the country."[10]

The action by Blehr precipitated considerable controversy, both about Wolfer and about the official conclusions in the Sirhan case. Investigations were launched by both LAPD and the district attorney's office. A grand jury investigation probed the integrity of the exhibits in the Sirhan case. And Wolfer sued Blehr for two million dollars. The court ruled that Blehr's letter was a public document and immune from libel action.

An example of how one of Wolfer's professional peers viewed his credibility is contained in a 1971 letter written by Marshall Houts, a former FBI agent and expert in legal medicine, who served as editor in chief of

Trauma, a magazine that dealt with issues of forensic science. Houts wrote to his friend Evelle Younger, who had prosecuted Sirhan and had since become attorney general for the state of California, to warn him about Wolfer's impending promotion:

> Dear Ev,
>
> This is an elaboration of our discussion last night at Bob Fullerton's.
>
> As I indicated then I have no personal interest in this matter, but do have a deep academic and professional concern over Wolfer's horrendous blunders in the past and those he will commit in the future if he continues on his present assignment. I am also concerned that you and the present District Attorney stand a strong chance of getting burned by Wolfer's misdirected hyperenthusiastic procedures and testimony. . . .
>
> Wolfer suffers from a great inferiority complex for which he compensates by giving the police exactly what they need to obtain a conviction. He casts objectivity to the winds and violates every basic tenet of forensic science and proof by becoming a crusading advocate. This is rationalized as being entirely legitimate since the accused is guilty anyway which makes the social objective worthy of the means to obtain it. . . .
>
> I will not elaborate on the details of the three cases under consideration by the civil service board (Sirhan, Kirschke, and Terry) other than to say that the real experts of integrity who have examined portions or all of the evidence are appalled at what Wolfer did. . . .
>
> Sincerely yours, Marshall Houts[11]

In October 1971, the results of the police and district attorney's investigations were made public almost simultaneously. Both endorsed Wolfer's expertise, attributing certain key discrepancies to "clerical errors," thereby clearing the way for his appointment. Despite Houts's scathing indictment and others like it, DeWayne Wolfer was given his appointment as forensic czar of the LAPD. But Marshall Houts's prediction that Wolfer would become an embarrassment would prove accurate.

In the summer of 1975, shooting victim Paul Schrade filed several legal actions relating to the assassination. He had firm legal status as an injured party in the shooting that took his friend's life. In one of these actions, Godfrey Isaac, representing Sirhan, got to question DeWayne Wolfer in front of superior court judge Robert Wenke.

Isaac was interested in Wolfer's account of his test bullets. Under his questioning Wolfer admitted that he had stored the bullets in an envelope in his desk drawer for nine months. Isaac asked why. Wolfer responded that he did it for security reasons, "because under the circumstances I knew which was Sirhan's and no one else did."

"Was it common procedure," asked Isaac, "for you to put test bullets into your desk drawer rather than somewhere else within the LAPD?"

"Oh, I would say probably not," replied Wolfer.

"May I see the evidence envelope that has your handwriting on it?" asked Isaac. He was handed the very same envelope that Fitts had introduced into evidence at Sirhan's trial. "Were bullets #55 in that envelope?"

"I would assume they were," replied Wolfer with hesitation. "I have no way of telling you positively if they were in the trial in this envelope. I would assume they were. I don't know. I can't tell you."

"Do you recognize the handwriting on this envelope?"

"Yes, this is probably my handwriting. Looks like it. It appears to be."

"Showing you down where it has 'Make: I and J.' That stands for Iver and Johnson?"

"That is correct."

"And below that the number H 18602. Is that number in your handwriting?"

"Yes, it is, but that is an incorrect number."

Incorrect indeed. The revolver taken from Sirhan had the serial number H 53725, but the bullets that were used for comparison and that established that the victims were shot "by this gun and no other" were marked as being from H 18602, another Iver Johnson Cadet model that the police were using for other test purposes. This discrepancy went unnoticed at Sirhan's trial. William Harper discovered it after the trial was over.

"When you put the H 18602 on that envelope," asked Isaac, "did you believe that was the number of the gun from which the bullets contained therein were fired?"

"Well, now, I don't know what you mean by that particular statement."

"Why did you put H 18602 on the envelope?"

"Because I asked a person for the number of the gun in the case of Sirhan; that was the number he repeated to me. I assumed that was the Sirhan gun and wrote those numbers down. . . ."

"From whom did you ask the number?"

"Here, today, I wouldn't recall."[12]

H 18602, like Sirhan's gun, was an Iver Johnson Cadet model .22 caliber revolver. According to Wolfer's reports, it was used for muzzle-distance tests on June 11, 1968, and for sound-level tests at the Ambassador Hotel on June 20. If H 18602 was really the source of the bullets in the envelope, Wolfer's test results would have to be a complete fabrication. If Wolfer mislabeled the envelope, as he maintained, because of a mistake by some associate whom he couldn't remember, other questions arise. According to a 1974 DA's office memo assessing the incident: "It is difficult to rely upon an individual's microscopic comparison of bullets, an obviously so-phisticated task, if that same person erroneously marks an evidence enve-lope in a matter of historical significance."[13]

Test-firing H 18602 and comparing the recovered bullets with the test bullets in People's exhibit number 55 would have been one way to deter-mine what had occurred here. Was that possible? During his testimony DeWayne Wolfer would assert that the test gun was still available, but an official police record indicated that it had been destroyed in July 1968—seven months before Sirhan's trial. In 1971, the record was "corrected" to show that the gun had been destroyed not in July of 1968, but in July of 1969.

During the hearing in front of Judge Wenke, Wolfer was also questioned by attorney Howard J. Privett, who was representing CBS, a co-petitioner with Schrade. Privett asked Wolfer if he had taken any photographs of bul-lets during his ballistic work.

"The record so indicates," answered Wolfer, "that there is an indica-tion that there was one set of photographs taken, that could well have been taken by me. . . ."

"Will you tell us, then, when and under what circumstances two photo-micrographs, that you believe were taken, were taken?"

"Well, I have to go back a ways. It wasn't—these photographs did not come to my attention until approximately a year ago when certain records were brought to me in the laboratory, and asked did I want these records. In these records, there was [sic] two photomicrographs of comparison of two bullets, under comparison microscope. Approximately a year ago this was brought to my attention, and I went to Jimmy Watson and he identi-fied the two bullets, and he said that I was the one that photographed these to the best of my recollection today."

Wolfer's story here was not one to inspire confidence. The photomicro-graph, as it was called, represented one of the few pieces of documentation of Wolfer's scientific analysis, but it had not been introduced at Sirhan's trial. According to Wolfer, he was not aware of the photograph until cer-tain evidence in the Sirhan case was presumably about to be disposed of in 1974. At that time he went to another officer, and that officer told him what the bullets were and told him that he had taken the photograph.

"Were those photographs that you have just identified," asked Privett, "are those marked either by exhibit number or item number, the bullets of which they represent?"

"No," answered Wolfer, "they merely indicate the fact that they are Kennedy bullets. So this would indicate to me by the fact that they are Kennedy bullets, one is Kennedy and one is one of my test shots."

"Does the photomicrograph indicate which one is the Kennedy and which is the test shot?"

"No, it does not."

"And so by looking at either the negatives or the prints or the jacket in which they are contained it is not possible to determine which photomicrograph represents a picture of the Kennedy bullet and which represents a test bullet?"

"That is correct."[14]

The admission that the bullets photographed were not even labeled as to which was which was another indictment of Wolfer's supposed scientific method. But this was only the first of several damaging revelations regarding this particular evidence. When the police files were opened in 1988 there was discovered a curious undated, unsigned memo concerning the photomicrograph in question. The document stated:

There exists a photograph of the Kennedy bullet and a test bullet taken through a comparison microscope. . . . The existence of this photograph is believed to be unknown by anyone outside of this Department. It should be effective rebuttal evidence should this case ever be retried. However, the release of this information at this time would be susceptible to criticism because lay people would in all probability have difficulty deciphering the photograph. The issue of its not being revealed at an earlier time may further make its authenticity suspect, particularly to the avid, exact assassination buff.

The siege mentality in this document is all too apparent, and yes, withholding the evidence does cast doubt upon its authenticity.

In 1974 deputy DA Dinko Bozanich wrote a forty-page memorandum to District Attorney Joseph Busch regarding a proposed examination of the Sirhan ballistic evidence by a panel of independent experts. The purpose of the memo was to evaluate "the present integrity or utility of the Sirhan firearms exhibits" and what risks there might be in having them examined. "The focal point of such an evaluation," stated Bozanich, "is predominantly the image of this office which is projected to the public, rather than any concern for the efficacy of Sirhan's conviction or the proved conclusion that one man acted alone in killing Kennedy."[15]

The Bozanich memo claimed that the allegation that the ballistic evidence suggests two guns

coincides with the precise area where this office is at a disadvantage because of doubts regarding the present integrity of the Sirhan exhibits and the lack of secondary evidence in the form of police photographs. . . . Wolfer never had any photographic reproductions prepared of the evidence and test bullets used in his microscopic comparisons during the Sirhan investigation.[16]

Toward the end of the memo Bozanich concluded:

As this office knows a refiring of Sirhan's gun at this date would not necessarily produce bullets with the same individual characteristics as those actually used by Wolfer during the Sirhan investigation. . . . Rather, the likelihood of inconclusive results is substantial, aside from the realistic possibility that a refiring of Sirhan's gun would produce sufficient differences in striations to conclude that the Sirhan bullet exhibits were not fired by Sirhan's gun.[17]

Bozanich's assertion that a test firing of Sirhan's gun had the realistic possibility of proving that the Sirhan bullets were not fired by Sirhan's gun is an extraordinary statement. He was trying to warn that there could be problems if an independent panel examined the bullets. Joseph Busch apparently took the warning and began damage control. As part of its defensive posture, the district attorney's office would assert that some of the Sirhan ballistic evidence had been tampered with, or bullets substituted, when certain outside parties had gained access to it in 1971. One internal DA's office memo marked CONFIDENTIAL and titled "Theory Behind Present Attempt to Discredit Wolfer" claimed:

The tampering of the Sirhan evidence could have resulted in three possible ways. First, [journalist Theodore] CHARACH, who had access to the exhibits 17 times, could have tampered with it. . . . Second, [criminalist William] HARPER could have done it, since he saw the exhibits 7 times. He is also a representative for HYCON, which is developing a new type of camera for ballistics work. If HARPER could utilize this camera to prove the two-gun theory, it would personally enhance him and promote sales of the HYCON COMPANY. Third, people who had a vested interest in the Black Panther cases could have tampered with the evidence, knowing there was a movement to discredit Wolfer, which of course could affect coming cases of Panthers.[18]

As if the offered range of possible motives for switching bullets was not broad enough, in the following paragraph of the memo an additional motive for tampering with the Sirhan evidence was put forward:

If the American public was satisfied that there was a grand design to eliminate the Kennedy family, there would be great public sympathy towards Ted Kennedy and the liberal Democrats.

On May 27, 1996, the then attorney for Sirhan Sirhan, Lawrence Teeter, wrote a letter to LAPD chief Willie Williams. In the letter Teeter maintained that he (in connection with Sirhan case researcher Rose Lynn Mangan) had "unearthed substantial evidence concerning the substitution of and tampering with bullets in the Sirhan case." One of Teeter's citations read:

Dr. Noguchi's autopsy report states that when a bullet was removed from the vicinity of Robert Kennedy's sixth cervical vertebrae, Dr. Noguchi inscribed "TN31" on the base of that bullet. That bullet later became People's Exhibit 47. However, the bullets were later examined by a court-appointed panel of seven firearms experts in 1975. At that time, the examiner who looked at the bases of the bullets noted that People's 47 contained the designation "DWTN" on the base. The fact that LAPD firearms expert DeWayne Wolfer ("DW") confirmed in 1975 that the bullets in the court's custody were the same ones he had examined in 1968 strongly suggests that the substitution of a stand-in neck bullet in place of the original took place prior to the trial.

The claims of evidence tampering and bullet switching have come full circle. Both sides in the Sirhan case have made serious charges against the other. As a result, what should be the most reliable evidence in the case, the bullets themselves, are now of very diminished value. The careful handling and documenting of this evidence by a trained and diligent forensic expert could have served to prove or disprove subsequent claims of tampering. Absent such demonstrated competence, the authors must agree with deputy DA Bozanich that "there is substantial question as to whether or not the Sirhan exhibits have been effectively preserved."[19]

In 1975, despite the opposition of the district attorney, as part of the action initiated by Paul Schrade, CBS News, and four other plaintiffs, Judge Robert Wenke ordered an independent panel to examine the Sirhan firearms evidence. The seven experts were jointly agreed upon by the plaintiffs and the defendants (the DA's office and the California State attorney general's office). The court issued a narrow mandate for the panel: it would examine the gun and bullets, but it was not to investigate bullet trajectories, eyewitness data, or the issue of possible extra bullets in the pantry ceiling and doorframe.

After two weeks of analysis, the forensic panel delivered its report to Judge Wenke. In one of its key findings the panel reported: "It cannot be concluded that Exhibits 47 [nonfatal Kennedy], 52 [Goldstein], and 54 [Weisel] were fired from the Sirhan revolver. The reasons for this are that there are insufficient corresponding individual characteristics to make an identification."

The panel also found that they were unable to conclude that a second gun was involved. The issue, in other words, at least as far as bullet markings, was still very much open. But DeWayne Wolfer had testified at Sirhan's trial that with his microscope he had managed to do what the seven forensic experts had been unable to do—conclude scientifically that the Goldstein, Weisel, and Kennedy bullets all came from Sirhan's gun and no other. Panelist Lowell Bradford stated, "The examination results contradict the original identification made at the trial of Sirhan B. Sirhan in that there is no basis for an identification of any of the victim bullets through the classical process of microscopically comparing them with test bullets. . . ."

Judge Wenke's forensic panel delivered their findings in a courtroom packed with reporters. What should have been a landmark event in the pursuit of historical truth in the Robert Kennedy case turned out to be an example of the media's unwillingness or inability to get beyond superficial impressions and the official spin.

The distortion resulted partly from the order in which the panel presented its findings. First up was the announcement that there was no evidence that a second gun was fired. The media had their headline, and the race was on to be the first to report it, not to discover its context or its more complex meaning. They rushed from the courtroom to call in their stories:

7 EXPERTS SAY RFK SLAIN BY SINGLE FIREARM (Associated Press)

RFK SECOND-GUN THEORY RULED OUT (United Press International)

NO SECOND GUN IN KENNEDY ASSASSINATION, PANEL SAYS (*Los Angeles Times*)

ONE GUN KILLED BOBBY: EXPERTS (New York *Daily News*)

This wave of case-closed headlines created the perception that, finally, the issues in the RFK case were settled—one gun, once and for all. Neither the public nor the media would perceive the gross inaccuracy. In reality, not one of the seven experts ruled out the possibility of a second gun (each wrote an individual report accompanying the collective one).

In response to the media coverage of the firearms panel, panelist Lowell Bradford issued the following statement:

The findings of the firearms examiners is being improperly interpreted by the news media.

1. The examiners found that the Sirhan gun *cannot* [emphasis Bradford's] be identified with the bullets from the crime scene.

2. The firearms evidence does not in and of itself establish a basis for a two gun proposition; likewise, this same proposition, on a basis of other evidence, is not precluded either.

Bradford would go on to recommend the examination of other evidence including "witnesses' statements that another gun was fired," "bullet pathways," and "evidence of more than eight bullets fired." This evidence, Bradford contended, deserved "the same kind of consideration and systematic analysis" as had been given the bullets.

Brushing aside Bradford's statement, Los Angeles authorities were quick to claim victory. "After years of unwarranted attacks on Criminalist DeWayne Wolfer," said LAPD chief Ed Davis, "his integrity and professional excellence have been vindicated."[20] City attorney Dion Morrow crowed, "It will be gratifying to LAPD criminalist DeWayne Wolfer, that his professional judgment and the quality of his work have been upheld." Morrow termed the panel report "a complete vindication of LAPD's ballistic work in the RFK case."[21]

The reprieve granted to DeWayne Wolfer's professional reputation following the firearms panel report would last only a few months. In December of the same year, the Jack Kirschke murder case came up for review by the California State Court of Appeal. (Ironically, this was the case Sirhan had discussed with his captors hours after the assassination.) During these proceedings, a three-judge panel censured the police criminalist for his testimony in the original trial. Wolfer had testified that enlarged photographs of bullets backed up his ballistic opinion, but the three-judge panel found that they didn't.

The appellate court, however, was most upset about Wolfer's other findings. "Unquestionably, Wolfer's opinion testimony on acoustics and anatomy was negligently false," wrote Justice Robert S. Thompson. "His testimony of his educational qualifications borders on perjury and is, at least, given with reckless disregard for the truth."[22]

In 1977 Wolfer would receive another rebuke by way of a reinvestigation of the assassination sponsored by the district attorney's office. The probe, run by special counsel Thomas Kranz, tried very hard to minimize the evidentiary discrepancies in the case and to praise the police work done in the investigation. Still, the *Kranz Report* was forced to admit to what it termed "the woeful lack of evidence reports and documentation concerning previous ballistics examination and trajectory studies, which had become evident during the examination of DeWayne Wolfer."[23] The report would continue:

> In light of the inability of Wolfer or other LAPD officials to produce substantial written documents, analyzed evidence reports or pertinent information regarding Wolfer's 1968 ballistics tests, his log report and laboratory work, it must be concluded that Wolfer is responsible for the sketchy and insufficient analysis or, if extensive reports and documents were prepared, Wolfer was negligent in permitting such reports and documents to be destroyed.[24]

The *Kranz Report* then went on to discuss missing tests reportedly performed upon the destroyed ceiling tiles.

> It appears that even in discussion between the LAPD Crime Laboratory and the District Attorney's Office prior to the trial, the reports of these x-rays and photographs were not given to the prosecution team. The explanation by the LAPD that these photographs and analysis "proved nothing," reflects the lack of judgment by the LAPD in fully co-operating with the prosecuting office. Even though it was anticipated that defense counsels' argument would center on diminished capacity at the trial, the fact that the actual murder bullet, People's #48, had been so badly damaged and fragmented and could not be linked to the murder weapon, necessitated a much more thorough, definitive, and complete documentation of ballistics, firearms and trajectory studies. The failure to do so reflects on the entire prosecution.[25]

In May 1980, DeWayne Wolfer would be back in the news again. LAPD SUSPENDS FORENSIC CHEMIST was the headline in the *Los Angeles Times*. The story by Myrna Oliver read:

> DeWayne Wolfer, head of the Scientific Investigation Division, was suspended by police chief Daryl Gates, May 23 for 30 working days without pay. Internal affairs investigators determined that Wolfer had failed to provide proper storage and analysis of bullets and other evidence and had improperly supervised firearms and explosives investigators.

Oliver reported that Wolfer had become "widely known for his forensic work," but that he had also become a figure of controversy. She noted that a district attorney's inquiry in 1971 had "cleared him of any wrongdoing" in the Sirhan case, but that in 1975, the California Court of

Appeal "concluded that Wolfer gave false testimony bordering on perjury in the 1967 murder trial of former Deputy District Attorney Jack Kirschke."[26]

In the testimony of DeWayne Wolfer at the trial of Sirhan Sirhan, Grant Cooper had the makings of a stunning cross-examination. Had Cooper been properly prudent, William Harper (or another private forensic expert) would have been seated at the defense table advising him.

Cooper might have asked Wolfer what caused him to be photographed pointing to bullet holes in the walls which he now said weren't genuine? What tests had Wolfer conducted to establish that the holes were caused by dish trays? Why were the doorframes removed and booked as evidence if they contained no bullet holes? Why were they to be subjected to trajectory analysis? How could Sirhan have shot Kennedy in the back when he was observed by many witnesses to be in front of the senator, and how could all four shots have been point-blank when most witnesses said the defendant fired only two shots before his gun was deflected? How could a bullet traveling at a sharp upward angle turn and enter Paul Schrade's head? How could bullets which were identified as having come from a pistol other than Sirhan's be used for firearms comparison purposes? And why was this evidence kept for nine months in Wolfer's desk drawer?

Cooper might also have demanded to see certain evidence. The doorframes and ceiling tiles should have been produced, as well as the results of the tests supposedly done upon them. The defense attorney could have run his own tests on the victims' bullets as well as on the enigmatic spent bullets allegedly found in Sirhan's car. He could have demanded to see the scientific backup for Wolfer's conclusion of a bullet match. He could have inspected the photomicrograph, and, with expertise of a forensic adviser, determined that it was not as the police represented.

But Grant Cooper was not in a combative mode when he rose to cross-examine DeWayne Wolfer. Quite the opposite. "Officer Wolfer," began Cooper, "let me ask you, what time are you leaving?" DeWayne Wolfer had an out-of-town professional commitment the following day, and Grant Cooper wanted to be sure not to inconvenience the criminalist.

"When we get through," replied Wolfer. "I'll go over and make my reservation for the first flight I can get on."

"We won't keep you," reassured Cooper.

Cooper then went on to ask several questions with no apparent purpose. Was the revolver used for test purposes still available? Wolfer responded that it was (although police documents would indicate that it wasn't). Cooper then asked Wolfer about any margins of error he might have built into his calculations of firing distance. In a very tangled reply

Wolfer asserted that he took his findings of distance and doubled them to create a tolerance for error.

But Grant Cooper had his own solution to the nagging firing-distance riddle. As will be seen later, the defense attorney seemed to have a recurring desire to clean up messy evidentiary situations as the trial progressed. Logically, these messes should have been the worry of the prosecution, but Cooper didn't like them. Sounding more like the prosecution on redirect than the defense on cross, Cooper applied his own logic to dismiss the conflicts in the evidence concerning gun-muzzle distance.

"Let me ask you this," said Cooper, referring to Sirhan's .22 caliber revolver. "With your experience of firearms . . . a weapon like this can cause death, and it did cause death, is that true?"

"Yes," said Wolfer.

"And it can cause death from one inch, two inches, three inches, six inches, one foot, three feet, six feet. . . . It could cause death if it were in the right place?"

"Yes."

And that was the cross-examination of DeWayne Wolfer. According to Grant Cooper, any questions about firing distance were irrelevant: a .22 caliber revolver could kill if it were fired from a distance of one inch or six feet.

DeWayne Wolfer could have been on the witness stand for the rest of the week answering questions and defending his testimony. Instead, he made his flight that afternoon.

SEVEN

Missing Persons

✳ ✳ ✳

ON THE AFTERNOON following the shooting of Robert Kennedy, the Los Angeles police found Sirhan's 1956 DeSoto illegally parked on New Hampshire Street, just a few blocks from the Ambassador Hotel. In the glove compartment was Sirhan's wallet. Also in the car were some matchbooks from Shakey's Pizza Parlor, a raffle ticket, and a book titled *Healing: The Divine Art* by Manley Palmer Hall. Most ominous, though, was a sales receipt for $3.99 from the Lock Stock 'n Barrel for .22 caliber ammunition, dated June 1, 1968.

The receipt had been issued by Larry Arnot, a retired Pasadena fireman who was working the shop's counter that day. When the police questioned Arnot, he told them that some time in the afternoon of June 1, three men, including one he identified as Sirhan, walked into his store. Sirhan, he recalled, bought two boxes of .22 caliber hollow-point Mini-Mag ammunition. One of the other men bought two boxes of Super-X Westerns. The four boxes were put on the same receipt.

Perhaps disturbed by his story, the police asked Arnot to submit to a polygraph examination. Arnot consented and the test took place. Apparently satisfied that any open questions had been resolved, prosecutor David Fitts called Larry Arnot to testify at the trial.

"Mr. Arnot," began Fitts, "directing your attention to the first day of June 1968, were you employed at a gun shop called the Lock Stock 'n Barrel in San Gabriel?"

Arnot said yes, and Fitts then asked him to describe the sale of bullets to Sirhan.

"You want me to relate the whole transaction?" Arnot asked, a little unsure. "The whole transaction?"

"Tell us what you know about it, sir," said Fitts. "If you remember."

"Approximately three-thirty in the afternoon three individuals entered the store, walked to the portion of the store where the ammunition was stored. I approached them, asked them if I could be of assistance, and in turn was given a request for .22 ammunition—"

"If the Court please," interrupted Fitts. "I don't think I'm going to let this go any further. If I may take this witness in my own way.

"Mr. Arnot, do you recall having a conversation with Lieutenant Enrique Hernandez of the Los Angeles Police Department with reference to
selling ammunition to three individuals?"

"Yes."

"Then he put you on the so-called polygraph, the lie detector, isn't that
true?"

"Yes."

"And he indicated to you with reference to the sale of what is reflected
on that slip that you were confused?"

"Yes."

"All right. And then you ultimately told Mr. Hernandez that so far as
selling the ammunition which is reflected on People's 22, that you had it
mixed up with a sale to three other people and were in your own mind
trying to connect it with the sale to Sirhan. Isn't that right?"

"I don't remember those words."

"Did you ultimately tell Mr. Hernandez that so far as that particular
transaction reflected in People's 22, that you didn't remember Sirhan and
you didn't remember anything other than that you had filled out that sales
slip with respect to a sale?"

"Yes."

"That's all I have."

The owners of the Lock Stock 'n Barrel, Ben and Donna Herrick, were
angered by Arnot's treatment by the police and the prosecution. They knew
Arnot to be an honest man and saw no reason for him to make up a story.
In addition, Donna Herrick had seen Sirhan in the store previously with
two companions, and she filed statements with both the police and the
FBI to that effect. But Donna Herrick was not called as a witness.

"They didn't want her to testify, because she wouldn't change her story,"
asserted Ben Herrick after the trial. Herrick then came to the defense of
Arnot: "The sales slip definitely proves the fact that he was telling the
truth and then they say the lie detector says he was telling a lie and they
throw him off the witness stand. It just discredited the man's testimony
and made a fool out of him, and for no reason because he was a prosecution witness to begin with. I just don't like the smell of it."[1]

There was nothing necessarily conspiratorial about Sirhan shopping for
.22 caliber ammunition with two others. Although no one had come forward and admitted to being with Sirhan, his companions might have been
his brothers or just friends with no relation to the Robert Kennedy murder. But to the police and the trial attorneys, even the barest mention of
possible accomplices had to be eliminated. The police had no evidence that
Sirhan was not accompanied by two others; indeed, Donna Herrick's story
tended to corroborate that of Arnot.

Prosecutor Fitts asked the jury to believe that Enrique Hernandez's polygraph discovered that Arnot had confused two separate sales. But a polygraph, if it can detect anything at all, is unable to detect confusion—only the physiologic reactions supposedly associated with telling a lie. It is clear from Fitts's interjection that Arnot's testimony was unexpected. Fitts then had to present Arnot as a man who had failed a polygraph test and had no memory of the sale. But if this was so, why did the prosecution introduce him as a witness?

A more likely explanation is that Arnot did see Sirhan with two others on June 1. Then, under pressure from polygraph operator Hernandez, he acquiesced to the police contention that he was confused. But later, under oath at the trial, Arnot's original memories of the transaction came spilling out despite his coaching. At that point, he had to be impeached by the very attorney who had called him to the stand.

As strange as this sequence was, defense attorney Grant Cooper's cross-examination of Arnot was equally bizarre. As if by instinct, Cooper opened his questioning, as he should, trying to exploit the inconsistency in Arnot's testimony. "Why did you tell us on direct examination that you sold this to Mr. Sirhan and two others?"

David Fitts immediately jumped up and testified for the witness. "I don't believe he said that."

Cooper accepted this answer, though Arnot had clearly made the statement. The defense attorney then, for no apparent reason, pressured Arnot into the nonsensical admission that he could remember the sale but not the individuals involved. He then closed with the kind of questions trial lawyers ask when they want to appear to be doing something.

"These two boxes that you sold, Mr. Arnot . . . how many cartridges would that be all together, sir?"

"One hundred."

"In other words, there are fifty in a box?"

"That's correct."

"And the two boxes of the other at ninety cents, is that also another one hundred?"

"Yes."

"In other words, all together there would be two hundred bullets?"

"That's correct."

"Thank you. I have no further questions."

Arnot's time in court was brief and barely noted by the press. Nevertheless, his appearance revealed much about the selective nature of the proceeding. Arnot's treatment at the hands of the LAPD was typical for witnesses with information relating to possible accomplices. Most of these witnesses would not appear at the trial.

•   •   •

One account of the assassination that should have at least provoked curiosity on the part of the police was that of Don Schulman, a runner for Los Angeles TV station KNXT. Immediately following the shooting, Jeff Brent of Continental News Service grabbed Schulman for a radio interview. Schulman was out of breath.

> BRENT: I'm talking to Don Schulman. Can you give us a halfway decent report of what happened within all this chaos?
>
> SCHULMAN: [ellipsis points indicate pauses] Okay. I was . . . ah . . . standing behind . . . ah . . . Kennedy as he was taking his assigned route into the kitchen. A Caucasian gentleman stepped out and fired three times . . . the security guard . . . hitting Kennedy all three times. Mr. Kennedy slumped to the floor. . . . They carried him away. . . . The security guards fired back. . . . As I saw . . . They shot the . . . ah, man who shot Kennedy . . . in the leg. . . . He . . . before they could get him he shot a . . . it looked like to me . . . he shot a woman . . . and he shot two other men.
>
> BRENT: Right. I was about six or seven people behind the senator, I heard six or seven shots in succession. . . . Now . . . is this the security guard firing back?
>
> SCHULMAN: Yes . . . ah, the man who stepped out fired three times at Kennedy . . . hit him all three times . . . and the security guard fired back . . . hitting . . . hitting him, and he [presumably Sirhan] is in apprehension.[2]

Despite the fact that Schulman reported that he saw a security guard behind Kennedy fire a gun at the assailant, a story that appeared on radio and TV and in some newspapers, the LAPD took no interest. This is curious because Kennedy was killed by a bullet entering the back of his head fired at close range, and security guard Thane Cesar was standing right behind Kennedy. Moreover, Cesar had an unholstered gun; he was not a friend of Kennedy's; he had been standing guard over the room where the ambush took place, and as Kennedy had passed by, Cesar had taken the senator by the arm.

Nevertheless, the Los Angeles police did not thoroughly examine Thane Cesar. They failed to clear up even elementary contradictions in the security guard's story, inconsistencies regarding his actions during the shooting. They also failed to verify the accuracy of his account regarding his disposition of a .22 caliber handgun. (Cesar told police that he sold it prior to the day of the assassination, but a receipt of this transaction subsequently recovered by journalist Theodore Charach listed the date of sale as four months after the assassination.) They failed to check Cesar's gun the night of the murder to see if it had been fired or even what caliber it was. (Cesar claimed he was carrying a .38 caliber pistol and that it was not fired.) And most strange, although he had been standing close to Robert Kennedy and had witnessed the assault, Cesar was not called as a witness at the trial of Sirhan.

An explanation as to why would be offered in a 1971 article in the *Los Angeles Times* entitled "Sirhan Case—Was There a 2nd Gunman?" In the article, reporter Dave Smith quoted an unnamed "official" who stated that the inconsistencies in Cesar's story were cause for dismissing him as a suspect or witness rather than investigating him further.

Said the official, "The guy's stories didn't jibe. He told conflicting accounts and it seemed obvious he hadn't really seen anything. He really had nothing to tell us."[3]

"Because of the variances in his story," wrote Smith, "the guard was dropped from any further questioning, his credibility questioned by officials who felt he was trying to inject himself into a sensational case he knew little about."[4]

The logic here is twisted. How can the police expect to solve any but the most obvious crimes if questioning ceases because a person who was close to the shooting and who played a security role gives "conflicting accounts?" Contrary to the assertion, Cesar had not tried to inject himself into the case. He was there at the scene, and considering the fact that the fatal bullet entered the back of Kennedy's head at close range, Cesar was worthy of scrutiny.

There were, however, people—unlike the police—who found Cesar's presence in the pantry suspicious. In researching what would become a film documentary on the assassination, Theodore Charach gained an interview in 1971 with Thane Cesar. Charach got the former security guard to speak candidly about his feelings on several subjects. When asked whom he would have voted for in 1968, Cesar revealed that he had no affection for the Kennedys.

"I definitely wouldn't have voted for Bobby Kennedy," Cesar said, "because he had the same ideas that John did and I think John sold the country down the road. He gave it to the commies, he gave it to whoever else he wanted. He literally gave it to the minority."

Cesar said he supported Alabama governor George Wallace. He then gratuitously offered his opinion on race relations in America.

The black man now for the last four to eight years has been cramming this integrated idea down our throats, so you learn to hate him. And one of these days at the rate they're going, there's going to be civil war in this country. It's going to be white against the black and the only thing I can say is the black will never win. . . . I can't see any other way to go.[5]

Thane Cesar's statements would appear in Ted Charach's documentary *The Second Gun.*★ With the advent of the documentary in 1971, witness Don Schulman was called down to the district attorney's office for his first properly documented interview with authorities since the murder. When the investigators asked the young man if he was certain that Cesar shot Kennedy, Schulman protested, correctly, that he had not said any such thing. "I never said I saw [the guard shoot Kennedy]. . . . Hell, I didn't even see Sirhan shoot Kennedy. I know what the newspapers and everybody say, but I didn't see him do it."

The men from the DA's office pressed Schulman some more. There was no talk about whether he was or wasn't in the pantry. The questions implied that he was there. Schulman was asked if he was "absolutely positive" about the security guard.

"I'm pretty doggone sure he fired his gun," Schulman answered.[6]

What is most odd about the police treatment of Schulman is the lack of documentation of any police interview with him during their original 1968 investigation. There does exist an LAPD memorandum, dated three years later, which refers to an interview Schulman supposedly had with LAPD sergeant Paul O'Steen on August 9, 1968. The document reports:

> Schulman . . . stated he was outside of the kitchen when he heard noises like firecrackers. He did not see the actual shooting or suspect due to the crowd. Mr. Schulman was reinterviewed on July 23, 1971. He stated during this interview that he was in the pantry about twelve feet from Senator Kennedy when the shots were fired. . . . Why Mr. Schulman has changed his mind or why his memory, which he describes as poor, has improved since August 9, 1968, is subject to scrutiny.[7]

The 1971 memo contains several odd leaps of logic. The memo would have one believe that Schulman, over a three-year period, gradually misremembered himself into the pantry. This conveniently overlooks the fact that just moments after the shooting Schulman asserted he was in the pantry and gave Jeff Brent's radio audience a detailed account of what took place in that room. In addition, whether or not he was correct about Cesar's

---

★After 1975 there was no recorded contact with Thane Cesar for fourteen years. Those interested in the assassination story were unable to locate him. Los Angeles authorities claimed that Cesar had died in Arkansas. In 1989, however, journalist Dan Moldea found Cesar working as a plumber in Southern California. After repeated requests, Cesar consented to be interviewed by Moldea. During these sessions he steadfastly maintained that he did not shoot Robert Kennedy. Ultimately, Cesar consented to Moldea's proposal that he take a polygraph exam concerning his guilt or innocence. According to Moldea's polygraph operator, Cesar passed the test.

firing his gun, Schulman accurately asserted that Cesar had displayed his gun, something admitted by Cesar but noticed by only a few others.

Over the years Schulman has been consistent in asserting that he did not see Sirhan shoot Kennedy, something the 1971 memo alludes to as if this diminishes his credibility. What the memo doesn't explain is how it makes sense to assert that a person "did not see the actual shooting due to the crowd" if that person is not even in the room.

Most strange is the apparent effort to make Don Schulman disappear altogether. Schulman, like other witnesses with disturbing observations, doesn't appear on the LAPD's list of those in the pantry when the murder took place. Moreover, there is no surviving record of his supposed interview with Sergeant O'Steen—no audiotape, interview transcript, or interview summary. And if the O'Steen interview did take place, why wasn't it reported in the LAPD *Summary Report,* which is supposed to summarize every police interview of consequence?

In October 1975, Schulman had his last official interview with special counsel Tom Kranz and his associate Bill Burnett. Kranz was working on an independent report, commissioned by the district attorney's office, which would reaffirm the official conclusions about the Kennedy murder. During the lengthy audiotaped session, Schulman made the following, slightly modified, statement about a second gun: "I thought I saw a security guard pull his gun and possibly fire." Later he would assert, "I saw other guns pulled and possibly fired."

Schulman's statement here about "other guns" is potentially significant, and he would not be the only witness to make this observation. In the same year in an interview with journalist Betsy Langman, Schulman would say that he was less certain that the security guard fired his gun but was "absolutely positive" that he saw other men in plain clothes with guns drawn in the pantry. Since there were no Secret Service agents present, and Kennedy had no armed bodyguards, who were these men?

The response to Schulman's assertion that he saw other guns drawn is representative of police reactions when confronted with difficult issues in this case. The normal investigative response might be, What did these other men with guns look like? What were they doing? Where did they go? Instead, to Schulman's assertion that he saw other guns, Bill Burnett responded, "No, there was no other guns."

"I thought I saw 'em," answered Schulman.

"Nope, you didn't."

After Schulman's departure Kranz and his colleague have a revealing discussion, putting down critics of the police version of the crime while the audiotape is still recording. Kranz then changes the subject back to

Schulman: "I never felt, particularly in light of the ballistics examination, that his statements about a security guard had much weight."

"Yeah," his colleague answers, "but he really has not changed his [story]; he's still sticking with, he still sees guns and this kind of shit. . . . I think if, if this thing is gonna go anyplace and he's gonna be a problem, I'd like to call him in and we'll interrogate him." Since Schulman had just been questioned for an hour and a half, the purpose of such "interrogation" would seem to be intimidation to get the witness to remain silent or change his testimony.[8]

Don Schulman would not be the only witness to merit peculiar treatment by the police.

On May 20, about two weeks before the California primary, a campaign luncheon was held for Robert Kennedy at Robbie's Restaurant in Pomona. Because of the size of the affair (four hundred guests), the night manager, thirty-five-year-old Albert LeBeau, was called in to help. After the murder, LeBeau saw Sirhan's picture on television and recognized him as someone he had seen acting strange at the luncheon for Senator Kennedy. On June 7, LeBeau contacted the FBI and told them what he had seen. Subsequently he signed a five-page statement to the Bureau describing his encounter with the man he believed to be Sirhan.

LeBeau's initial duty at the luncheon was to act as ticket taker on the staircase leading into the restaurant. While collecting tickets on the crowded staircase, LeBeau heard a noise and turned to see a woman who "had to climb over the rail from a booth and over a brick flower casing in order to get behind me. I saw a man coming over the rail and dropping onto the stairs behind the girl."

LeBeau intercepted the couple. "Do you have tickets?" he asked.

"We are with the senator's party," the woman answered.

LeBeau told them that tickets were still necessary. The woman then claimed, "We are part of the senator's party. He just waved us to come upstairs."

The woman, as described by LeBeau, was Caucasian, twenty-five to thirty years old, with "medium blond" shoulder-length hair. She appeared to be five feet six, somewhat taller than the man she was with. She also had a "nice shape, built proportionately."[9] Her companion, whom LeBeau later recognized as Sirhan, said nothing during this exchange, but LeBeau did notice a coat draped over his right hand and forearm, this on a very warm May afternoon.

LeBeau sent the couple back down the stairs away from the luncheon. Later, however, as Robert Kennedy was giving his speech, he saw the couple once more standing against the back wall of the dining room among the hundred or so standees.

Whether the man he encountered was actually Sirhan could not be independently proved or disproved, but the basic facts of LeBeau's story were corroborated. William Schneid, a police officer from Pomona who was on duty in the restaurant, reported to the FBI that he had seen the couple cross over the "brick facade adjacent to the stairs and over the stair railing behind persons apparently checking for tickets at the foot of the stairs." He witnessed LeBeau stop the couple.

Schneid told the FBI that the man he saw bore a likeness to Sirhan, a slim Latin or Mexican man with dark curly hair, five feet six to five feet seven. Despite this, Schneid's FBI summary strangely states, "He did not feel the man observed by him would have been Sirhan Sirhan." The woman Schneid observed on the stairs was described as a Caucasian in her mid-twenties, five feet four to five feet seven with medium- to light-brown hair, an "attractive" woman who was "proportionate [in figure]," and "officious." Schneid had encountered her earlier, just prior to the arrival of Senator Kennedy. She had been standing by the kitchen door of the restaurant, apparently trying to get in. When Schneid told her that entrance was closed, the woman asked the officer which way Senator Kennedy would enter the luncheon. Schneid replied that the senator "would probably go up the stairs to the second floor." Schneid was never taken to a police lineup to see if he could identify Sirhan. He was not even interviewed by the LAPD.[10]

On June 12 Albert LeBeau picked Sirhan's mug shot for the FBI as a man "closely resembling" the man he saw on the stairs. Despite this, LeBeau was never afforded the opportunity to view Sirhan in a lineup for positive identification. Moreover, there are disturbing irregularities in LeBeau's police file.

Albert LeBeau was interviewed by the LAPD on June 26. A transcript of this session has not survived in police files. Nor has a tape recording, if one was made. What does survive is a "summary" of the interview, a convenient device if one is intent on shaping or spinning information given by a witness. The June 26 summary states that LeBeau had been previously interviewed by "Officer Thompson," but no record of that session exists in the files.

The summary of LeBeau's interview is a lengthy three-page, single-spaced document. It is unusual in that it is peppered with frequent quotations from LeBeau, which would indicate that the session was recorded, then excerpted. During the interview LeBeau apparently successfully picked Sirhan from a batch of twenty-five photos of dark-skinned young males. The summary, however, makes special mention of the fact that LeBeau failed to pick out another picture of Sirhan, this a Racing Commission ID photo, as though this failure seriously injured the witness's credibility.

The final sentence of the interview summary is uncharacteristically dramatic: "Just before the conclusion of the interview LeBeau was asked,

'Could you under oath swear that Sirhan is the man involved in the incident on May the 20th?' LeBeau hung his head and stared at the floor for several long moments and replied, 'No.'"[11]

The LAPD's *Summary Report,* the fifteen-hundred-page document that summarized the police investigation, but which was not released to the public until 1986, puts an entirely different spin on the LeBeau interview. The report says LeBeau "initially stated the man was Sirhan, but later admitted he lied."[12] There is no record of any such admission in police files. If the synopsis in the *Summary Report* chose to portray the lack of absolute certainty as a confession of falsehood, then the honesty of the entire investigation is called into question.

On July 19 the FBI would be informed of another incident in which Sirhan appeared to be stalking Robert Kennedy. This incident took place in the Kennedy campaign headquarters in Azusa, California. Laverne Botting, a forty-one-year-old volunteer, told the Bureau that on May 30 she observed two men and a woman enter the office. One of the men approached her desk. This man, whom she would later recognize as "Sirhan or a person who very closely resembles Sirhan," said he was from the RFK headquarters in Pasadena (Sirhan lived in Pasadena) and asked if Robert Kennedy would be visiting the area. Botting replied that he would not. While the other two remained at a distance, Botting was able to describe the woman as a twenty-two- to twenty-five-year-old Caucasian, five feet seven inches tall, with an "excellent figure" and "dishwater blond hair."[13]

The Los Angeles police interviewed Botting three weeks later. Though she had told the FBI she would be able to make a definite judgment on her sighting if she saw Sirhan in person, she was never given the opportunity. Botting picked out Sirhan from a photo lineup and then told Officer C. B. Thompson that the man she thought was Sirhan was five feet four, twenty to twenty-five years old, with dark eyes and kinky black hair (characteristics closely resembling Sirhan).

In the interview summary Officer Thompson reports that Botting claimed that she had received a strange phone call: "I hear you think you saw Sirhan," her anonymous caller said in a threatening manner. "You had better be sure of what you are saying." If this call actually took place, it raises the question of who, besides the Los Angeles Police Department, would have an interest in exerting pressure on Botting's degree of certainty. Who beyond the LAPD even knew of her sighting?

Despite Botting's having given a description of the man she saw as closely resembling Sirhan, Officer Thompson's summary makes special note of the fact that Botting described the man she saw as having a broad nose and shoulders. This leads Thompson to ultimately conclude: "Witness has obviously made an honest mistake."[14] As with LeBeau's session, there exists no transcript nor audiotape of this interview.

If there had been no corroboration of her story, the police might be forgiven for dismissing Botting's story as "an honest mistake." But there was a witness to the events described by Botting. Another volunteer at Kennedy headquarters that day, forty-five-year-old Ethel Creehan, called the police on June 7 and told them of the incident. She told them she was "fairly certain" the man she saw was Sirhan, but that she would not want to "testify to the fact without first seeing Sirhan in person."[15] Like Botting and LeBeau, she would not be given the opportunity.

Ethel Creehan would be reinterviewed a month later by Officer Thompson. At that time she picked out Sirhan's photograph as resembling the man she observed with her coworker, Laverne Botting. Creehan described the man as being five feet eight. She described the girl as perhaps nineteen, but with makeup that made her appear twenty-three to twenty-five. According to Creehan she had brown or blond shoulder-length hair. She also had a "prominent" nose. (Note: witness Sandra Serrano said that the woman in the polka-dot dress had a "funny nose"; witness Vincent DiPierro said that she had a "pudgy" nose.)

In his summary of Creehan's interview Officer Thompson reports that he checked with a woman from Kennedy headquarters in Pasadena, who said there was no reason why they would have sent anyone to Azusa to inquire about the senator's schedule. Thompson states this as if it casts doubt upon the stories of Botting and Creehan, when in fact it makes the afternoon visitors to Azusa all the more suspicious.

Thompson's conclusion on Creehan is also quite remarkable: "The person described by Mrs. Creehan as possibly being Sirhan is 4 inches taller than Sirhan. It is doubtful if the person she observed was Sirhan."[16] Botting, remember, was given no credence for describing the mystery man as five feet four, but Creehan is apparently discredited for misestimating by a few inches the height of a man she viewed only casually some weeks earlier. It is difficult to escape the conclusion that the interviewing officer in these cases was searching diligently for anything at all to dismiss the witnesses' testimony.

The Los Angeles police found it easy to dismiss or discredit witnesses who reported seeing Sirhan in the company of possible accomplices, even though, in many of these pre-assassination stories, the same image (a woman in her early twenties with a good figure) appeared with regularity. More alarming is the LAPD's conduct toward a number of other witnesses who reported suspicious activity in or near the pantry of the Ambassador Hotel the night of the shooting.

On the night of the murder, Nina Rhodes was at the Ambassador Hotel with her husband to celebrate Robert Kennedy's primary victory and attend a private party in the senator's suite. She was in the pantry when Robert Kennedy was shot. She was interviewed by the FBI, but no recording or transcript has survived. In their place is a summary report which said the following:

> She had just left the entrance to the kitchen and noticed the Senator shaking hands with various kitchen employees . . . when she suddenly heard a sound like a firecracker. . . . She instantaneously realized that . . . shots were being fired. She later recalled hearing eight distinct shots. Everything appeared to her like still frames in a stop-action movie. . . . [T]he individual who fired the shots at the Senator appeared to her to be wearing a powder blue jacket.[17]

When shown her FBI interview summary in 1992, Nina Rhodes took issue with no fewer than fifteen items as stated in the report, some minor, some not. Most relevant, Rhodes claimed in writing, "I never said I heard 8 distinct shots. From the moment the tragedy began I knew that there were at least 10–14 shots and that there had to be more than one assailant. The shots were to the left *and* [emphasis added] right from where I was."[18]

Nina Rhodes's perceptions that ten to fourteen shots were fired and that they came from two separate sources were the items of greatest forensic value in her testimony. It is significant, then, that in the FBI summary of her interview she is portrayed as hearing "eight distinct shots." It is also significant that despite her rather detailed account of the murder given to the FBI, the Los Angeles police do not include Nina Rhodes on their list of witnesses whom they say were in the pantry at the time of the murder.

One person definitely on the list of pantry witnesses was Evan Freed, who was standing near Robert Kennedy when the shooting started. Freed was a part-time news photographer in 1968. He is now a deputy city attorney for the City of Los Angeles. In 1992 he, like Nina Rhodes, swore an affidavit in support of the petition to the Los Angeles County Grand Jury.

In his detailed, four-page declaration, Freed said that in 1968 he had been assigned to cover the Robert Kennedy campaign. He described the events at the Ambassador Hotel leading up to the shooting.

Freed said that during the evening he had been on the fifth floor of the Ambassador Hotel, where the Kennedy campaign had rented a suite of rooms. He said he accompanied Kennedy on the elevator that took the senator down to the second floor, where he would speak to the crowd gathered in the Embassy Room. Some minutes prior to the end of Kennedy's speech, Freed said he wandered into the pantry. There he noticed two men "very similar in appearance" moving around. One of these men would turn out to be Sirhan. The two men did not stand together but seemed to look at each other every now and then. Freed thought they might be brothers.

When Senator Kennedy entered the pantry after his speech, Freed began to walk beside him. When the shooting started he was "about 4 feet away," facing Kennedy. "I saw the 2nd man (wearing darker clothing) who had been in the pantry with Sirhan during the speech pointing a gun in an upward angle at the Senator. Based on the sound I heard, I believe the first shot came from this man's gun. In the background I could see Sirhan firing a revolver held in his right hand in the direction of the Senator. People in the crowd were screaming and grabbing Sirhan. . . ."

In his affidavit Freed said that as the crowd rushed forward toward Sirhan, they passed by the second gunman, who was backing away. Moments later he saw the second gunman running in his direction, pursued by another man yelling, "Stop that guy, stop him!" According to Freed, the pursuer made an attempt to grab the gunman but failed. Then both men ran out of the pantry.

When Freed met with police detectives he said he told them the story he had related in his affidavit. "I was asked whether or not the man pursuing the 2nd gunman could have been yelling, 'Get an ambulance' or 'Get a doctor.' I told them that was not correct, *but they insisted that I had been incorrect in what I heard* [emphasis added]."

Freed said that although he had given a description of the man who was pursuing the second gunman, there was never a request from the police that he produce a drawing of the man or look for him in photographs.

"I made it very clear that the 2nd gunman looked very much like Sirhan, except that his clothing was darker in color and coordinated."

Freed related that he had also been contacted by the FBI, but that they "seemed to be avoiding asking me questions about the 2nd gunman, although I told them the same things I have stated above." Freed ended his declaration saying that he had never desired any publicity in the case and had no opinion as to who fired the fatal shots into Robert Kennedy. "My purpose in making these statements now is to help insure that a fair investigation is conducted in this case. I declare under the penalty of perjury that the foregoing is true and correct."[19]

Evan Freed's first police interview dated June 14 asserts that Freed claimed to have seen two men and a woman leave the pantry in a hurry after the shooting. The woman was described as "possibly wearing a polka dot dress."[20] In a "reinterview" dated August 1, Freed's pantry story is retold but with no mention at all of the suspicious trio he had reported before. On September 11, Freed would be interviewed by the FBI. The summary of this interview reports: "He [Freed] looked up and saw a man shooting a gun. . . . The man who was doing the shooting was subsequently identified as Sirhan Sirhan. *Sirhan was the only person Freed saw shooting* [emphasis added]."[21] The authors are aware of no other interview summary in the FBI files that asserts that the witness saw only one person shooting.

From their interview summaries, the police and the FBI seemed quite willing to discount the story told by Evan Freed, but if they truly believed that no one was able to substantiate Freed's story, then they can't have been very diligent in their search.

On the night of the murder Dr. Marcus McBroom was standing right outside the kitchen in the Embassy Room. McBroom told his story in detail to researcher Greg Stone in 1986.

> The first inference that we had that anything was awry was that we heard the first one or two shots. And then a woman in a polka dot dress ran out of the kitchen shouting "We got him" or "We shot him." No one really was even certain as to what she had said because no one initially really comprehended what was really happening. Immediately after she ran out, a man with a gun under a newspaper ran out in a very menacing way and myself and a man by the name of Sam Strain and the man running the ABC camera we drew back instinctively when we saw the gun.[22]

McBroom described the woman in the polka-dot dress as between twenty-two and twenty-four years of age, brunet, fairly attractive, between five feet three and five feet four, and "proportionate." The man with the gun he described as an "Arab looking person" in a blue suit (Freed described the man in blue "coordinated" clothing), perspiring profusely, with a newspaper draped over his arm and a pistol visible underneath it. When McBroom was asked by police to pick out from a series of mug shots someone who looked similar to the menacing man, McBroom picked a photograph of one of Sirhan's brothers, thus confirming Freed's description of the man bearing a familial resemblance to Sirhan.

Freed's and McBroom's accounts of seeing suspicious persons flee the pantry would be corroborated by a number of witnesses in or just outside the hotel kitchen.

George Green, a thirty-three-year-old real estate salesman, reported to the FBI that at about 11:15 to 11:30 he was at the Ambassador Hotel observing Kennedy press secretary Frank Mankiewicz talk with reporters in a corridor leading to the pantry area. At that time Green saw a man whom he would later identify as Sirhan standing at the edge of the crowd. He was standing near a tall thin man and a female Caucasian in her early twenties.

Green told the FBI that the woman had "a good figure" and wore a white dress with black polka dots.

Green entered the pantry area just as the shooting began. At first he couldn't identify the popping noises he heard, but then he recognized them as gunfire. Before Green joined the struggle to subdue the apparent assailant, he noticed a man and a woman rush out of the pantry. Their actions were conspicuous because everyone else seemed to be trying to get into the room. The woman wore a polka-dot dress.[23]

Jack J. Merritt, a uniformed security guard working for Ace Guard Service, reported to both the police and the FBI that he saw "two men and a woman leaving the kitchen." He described the woman as approximately five feet five inches tall, with "light colored" hair. The men who were leaving wore suits; the woman, a polka-dot dress. According to Merritt, "They seemed to be smiling."[24]

Twenty-one-year-old Kennedy supporter Richard Houston was standing outside the pantry when the shots were fired. He told the police that shortly thereafter he saw a woman run out of the room. Houston said the woman wore a black-and-white polka-dot dress "with ruffles around the neck and front." As she hurried by, Houston heard her say, "We killed him," after which she "ran out onto a terrace area outside."[25]

Kennedy campaign worker Darnell Johnson was in the pantry ahead of the senator's party. While there he noticed a group of five people standing near each other. One of these would turn out to be Sirhan. Near him Johnson saw a six-foot-one man in a light-blue sports coat, and a white female. Johnson described the woman as twenty-three to twenty-five years old, with light-brown hair, five feet eight, 145 pounds, and "well built." The woman wore a white dress with quarter-size black polka dots. Johnson noticed that the three men and the woman left the room as Sirhan was being subdued.[26]

Booker Griffin, a twenty-nine-year-old Kennedy supporter and director of the Negro Industrial and Educational Union, told police he thought he saw Sirhan on three different times during the evening. On two of those occasions Sirhan was standing next to a woman, and although Griffin did not observe them talking, it was his impression that they were together. He noticed the two because they seemed "out of place." The woman he recalled was wearing a "predominantly white dress that may have had another color on it."

When the first shots were fired, Griffin was standing just outside the pantry. He noticed the woman and another man whom he had seen earlier with Sirhan run out of the pantry. Something in their motion and demeanor made Griffin blurt out, "They're getting away!"[27]

Jose Carvajal was working as a busboy the night of the murder. He told reporter Fernando Faura that he had entered the pantry in time to see a girl in a polka-dot dress running away. He said that a fellow worker, Jesse Gonzales, had seen Sirhan with the girl earlier, and that another kitchen worker, Jose Luis Miranda, had been standing near Sirhan before the shooting and had seen everything. But Miranda had been picked up by the FBI and had not returned to work. He was undocumented, and according to Carvajal, people in the kitchen believed he was sent back to Mexico as a warning to keep quiet about what they saw.[28]

There were also people who had noticed the woman in a polka-dot dress earlier in the evening. Lonny Worthy, Margaret Hahn, Judith Groves, John Ludlow, Pamela Russo, Greg Clayton, Eve Hansen, Nina Ballantyne, Susan Locke, Carol Breshears, and Jeanette Prudhomme were witnesses who reported seeing such a woman, either with a man resembling Sirhan or in suspicious circumstances.

Kennedy volunteer Susan Locke reported to the FBI that she saw a suspicious woman in the Embassy Room just before Kennedy's speech. According to Locke the woman seemed "somewhat out of place" and stood "expressionless" amid the crowd celebrating the apparent victory. Locke also noticed that the woman did not have the yellow badge necessary for admission to the Embassy Room, and she pointed the woman out to Carol Breshears, a woman in charge of the Kennedy support organization called the "Kennedy Girls." The mystery woman, according to Locke, was in her early twenties, "well proportioned," and wore a white dress with blue polka dots.[29]

Jeanette Prudhomme, a junior high school student and a Kennedy volunteer, reported to the police that she believed she saw Sirhan with a woman and another man in the Ambassador Hotel. She described the woman as a female Caucasian, twenty-eight to thirty years old, five feet six, 130 pounds, with brown shoulder-length hair and wearing "a white dress with black polka dots."[30]

While the description of the mystery woman offered by these witnesses varies in some respects, especially regarding hair color, a fairly consistent image emerges of an attractive woman in her early to mid-twenties, with a good figure, and wearing a white dress with black or dark-blue polka dots. There is also a rough but significant symmetry to the sightings by witnesses at the Ambassador: earlier in the evening in the Embassy Room, then near the pantry, then in the pantry, then running from the pantry across the Embassy Room, then outside the hotel.

There is also a story about something that happened earlier in the day that may have involved the same woman. A week after the murder, a man named John Fahey nervously approached Fernando Faura in his newspaper office and told the reporter about his chance meeting with a woman at the Ambassador Hotel the morning of the murder. By Fahey's description the woman closely resembled the young woman seen later that night in a polka-dot dress, but more alarming, she said to Fahey over breakfast, "They're gonna take care of Kennedy tonight."[31] Fahey and the woman then spent a bizarre day together, with the woman repeating her prediction and even inviting Fahey to come watch. At the time, Fahey didn't know what to think, but now that the foretold murder had happened, he was afraid to even go to the police.

Faura was a good reporter and a good citizen. He sat Fahey down, made an audiotape of his account of his day with the mystery woman, and typed out a transcript. He then gave the transcript to the police and said if they were interested in talking to this witness, he would escort him to the station. The police called and asked to see the man. They also asked for Faura's interview tape, so they could make a copy. The next day the police interviewed John Fahey, while Fernando Faura waited for his tape to be copied, but the tape was never returned.[32]

Faura then did what the police should have done. He had a portrait of the woman drawn from Fahey's description. Faura was able to get the portrait in front of Vincent DiPierro, who had reported seeing Sirhan moments before the shooting with a girl in a polka-dot dress. DiPierro looked at the portrait and offered a few small corrections. "But that's the girl," he said.[33]

What followed was an LAPD campaign against both Faura and Fahey, complete with slander, threats, hostile interviews, and a phony polygraph session with Sergeant Enrique Hernandez.[34] Both Fahey and Faura were followed each day. Fahey finally became frightened into giving the police a revised statement, which, at their suggestion, pointed the finger at Faura as the originator of the story, something that, as the evidence showed, could not be true.★

The commanding officers of the LAPD were certainly aware that their work would be scrutinized. They were also aware that the image of the Dallas police had suffered in reaction to what was seen as a very poor handling of the murder of President Kennedy. Thus, from the beginning, great emphasis was placed on public declarations pledging a thorough and professional investigation.

"Only those officers whose personal traits indicated complete dependability, ability to work with little supervision and flair for analyzing facts

---

★In 2016, at the urging of his children, Fernando Faura published *The Polka Dot File,* a book in which he describes in detail the story brought to him by John Fahey, how he went about verifying that story, and how the LAPD went to great lengths to discredit him. Fernando Faura was one of the only reporters who was actually following leads, and his treatment at the hands of the LAPD is as revealing as the startling story that John Fahey brought to him.

were chosen," declared the chief of detectives Robert Houghton.[35] Houghton would later describe the police investigation as "the most extensive search for truth ever launched by a local law enforcement agency."[36]

Houghton's praise for the police would be echoed by that of chief prosecutor Lynn Compton. "The FBI and the Los Angeles Police Department have interviewed literally thousands of people running out every suggestion, lead or possibility," said Compton during the trial, "and they have failed to find any connection between Sirhan and anyone else."[37]

The assertion by the police that in their thousands of interviews they discovered no evidence to support the story of the polka-dot-dress woman or other murder accomplices is simply untrue. There were many such witnesses, and the police did not have to look far to find them. But never were the accounts of these witnesses collated by the police, to be compared, cross-referenced, and studied. Instead, the "flair for analyzing facts" consisted of passing this evidence through a series of filters, such as interview summaries and summary reports, whereby the unwanted material would either disappear or be diluted, discredited, rephrased, screened, isolated, or ignored.

In the case of George Green, his story of seeing Sirhan standing near a woman in a polka-dot dress would strangely disappear between his FBI interview and his later LAPD interview. Lonny Worthy's story would also be lost somewhere between the FBI and the LAPD interviews, and the same would be true of the information given by Susan Locke; this is particularly odd because Locke's details on the polka-dot-dress woman comprised about a third of the information she gave to the FBI. Jeanette Prudhomme's account of Sirhan with the woman in polka dots is discounted in the LAPD *Summary Report*. "She was shown photographs of Sirhan," it states, "but was unable to make an identification." Considering liberties taken elsewhere, one might wonder what "make an identification" meant to the police in this instance.

The account of Richard Houston was left out of the LAPD *Summary Report*. Guard Jack Merritt's story of the woman in polka dots is stated briefly, without comment. That of Judith Groves is not reported at all. A terse sentence in the *Summary Report* states that Darnell Johnson says he saw Sirhan and the woman in the polka-dot dress. The report then says, "Note: Investigators believe Johnson's statements unreliable and contrary to fact." The basis for this belief is not explained.

Marcus McBroom's polka-dot-dress story is also not mentioned in the *Summary Report*. After reporting that McBroom had noticed Sirhan because he looked "out of place," the report states, "All additional statements made by McBroom were later retracted and are not reported here." McBroom denies any retractions.

The LAPD *Summary Report* would dismiss Booker Griffin by stating that

Griffin confessed "that the story of the male and female escaping was a total fabrication on his part." In June of 1987, Phil Melanson interviewed Griffin in the offices of the talent agency he ran on Sunset Boulevard in Hollywood. He repeated his account of seeing Sirhan and the woman. He was then shown the recently released *Summary Report* alleging he had admitted he had lied.

Griffin reacted with disbelief. "This is not true," he said forcefully. "This is totally untrue. . . . I'm not blind. I'm not a dishonest person. I know what I saw."

Whether or not a witness's story made it into the *Summary Report,* altered or otherwise, the report itself was not made public until 1986, and the investigation files were not made public until 1988—twenty years after the murder. Thus no witness was in a position to know whether his or her statements had been accurately represented in the interview summaries or the *Summary Report.* Also, no witnesses were, and no one else was, in a position to know exactly how many others had seen another man with a gun or Sirhan with possible accomplices. Each witness was isolated and made to feel that he or she was the only one reporting anomalous information.

Through careful manipulation of the press, the Los Angeles police successfully painted the story of the woman in the polka-dot dress as the hallucination of one "overwrought" young woman. The truth was that many apparently reliable witnesses saw this woman and reported their sightings to the police.

Evan Freed, Nina Rhodes, and Dr. Marcus McBroom are, presumably, responsible citizens. None of them has sought publicity or gain concerning what they saw the night of the murder. None could be considered an assassination buff or a conspiracy theorist. They merely reported to the police what they saw. But despite supporting evidence, the testimonies of these witnesses, and others like them, were systematically erased or ignored by the police.

If there was a short-term payoff to the manipulation of unwanted witnesses, it came the day defense attorney Russell Parsons stood before Judge Walker and requested under the California rules of discovery the right to examine the police files of these witnesses and others who had contact with Sirhan or who otherwise had witnessed the events of the murder. Prosecutor David Fitts later revealed that the LAPD was extremely reluctant to let go of these documents, but there was really no choice. He walked over to Parsons and placed the daunting pile of reports in front of him. "Do you want to count them?" he asked.

When the prosecution was finished turning over what they had to the defense, prosecutor Lynn Compton approached Judge Walker.

"I wonder if I might state something for the record which may be of assistance to Court and counsel."

Compton went on to say that the material in possession of the district attorney's office had been put into three categories: information pertaining to witnesses they planned to use at the trial, witnesses who provided background information who would not be called at the trial, and, third, "miscellaneous type of information which deals mainly with the subject of investigations that have been conducted concerning other possible suspects as to the existence of conspiracy and that sort of thing which I might indicate is all negative."

After his assertion that the witness interviews were conspiracy negative, Compton said, "We want to make perfectly clear to this Court and the record that there is nothing in our possession which we seek to conceal or withhold from the defense. . . . We believe that we have furnished the copies of statements of people *who could possibly be of any value at this time* [emphasis added]."

Despite these assurances, the prosecution may not have been as forthcoming with the defense as they pretended to be. On May 16, 1969, a post-trial meeting was held in the chambers of assistant presiding judge Charles A. Loring. There it was revealed that the prosecution had used some amount of discretion in deciding which files would be passed on to the defense. The purpose of the meeting was to discuss the appropriate resting place for evidence presented and not presented at the trial. Assistant district attorney David Fitts and deputy chief Houghton had this exchange in front of Judge Herbert Walker:

> FITTS: [talking about the discovery motion] They had a lot of specific names so they got that stuff and let me assure you here and now that which was delivered on discovery and that which was filed with the court was *scaled* [emphasis added] to this extent. They asked for interviews and interviews they got, but when it came down to embodying conclusions of investigative personnel you know and we believed, after examining this, that and the other, that even this [particular witness with information relating to a possible Sirhan accomplice] is a self-seeking son of a bitch—let it stay in the record. *Material of that kind I abstracted from the file* [emphasis added].
>
> HOUGHTON: We got a lot of actually what was summaries of interviews, not Q's and A's. . . .
>
> FITTS: *Where possible the stuff was not made a matter of record* [emphasis added].

Fitts and Houghton here appear to admit to screening the evidence handed over to the defense, particularly in regard to witnesses with accomplice-related information—a serious violation of due process. They also appear to refer to the excluding of raw information from the case record by use of interview summaries.

Is our reading of this conversation too harsh? The normally mild-mannered defense attorney Grant Cooper did not think so. He presented a declaration to the court in late May 1969 in which he claimed to be "astonished" by the meeting that included the police, the prosecution, and the trial judge, but that excluded representatives from the defense.

"I am, of course, disturbed . . . as to why the police department and the District Attorney's Office 'abstracted from the file' some materials pertaining to their assessments of various witnesses with whom they conducted interviews and why some items of investigation were regarded too secret that they were barred from anyone, except the District Attorney, the F.B.I. and the Los Angeles Police Department." Cooper ended his affidavit by declaring this conduct "a colossal violation of the Constitutional and statutory rights of the accused."[38]

From their own statements in Judge Loring's chambers after the trial, one can fairly conclude that the prosecution was not entirely forthcoming when it handed over its files to the defense on October 14. If this conduct was designed to limit the scope of inquiry in the case, it was immensely successful. Prosecutor Compton's pronouncement in court that the witness interviews did not support a conclusion of conspiracy, and Russell Parsons's hasty reiteration of that view later in the day provided the front-page headline in the following morning's *Los Angeles Times:* BOTH SIDES AGREE, SIRHAN WAS ALONE.

That headline would signal the end of public consideration given to any witness with accomplice-related information. Though numerous, apparently reliable witnesses had seen Sirhan in suspicious circumstances before the shooting, most would be ignored from this point forward. But there were two witnesses who saw Sirhan with a woman in a polka-dot dress the night of the murder who could not be dispatched with a shuffling of papers, an interview summary, or a morning headline. The Los Angeles Police Department would direct inordinate resources to handling these witnesses, and their resulting testimony would undergo an extraordinary and tortured transformation.

EIGHT

The Spotted Ghost

✳ ✳ ✳

ON FEBRUARY 17, Jesus Perez was called as a witness for the prosecution. A busboy at the Ambassador, Perez had exchanged greetings with Robert Kennedy in the hotel pantry only moments before the murder. The young man also claimed to have exchanged words with the assailant before the shooting. Perez, however, spoke broken English, so his testimony at Sirhan's trial was given through a court interpreter.

"Mr. Perez," began John Howard, "I would like to direct your attention to the defendant in this case, the gentleman seated to my left at the extreme end of the counsel table. Did you see that individual in the pantry area before the senator made his speech?"

"Yes."

"How long before?"

"About a half hour, more or less. I don't remember very well."

"You talked to the defendant before the shooting?"

"Yes."

"What did you say?"

"That I didn't know anything whether he [Kennedy] would come through there or not."

"Was there any further conversation between you and Mr. Sirhan?"

"Some boys spoke in Spanish and he asked me what they were saying. I told him they weren't talking about him, they were talking about *some pretty girls* [plural, emphasis added]."

Perez's testimony, as translated by the court interpreter, differed from that which he gave to the Los Angeles County Grand Jury a few days after the crime. At that time Perez recounted in his own words the brief conversation he had with Sirhan in the pantry before the shooting. According to Perez, Sirhan had apparently been bothered by glances and bits of conversation among the busboys that he felt were directed at him. Sirhan approached Perez and asked him what the boys were talking about.

"And I tell him," Perez testified, "'he is talking about *the beautiful girl* [singular, emphasis added]. He no talking about you.'"[1]

The difference between Perez's grand jury and trial testimony is slight. It would be unworthy of mention if it didn't touch on one of the central mysteries of the assassination. Was Sirhan in the company of an attractive woman moments before he fired a gun at Robert Kennedy?

The same day that Perez testified, another hotel employee, Vincent DiPierro, would be called to the witness stand. DiPierro was a student at Santa Monica Community College, employed part-time as a waiter at the Ambassador Hotel, where his father, Angelo, was one of the maître d's. Like Perez, he was questioned by assistant DA John Howard.

"Directing your attention to June 4, 1968," commanded Howard, "did you have occasion to go to the Ambassador Hotel?"

"Yes, I did."

"Did you go to the hotel for some reason?"

"Yes, my father called me and said if I'd like to see Senator Kennedy I could come down."

Howard's courtroom examination of DiPierro was not the first time the assistant DA had questioned the young man about the murder of Robert Kennedy. The night of the shooting Howard had participated in DiPierro's 4 A.M. debriefing, along with LAPD officers Patchett and Melendres.

That night, DiPierro had told the police that as Kennedy stopped to shake hands with busboys Romero and Perez, he noticed a young man, who would turn out to be Sirhan, hanging on to a tray stand. DiPierro's eye had been drawn to the young man, he said, because he was standing next to an attractive woman. "It looked like she was almost holding him," DiPierro had reported. DiPierro then watched as the young man got down from the tray stand, advanced on Senator Kennedy, and fired his gun. Blood hit the young hotel employee in the face, and Kennedy aide Paul Schrade fell wounded against him.

During the interrogation at the police station, John Howard had asked DiPierro if he had seen the assailant and the woman talk to each other.

"He turned as though he did say something," DiPierro had answered.

"Did she move her mouth like she was speaking to him?"

"No, she just smiled."

"And would it seem as though she smiled at something that had been said?"

"Yeah."

DiPierro had then described the woman to Howard as being "good-looking" with "a pudgy nose" and wearing "a white dress with black or purple polka dots."

Two days later DiPierro would tell the same story in testimony before the Los Angeles County Grand Jury. "I noticed there was a girl and the accused person standing on what we call a tray stacker. . . . [S]he had a very good-looking figure—and the dress was kind of lousy. It looked as though it was a white dress and it had either black or dark purple polka dots on it. . . . He looked as though he either talked to her or flirted with her, because she smiled. . . . In fact, the minute the first two shots were fired, he still had a sick-looking smile on his face. That's one thing—I can never forget that."

Because he was so close, and because he was watching the assailant before the shooting began, DiPierro was perhaps the best eyewitness the prosecution had. Seemingly impressed with DiPierro's clarity and sincerity, Sergeant Patchett praised him in the initial report as a "very very good witness." But during the trial of Sirhan, John Howard did not ask the same questions he asked the night of the murder. And Vincent DiPierro's testimony would undergo a startling transformation.

At 12:30 P.M. on June 5, the Los Angeles Police Department put out the following teletype bulletin to law enforcement agencies all across the country.

> I RAM 6-5-68 APB EMERGENCY
> ASSAULT WITH INTENT TO COMMIT MURDER. IN
> CUSTODY SUSPECT SIRHAN BISHARA SIRHAN AKA
> SIRHAN SHARIF BISHARA. . . . PRIOR TO SHOOTING,
> SUSPECT OBSERVED WITH A FEMALE CAUC. 23–27, 5–6,
> WEARING A WHITE VOILE DRESS, ¾ INCH SLEEVES, WITH
> SMALL BLACK POLKA DOTS, DARK SHOES, BOUFFANT
> TYPE HAIR. THIS FEMALE NOT IDENTIFIED OR IN
> CUSTODY. . . . ANY INFORMATION ON SUSPECT AND
> DESCRIBED FEMALE CAUC. RUSH RAMPART DETS.[2]

This was not the first all-points bulletin to describe a possible accomplice. Only minutes after the shooting, an APB carrying a similar description went out over police radio. Its source was Sergeant Paul Sharaga, a forty-year-old police veteran with an excellent record. Sharaga was in his patrol car one block from the Ambassador when news of trouble at the hotel came over his radio. He drove quickly to the parking lot behind the hotel, where he encountered a distressed older couple who had seen a woman in a polka-dot dress and a young man run from the hotel laughing and shouting, "We shot him! We shot him!"

Sharaga immediately went to his car and put out an APB on the two suspects. Sharaga's APB apparently did not stand long. Sharaga asserts that a senior officer requested that he cancel it. Sharaga refused. It was canceled anyway.

Police radio communications tapes (released in LAPD files) show that at 1:41 A.M. a patrol car radioed the dispatcher and asked for clarification: "Is there still an outstanding suspect, and, if so, can I have the descriptions?" After some cross talk, the dispatcher responded: "Disregard that broadcast. We got Rafer Johnson and Jesse Unruh who were right next to him [Kennedy], and they only have one man and don't want them to get anything started on a big conspiracy."[3]

After Sergeant Sharaga put out his APB, he set up a logistics "command post" as required by departmental procedure. He took the name and address of the couple in the parking lot, whom he remembers as "the Bernsteins," and gave a handwritten memo with this information to a courier, who took it to headquarters. It subsequently disappeared, and Sharaga had no copy. There is no official record of anyone ever finding or talking to "the Bernsteins."

In the days that followed, Sergeant Sharaga wrote up a report of his encounter in the parking lot. Copies were filed with the watch commander and the sergeant's office. In a 1993 interview with the authors, Sharaga described what happened next: "A few days later, I wanted to go back and refer to the reports for one reason or another, but they were all gone. I asked the day-watch sergeant if he knew anything about it, and he said the several agents from SUS [Special Unit Senator, the elite police task force set up to investigate the crime] had come that morning and cleaned out all the reports. I called SUS and they denied they'd even been there."[4]

Unknown to Sharaga at the time, in place of his report would appear a summary report of an alleged interview of Sharaga by two SUS detectives. (Recall that many witnesses with accomplice-related information had summary reports of interviews in their files instead of transcripts of the actual interviews. The alleged misrepresentations in the report in Sharaga's file are typical of those experienced by these same witnesses.) According to this summary report, Sharaga is supposed to have said that he believed the older couple heard the woman shout, "They shot him" instead of "We shot him."[5]

In 1988 Paul Sharaga was shown a copy of his reported interview with the SUS detectives. He was quite angry and signed an affidavit saying that the document "contained false and deliberately misleading statements."[6] Four years later his anger was still apparent. "That report is phony," he said from his home in Missouri. "No one ever interviewed me, and I never retracted my statement from 'We shot him' to 'They shot him.' This is just how things were done. If they couldn't get you to change your story, they'd ignore you. If they couldn't ignore you, they'd discredit you, and if they couldn't do that, they'd just make something up."[7]

If someone in the LAPD was trying to make the shouting woman on the stairs disappear by "losing" Sergeant Sharaga's report of the incident, they had a much thornier problem in the person of twenty-year-old Kennedy campaign worker Sandra Serrano. Serrano, recall, was on a fire staircase outside the Embassy Room when she was passed by a man and a young woman who was shouting exuberantly, "We shot him! We shot him!"

A little while later Serrano would be interviewed by Sander Vanocur on national TV, where she would tell her story and describe the woman as wearing a "white dress with polka dots" and having a "funny nose."

Vanocur was not the first person to whom Serrano told her story. She had first approached a guard, then a close friend, and then a man who seemed to be in authority, John Ambrose, who happened to be an assistant district attorney for Los Angeles. He calmed Serrano down, then listened to her account. On June 7, deputy DA Ambrose would file with the FBI a report of this encounter with the distraught young witness. In the report Ambrose recalled Serrano's description of the mystery woman as "between 22 and 26 years of age, approximately 5'5", wearing a white dress with black polka dots and heels, with a good figure." Ambrose concluded, "Serrano impressed me as a sincere girl who was a dedicated Kennedy fan, not interested in publicity."[8]

The Los Angeles police interviewed Serrano twice in the early morning hours of June 5. Two days later she returned to the hotel to reenact her story for police, FBI, and Secret Service investigators. The next day she was reinterviewed by FBI agents and taken to police headquarters to view Kathy Sue Fulmer, one of several women whom the LAPD would offer as a possible, nonsinister polka-dot-dress woman. Fulmer had told police she was at the Ambassador with an orange polka-dot scarf. Serrano immediately asserted that Fulmer was not the woman she had encountered. Then it was on to NBC Studios in Burbank for a screening of television footage of the crowd at the Ambassador. Neither Sirhan nor the other two persons showed up on the screen. On June 10 Serrano was again interviewed by investigators from three agencies. She performed a filmed reenactment. Then she was taken to police headquarters to inspect eight polka-dot dresses assembled by the LAPD.

The handling of Sandra Serrano by the LAPD was a campaign within a campaign. With other witnesses who had seen the woman in the polka-dot dress either ignored, sworn to silence, intimidated, or otherwise discredited (and their files closed for the next twenty years), the police could pretend that Sandra Serrano was the only one who had claimed to see this woman. And the only reason they had to pretend about that was that Serrano had made her claim on national TV; otherwise she could have been ignored like the others. If Serrano could be broken, then the whole inconvenient issue of the mystery woman could be put to rest. In pursuing their objective, the police would attack Serrano's credibility on all fronts. Serrano's consistency, her going on record before any controversy was known, the sincerity perceived by assistant DA Ambrose, and the corroborating accounts of other witnesses would count for nothing. She would become the case's most interviewed witness.

In her original interview Serrano had said that she heard "backfires" just before she saw the fleeing couple. The LAPD investigators began referring to the sounds Serrano heard as "gunfire." The fact that this was their word, not hers, would be irrelevant: they would put the word in her mouth and then bludgeon her credibility with it.

In a burst of investigative zeal, the LAPD brought Serrano to the Ambassador Hotel and fired a .22 handgun (similar to Sirhan's) inside the pantry. At the same time they recorded the event with a tape recorder and decibel meter from the steps outside, where Serrano had rested. The verdict: it was impossible to hear shots from her position. During the experiment, audiotaped by the LAPD, Serrano protests (her voice choked with emotion): "It sounded like backfires of a car, and I never heard a gun. I don't know what a gun sounds like."[9] No matter. From that time forward every police report on Serrano would begin with the litany that it was impossible for her to hear pantry gunshots, as though that fact alone was enough to discredit her story.

During the fire-escape sound tests, FBI agent Richard Burris began pressing Serrano again.

"On television, with Sander Vanocur," Burris challenged, "you didn't say anything about seeing a girl and two men going up the fire stairs. You only said you saw a girl and a man coming down. And later you told the police you saw two men and a girl going up together and one of them was Sirhan Sirhan. That was the most significant thing you had to tell the police and yet you didn't say anything about this in your first interview, your interview on television."

"I can't explain why," a confused Serrano cried. "You're trying to trick me. You're lying and you're trying to trick me."[10]

Although she wasn't thinking clearly enough to know the answer, Serrano's instincts were correct—it was a trick question. During her first accounts to Ambrose and Vanocur, Sirhan's face and identity were not known to her, and she had no way to know at that time that the man she saw on the stairs was the alleged assassin. The most important fact then was that the woman said, "We shot him."

On June 12, Serrano tried to defend herself. She phoned the FBI and informed Agent Burris that she was in the process of retaining legal counsel and would not talk to investigators again unless her lawyer could be there. But on June 20, without counsel, Serrano would be scientifically certified as a liar by the LAPD's instrument of choice for dealing with conspiracy witnesses—Sergeant Enrique Hernandez and his "truth machine."

The device that has become known as the polygraph, or "lie detector," was first developed in the early part of the twentieth century. It was initially greeted with great skepticism, but after helping solve some of

Chicago's notorious gangland killings in the 1930s, it gained acceptance, gradually taking its place in the public mind as a legitimate weapon in the modern law enforcement arsenal.

Had the polygraph remained in the arena of law enforcement, it would command more respect than it does today. But by the mid-1980s the machine had descended upon mainstream America, with as many as two million exams performed each year, most of these done by employers on current or would-be employees. The question of whether the polygraph was a legitimate scientific device or merely a sophisticated carnival trick was now relevant to a growing constituency.

Accurate scientific data on the validity of the polygraph have always been difficult to come by, but in 1983, the U.S. Office of Technology Assessment declared the device "virtually useless" for preemployment interviews, and more opposition to its widespread use developed. Critics such as psychologist David Lykken of the University of Minnesota claimed that, for discovering truth, the polygraph is "little better than flipping a coin."[11] In 1989 Congress responded by making it illegal to use the polygraph for screening potential employees. Yet, paradoxically, the polygraph has played a useful role in solving crimes. Over the years, perhaps due to the belief that the device really works, the "lie detector" has been quite effective in eliciting confessions.

The principal problem with the polygraph is that it does not measure lies but, instead, measures physiological responses that anxiety supposedly produces when telling a lie. The commonsense difficulty here is that many different things can cause anxiety, among them being asked questions that might lead to the suspicion that one has committed a crime even if one hasn't.

The inability of the polygraph to detect liars successfully is not its chief liability; it is the propensity for false positives—that is, labeling people liars because they are nervous or simply because the examiner has misinterpreted the various squiggles on the graph paper. Moreover, the validity of a polygraph test depends not only upon whether the technology is valid, the subject appropriate, or the examiner properly trained, but also upon the examiner's integrity—for an improper test based upon an examiner's prejudice, or malice, is almost impossible to prove.

Although dishonest polygraph exams in criminal investigations can lead to great injustice, the chances that an innocent person will confess to a serious crime when confronted with dishonest results are slight. An unfortunate side effect to this reality is that it may actually encourage zealous operators to habitually present suspects with "guilty" results, hoping to flush confessions from those who truly are. But when the same game is played with a witness to a crime, instead of a suspect, the equation is changed. With little in the way of a personal stake in the truth, the witness may well decide to end the aggravation and be done with the whole thing. In this circumstance, overzealous application of the polygraph is tantamount to tampering with evidence.

As Chief Houghton described in *Special Unit Senator,* on June 20, Lieutenant Manny Pena suggested to Sergeant Hernandez that he might "like to take Sandra Serrano out for an SUS bought steak."[12] After what must have been a delightful dinner for Serrano, she was polygraphed between nine and ten P.M. Although many tapes of LAPD witness interviews have been either lost or destroyed, a tape of Serrano's session with Hernandez has somehow survived. That the tape contained information potentially embarrassing for the police is indicated by the embargo order placed upon it: "Do not play or have transcribed without the express permission of Capt. Brown [second in command of SUS]."[13] During the pre-interview phase of the polygraph session, Serrano's aunt is present (her parents lived in Ohio). After her aunt departs, Hernandez gives a glowing explanation of the wonders and workings of the machine. He then hooks Serrano up and asks her in several different ways if she was telling the truth about the girl in the polka-dot dress. Serrano answers that she was. The questions end.

"Sandy," says Hernandez in a confidential tone, "I'm not gonna ask you any more questions, not a single one. I do want to talk to you like a brother. Look, I presume, I don't know what religion you are, I'm Catholic. Are you Catholic?" And with that Hernandez launches into a solo rendition of "good cop, bad cop," showing a patronizing concern for Serrano on the one hand, and hinting heavily on the other at unpleasant things to come if she doesn't change her story. What follows is a series of excerpts from this emotionally charged session.[14]

Hernandez informs Serrano, falsely, that "nineteen girls" have come forward with stories, but only two "really loved Kennedy as a person." The rest were gold diggers or publicity hounds. He tells Serrano that she is one of the two who loved Kennedy, and she is honestly mistaken about what she saw. Then he becomes assertive.

"Nobody," he says, "told you, 'We have shot Kennedy.'"

"Yes," Serrano responds, "somebody told me that 'We have shot Kennedy.'"

"No, Sandy."

"I'm sorry, but that's true. That is true."

Hernandez invokes a wide range of themes for his game of "truth or consequences." "One of these days, you're gonna be a mother," he tells Serrano. "You're gonna be a mother, you're gonna have kids, and you know that you can't live a life of shame, knowing what you're doing right now is wrong."

"But I seen those people," Serrano protests.

"Sandy, you know that this is wrong."

"I know what I saw. . . . I remember seeing the girl!"

"No, No. I'm talking about what you have told here about seeing a person tell you, 'We have shot Kennedy.' And that's wrong."

"That's what she said."

"No, it isn't, Sandy. Please don't."

"No! That's what she said."

"Lookit, I love this man."

"So do I."

"And you're shaming, you're, he, if right now, if he can't even—"

"Don't shout at me."

Hernandez then tells Serrano of his personal affection for Kennedy "the man," how Kennedy allegedly gave him a commendation that he greatly cherished. He accuses Serrano of thwarting the investigation. He repeatedly invokes Robert Kennedy and his family.

"You don't know and I don't know if he's a witness right now in this room watching what we're doing in here," he says. "Please, in the name of Kennedy . . . don't shame his death."

"Don't, don't come on with this sentiment business," responds Serrano, acting more professionally than her interviewer. "Let's just get this job done."

But Hernandez won't be deterred. He invokes history, the nation, the Kennedy family, the senator's ghost, the Catholic Church, law and order, good health, redemption, and Serrano's children-to-come in an effort to persuade the witness to change her story.

"The Kennedys have had nothing but tragedy," he says, and then he sweetens the pot. "And I'm sure—you mark my words—that one of these days, if you're woman enough, you will get a letter from Ethel Kennedy—*personal*—thanking you for at least letting her rest on this aspect of this investigation."

Serrano, one must remember, was merely a witness. She was not a person accused of a serious crime, clinging to a flimsy story in the hope of escaping punishment. She had no reason to make up such a story, but more important, other witnesses (the "Bernsteins," by way of Sergeant Paul Sharaga) described the very people and, word for word, the conversation Serrano was reporting. Nevertheless, Hernandez kept attacking.

"This didn't happen," he says forcefully.

"It happened," Serrano replies.

"No, it didn't happen."

"Yes," she affirms, her voice fading.

At another point, when Hernandez again states flatly that she did not hear the phrase "We shot him," Serrano again disagrees and laughs nervously (sounding on the verge of breaking into tears).

"Don't you be laughing it off with a smirk on your face," Hernandez says in a menacing tone. He then implores Serrano to "redeem something that's a deep wound that will grow inside of you like cancer."

Serrano sighs and says in a low voice, "Damn cops, why don't you just leave me alone?"

"The only time you will be left alone," says Hernandez, "is when you tell me the truth about what happened outside on the staircase."

Hernandez keeps telling Serrano that he can fix this thing by himself if she will just change her story. But if not, he will be forced to tell the world that she is a liar, and the interrogations will continue because he'll have to turn her over to other investigators "upstairs" who are presumably not as nice or as understanding as he.

"Now you see what happens," he warns her; "there's two ways to approach this thing. The first is for me to appeal to you as a decent woman who campaigned for Senator Kennedy. The other way is for me to hold up the paper [the polygraph results], go out there and tell these people, and have them tell whoever they're going to tell upstairs . . . and they're gonna want to talk to you again and again."

"To tell you the truth," Serrano answers wearily, "I don't know anymore what happened. I just don't know. It's all such a big mess."

"Sandra, look. I don't know how we can do it to stop this thing. The easiest way for you, so we can stop it, nobody ask you anything else, you go home, be relieved of this thing. I don't know how we can do it. Possibly if I ask you right now and I get a report and we dictate it to someone, you and me, maybe we can stop it there."

Hernandez finally gets his way. After an hour of agonizing confrontation, he wears Serrano down to the point where she agrees to having been "messed up." With the stenographer present, Hernandez leads Serrano through a series of questions after which she agrees that she had been confused and pressured by the expectations of the media and the public. Now that he had Serrano rolling downhill, Hernandez is eager to accelerate the process by finding scapegoats for her.

"The facts that you saw," he offers, "were apparently misquoted, or misprinted, or mistelevised to the actual true facts."

This was too much for Serrano even in her distraught state. "Well, they can't have been mistelevised because I said that. I actually said that. . . . I really thought there was something behind it. I was scared. I tell you I've been scared all this time."

Hernandez tries to help Serrano reconstruct where she heard it. In his version Serrano was sitting on the staircase when someone came down and said something about Kennedy being shot. When she was down at the Rampart Street police station, she spoke to Vincent DiPierro, who told her his story of the girl in the polka-dot dress.

"So, that's where that thing about the polka-dot dress, that's where it started," says Hernandez, asserting more than asking.

"I guess," answers Serrano, seeming not to care anymore.

The very next day the LAPD called a press conference. At the meeting Inspector John Powers, assistant commander of the detective bureau, publicly canceled the all-points bulletin for the girl in the polka-dot dress. "It was determined that the person who originally described the female in the white polka-dot dress was erroneous," explained Powers, apparently referring to Sergeant Hernandez's session the day before. Powers explained that "the key witness, the one who caused the alert to be put out," had been "overwrought" after the slaying. He then dismissed other reports of a girl in a polka-dot dress at the Ambassador Hotel. "The room apparently was full of them,"[15] he said, as though the very number of these reports was reason to believe that they were untrue.

According to chief of detectives Robert Houghton in his book *Special Unit Senator,* the breaking of Sandra Serrano was the "turning point" in the Robert Kennedy murder investigation. "SUS closed the vexing case of the polka-dot-dress girl," Houghton wrote proudly. "In police work, for lack of a better word, we say a witness was 'contaminated.' "[16] The congratulatory mood within the police investigation was contagious, and Sergeant Hernandez's work with Serrano would draw special praise from senior police officials. In a little over an hour Enrique Hernandez and his "truth machine" had managed to take what appeared to be a sincere and coherent witness (albeit fatigued by two weeks of adversarial attention) with a story that was corroborated by a number of independent sources and, in exchange for his promise to stop with the repeated interrogations, got her to agree to Hernandez's version of events, which could not possibly be true. Serrano could not have gotten the polka-dot-dress story from Vincent DiPierro, because she told it to assistant DA Ambrose before she ever met the young waiter. In their supposed search for truth, an inconvenient fact such as that didn't bother the police. Several weeks later Enrique Hernandez would be promoted to the rank of lieutenant.

Twenty-five years after the fact, Enrique Hernandez's superior Manuel Pena still defends Serrano's treatment at the hands of the polygraph operator. "It was a necessary move on my part," he told William Klaber. "We tried every way in the world to find this gal in the polka-dot dress to see if we could substantiate her [Serrano's] story. And we couldn't do it. I wasn't about to leave the case hanging there."[17]

Pena's words illustrate quite clearly the police mind-set. First, if they were really trying to substantiate Serrano's story, they had plenty of witnesses to draw upon. Second, they took their own inability to locate the girl in the polka-dot dress as evidence that Serrano was lying. But that fact should have helped confirm her story. If, as Pena asserted, Serrano misheard the woman who actually said, "They shot him," then one might have expected that woman to come forward after all the publicity. That she didn't would support Serrano's more sinister interpretation of events. But Pena and the police seemed unwilling to leave any questions unanswered. "We got to a point," he said, "where we had to establish something on an investigative basis that she was mistaken."[18]★

While other witnesses with accomplice-related stories were dismissed or ignored, Serrano and DiPierro were given special attention by the Los Angeles police. They were both invited to fashion shows, where they viewed and compared a variety of white dresses with black polka dots. Sandra Serrano's special status came from the fact that many thousands of people had seen her on TV describing the girl in the polka-dot dress. DiPierro was important in that he had actually seen Sirhan fire his gun. Thus, while both witnesses, according to the LAPD, were telling stories that were untrue, Serrano, because of her high profile, would be discredited, while DiPierro, because he was needed as a witness, would be rehabilitated.

By July 1, when Vincent DiPierro was reinterviewed by police, polka-dot-dress stories were unwelcome, smoking gun or not. As a result, he earned, as did most witnesses with accomplice-related information, a session with Sergeant Enrique Hernandez. An audiotape of this interview has survived, but it is of such poor quality that little more than an occasional word can be understood. Nevertheless, it is known that DiPierro took the polygraph test and was then told by Hernandez that he failed the part about the woman with Sirhan. From all indications DiPierro seemed less inclined to fight the police than Serrano, and most likely Hernandez had to invoke a shorter list of deities to get DiPierro to do his duty and admit that he was confused. As with Serrano, Hernandez then called in a stenographer to record the postpolygraph session.

"As a matter of fact," said Hernandez once the notes were being taken, "you have told me now that there was no lady that you saw standing next to Sirhan."

★The police efforts in regard to Serrano were quite far reaching. On July 22, 1968, according to an August 2 police "progress report," the LAPD contacted the Internal Revenue Service and requested that they "run a financial background" check on Serrano and five other witnesses. The stated purpose of the check was "to eliminate any possible connection with suspect Sirhan regarding money matters." A more realistic view was that they were looking for something to frighten a witness into changing her story.

"That's correct," responded DiPierro.

"Okay. Now, I can appreciate what you would have or could have been going through on that evening." Hernandez here seems to be fluffing up the bed for DiPierro's change of heart; but, here again, a polygraph does not detect confusion, if it detects anything at all. "But I think what you have told me," Hernandez continued, "is that you probably got this idea about a girl in a black-and-white polka-dot dress after you talked to Miss Sandra Serrano."

"Yes, sir, I did."

Hernandez had now pulled a coup of investigative logic: ten days earlier he had gotten Sandra Serrano to admit that she had originally cribbed the polka-dot-dress story from DiPierro; now Hernandez had DiPierro confess that he had gotten the story from Serrano. But as Hernandez tried to wrap up the session, DiPierro's words seemed to betray his eagerness to cooperate.

"You did not see a girl in a polka-dot dress," said Hernandez, seeking to cement his victory. "You did not see a girl in a black-and-white polka-dot dress standing behind Sirhan on that evening?"

"No."

"Is there anything else that you have told me previously or that you have told Sergeant Patchett or anyone else that . . . is not the truth?"

"No. Nothing," he answers. "Only about the girl."

"Only about the girl?" repeated Hernandez.

"Yes, sir. That good enough?"[19]

The problems the police had with witnesses who had seen the mysterious girl brought no comfort to the defense lawyers. They were as much a bother to the defense as they were to anyone else. Grant Cooper and Emile Berman had both entered the case late, and Russell Parsons, although he had been on the case from early on, spent most of his energy filing motions and worrying about how the defense was going to raise money. Only the two defense investigators, Mike McCowan and Robert Blair Kaiser, did any real work as far as reviewing witness statements.

Kaiser, in particular, was quite critical of what he perceived as a pattern of bullying by Hernandez, and of the LAPD's rush to dismiss witnesses who had seen things that didn't agree with the official version of events. One evening as Kaiser listened to a tape of Grant Cooper's long interview with Sirhan in his jail cell, he felt compelled to sit down and write Cooper a memo. "Before we do too much more research on the death penalty," he wrote, "or call in too many more experts, we ought to do a little suggesting of our own—that maybe Sirhan has been programmed to do

something he now considers 'stupid'—possibly without his complete awareness that he was being so used."[20] This idea, however, was never seriously
considered by the attorneys.

To reduce the crime to its essentials, one could say that Sirhan either
acted alone or as part of a conspiracy, and that his actions were either willful
or unwillful. Looked at this way, there are four possibilities. The prosecution maintained that Sirhan acted willfully and alone. The defense argued
that Sirhan acted alone but without the necessary volition to constitute legal
premeditation. But to Sirhan's attorneys any evidence of accomplices would
only indicate willful concerted action, which would destroy the defense
contention of an act committed without premeditation. Never did the
lawyers consider the fourth possibility: that evidence of others involved
might exonerate Sirhan if his participation were involuntary.

The defense attorneys' lack of curiosity in this direction may have been
abetted by the report of defense investigator Michael McCowan. In his
report to Cooper, McCowan asserted that DiPierro

> stated that he saw Sirhan with a girl in a polka-dot dress standing
> with him by some stairs prior to the shooting. He later admitted that
> he made up the story and that it was Sandy Serrano who had told
> him that she saw a girl in a polka-dot dress running out of the kitchen
> yelling, "We shot him! We shot him!" Miss Serrano's testimony was
> also proven false.

McCowan, recall, was a former police officer turned private investigator who offered his services, free of charge, to the defense team. His
propensity to accept and pass on to Sirhan's attorneys the shabby police
interpretation of these witnesses' testimony is noteworthy for its brevity
and lack of analysis.

Vincent DiPierro was called to the witness stand by the prosecution on
February 17, to dramatically point to the defendant as the man he had seen
shoot Kennedy, and under John Howard's direction he did just that.

"Now this person you observed on the tray rack," asked Howard, "would
you describe him for us?"

"Yes," replied DiPierro, "he had dark hair and a white shirt or possibly
a light blue shirt, with dungarees or dark blue pants."

"Do you see that person in court?"

"Yes, sir, I do."

"Would you indicate him, please?"

"This gentleman seated here."

"May the record indicate Mr. Sirhan, Your Honor?"

Under Howard's direction, DiPierro's story was told in great detail, but the girl he had originally seen with Sirhan was never mentioned. Normally, a witness who had failed a lie detector test concerning the second most important element of his story might have been scratched as a witness by the prosecution or savaged by the defense. Not here. Nevertheless, there were some surprises during cross-examination. Grant Cooper asked a routine question, and despite the lie detector and the apparent coaching, the story of Sirhan and the girl came spilling out.

"What was there that caused you to notice him?" asked Cooper.

"At the time," replied DiPierro, "there was there, I believe, a girl standing within the area of Sirhan. . . ."

"Then you did see a girl standing there by him at that time?"

"Not definitely by him, in the area of him."

"Pardon me. Can you tell us where she was?"

"I would say around the area of the tray rack where he was, but I cannot say."

"And you observed the girl first, did you?"

"Yes, I did."

"And you observed this girl because she was pretty?"

"Correct. . . ."

"Did you observe how the girl was dressed at that time?"

"Well, I can recall she was wearing a polka-dot dress. . . ."

"And what kind of polka dots were these, were they black or—"

"Black."

After having elicited from the witness the "girl with Sirhan" story, Cooper referred DiPierro to the transcript of his July 1 interview with Sergeant Enrique Hernandez. Cooper then read to the court the entire transcript of Hernandez's recorded session with DiPierro, wherein the witness confessed that the story he was telling about the girl was false. Cooper finished with Hernandez's assertive question:

Q: You did not see a girl in a polka-dot dress. You did not see a girl in a black-and-white polka-dot dress standing beside Sirhan on that evening?

A: No.

"Now let me ask you first," said Cooper when he was done reading, "was this statement that you gave to Sergeant Enrique Hernandez on July 1, 1968, the truth?"

"Yes, it was," said DiPierro.

Only minutes before, DiPierro had testified that he first noticed Sirhan because of the pretty girl in a dress with black polka dots standing beside him. Now he was saying once again that the story was false. On redirect examination by prosecutor David Fitts, DiPierro's testimony would become schizophrenic.

"Are you telling us in substance," questioned Fitts, "there was a girl standing near Sirhan at or near the time of the shooting, sir?"

"Yes, sir," answered DiPierro.

"With a polka-dot dress?"

"Yes."

"And the kind of girl that attracted your attention, is that right?"

"Yes, sir."

And there it was. After all the screening, summary reports, polygraph tests, supposed witness retractions, witness selections, and coaching, the story the police were most trying to kill, that of the woman in the polka-dot dress, was now part of the trial of Sirhan Sirhan. David Fitts, however, was ready for this eventuality.

"I have a photograph, Your Honor," he said, addressing Judge Walker, "three views of a girl in a polka-dot dress."

After the photographs were admitted into evidence, Fitts went back to Vincent DiPierro.

"Mr. DiPierro, first I direct your attention to the black-and-white photograph, 10A. . . . Do you recognize that individual as anyone you have ever seen before?"

"Yes, I believe I saw her that night."

"Are you telling us that this appears to be a picture of the girl that you saw in the pantry at or near the time of the shooting?"

"Yes, but I believe she had darker hair than that."

"I didn't hear the answer, Your Honor," Grant Cooper interjected.

"He said, 'But I believe she had darkened her hair,'" replied Judge Walker, giving a somewhat inaccurate account of what the witness had said.

Fitts was eager to glide over this point.

"In any event," he said to the witness, "she seems to be pretty blond in the picture, doesn't she?"

"Yes, she does."

"Other than the difference in the color of the hair that you noticed, does she seem to be the girl?"

"Yes, I would think she would be."

"If the Court please, I believe that Mr. Cooper will stipulate with me that the girl depicted in these photographs is one Valerie Schulte, I understand, a Santa Barbara girl.

"I have nothing further."

To any juror paying attention it must have appeared that the testimony of

Vincent DiPierro had in a short period undergone a tortured odyssey. First, he identified Sirhan as the murderer, without having his testimony crushed by his alleged failure of a lie-detector test. Next, he told his entire story without ever mentioning the girl with Sirhan. Then in dizzying succession, he admitted to defense counsel Cooper that there was indeed a pretty girl in a polka-dot dress with Sirhan the night of the murder, a dress with black polka dots; then he admitted that this story was false. Finally, on redirect, DiPierro agreed with prosecutor Fitts that there *was* a girl with a polka-dot dress in the pantry standing near Sirhan, but it was "Kennedy girl" Valerie Schulte.

The following day Valerie Schulte would be called to the witness stand. The attractive blond young woman stood up and then, using a crutch, limped slowly to the witness stand—one leg in a brace, the result of a nasty skiing accident she had suffered *before* the assassination.

"Miss Schulte," said David Fitts, "directing your attention to the fourth day of June 1968, which was Election Day, did you go to the Ambassador Hotel on that evening?"

"Yes, I did."

Valerie Schulte had indeed been at the Ambassador Hotel. After Kennedy's speech she had followed some distance behind the senator into the pantry where the shots were fired. After Schulte described the shooting from her vantage point, prosecutor Fitts asked another question.

"Would you tell us what you were wearing on this evening in question?"

"Yes, I was wearing a green dress with yellow polka dots."

"Did you bring the dress you were wearing that evening to court with you?"

"Yes, I did."

The witness was then handed a plastic bag containing the green dress.

"Would you just hold it up so that everybody can see it?"

In a trial filled with odd moments, this would be one of the most bizarre—symbolic for the extreme disregard for the truth manifested by both the prosecution and the defense. By any measure, the claim that Valerie Schulte was the mysterious polka-dot-dress woman was silly. She was never standing near Sirhan, which contradicts DiPierro's detailed account given the night of the murder of seeing Sirhan and the woman apparently talking. But most important, Schulte had her leg in a cast and was using a crutch. Moreover, she was wearing a dark-green dress with large yellow lemon-shaped splotches.

At this point the prosecution's position on the polka-dot-dress woman defied all logic. Recall that Enrique Hernandez and his polygraph had already determined that Vincent DiPierro had lied when he said he saw a woman in a polka-dot dress that night. Now, apparently, he had been telling the truth—he just had a few of the facts wrong.

And what of the other witnesses who mentioned a mystery woman and who had already been branded as liars? Were they now to be brought back and told that they were merely confused, that the dress they saw as white was really green, the polka dots they saw as black were really yellow, and the woman they saw running from the scene was really on crutches? No, it wouldn't be done. The police had a woman, and they had something they called polka dots, and to most everyone involved, including the press, that would do.

On the following day a picture of Valerie Schulte dominated the front page of the *Los Angeles Times*. After eight months of byzantine investigation, the case of the woman in the polka-dot dress was now publicly solved.

Though he had tried his best to do what was expected of him, the constant pressure upon Vincent DiPierro apparently wounded his sense of self. Just a little over a month after Sirhan was convicted, DiPierro wrote a letter to local radio (KHJ) reporter Art Kevin, who was broadcasting a series on the unanswered questions in the Robert Kennedy murder. It was Kevin's segment on the polka-dot-dress woman that DiPierro found most interesting. Kevin had reportedly resisted police pressure not to air this segment, which raised, once again, despite the public resolution of the controversy at Sirhan's trial, the specter of the woman in the polka-dot dress. It was, said DiPierro, "the first 'real true' report" of the incident, and he praised Kevin for "the extensive research and brilliant job of reporting a factual story."

DiPierro told Kevin that the polka-dot-dress story "concerned my character personally, [and] I was deeply interested in *hearing the facts straight for a change* [emphasis added]." DiPierro then offered to assist Kevin on the story in the future.

But when Art Kevin drove out to the DiPierro residence a few days later he discovered that someone had been there before him. The door was answered by Angelo DiPierro, Vincent's father and a maître d' at the Ambassador Hotel. Vincent stood nearby. Kevin reported that both men "looked all shook up." Angelo DiPierro then told Kevin that the FBI had come by and explained in great detail how hard the police had worked in reconstructing the events in the pantry. The father hinted that he had some reason to believe there was some threat to his son's life, and he pleaded with Kevin to forget the whole thing. The door was then shut.[21]

Shortly after her dramatic session with Sergeant Enrique Hernandez, Sandra Serrano quit her job and moved back to Ohio. Later she returned to California, but she avoided comment on the Robert Kennedy case for twenty years. Then in 1988, a week after the LAPD files on the case were made public by the California State Archives, a forty-year-old Sandra Serrano Sewell talked briefly to radio interviewer Jack Thomas about her treatment as a witness at the hands of the Los Angeles police. "I don't ever want to have to go through that again," she said, "that kind of everyday harassment, you know, being put in a room for hours with polka-dot dresses all around you. It was a bad scene and one that as a young person I was totally unprepared to handle. . . . I was just twenty years old and I became unglued. I said what they wanted me to say."[22]

NINE

Malice Aforethought

✳ ✳ ✳

F OR THE REPORTERS covering the Sirhan trial, the first weeks of testimony had been difficult to translate into exciting copy. Grant Cooper hadn't challenged the prosecution's reconstruction of the crime, and he had cooperated in the bizarre presentation of Valerie Schulte as the girl in the polka-dot dress. Hope for real drama now centered on the moment when Sirhan Sirhan would take the witness stand. How would the accused assassin conduct himself? How would he justify his actions? Why had he murdered Robert Kennedy?

Under California law, motive, unlike premeditation and malice, is not an element of murder. "Presence of motive may tend to establish guilt," Judge Walker explained to the jury. "Absence of motive may tend to establish innocence. But the state does not carry the burden of proving any motive at all." Still, whether it leads to unknown perpetrators or satisfies a jury's curiosity, answering the question of motive is central to any case.

Since the captured assailant of Robert Kennedy was not providing information to anyone directly after the shooting, the initial question of motive was up for grabs. As has been noted, public officials, including President Johnson, Governor Reagan, and Mayor Yorty, quickly stepped in with explanations. Others did also. The day after the assassination, U.S. attorney general Ramsey Clark held a press conference and declared that there was no evidence of conspiracy, even though the Los Angeles police had just put out an APB for a woman seen with the assailant before the shooting. In another story, a Cuban refugee named Jose Duarte said he had a scuffle with Sirhan several weeks before at a political meeting where Sirhan had declared support for Fidel Castro, this echoing Mayor Yorty's assertion that Sirhan was a communist.

A very different view came from John M. Lawrence, chairman of something called Federated Americans against Israeli Racism (FAIR) headquartered in New York. At the end of a long article in *The New York Times* about the notebooks found at Sirhan's home, Lawrence was quoted as saying, "There are no tears in us for Robert Kennedy . . . the advocate of sending American bombers to Israel so Jews may kill more Arabs."[1]

Lawrence's statement was the first suggestion that the January 1968 deal to sell jet planes to Israel (negotiated by President Johnson and Israeli prime minister Levi Eshkol) was the motivating factor in the murder of Robert Kennedy. In time, this explanation would be embraced by the police, the prosecution, the defense, the press, the Arab community, the defendant, and the defendant's family. It was simple, easily understood, and seemed to serve the basic needs of all parties. But there were serious problems with this explanation, problems that almost everyone was willing to ignore.

For example, if Sirhan murdered Robert Kennedy to make a political gesture on behalf of the dispossessed Palestinian Arabs, why didn't he shout, "No bombers to Israel!" as he fired his gun? Why would he remain silent in police custody? Why would he withhold his identity? Having accomplished his task with no chance of escape, wouldn't he be eager to take credit for his deed and speak to the world about the injustices suffered by his people?

But for weeks after the shooting Sirhan did not announce any motive, political or personal. He never said meekly, much less with bravado, that he had killed Kennedy for the Arab cause. He did not deny the killing—he simply could not offer an explanation for it. In short, Sirhan did not act like a political assassin.

There is also a timing problem in the "jets to Israel" theory. The official story was that on May 18 Sirhan saw Robert Kennedy on television promising to sell fifty jet planes to Israel. This supposedly so enraged Sirhan that he made up his mind to kill Kennedy and wrote, "RFK must die" in his notebook. This story has been told and retold many times. Those on Sirhan's defense team were as effective in propagating the tale as those on the prosecution. During his final argument, defense attorney Emile Berman said, "We come down to May 18 of 1968, and I told you about his blowing his stack when he heard this on television about the Phantom jets—pounding the TV, stalked to his room; he wrote and said and indicated that he, who had loved and admired Kennedy, had been betrayed; and he was outraged."

The power and longevity of this story was evidenced in 1988, when Sirhan's then-attorney Luke McKissack gave his own rendition: "He felt after seeing Kennedy make the statement that he was gonna send . . . with the yarmulke on him in the temple . . . he was gonna send fifty Phantom jets to Israel, that was interpreted by Sirhan as basically sending planes to bombard and kill his own people."[2]

May 18 was a critical date in all this, because the incriminating notebook entry "RFK must die" bore that designation. If the notebook date is correct, then the intent to murder had to exist at that time as well as the motive behind that intent. The difficulty here is that the documentary on Robert Kennedy that Sirhan supposedly watched was aired in Los Angeles on May 20, two days after the notebook entry. More important, it contained no references at all to sending jets to Israel.

The documentary was a relatively standard recapitulation of Senator Kennedy's political career. It reviewed his tenure as U.S. attorney general and touched on his relationship with President Kennedy and his ascent to the U.S. Senate. In searching for segments that might have disturbed Sirhan, one can find brief footage of Robert Kennedy as a reporter in Israel in 1948, "helping to celebrate their independence." Later, an announcer talked of Kennedy's desire to "play a role in the affairs of men and nations" as an Israeli flag was shown in the background. This imagery may well have angered Sirhan, but it could hardly be considered a catalyst for murder, and it is very different from the reported vision of Kennedy wearing a yarmulke in a temple and promising to send bombers.

On May 20, Kennedy was at the Temple Isaiah in West Los Angeles, but his statements there were anything but inflammatory. He spoke mostly about a negotiated settlement between Israel and her Arab neighbors. When Kennedy did mention arms, it was in response to the increased Soviet threat in the Mediterranean. "We must assist with arms, if necessary, to meet the threat of massive Soviet military buildups. . . . But in the long run, an arms race helps no one. What we need is an agreement . . . to defuse the Middle East and to stop on all sides further shipments . . . a small but important step toward peace in the world."

Kennedy also spoke of making the "desert bloom" by a peaceful sharing of the waters of the Jordan River. When someone asked where he stood on the city of Jerusalem, Kennedy did not take a pro-Israel position. "I stand here," he said, "in Los Angeles."[3]

It's possible that Sirhan's bomber motive didn't begin in May with the television documentary but began in January 1968 when the Johnson/Eshkol deal was announced. But if Sirhan had harbored a death wish for Kennedy from January, he certainly hid it well. In the dozens of police interviews conducted with virtually everyone who had contact with him during the year prior to the assassination, there emerged not a single recalled instance of Sirhan having commented on Kennedy's support of Israel, on jet bombers, or on anything at all relating Kennedy to Jews, Israelis, or the Middle East. Moreover, nowhere in Sirhan's notebooks, before or after May 18, is there any mention of jet bombers for Israel. In addition, Sirhan has always maintained that until shortly before the murder he was an admirer of Kennedy.

In one of his jail-cell interviews with prosecution psychiatrist Dr. Seymour Pollack, Sirhan is emphatic about this point.

"Now that was in May of '68, that you saw the television program, is that right?" asks Dr. Pollack.

"Right."

"He was already running in the primaries. Now you mean until that [TV documentary], up until that time, you were for Kennedy?"

"Hell, I was for him, sir."[4]

The only testimony the prosecution was able to present regarding Sirhan's prior intent came from Alvin Clark, a Pasadena sanitation worker. Clark had collected trash on East Howard Street and over time had gotten to know Sirhan, because Sirhan on occasion had brought him coffee and then engaged him in conversation. Clark testified that on one of these occasions Sirhan had threatened to murder Robert Kennedy. On cross-examination Emile Berman dented Clark's credibility by having him acknowledge that during his FBI interview he had said he did not want to take an oath when testifying at the trial because he was willing to say anything to see Sirhan convicted.

If one accepts for the moment that the U.S. plan to sell jets to Israel was some sort of substitute motive, when might that idea have entered Sirhan's head, and how did it get there?

On August 14 the accused assassin was interviewed by his attorney, Russell Parsons, and journalist Robert Blair Kaiser. It was the first of more than a dozen interviews Kaiser would conduct as a nominal defense investigator. In Sirhan's breast pocket during the interview was the *New York Times* article about the assassination, sent to him by John Lawrence, director of Federated Americans against Israeli Racism in which Lawrence was quoted as saying that he had no tears for Kennedy, because he was an advocate of sending bombers to Israel to kill Arabs.

Sirhan had received the clipping on June 10. It accompanied a letter by Lawrence, five dollars in cash, and three issues of *Insight,* the official newsletter of FAIR. In his letter Lawrence told Sirhan that he ought to be forgiven for his mistake, because he made it in the pursuit of justice. He also called Sirhan a soldier in the cause of justice for the Arab people.

Lawrence followed his letter with three telegrams on June 10, June 11, and June 13, each offering encouragement and advice. Sirhan replied by wire on June 13.

RESPECTED SIRS: GRATEFUL FOR MONEY ENJOYED "INSIGHT" PLEASE SEND MORE ISSUES ANXIOUS ABOUT MIDEAST REACTION. SIRHAN.[5]

On June 14, John Lawrence responded with another letter. In it he advised that Sirhan defend himself by putting American society and Robert

Kennedy on trial for their sociopathic conduct. He advised against a psychiatric defense. If Sirhan pleaded insanity, he cautioned, all those who subsequently spoke out against the injustices suffered by the Palestinian people would also be judged insane.

Sirhan, understandably, was not receiving encouragement or support from many quarters. The little he did receive was from the Arab community, but that was conditional: Sirhan should behave like a loyal, although perhaps misguided, Arab nationalist.

In his August 14 meeting with Parsons and Kaiser, the accused assassin cautiously began to do that. He wasn't very convincing. As Sirhan spoke about Kennedy's betrayal of the Arab people, Kaiser noted, "he didn't *sound* upset [emphasis Kaiser's]. His dislike of Kennedy—you could hardly call it so much as anger—seemed remote and detached."[6]

This was Sirhan's first attempt to give political coloration to the murder. It is significant that at this moment he carried the John Lawrence clipping linking Kennedy to the jets-for-Israel deal. Had this truly been Sirhan's motivation, it would hardly seem necessary to carry the article. But if this were a new idea, Sirhan might want to carry it for reassurance. The article in Sirhan's pocket and his unconvincing words led defense investigator Robert Kaiser, who would spend many hours with Sirhan, to the stunning conclusion that it was "doubtful that Sirhan heard anything about Kennedy's 'promise' to send fifty jet bombers to Israel until John Lawrence told him about it *after* [emphasis Kaiser's] the assassination."[7]

Sirhan's amnesia presents yet another difficulty for the question of motive. If the accused assassin was making a heroic gesture on behalf of his people, why would he not remember the crime or say he did not remember the crime, while at the same time not denying or challenging his guilt? Sirhan's lack of memory simply does not fit with the act as a political event. If one has no memory of planning to kill, then a subsequent offer of motive must be an after-the-fact rationalization. A careful examination of Sirhan's interviews with his lawyers and doctors exposes this process. These conversations do not show a politically motivated assassin, but rather a man who remains confused about what happened and who adopts a particular motive as his best choice.

During December 1968, while others were on Christmas break, Robert Kaiser scheduled several private interviews with Sirhan. During these recorded sessions Sirhan was relatively relaxed and cooperative with the defense investigator. After some conversation about books Sirhan had in his cell—he had just finished Whittaker Chambers's *Witness,* and was reading Victor Hugo's *Les Misérables*—Kaiser asked Sirhan about his father, Bishara, who had abandoned his family and gone back to Palestine.

Sirhan tried to explain and then spoke of his alienation:

"I was raised here. My whole mind is engulfed in the American way of life, American line of thinking, my mind operates American. Now my father . . . he is all Arab. One hundred percent Arab. Today he would be a complete stranger to me. His line of thought, his background and heritage are not mine. I don't think I could reconcile myself with him, you know, on a cultural basis.

"I don't identify with the Arabs politically or any other way except for the fact that their blood flows in my veins. Their food I don't go for. Their clothing I don't dig. Their robes and all that bullshit. Their politics I can't understand and don't want to understand. Their religion? I'm a Christian. Their language I don't speak very well. Hell, I'm an American. That's the way I look at myself."[8]

For a man who is supposed to be the Arab avenger, this is a remarkable statement.

A little later Sirhan would say, "I'm not psychotic. I don't think I am. Except when it comes to Jews."

"I'll tell you something," said Kaiser. "Sometimes when we are talking about this . . . I feel you are putting me on. As if you are overplaying that."

"I could be sometimes," admitted Sirhan. "But it's in me."

"At times I think you are overdoing it."

"I could be. I could be. But I have to prove my point. That is my main weakness."

"You can't come across as one big mad-on against the Jews," replied Kaiser. "That's unbelievable."[9]

Kaiser's conversations with Sirhan continued. To Sirhan's discomfort, the defense investigator attempted to discuss the prisoner's sex life. Sirhan resisted but was more or less challenged into revealing that he had "gotten his share." He described to Kaiser several sexual encounters that served only to reinforce Kaiser's notion that Sirhan had not had frequent or fulfilling sex.

"I don't want to talk about it," said Sirhan. "You know women, money and horses were my thing, but I still maintain this thing had a political motivation. There was no other . . . involving factor. And I will keep it political."[10]

Sirhan's sex life had already been probed by the psychologists, and Sirhan understandably found this scrutiny uncomfortable. In these situations the political motive seemed to serve as a defense against these distasteful inquiries.

For example, when Kaiser brought up Sirhan's difficulties with women, the defendant responded, "Don't talk about women to me . . . If I had need of some sexual outlets, I'd go out and get a girl. I wouldn't go out and shoot that bastard."

"You weren't all tied up?" asked Kaiser.

"I *was* all tied up," said Sirhan. "The Arab-Israeli—"

"Well, you had a real burning gripe."

Sirhan, sounding confused, then replied in a manner quite unlike a political terrorist. "This is what puzzles me," he said. "I have had hatred, but not that much. Hatred was very foreign to me. That bothers me. I can't understand it."[11]

Sirhan's continued confusion about the crime was quite evident during his first full interview with attorney Grant Cooper in December 1968.

"One of the most important things in the world for a lawyer," began Cooper, "and more important for you, is that I get the complete truth, I can't operate any other way. . . . I am interested in when you first decided you were going to kill Kennedy, because it is written down in books and everything, and they have it, so you tell me. . . ."

"I honestly did not decide to do it, sir," replied Sirhan. "Objectively, I had no awareness of what I was doing that night. . . ."

"Well," said Cooper, "who do you think killed him?"

"Obviously I must have—but I have no exact—no objective of what I was doing."

Cooper was skeptical. He offered instead what had become the accepted motive. "As I view it," he told his client, "you heard Kennedy make a statement, in substance that he wanted to send these airplanes to Israel. This burned you up, and then you write down in the book 'Kennedy must go,' 'Kennedy must go,' or words to that effect."

To Cooper's chagrin, Sirhan continued to maintain that he had no recollection of ever intending to murder Robert Kennedy. Cooper then asked Sirhan if he was angry at Kennedy when he went to see him at the Ambassador Hotel reception on June 2.

"No, I wasn't," said Sirhan.

"Why not?" asked Cooper.

"This is—well, you have to hit me at the time. At the time I heard these things I was mad, but again sir, the madness, this feeling, this emotion or whatever had subsided . . . and that's why I thought I decided to like him again when I went down there to see him."[12]

In a subsequent session Grant Cooper presented Sirhan with photocopies of pages from his notebooks. Emile Berman and Robert Kaiser were also present. Cooper began reading randomly from the notebooks.

" 'Nasser is the greatest man who ever lived in this world. Nasser is the greatest man who ever lived in this world. Nasser is the greatest man who ever lived in this world. Lived. Lived. Lived.' What about that?"

"All this repetition!" said Sirhan, as though it were the first time he had heard these words.

" 'Tonight. Tonight. Tonight. We. I must buy a new Mustang tonight. Tonight. Tonight. Tonight. Tonight. Meet me tonight.' "

"I must be psychotic," said Sirhan, laughing, but with no better explanation for the strange writing.

"'Let us do it. Let us do it. Let us do it do it it it. Let us do it. Please pay to the order of 50. 50. 50. 50,000. 5. 500,0000. Very good. Very good. One hundred thousand dollars.'"

"Whew!" exclaimed Sirhan.

"How much did you say you made a week?" asked Emile Berman.

"Seventy dollars a week," said Sirhan, who had briefly made that much as a racehorse groom.

"'Please pay to the order of Sirhan Sirhan the the the the amount of 15 15 15 15 death life 15. $15,000. Must die. Die. Die. Die. Dollar sign. Life and death.'"

"For Christ's sake," interrupted Berman. "Were you smoking hashish? What kind of writing involves this constant repetition of a word?"

Sirhan had no answer. "That's what I've been wondering."[13] Once again, in the confidential company of his attorneys, Sirhan was more like a confused boy than a political assassin.

If Sirhan seemed unsuited for the role of political assassin in his sessions with Grant Cooper, he positively flunked the audition in his sessions with Dr. Seymour Pollack. Recall that Dr. Pollack was a renowned psychiatrist from the University of Southern California, who had been brought into the case by the district attorney's office to provide the expertise needed to refute the defense's claim of diminished capacity. Pollack was given unprecedented access to Sirhan when Grant Cooper thought his input would help bring about a successful plea bargain for Sirhan.

Trial testimony, audiotapes, and documents released by the DA's office (in 1985–1986) reveal that Pollack was not merely invited in for a supervised evaluation of the defendant. He got to work with Sirhan extensively. Pollack spent approximately twenty hours in Sirhan's cell, in eight sessions lasting from one and a half hours to a marathon five and a half hours. At some of the sessions, Grant Cooper and Dr. Bernard Diamond, the defense psychiatrist, were present. At others, the prosecution psychiatrist had Sirhan to himself.

Pollack was aware of the conflicting nature of this role: "I'm doing my damnedest to bend over backwards to find something that would exonerate him, and I have to watch myself," he confided to Dr. Diamond. ". . . How the hell can I be so deceitful? Here I am the prosecution consultant, and yet at the same time—you get my point?"[14]

Pollack's sessions with Sirhan raise serious questions as to the increasingly porous boundaries in this case between the prosecution and the defense, and also between the medical and the legal professions. As the audiotapes reveal, Pollack does not merely assess: he hypnotizes the prisoner, challenges him, and gives fairly impassioned mini-speeches. Often he appears to be coaching a somewhat passive or reluctant Sirhan on his motive.

"I have a clear picture of what you did," lectures Pollack. "You were waiting for Kennedy. You were actively looking for him. . . . Apparently what was eating at you was these elections and how strongly you felt about the American political figures letting the Arab world down. . . . It isn't just letting the Arab world down, it's building up Israel."

Sirhan agrees, and Pollack goes on to preview the upcoming trial in terms of its political theme.

"The trial is a trial in which you are sort of accusing America of . . . burying a million Arabs."

"In fact!" Sirhan seems pleased.

"And that's, that's, that's your—in a sense—that's your plea."

Sirhan says nothing and continues to listen to Pollack's sudden insight about the trial as a political showcase: "I assume . . . that you really want . . . the world to see the Arab suffering, the Palestinian Arabs particularly, but all of the displaced Arabs . . . to see that American policy has helped [cause] that suffering."

That Sirhan had not acted like a political assassin before or after the murder didn't bother Dr. Pollack. These inconsistencies could be dismissed by viewing Sirhan as an amateur: "I don't really think you thought the whole thing out," Pollack says. "You certainly didn't work out a good way of killing him, in the sense that it was, uh, a good plan."

"That's what I don't understand," replies Sirhan. "If I wanted to kill a man, why would I have shot him right there where they could have choked the shit outta me?"

"It might be that you wanted to be caught, if you wanted the world to know it was an Arab who did it," answers Pollack, offering an escalated version of the alleged motive. There was nothing in Sirhan's behavior after the murder to warrant this opinion, and in his jail cell eight months later, Sirhan wasn't buying it either.

"You don't think so?" asks Pollack.

"If I had wanted to kill him," says Sirhan, again questioning whether he ever had planned to murder Robert Kennedy in the first place, "would I, sir, be so stupid as to leave that notebook there, waiting for those cops, sir, to pick it up?"

"It would seem not," Pollack agrees. "It would seem that if you planned to kill him you wouldn't leave things around."

"That's what puzzles me," says Sirhan.

"Only you're not a killer," says Pollack, returning to his earlier insight. "You see, a person who isn't a killer doesn't think about all those things. If I were to kill somebody, I could do something as stupid as that, too, and I'm not stupid either. And looking at it from your eyes, I don't think killing Kennedy was stupid. You see, I think Kennedy's assassination was a political assassination."

But Sirhan refuses to fit neatly into Pollack's puzzle.

"My own conscience doesn't agree with what I did."

"Your conscience?" says Pollack. "In what way?"

"It's against my upbringing," says Sirhan in what by any measure is an extraordinary moment. "My, my, my childhood, family church, prayers . . . the Bible and all this, sir. 'Thou shalt not kill.' Life is the thing, you know. Where would you be if you didn't have life? And here I go and splatter this guy's brains. It's just not me."[15]

Dr. Pollack and Sirhan went around in circles for hours. Eventually Pollack would throw up his hands and exclaim, "Ah, what a crazy mixed-up case!" But the doctor would overcome these feelings of confusion. On the witness stand two months later, Seymour Pollack would turn on Sirhan in a most callous way.

In the trial of Sirhan Sirhan the political motive became an article of faith. Its disciples were drawn from those prosecuting Sirhan, and those most active in his defense—the Arab-American community. On June 11, Dr. M. T. Mehdi, secretary-general of the Action Committee on American-Arab Relations, wrote a letter to *The New York Times*. In the letter Mehdi once again mentioned the fifty jet bombers promised to Israel. "As we condemn Sirhan's act," he wrote, "we must [also] condemn the Zionist pressures which forced Senator Kennedy to support Israel wrongly against the Arabs. Senator Kennedy is in a very real sense an indirect victim of Zionism. The Senator was morally wrong; Sirhan was legally wrong."*

Later in the day Dr. Mehdi would tell newspaper reporters that he did not believe the assassination was an act of insanity, but that it was "a politically calculated thing." Sirhan, Mehdi said, "was not insane. Just as the man who decided to drop the A-bomb over Hiroshima was not insane."

Mehdi's ideas about an unconventional defense had its proponent in defense consultant Abdeen Jabara. Recall that in October of 1968 attorney Russell Parsons met with Jabara in Chicago and agreed that some amount of Palestine history from the Arab point of view would make its way into the defense of Sirhan Sirhan.

The Parsons-Jabara arrangement went undisturbed until January, when attorney Emile Berman joined the defense team. Berman believed that em-

---

*Note: the continued identification of Sirhan's motive with Dr. Mehdi's words was demonstrated in 1994 when excerpts from Dr. Mehdi's letter were read at Sirhan's parole hearing as evidence of why he should not be released, as though Sirhan himself had written these words.

phasizing the accused's political motivation was not going to help Sirhan. At one meeting Berman voiced this reservation: "To put on Arabs as a counteroffensive in court," he said, "would be a very serious step."

Parsons didn't agree. "In the defense of diminished capacity," he replied, "damn near anything that influences a man is admissible."[16]

Parsons was technically correct. The defense of diminished capacity is not automatically incompatible with a political motive. But Berman believed that a jury would be able to understand only one or the other. If the defense got the jury to accept Sirhan's political motivation, he reasoned, in the process they would reject diminished capacity.

The rift between Parsons and Berman over this issue was permanent, and the two-minded nature of the defense was evident throughout the trial. Grant Cooper may have felt uncomfortable introducing the Arab-Israeli conflict into the case, but he had little choice: the Arab community already had Sirhan's ear, and Cooper had already agreed to have an Arab observer at the trial.

The friction continued. During a jail-cell visit with Sirhan, Abdeen Jabara told the defendant that it was Emile Berman who was preventing the Arab-Israeli situation from coming out at the trial. Having rallied Sirhan to his cause, Jabara then invited Berman to have lunch. Robert Kaiser joined them.

As Kaiser reports in *"RFK Must Die!"*, Jabara didn't touch his food. "This is a serious matter," he told Berman. Jabara then delivered a well-spoken history of the Arab-Israeli conflict, beginning with Theodor Herzl and the foundation of the Zionist movement and right up to the Arab defeat in the Six-Day War of 1967.

Berman was polite, but he wanted to know how the pieces fit. "How do we bring it home to Sirhan? The judge isn't going to let us present a history lesson in court."

"The conflict," said Jabara emphatically, "has to come into the trial."[17]

When the defense began to call its witnesses, Grant Cooper's Arab observer arrived in Los Angeles.

"If Your Honor please," said Cooper in court, "I would like to introduce Mr. Issa Nakhleh, who is a director of the Palestinian-Arab delegation to the United Nations. He is a member of the English bar, having been admitted at Lincoln's Inn and also a lawyer in Palestine, and I would move his admission in the case simply as an adviser for the period of time that he will be here."

"It is your desire?" Judge Walker asked Nakhleh.

"Yes."

"The motion will be granted and we are glad to have you here."

Ambassador Nakhleh would sit as an adviser to the defense for three weeks. He visited Sirhan in his cell. But, just as it had between Jabara and Berman, animosity soon developed between Nakhleh and Berman. Berman had threatened to withdraw from the case if more political material were introduced. At a meeting of the defense attorneys Nakhleh spoke out; as leader of the nonvoting Palestinian UN delegation, he wanted more on the plight of the Palestinian refugees to "create a balance in the jurors' minds."

"My friend Mr. Berman's objections," said Nakhleh, "were motivated by political reasons, not by a desire to help your client. He threatened to withdraw from the case—"

"So did you, Mr. Nakhleh," interrupted Cooper. "This morning."

Berman, who had remained quiet, now spoke. "Political assassination isn't exactly diminished capacity."

"Mr. Berman has stopped you from doing what you must," Nakhleh answered. "He's acting for political motivations."

"And you," Berman replied, "are sending Sirhan to the gas chamber."[18]

The standard way to make sense out of the Sirhan enigma—the way promoted by the prosecution and the Arab community and adopted by the defense attorneys, the press, and the public—is to accept Sirhan's assertions of political motivation and to disbelieve his professed lack of memory. Of all those connected to the case, only two—Robert Kaiser, and to a lesser extent, Dr. Bernard Diamond—understood Sirhan in reverse: giving credence to his lack of memory and disbelieving his political motive. While this reverse view needs additional clarification, it explains, far better than the official version, Sirhan's behavior before and after the shooting, as well as his words and actions once incarcerated.

It is important to understand that in the reverse model, Sirhan is not lying about his political motive. He awakens one morning to discover he has murdered an important political figure. He has no memory of the event or of planning the event. Why then did he do it? As much as anyone, Sirhan needed to answer that question.

Sirhan's choices were two: either he was crazy, or he murdered Robert Kennedy to defend his people. A third possibility, that he had been an involuntary dupe, was not seriously considered. When this possibility was suggested to him in his jail cell by Robert Kaiser, Sirhan rejected it. He had no memory of anyone bending his mind toward murder.

Though a finding of mental illness was within Sirhan's best interest in terms of escaping maximum punishment, Sirhan, without variation, rejected that idea. Throughout the trial he continually undermined his attorneys' efforts at establishing a psychiatric defense. Almost everyone noted that Sirhan seemed to favor the gas chamber over being judged insane.

Part of this rejection may have been cultural. Sirhan's brother Adel spoke to the authors about this in 1993. "In Arabic culture," he said, "there is a great stigma attached to mental illness. Not only is the person involved outcast, but also his family. Here it is a somewhat romanticized notion, but in the Middle East it is better to be a thief than to be thought of as crazy."

An example of this cultural bias can be seen in an incident that took place at the Hall of Justice. Sirhan's mother, Mary, was in an elevator and overheard defense attorney Emile Berman tell a reporter, "Oh, Sirhan is obviously mad. That notebook shows nothing but madness."

Berman, of course, was trying to demonstrate to anyone who would listen that the very strange writing in Sirhan's notebooks did not constitute legal premeditation. He was fighting for Sirhan's life. Mary Sirhan, however, would have none of it.

"What are you saying?" she demanded of Berman. "I don't like that. You cannot say that, that my boy is mad. What he did he did for his country."[19]

From Taibeh, on the West Bank, Sirhan's father echoed the same words. "If he did this," Bishara said, ". . . it was because he was doing something for his country. We know he is a hero."[20]

Sirhan's father had not always felt that way. The day after the murder he had said that news of the crime made him sick. "If my son has done this dirty thing," he proclaimed, "then let them hang him."[21]

Bishara Sirhan's change of outlook may be seen as parallel to that of his son. The political motive made the crime understandable and, within a certain context, even acceptable.

If one believes Sirhan, that he has no memory of the crime, then one must imagine the young immigrant waking to find himself in prison, and not only the perpetrator of a foul murder but the focus of an international debate on the injustices suffered by his people. Until this moment, his life had been one of unending failure and mediocrity. But now his likeness is on thousands of Al Fatah posters; the ambassador of the Palestinian UN delegation attends his trial; he receives adoring letters from Palestinian girls. Is it so strange that this young man comes to embrace the political motive?

Through the careful examination of his words and behavior, it would appear that Sirhan adopted the political motive after the fact. As has been shown in his conversations with his attorneys and doctors, Sirhan was quite puzzled by the crime. These private moments, not those when he was grandstanding before the public, are the clearest windows into the defendant's mind.

Sometimes the clue is in the phrasing of a statement. For example, when defense psychiatrist Dr. Bernard Diamond tries to persuade Sirhan that he is sick, Sirhan takes issue. He says he is not sick and doesn't want anyone to mess around with his mind or portray him as stupid. "I'd rather die," he says, "and *say* I killed that son of a bitch for my country, period [emphasis added]."[22]

A similar moment occurred in his cell in the presence of his attorneys when Sirhan confronted the fact that he might die for this crime. "Well," he said, "if it is going to cost me my life, I want to help the Arabs."[23] This is not a statement a man would make if he had done the deed to help the Arabs in the first place.

In another private conversation in his cell, Sirhan was asked how he felt about being portrayed as a hero on an Al Fatah poster. Had he carried out a political murder on behalf of the Palestinians, Sirhan might have greeted such news with enthusiasm. Instead he replied, "The shot was expended. I might as well make the most of it."[24]

TEN

Sirhan Bishara Sirhan

✻ ✻ ✻

T HE AFFIRMATIVE DEFENSE of
Sirhan Sirhan began on Friday,
February 28. Grant Cooper's initial strategy was to present witnesses
who could enlighten the court about Sirhan's life and, when possible,
present an Arab view of the Palestinian-Israeli conflict. Toward this end
Mr. Baron Sarkees Nahas was called to the witness stand.

Mr. Nahas had been born in Jerusalem, where he lived until 1949. Then
he moved to Beirut, where he worked for the United States Information
Service and, following that, the United Nations agency that organized relief for the Palestinian refugees. Under Cooper's guidance Nahas testified
about conditions in Jerusalem at the time of the Sirhan family's residence.

Following Nahas was Ziad Hashimeh. Hashimeh resided in Chicago,
but in 1949 his family and the Sirhans were two of nine families who
shared a house in the Old City of Jerusalem. Both families had been forced
from their original homes by the fighting between Arabs and Jews.

"Was it a very old house?" asked Grant Cooper.

"Well, I would say eight hundred years," answered Hashimeh, who then
described the privations suffered by those living there.

Hashimeh was born in 1944, the same year as Sirhan, and the two boys
were friends. Hashimeh told the court that he frequently visited the single
room that sheltered the Sirhan family. He also described the violence that
Sirhan had received at the hands of his father.

"Did you ever see him strike Sirhan?" Cooper asked.

"Oh, yes, quite a few times."

"I take it because he was a bad boy, or something."

"Well, no. The husband, the man, was too emotional, you know. . . .
Quite a bit of times he beat him."

"Did he strike him with his hands?"

"He used all sorts of sticks and hands."

Cooper asked Hashimeh if he remembered another time that he saw
Sirhan crying.

"I was in the room and I heard him shouting, 'Mother, mother.' . . .
The whole apartment they goes out and he was shaking, you know, like

that, moving his body and he was crying, 'Hand, hand,' so we all had to go to the well."

"What did you see?"

"We saw hand in—"

"You mean a human hand?"

"A human hand."

"That was in the bucket?"

"In the bucket, yes."

Hashimeh remembered the young Sirhan as a "sensitive" boy who chastised him for telling a lie. "He told me, '[I]if you lie, people are clever enough to lie back to you. . . . Do not lie.'"

Hashimeh also recalled a time when Sirhan talked him into coming to hear his mother speak about religion. "I am a Muslim and he is a Christian, and I said, 'I do not believe in religion, religion means nothing to me,' and then he said, 'You don't have to believe in religion, but you can believe in God. My mother is not speaking to people to make them follow a religion. She goes to make them follow God.' So I had a good feeling for those words, you know, so I went with him to his mother."

When Hashimeh stepped down, Grant Cooper introduced John T. Harris, an officer of the Pasadena School District, who testified about Sirhan's mediocre scholastic performance in high school. During Harris's testimony Russell Parsons broke in and asked to speak to Judge Walker. "This morning he was wonderful," he said, speaking about Sirhan. "Since lunchtime he has been quite disturbed. For some reason he doesn't want this information that is going on to go into the Court. He has some objection to it, and he says he would like to talk to you in chambers."

"He will not talk to me in chambers," Walker insisted.

Grant Cooper then suggested that the jury be excused. "We might as well face this sometime," he sighed.

After the jury left, Cooper spoke. "Mr. Parsons just interrupted us quite properly to inform Your Honor that the defendant has objected to our calling this witness. . . . The defendant has objected to our calling approximately a dozen witnesses, whom we as lawyers all agree are relevant and proper to the issues in his best interest and for the defense. Nevertheless, he has indicated to us last week that he would forbid us to call those witnesses.

"Now I am informed—he informed me just before we started at two o'clock—that again he forbade us to call these witnesses whom in our judgment we deem proper. . . . Have I recited it correctly, Mr. Sirhan?"

"Yes, you have."

"There is something you want to say?" Judge Walker asked Sirhan.

"May I address the Court in chambers, sir?"

"No," replied Walker.

Since his youth Sirhan had suffered a nervous condition that made him tremble in difficult moments. Now, gripping his chair, he struggled to maintain control. "I, at this time, sir, withdraw my original plea of not guilty and submit the plea of guilty as charged on all counts. I also request that my counsel disassociate themselves from this case completely."

Judge Walker had been caught off guard: "Do I understand—stand up—do I understand that you want to plead guilty to murder in the first degree?"

"Yes, sir, I do."

"All right, and what do you want to do about the penalty?" queried Walker,

"I will offer no defense whatsoever."

"The question is," repeated Walker, "what do you want to do about the penalty?"

"I will ask to be executed, sir."

At this the wire-service reporters hurried for the courtroom door. Judge Walker appeared awkward as he sought to keep control of the proceedings.

"I know of nothing in the law that permits a defendant under any circumstances to enter a plea of guilty to murder of the first degree and ask for execution."

"Well, I have, sir," replied Sirhan.

"Well, now, just a minute. Why do you want to do this?"

"I believe, sir, that is my business, isn't it?"

"You just believe it is your business?" said Walker, searching for leverage.

"That is my prerogative."

"No it isn't," argued Walker. "Now when we come to accepting a plea, you have to give me a reason."

Thus challenged, Sirhan replied, "I killed Robert Kennedy willfully, premeditatively, with twenty years of malice aforethought: that is why."

"Well, the evidence has to be produced here in court," said Walker, appearing to invent new law. Normally a plea of guilty relieves the prosecution of proving anything. Certainly, the burden of proof does not fall on a defendant as a prerequisite for making a guilty plea.

"I withdraw all evidence, sir," said Sirhan.

"There is no such procedure."

"To hell with it."

Walker had heard enough. "Well, the Court will not accept the plea. Proceed with the trial. Let me give you to understand here and now that this Court will not put up with any more of your interrupting. You are to follow the advice of counsel and just sit down there. Any further interruptions by you in this trial will result in you being restrained. You understand that?"

"Sir?"

"I mean by that that you will have a face mask put on you which will prohibit you from talking and, further, your arms will be strapped to your chair and the trial will proceed. You understand that?"

"I understand. However, sir, I intend to defend myself *pro per*," said Sirhan, using the legal term for self-representation. "I don't want to be represented by these counsel."

"You have retained counsel," answered Walker. "Counsel is staying in the trial."

"What I have said, I don't want anyone to have a trial shoved down my throat, sir, and you are not going to shove it down my throat, sir, in any way you want."

"You say you want to go *pro per*?" asked Walker.

"Yes."

"What are the defenses; let me ask what are the elements of the crime of murder?"

"Sir, I don't know. I don't understand all of this legality. You let me—"

"I am conducting these proceedings, not you. What are the defenses to murder in the first degree?"

"I don't know."

"I find you are incapable of representing yourself. Sit down and keep quiet and, if not, I intend to keep you quiet."

"No, sir. I still maintain my original point. I plead guilty to murder and ask to be executed."

"I thought I made it clear. The Court will not accept the plea."

"I am sorry," answered Sirhan. "I will not accept it."

"The law tells me what I can do and cannot do. Now you understand from here on out you keep quiet, and if not, I will see to it that you are kept quiet."

"I am sorry, but my original position stands."

"Get the jury down."

"Why not let me go into chambers. I insist."

"You are not going to go in chambers. I let you go in there once and that was the beginning and the end. That procedure is over as far as I am concerned. We will proceed with the trial. Again, I will tell you to keep quiet and consult with your attorneys."

"Can I consult with them a minute?"

"We will proceed with the trial. Do you want to consult in the hold tank, Mr. Cooper?"

"Yes, Your Honor," Cooper replied. Judge Walker then called the afternoon recess.

What had caused this outburst? Why did Sirhan ask to be executed? Did he now suddenly remember the crime? Did he believe that his lawyers would not properly represent the Palestinian cause? Did he want to martyr himself in a more dramatic fashion? No, Sirhan sought to enter a plea of guilty because he was embarrassed at the thought that two young women would be called as witnesses.

"I told you not to bring those two girls in here,"[1] he screamed at his attorneys once they were in the holding cell. Sirhan had misidentified two women sitting in the courtroom as Gwen Gumm and Peggy Osterkamp, both of whom had been the subjects of ramblings in his notebooks. Gumm had been a fellow student at Pasadena Community College, while Osterkamp had worked at a horse farm where Sirhan was also employed.

Peggy Osterkamp's name appeared in the notebooks dozens of times. What would be labeled as page 31 was devoted entirely to her:

P Peggy Osterkamp is I love you I love you sterkamp Miss Peggy P
P P P I love you I love you . . . y y you P Miss Peggy Osterkamp
Miss yo y you you you I your children Sol & Peggy I love you I your
I I love love y y your children Sol & Peggy Peggy[2]

Sirhan had not dated Peggy Osterkamp or Gwen Gumm. Neither woman had been any more than fleetingly aware of his existence. The public exposure of his notebooks had already caused Sirhan acute embarrassment, and having two women whom he fancied testify to the world that he meant nothing to them would have been the ultimate humiliation. To insure that this would not happen, Sirhan was ready to fire his lawyers, plead guilty, and suffer the gas chamber.

When court resumed with the jury absent, Grant Cooper was the first to speak.

"If your Honor please. Since Your Honor declared the afternoon recess, we as counsel have conferred with our client in the holding cell and he has advised us definitely, positively, and unequivocally that he does not desire us to continue to represent him as counsel. I have conferred with my brethren of the defense, Mr. Parsons and Mr. Berman, and none of us have any desire to continue representing a client who does not desire our services.

"I think I should state this into the record historically," Cooper continued. "We were asked to represent him and each one of us has volunteered our services without compensation and we feel that we have prepared what we feel, based upon the facts and the law, is a legitimate defense of diminished responsibility."

Cooper told the court that Sirhan was quite capable of communicating with his attorneys; it was just a "violent difference of opinion as to how the defense should be conducted. . . . At this time, since the defendant does not desire us to represent him, we are perfectly willing, as a matter of fact

I might say anxious, to withdraw from the case and let him either represent himself or be represented by other counsel. . . . Neither one of us wants to desert him. We are still willing, if Your Honor please, to represent him as conscientiously as we know how. With that I must leave it up to the court."

Judge Walker had already made up his mind. "I know of no law that permits counsel to withdraw in the middle of proceedings except for good cause. I have examined the law and I don't feel that this situation is good cause. . . . He is incapable of representing himself. This is proven by the two questions I asked him. I will deny your motion to withdraw. . . . I think you have prepared a good defense, if not the only logical defense that could be presented."

"We are prepared to go forward."

"All right, we will proceed. Bring the jury down."

The afternoon session did not last long. Russell Parsons called Mary Sirhan. Dressed in a black suit, the diminutive Mrs. Sirhan walked bravely to the witness stand. She was in obvious distress, and the strain of the past year's events made her look older than her fifty-six years.

"Are you the mother of Sirhan Bishara Sirhan?" Parsons asked.

"Yes," answered Mrs. Sirhan in an unsteady voice.

"And when was he born?"

"He was born in 1944. March."

"March 1944?"

"Yes."

"And where was he born?"

"In the city of Jerusalem."

"And how long had you lived in Jerusalem before he was born?"

"Well, I'd say thousands of years. My family from generation to generation . . . the City of Peace."

"Is that what you called Jerusalem?"

"Yes," answered Mrs. Sirhan, crying now, "all over the whole world we call it the City of Peace. . . . Please don't mind if I look this way."

"If Your Honor please," interjected Grant Cooper, "may we approach the bench."

Cooper told Judge Walker that Sirhan's attempt to change his plea had shaken Mrs. Sirhan badly. He asked if the court could be recessed until Monday. Walker, sympathetic to Mrs. Sirhan's position, agreed.

On Sunday, March 2, Grant Cooper took Ambassador Issa Nakhleh up to see Sirhan in an effort to get the defendant to cooperate once again with his lawyers. Nakhleh asked Sirhan what was troubling him. Sirhan replied that there were witnesses scheduled to testify that he did not want called. Nakhleh discovered that the witnesses most objectionable were the two girls Sirhan had mistakenly believed were present in the court Friday. He then asked Sirhan if those two were excluded would Sirhan reunite with his counsel? Sirhan agreed. Nakhleh then got Cooper to agree not to call the two women.[3] The courtroom crisis, sparked by adolescent embarrassment, not Middle East politics, was over.

On Monday, Mary Sirhan assumed the witness stand once again, followed by Adel, the defendant's brother. Each told the court what they could of Sirhan's life in Palestine and in the United States. Late in the day Grant Cooper called his next witness. Court clerk Alice Nishikawa administered the oath.

"Do you solemnly swear the testimony you are about to give in the case now pending before this Court shall be the truth, the whole truth, and nothing but the truth, so help you God?"

"Yes, ma'am."

"Be seated. State your name, please."

"Sirhan Sirhan."

Trial testimony of a murder defendant carries with it some risk, because it leaves the witness open to cross-examination. In this case, since the defense had already conceded most of the facts, Grant Cooper felt there was little to lose. The jury, he reasoned, should see a human face on the accused. Other than that, however, Cooper didn't appear to have a clear idea of what he was trying to accomplish with his client. And his client had some ideas of his own. As he had in February, Sirhan once again took the oath with his arm upraised and fist clenched.

"Mr. Sirhan," Cooper began. "It is alleged that on the fifth day of June 1968, you killed and murdered Senator Robert Francis Kennedy, a human being. Did you on or about that date shoot Senator Kennedy?"

"Yes, sir."

"Do you have any doubt but that you did it?"

"No, sir, I do not."

"Now, you were born in New Jerusalem on March 1944, and you moved to the Old City of Jerusalem within the walled city, sometime during the year 1948?"

"Yes."

"Do you, yourself, have any recollections of your childhood . . . ?"

"A little bit, yes."

"What do you remember?"

Sirhan's memories as a young boy were dominated by the brutal conflict in Palestine between the Arabs, the immigrating Jews, and the then-governing British. His young eyes saw the disembowelment of a man by a bomb, a group of Arabs blown apart while waiting for a bus, and, most traumatic, his older brother being crushed to death by a truck swerving to avoid sniper fire.

At that time the Sirhan family lived in a ground-floor apartment just outside Musrara, a mixed middle-class Arab and Jewish quarter. Sirhan's father, Bishara, a Greek Orthodox Arab from the nearby town of Taibeh, had a position with the British Mandate Government. But both the family home and Bishara's job would be lost when Israel declared its independence in 1948 and the Arabs in their neighborhood were forced from their homes. What followed were eight difficult years as refugees.

After extended testimony on Sirhan's recollections of war-savaged Jerusalem, Grant Cooper changed venue. "Now there came a time," he asked the defendant, "did there not, Sirhan, when the family decided to leave Old Jerusalem and come to the United States of America?"

"Yes, sir."

"What were your feelings about leaving?"

"I was very hesitant, sir. I didn't want to leave. I wanted to stay in my own country, sir, with my own people."

In 1956 the Sirhan family emigrated to the United States, sponsored by a California family Bishara had met in Jerusalem. The family traveled to California by rail and settled in Pasadena, but after seven months, Bishara returned to Taibeh. According to Mary Sirhan, her husband returned "because of his mother," who was old and ill. An alternate explanation was that Bishara simply abandoned his family, unable to adapt to the new American culture. Neither Mary nor Sirhan would ever see him again.

After Bishara left, Sirhan's older brother Adel became the primary bread-winner. Mary Sirhan described it in court: "We were busy all the time trying to support the little ones and everything. It was really hard because Father had left and we were alone in a strange country. We didn't know *enough* of the customs of the language, and we just tried our best to live and to do right."

Mrs. Sirhan finally landed a job at the Westminster Nursery School. At age thirteen Sirhan took on a paper route. He delivered the *Independent Star-News* for four years, often delivering both the morning and evening editions. According to his mother he was proud of his economic contribution to the family. She got compliments on his work from neighbors who were customers.

Sirhan started his U.S. education in the sixth grade at Longfellow Elementary School. He especially liked geography and wrote that his occupational goal was to be a doctor. At John Muir High School, Sirhan studied history and government as well as Russian and German. He now thought about living life as a diplomat in the foreign service. But it was also at John Muir that Sirhan began to feel separate. He noticed that the popular kids were tall and blond, that they wore different clothes every day and had cars of their own.

In September of 1963 Sirhan enrolled in Pasadena Community College.

His interests in government and foreign languages continued, and he joined the International Club (comprising one hundred and fifty or so students interested in foreign affairs). But Sirhan's academic performance at Pasadena was poor. Soon he was barely passing and sometimes failing his courses. According to his mother, the cause of his academic tailspin was the fatal illness of his sister Ayda. She was diagnosed as having leukemia in 1962 and became gradually worse until her death in 1965. Sirhan became preoccupied with the family tragedy. He dropped out of college after two years.

"Now after you were discharged or dismissed as a result of your poor grades and your absences," asked Grant Cooper, "what did you do then?"

"Having developed, sir," Sirhan replied, "a likeness [*sic*] for horses, and a love for horses, I decided to try to ride them, to become a jockey."

"I take it by this time, having flunked out, you gave up your ambition to be a diplomat?"

"I gave up my scholastic ambition completely, sir."

In 1966 Sirhan landed a job as an exercise boy at Granja Vista Del Rio Ranch near Corona. He wanted to be a jockey. On the morning of September 25, several owners had gathered at Granja Vista to see their horses run on the training track. But the track was foggy and some owners backed out. A three-horse race then shaped up, with Sirhan on a filly named Hy-Vera. At full gallop the horses disappeared into the fog and ran into the rail. Sirhan fell and was taken to Corona Community Hospital, where he was found to be intact, but he continued to complain of fuzzy vision and headaches. He sought the advice of at least eight medical doctors. None could relieve his pain.

"The eye kept bothering me," Sirhan recalled at his trial. He tried to return to work, and even summoned the courage to ride again. But his dream of being a jockey was finished. Sirhan would eventually receive seventeen hundred dollars in workmen's compensation insurance. According to his friends and family, he became a different person—withdrawn and irritable.

Once again Sirhan redirected his energies. He became interested in the occult. When, in court, Grant Cooper asked how that came about, Sirhan responded, "I have always asked the question myself, sir, 'What is this life about? What is this reality, this world?' I always wanted to know what was behind it."

Perhaps to fill the void created by his lost dream, and to overcome the physical pain that his numerous doctors could not abate, Sirhan fervently embraced the realm of the mind: self-hypnosis, mind control, mysticism. He practiced the mental projection of images and ideas. He frequented one Pasadena bookstore that specialized in the occult and got a part-time job at another. There he read books he could not afford to buy, books with titles like *The Laws of Mental Domination; Meditations on the Occult Life; and Thought Power: Its Control and Culture.*

In May 1968 he paid twenty dollars to join the Rosicrucians, a self-described "ancient mystical order," after seeing an ad in a newspaper. He attended one meeting of the local "lodge." Sirhan participated in one of the evening's "experiments," an exercise in tactile, sensory perception, but he left immediately after the meeting was over. This fleeting, superficial contact with the Rosicrucians would be magnified to an event of great significance by his own attorneys and those prosecuting him.

Cooper next asked Sirhan about the day of the shooting.

"What were your plans for that Tuesday?"

"Well, Tuesday, sir, I planned to go to the races."

"What races were on?"

"At Hollywood Park."

Sirhan told Cooper that he had been going to the races for several weeks. Cooper asked how he had fared in the betting. Sirhan replied "good and bad," then conceded that he had lost more than he had won. Sirhan then told Cooper that he had looked at the racing entries in the newspaper and decided not to go to the track because he wasn't interested in any of the horses. It was then, he said, he decided to take his gun and go to a shooting range.

"All right, and then you drove where?"

"I drove to the San Gabriel Valley Gun Club range."

Sirhan told Cooper that he had stayed the afternoon at the range, a fact borne out by a number of witnesses who saw him there. Sirhan reportedly left when the range closed at 5 P.M.

Sirhan said that he had planned to go to another Rosicrucian meeting scheduled for that evening, but as he looked through a newspaper while eating at Bob's Big Boy, he saw an advertisement for the Miracle March for Israel, a parade on Wilshire Boulevard to celebrate the Israeli victory over the Arabs in the Six-Day War a year earlier. Sirhan told Cooper that just seeing the ad gave him "a burning feeling inside."

"What did you decide to do?"

"I commenced to go down to Wilshire Boulevard on Miracle Mile where they were having that parade."

In his anger Sirhan had failed to notice that the parade was scheduled for the following night. Instead of a parade, all Sirhan found was a store-front campaign party for U.S. senatorial candidate Thomas Kuchel. Sirhan stopped in and overheard that there were several larger parties going on at the Ambassador Hotel, a short distance away. He then made his way to the Ambassador.

Sirhan told the court that when he first entered the hotel, he noticed a sign for the Max Rafferty headquarters in the Venetian Room. Rafferty was the U.S. senator against whom Kuchel was running. Sirhan had attended classes in high school with Kathleen Rafferty, the senator's daughter, and he testified that he hung around the Rafferty party for about an hour hoping to spot Kathleen. During this time he said he consumed several Tom Collins drinks.

"Do you have any specific recollection of how many drinks you had?" Cooper asked the witness.

"No, sir, I don't."

"Do you know whether you had more than two?"

"I don't really know, sir."

Sirhan told Cooper that after an hour or so he left the Rafferty party and wandered around a bit.

"Now, at some point did you decide to go somewhere?"

"Yes, sir. I felt that I was quite high, and if I got any more drunk there was nobody with me to take care of me. So I decided to go home."

Sirhan then described walking back up Wilshire Boulevard to his car, getting in, and then deciding that he was too drunk to drive.

"What did you do then?"

"Then I decided, sir, to go back to the party and sober up, drink some coffee."

"Did you pick up your gun?"

"I don't remember, sir, if I did pick up my gun."

"As a result of what happened, you know you must have picked it up?"

"I must have, sir, but I don't remember picking it up."

"And where did you go when you got to the Ambassador?"

"I was in search of coffee, sir. I went in search of coffee. I tried to—I don't know where I found it, but eventually I found some coffee."

Sirhan described finding a large silver coffee urn and then meeting a dark-haired young woman and pouring coffee for her.

"Do you have any idea approximately how old she was?"

"About my age."

"A good-looking girl?"

"Beautiful."

"What happened next."

"I don't remember."

"What was the next thing you did?"

"The next thing I remember, sir, I was being choked."

"Do you remember anything between the time you had the coffee, anything?"

"No, sir. No, I don't remember."

"Now you have heard the testimony in here of at least a dozen witnesses . . . that you walked up to Senator Kennedy and put a gun toward his head, possibly within an inch or two, and you pulled the trigger and he eventually died?"

"Yes. I was told this. . . ."

"And you did kill him?"

"Yes, sir. I did."

"How do you account for all these circumstances?"

"Sir, I don't know."

After running through the events of the night of the murder, Grant Cooper asked Sirhan to explain what his feelings were toward President John Kennedy.

"I loved him, sir," Sirhan replied. "More than any American would have."

"Why?"

"Because just a few weeks before his assassination he was working, sir, with the leaders of the Arab government, the Arab countries, to bring a solution, sir, to the Palestinian refugee problem, and he promised these Arab leaders that he would do his utmost and his best to force or to put some pressure on Israel, sir, to comply with the 1948 United Nations Resolution, sir; to either repatriate those Arab refugees or give them back, give them the right to return to their homes. And when he was killed, sir, that never happened."

Cooper next asked Sirhan to relate to the court what he knew about the origins of the Palestinian conflict. Sirhan responded with a detailed account of the history of the region. He started with the 1897 conference in Switzerland that spawned the Zionist movement. He explained how the politics of Palestine became polarized during the First World War, when, seeking help in its fight against Turkey, Great Britain made conflicting promises to both the Arabs and Jews in the region. He explained to the court how the 1917 Balfour Declaration pledged British support for a Jewish national home in Palestine, and how the British Mandate Government that followed facilitated the immigration of European Jews into the area.

Sirhan finished by providing some demographics for the court: the 1917 population of Palestine was, he said, "seven hundred thousand Palestinians . . . seventy thousand Christians, of whom I am one . . . and some fifty-six thousand Jews." By 1948, Sirhan asserted, the Jews numbered 650,000, and were militarily strong enough to declare themselves a separate nation and expel the native Palestinians.

When Sirhan was done with his history lesson, Grant Cooper changed the subject.

"Now, Sirhan," he said, "you had some notebooks."

A week earlier the prosecution had tried to introduce Sirhan's notebooks into evidence. As they approached the subject, Sirhan started whispering loudly to Russell Parsons, "Those notebooks are private. They're my property. The police had no right to take them. They had no search warrant."

Since it was already late, Judge Walker adjourned for the day to avoid a scene. The next morning Grant Cooper entered Judge Walker's chambers accompanied by his client.

"Mr. Sirhan," Cooper scolded, "put out your cigarette, please. Court is in session. You wanted to make a statement?"

"Your Honor," began Sirhan.

"[I]f these notebooks are allowed in evidence, I will change my plea to guilty as charged. I will do so, sir, not so much that I want to be railroaded into the gas chamber, sir, but to deny you the pleasure, sir, of after convicting me turning around and telling the world: 'Well, I put that fellow in the gas chamber, but first I gave him a fair trial,' when you in fact, sir, will not have done so. The evidence, sir, that was taken from my home was illegally obtained, was stolen by the district attorney's people. They had no search warrant. I did not give them permission, sir, to do what they did to my home. My brother Adel had no permission to give them permission to enter my room and take what they took from my home, from my own room."

As has been demonstrated, Sirhan here was probably motivated more by the prospect of personal embarrassment than by juridical principle.

"Now, Mr. Sirhan, let me tell you this," answered Judge Walker. "The Court has ruled on the admissibility of this evidence in court, and, if there is an error, the upper court can reverse this case. . . . You have got three counsel and they are running the lawsuit to your very best interest and there is no question in the Court's mind about that."

Sirhan reluctantly accepted the judge's view, and Grant Cooper fought the notebooks in open court. As a result, only four of the most incriminating pages were entered into evidence. On Cooper's motion, several other pages containing angry rhetoric but no mention of Robert Kennedy were excluded as being inflammatory.

But now, with Sirhan on the witness stand, Grant Cooper had a different idea. He wanted to introduce all the remaining pages of the notebooks into evidence, so that the jury could better understand the portions they had already seen. "I am going to read them," Cooper said, "one page at a time."

Grant Cooper began by reading passages and then asking for comments from Sirhan. Some of the entries were clearly classroom notes, but many were not. There was a great deal of material that Sirhan could not explain.

The best he could do was say that the handwriting appeared to be his. In some cases he could not even say that.

"Now, page thirteen, at the top," read Cooper. " 'Jockey, alcohol,' then 'alcohol' and then 'love love love love love love,' and this is in this space here and then there is 'feed, feed feed' and then 'Sirhan Sirhan' circled and then 'feed feed feed feed feed feed feed feed feed feed feed feed feed.' Do you know why you wrote that down and kept repeating feed, feed, feed?"

"No, I don't."

When Cooper got to page 15 he read the "RFK must die" passage. He went to the entry below it. "Do you remember writing this: 'Please pay to the order of of of of of of of of of of of of this or that'?"

"No, sir," replied Sirhan, "I don't remember that."

"What significance does it have for you?"

"Nothing to me. I don't have a bank account. I don't understand it."

"Now let me ask you this. There is a date on there?"

"Yes, sir."

"May 18, nine forty-five A.M., and you recall what your feelings were about Robert F. Kennedy on or about May 18, which would be about three weeks roughly before June 5, approximately three weeks?"

"It could have been a time, sir, when he came out and said, when he said he would send fifty planes to Israel."

Cooper was now coloring in the official motive for the benefit of the jury. Sirhan cooperated in this effort, although his tentative answers reveal his uncertainty. Although no one appeared to notice, Sirhan correctly recalled that the television documentary did not mention any bombers to Israel. Still, the program had angered him.

"When I watched him on television, it burned me up, sir. And that is most likely, sir, the time I had written this."

"But you don't remember writing it?"

"I don't remember writing it."

From page 22, Cooper read another disturbing passage:

" 'The author expresses his wishes very bluntly to be recorded by history as the man who triggered off the last war. Life is ambivalence. Life is struggle. Life is wicked.

" 'If life is in any way otherwise, I have honestly never seen it. I always seem to be on the losing, always the one exploited to the fullest.' "

"All of that is in your handwriting?"

"Yes, sir, it is."

"You wrote it?"

"I wrote it."

"Now what was on your mind when you wrote that?"

"I must have been a maniac at the time. I don't remember what was on my mind. . . ."

"That is what you said, isn't it?"

"That is what I said, but it's not me, sir. It's not Sirhan sitting right here who wrote that."

"Well, who wrote it?"

"I did."

"What do you mean, it isn't Sirhan writing this?"

"I can't explain."

On a subsequent page Cooper read the phrase " 'Second group of American Sailors must be disposed of.' "

"What group of sailors did you have in mind?" Cooper asked.

"I don't know, sir, what group of sailors. I don't remember."

"Were there any group of sailors that you were angry at?"

"I am not mad at any sailors. I am not mad at any. I don't know."

"Do you have any idea why you wrote that there?"

"No, sir, I don't."

"Now you say here in the plural, 'We believe that we can effect such action and produce such results.' Was there somebody else that was going to join with you in doing what you wrote down there?"

"I did the writing myself, sir. I don't know who else it could be."

"Well, do you have any idea, did you have anyone with you as an accomplice?"

"No, I did not."

"Did anyone hire you?"

"No."

"What does that mean there, the 'we' that was in there?"

"I can't explain it. I have no explanation."

"That is an editorial 'we'?"

"It must be."

Cooper read Sirhan another passage: " 'Sirhan Sirhan, Jet Spec, please pay to the order of Garner Ted Armstrong.' "

"Do you know who that is?"

"I don't know, sir."

"Do you know who Ted Armstrong is?"

"The only thing I can think of is the tire company."

"The tire company?"

Strangely, Sirhan Sirhan could not identify the then well-known television evangelist whose name appeared in his notebook. But he did know who Jet Spec was. In fact, the most enigmatic names in the notebook—French Cargo, La Laguna Doll, King's Abbey, Jalousie—unrecognized by anyone else, were easily and willingly identified by Sirhan. They were racehorses.

Just as strange, there was a page of Arabic writing that Sirhan could not decipher. Issa Nakhleh, head of the Palestinian delegation to the UN, was called to the stand and read the page of what turned out to be gibberish. Once again Cooper had Sirhan admit his authorship.

"You wrote this, didn't you?" Cooper asked.

"Yes, sir, I did."

"Can't you read that? Or you just didn't want to make the effort?"

"No, I really couldn't read it."

"You couldn't read it?"

"No, sir."

Cooper continued, and again, the exchange between attorney and client was bizarre.

"'Workers of the world unite. You have nothing to lose but your chains.' You wrote that, did you not?"

"It's my handwriting, yes."

"You believed that when you wrote it?"

"I must have, sir. At the time I wrote it. I don't feel so now."

"Why don't you feel that way now?"

"It sounds queer to me. It sounds queer to me."

"It sounds queer to you?"

"I don't remember writing it, but it is my handwriting, but I have actually no memory of writing it, sir. I don't have."

"Was there a time you felt that way?"

"There must have been at the time I wrote it, I must have felt that way."

"What caused you to feel that way?"

"I don't know."

But Grant Cooper had an explanation for the writing in Sirhan's notebooks. Holding up a magazine, he approached Sirhan.

"I show you a *Rosicrucian Digest* for May 1968. . . . Did you read this article on page one ninety-one?"

"Yes, sir, I did."

The article on page 191 was by Arthur J. Fettig. It was titled "Put It in Writing." Grant Cooper read the article to the jury:

"Plan to dare something different—something exciting! Plan to become a success in some endeavor and be ready to jump barefoot into the excitement of living. But here's a word of advice: put it in writing! Put your plan, your goal, your idea in writing, and see how it suddenly catches fire. See how it gains momentum by the simple process of writing it down."

The author then quoted several people whom he termed "outstanding successes," such as bandleader Stan Kenton and Les "Jugger" Gervais, "one of the United States' finest professional archers," who attested to the power of putting one's goal down on paper. Cooper continued:

"Try it. Pick a goal. Set a target date. Now start working to make it come true. But one more thing: BELIEVE—believe that it will come true! Start acting as if you are certain you will achieve your goal. . . . I DARE you to write it down!"

Cooper put down the magazine and approached Sirhan.

"Did you write these things down at the time you wrote them with the objective in mind of accomplishing your goal?"

"Yes, sir," answered Sirhan, "in reference to that, the assassination of Robert Kennedy."

In this exchange Grant Cooper, by reputation a superb criminal defense attorney, demolished his chosen defense of Sirhan and handed the case to the prosecution. As has been shown, Grant Cooper throughout the trial had demonstrated an incomplete knowledge of the physical facts of the murder. Some important evidence had clearly been hidden, and Cooper's late entry into the case did not aid his understanding. But Grant Cooper also had a poor understanding of his client.

When the two first met, Cooper asked Sirhan why he had committed the crime. When Sirhan answered he didn't know, Cooper didn't accept this answer but instead offered Sirhan the jets-to-Israel motive. At the trial Cooper presented that motive to the jury.

Cooper was particularly embarrassed by Sirhan's lack of memory. "I just don't know why he blanks out on so many things," the frustrated attorney told reporters during a recess. "We'd rather he remember everything that happened."[4] Cooper most of all wanted to keep his credibility with the court and public. He sought desperately to make sense out of the crime. But in this attempt, Cooper undermined the defense of diminished capacity.

By California law, if a defendant does not have the capacity to reflect maturely and meaningfully upon the gravity of the crime, he would be guilty of no more than second-degree murder. This was Cooper's chosen defense for Sirhan, and given the attorney's understanding of the case, it was the logical choice. The bizarre nature of the scribbling in Sirhan's notebooks—the sheer nonsense of much of it, the strange repetition, and Sirhan's apparent inability to remember the entries certainly did not suggest mature and meaningful reflection. But by proposing that Sirhan's writings were a rational effort to bring into being his murderous intent, and getting Sirhan to agree to it (one wonders if the notebooks of Stan Kenton and Jugger Gervais looked anything like Sirhan's), Cooper simply gave the case to the prosecution.

Cooper seemed oblivious to the fact that his examination of Sirhan was ripping apart the defense. Emile Berman was not. Promoting the political motive made no sense to him at all. "This is embarrassing to me," Berman said during a recess as he considered resigning from the case. "I thought we weren't going to make a political thing out of this. This makes it a political assassination, and that's no defense to murder."[5]

When prosecutor Lynn Compton initiated his cross-examination, he questioned Sirhan about the anti–United States rhetoric in his notebooks:

"You don't deny that at some point in your career you felt very strongly about the overthrow of the United States government?"

"As I said, at that time, sir."

"At the time you wrote the material down?"

"Yes, sir, when I wrote it down and only at that time, sir. I don't remember entertaining it after or before. I don't even remember that itself right then."

Compton then went on to explore Sirhan's interest in the occult.

"Now, let me talk to you a minute about these studies of your books about how to improve your mind. When you read these things, you didn't really expect to acquire some supernatural power, did you?"

"Sir, that is what they claimed, sir, that you would."

"I know what they claim, but you didn't really expect to do that, did you?"

"You're wrong, sir. I did."

"You did?"

"Surely."

Compton's foray into the occult had a destination in the *Rosicrucian Digest* article that Grant Cooper had introduced the day before.

"You read in this book from the Rosicrucians that if you write things down and think about them enough it will help accomplish the goal, right?"

"That's what the book said, yes."

Sirhan, once again, appeared to be accepting the *Rosicrucian Digest* article as a possible explanation for the writings in his notebooks. All parties were apparently willing to overlook the fact that most of the strange writing in Sirhan's notebooks predated the article.

"So when you wrote down in your notebook 'Kennedy must die, Kennedy must die, Kennedy must die,' you were practicing the Rosicrucian approach?"

"I don't know what I was practicing, sir."

Compton would now lead Sirhan back to the well that Cooper had made him drink from the day before.

"Well, yesterday you remember what you said—your counsel said: 'Did you write these things down at the time you wrote them with the object in mind of accomplishing your goal?' and you said, 'Yes, sir, in reference to that, the assassination of Robert Kennedy.'

"Do you remember telling us that yesterday? Yes or no?"

Compton had Sirhan read that portion of the trial transcript.

"Now is that what you told us yesterday?"

"Yes, sir."

Compton then questioned Sirhan regarding his purchase of the Iver Johnson Cadet pistol he had acquired in the winter of 1968 from his brother's friend.

"Did it look like a pretty good gun to you?"

"I thought it did, yes."

"You said you had shopped for guns in other places?"

"I didn't necessarily shop. I had looked at guns in other places, yes. . . ."

"Did you ever try to buy a gun in a gun store?"

"No, sir, I never had enough money to buy a gun from a gun store."

"As a matter of fact you knew they wouldn't sell you one, didn't you?"

"I did not know they would not sell me one."

"You knew that as an alien in fact you could not have one?"

"No, sir, I did not know that."

Compton then asked Sirhan about his practicing at the gun range. Did Sirhan remember signing his name at the registry?

"No, I don't remember exactly, sir—sir, you are asking me—this is just in the process—this is part of the process, sir. I don't exactly remember when I opened my gun and when I put in every bullet. Your asking me when I wrote my name, sir, is the same as asking me about every bullet that I put in that chamber. That's stupid."

"I confess sometimes I do ask stupid questions."

"Yes, sir, you do."

"Thank you."

Compton next turned to Sirhan's conduct while in police custody the night of the murder.

"Everybody was very friendly?"

"They were extremely friendly, sir."

"Officer Jordan was a real nice guy?"

"He was."

"So he asked you what your name was, didn't he?"

"I don't remember if he did."

"You don't recall anybody asking you your name that night?"

"It was Mr. Howard asking me my name. Then he started with this 'If you say'—gave me those constitutional rights, whatever they were, and he said, 'If you give your name or say anything it can be used against you,' and I kept my mouth shut. . . ."

"Did you wonder why you were there?"

"The people said—and this Mr. Jordan was so friendly, sir, and at the time nothing was mentioned about the case. I didn't know what happened, sir."

"But you never were curious about why you were there, why you were handcuffed or why you were in the police station?"

"No, sir. I wasn't myself, sir. I didn't know what was going on."

"That is because you were still suffering from the effects of that liquor?"

"I don't know from the effects of what, sir. I was not myself, sir, as I am now."

"You were quite a bit different than you are now?"

"I must have been, otherwise I would have remembered all those things that happened, and what happened. . . ."

"Do you remember later on in that same conversation you said to Mr. Howard, 'I have been before a magistrate, have I or have I not?' Mr. Howard said, 'No, you have not. You will be taken before a magistrate as soon as possible. Probably tried.' . . . You didn't ask Mr. Howard at that time 'Tried for what?' did you?"

"I don't remember, sir, if I did or not."

Sirhan had not said, "Tried for what?" to Mr. Howard, but his question as to whether or not he had been before a magistrate was a clear indication that he was disoriented. He appeared to be normal, yet he did not know if he had been before a judge. What did this mean? Had Grant Cooper been running an aggressive defense, Mr. Howard would have been on the witness stand explaining what in Sirhan's behavior just hours after the murder had caused the assistant DA to repeatedly ask the prisoner if he knew where he was.

But since Cooper was embarrassed by Sirhan's lack of memory, he did not press the point. Nor was it necessary for the prosecution to explore the subject. They already had the defendant neatly packaged, as Mr. Compton's final exchanges with Sirhan demonstrate.

"Now, Mr. Sirhan, . . . you told us earlier this morning that as far as you were concerned you were willing to fight for the Arab cause, right?"

"Yes, sir. The Palestinian Arab cause."

"And do you think that the killing of Senator Robert Kennedy helped the Arab cause?"

"Sir, I'm not even aware that I killed Mr. Kennedy."

"Well, you know he's dead?"

"I know he's dead. I've been told that."

"In other words, the killing of Senator Kennedy would have only helped the Arab cause if you did it, right?"

"How do you mean that, sir? 'If I did it'?"

"Let me ask you this—again; I will repeat the question. Do you think that the killing of Senator Robert Kennedy by anybody helped the Arab cause?"

"I'm in no position, sir, to explain that. I am no political observer to say."

"There's no question in your mind but that you did it?"

"All the evidence has proved it. Your evidence."

"Are you glad he's dead?"

"No, sir, I'm not glad."

"Are you sorry?"

"I'm not sorry, but I'm not proud of it either."

"But you are not sorry?"

"No, sir, because I have no way of—no exact knowledge, sir, of having shot him."

"Well, the other day right here in this courtroom did you not say, 'I killed Robert Kennedy willfully, premeditatively, with twenty years of malice aforethought'—did you say that?"

"Yes, sir, I did."

Grant Cooper jumped to his feet. "If Your Honor please . . ."

Cooper began to object that Sirhan's statement had been made out of the presence of the jury and in a fit of anger directed at his own attorneys. Compton pointed out that the statement was made nevertheless and was admissible.

"One last question, Mr. Sirhan," said Compton, continuing where he had left off. "You said you would be willing to do what you could to help the Arab cause and fight for it. Are you willing to die for it?"

"When did I say, sir, that I wanted to attempt to fight for the Arab cause?"

"This morning, I think—may I ask you again: Are you willing to fight for it?"

Sirhan Sirhan was now caught in a box that had been constructed with the encouragement of his Arab supporters, his family, and his attorneys. He would have to respond to Compton with the head of the Palestinian UN delegation present and millions of other Arabs observing from a distance.

"I am willing to fight for it," Sirhan answered.

"Are you willing to die for it?"

"I am willing to die for it."

In a handful of questions Buck Compton had summarized the prosecution case against Sirhan Sirhan. He was to be convicted and sentenced on the basis of his motive: political assassination. Despite the fact that the defendant professed no memory of the crime, Compton had gotten Sirhan to admit to the jury that he was willing to fight and die for the Arab cause. Nothing else needed to be said.

In putting Sirhan Sirhan on the witness stand, Grant Cooper had accepted the risk of cross-examination. Unfortunately for Sirhan, much of the damage done to the defense during his testimony was done by his own attorney. Cooper had actively promoted the political motive. He had tried to make sense out of Sirhan's strange writings by posing the bombers-to-Israel hypothesis. He had also tried to rationalize the notebooks by dragging out the article in the *Rosicrucian Digest*.

Sirhan's notebooks were quite clearly written in an abnormal state of mind. They should have represented very poor evidence of premeditation. But Cooper helped the prosecution skip over that difficulty by reducing the bizarre writing to some occult version of positive thinking. Thanks in great part to the defense attorney's efforts, the jury now had all the shorthand they needed. Sirhan had shot Senator Kennedy for advocating the sale of bombers to Israel; the writing in his notebooks was to strengthen his murderous resolve; he was willing to die for his cause. In such a syllogism, the questions of guilt and punishment were already decided.

ELEVEN

Rorschach and Freud

✻ ✻ ✻

ON SUNDAY, MARCH 2, the doctors on the defense team again met at Grant Cooper's office, this time to coordinate their trial testimony. The defense that Cooper had selected for Sirhan, diminished capacity, was a relatively new wrinkle in California criminal law. Cooper wanted to be sure that everyone was up to date.

In the preceding decade, decisions by the California Supreme Court had dramatically modernized the intersection between law and psychiatry. Prior to that the law had remained virtually unchanged for a century, its precedent an 1843 case in which a man named Daniel M'Naghten murdered one Edward Drummond, who happened to be secretary to the British prime minister, Sir Robert Peel. At M'Naghten's trial the defense introduced evidence of the accused's insanity, focusing on his obsession with certain morbid delusions. Lord Chief Justice Tindal, in his charge to the jury, stated, "The question to be determined is whether at the time the act was committed, the prisoner had or had not the use of his understanding, so as to know that he was doing a wrong or wicked act."

The jury returned a verdict of "not guilty, on the ground of insanity."

For one hundred years the knowledge of right and wrong, the "M'Naghten rule," was the test for insanity in criminal law. But modern psychiatry eventually caught up with the concept, and by the 1950s and 1960s there was a string of cases in California that recognized gradations in criminal responsibility. In two of the earliest cases, *People v. Wells* and *People v. Gorshen*, Dr. Bernard Diamond, the psychiatrist that Grant Cooper had selected to anchor the Sirhan team, testified as a witness for the defense. In each case the defense was successful in establishing the relevance of the defendant's state of mind or mental health to his formation of criminal intent.

In 1964 the California Supreme Court heard *People v. Wolff*. In this case a fifteen-year-old boy named Ronald Dennis Wolff had murdered his mother with an ax handle. There was evidence of both prior planning to the murder and evidence that Wolff understood his actions to be wrong, but he had also been diagnosed as "schizophrenic." In reviewing the case the California Supreme Court ruled ". . . there is no question that the defendant had the intent to kill; but . . . the true test must include consideration of the somewhat limited extent to which this defendant could maturely and meaningfully reflect upon the gravity of his contemplated act."

The court reduced Wolff's conviction of first-degree murder to murder in the second degree, and in so doing redefined "premeditation" and established the defense of "diminished capacity."

After reviewing the case law for the doctors gathered in Grant Cooper's office, Emile Berman, who would conduct the questioning during this part of the trial, said that he wanted Dr. Roderick Richardson to lead off for the defense. Dr. Martin Schorr, however, insisted that he should testify first. Richardson voiced no preference. Seeking to keep peace, Berman changed his lineup.

Martin Schorr was a clinical psychologist who screened prison inmates for the county of San Diego. He was on the staff of a half dozen hospitals and clinics in Southern California and was a member of numerous professional organizations, some arcane, including the Rorschach Research Exchange, the Society for Projective Techniques, and the International Transactional Analysis Association. He had testified in court as an expert witness on numerous occasions and had been invited into the case by Russell Parsons in June of the preceding year. All of this was told to the jury on Monday, March 10, 1969, by Dr. Schorr under defense counsel Berman's direction.

Dr. Schorr had examined Sirhan Sirhan in his cell on the thirteenth floor of the Hall of Justice on November 25 and 26. He had administered five tests: the Wechsler Adult Intelligence Scale (commonly known as the "IQ Test"), the Minnesota Multiphasic Personality Inventory (MMPI), the Thematic Apperception Test, the Bender Visual-Motor Gestalt Test, and the Rorschach (inkblot) Examination. All of these tests, according to Schorr, were "projective," something he likened to "a mental X-ray," penetrating the "mask of sanity or conformity and getting down to the root feelings and attitudes of the true personality."

Dr. Schorr diagnosed Sirhan as being in "a paranoid psychosis, a paranoid state." He told the court that his tests revealed a man trapped in "a rigid, persistent, persuasive system of delusional false beliefs," with a personality structure that was in a "high degree of fragmentation." Later, under Berman's questioning, Schorr would agree that prior to the murder, Sirhan was not able to "maturely and meaningfully reflect upon the gravity of his crime."

If Schorr had been able to say all of this in an hour or two, the defense might have benefited from his testimony. But the apparent defense strategy was to overwhelm the jury with expertise. Together, Berman and Schorr plodded through all of Schorr's tests, Sirhan's responses, how they were scored, and what they meant.

"But this is most significant," said Schorr in the midst of one endless explanation. "Here we have forty-one percent—and the total here should always be under ten; less than ten. It's forty-one. So taking the upper limit of the norm, ten, forty-one is four times excessively wrong."

"Four times excessively what?" asked Berman.

"Wrong," replied Schorr. "Four times excessively abnormal. This is what I tried to say earlier; there are no right or wrong things; there are no good or bad. This is bad in terms of the norm, but it is not bad in and of itself; it depends on what kind of value you place on this kind of a personality profile. I haven't even given it a name yet."

As Schorr went on, the members of the jury heard all they cared to about the "psychodynamics of personality adjustment," "F percent columns," "projective psychodiagnostic techniques," "C primes," and "fantasy manifestations." At times Schorr's jargon confused his own lawyers as well as the presiding judge. Schorr said that during the murder he believed Sirhan was in a "dissociate state."

"Dis-associate?" asked Judge Walker

"Dissociate," said Schorr.

"Dis-associate state?"

"Dissociate state."

On Tuesday afternoon, after a tedious day and a half of charts, diagrams, and technical language, assistant district attorney John Howard began his cross-examination of Dr. Martin Schorr. Howard pressed Schorr on his definitions; he asked specific questions about the murder. When did Sirhan go into his dissociate state? What induced that state? At what moment did he emerge from it?

Under this questioning Schorr became uncomfortable. When Howard suggested he expand upon an answer, Schorr replied, "Well, I would rather get through and go home and get back to work." The doctor, it seemed, was beginning to lose his taste for the attention he had craved only days before.

Schorr sensed that he was being stalked, and his answers to Howard's questions were filled with qualifications, always leaving himself a route for retreat. When, on occasion, he was cornered, he would escape down a ladder of words, but at a cost. To the juror listening, Schorr's concepts and theories, difficult to understand to begin with, became less worthy as they changed contour according to the need of the moment. For example, Howard challenged Schorr on his split-personality model of Sirhan.

"Now are you telling us the Hyde and Jekyll Sirhan are the same?" he asked.

"The same person."

"The same personality?"

"The same personality structure."

"I got the impression yesterday they were different; have they merged together?"

"Maybe I better make that more correct. I didn't say that. The personality structure of this individual is essentially that of a paranoid state or paranoid psychosis, and the paranoid state itself doesn't matter whether he is in dissociate reaction or he is a paranoid psychotic, though psychotic disturbances, the paranoid state, personality structure, when in the dissociate reaction or not, it still is there."

When he came to questioning Schorr on his Rorschach Examination, Howard increased the pace. He was superbly prepared and at times seemed to demonstrate a better knowledge of Rorschach than did Schorr. Howard picked particular "inkblots" and asked Schorr how he had come to score them the way he did. Schorr stubbornly held to the idea that the test left little room for interpretation. "He makes his own diagnosis by the way he sees things," he said, referring to Sirhan.

"Well, Doctor," replied Howard, "I am suggesting you made the diagnosis, not he, so I am inquiring what you did." Howard's point was that there was considerable discretion in how a response was scored, yet if only one or two responses were scored differently, the results of the test would change dramatically because the base of the test was so small.

"If you get a different scoring or a different interpretation," insisted Schorr, "you are not going by Rorschach; you are developing something that has no correspondence with the reality of Rorschach."

"All right, Rorschach himself," challenged Howard. "Will you tell me in what book I can find that he ever suggested there was a scoring system for it?"

Schorr had to concede that the scoring systems for the examination had been developed by Rorschach apostles in more recent years, but, he added proudly, "I used the scoring system that is consonant with what is used in the state of California . . . only one of twenty-one possible scoring systems."

"Which one is it?"

"Klopfer."

Schorr might have thought it sounded impressive that there were twenty-one possible scoring systems, but the fact merely supported Howard's contention that the test demonstrated as much about the doctor as it did about the subject.

In the end Howard would catch Schorr in a trap the doctor had set for himself. During cross-examination Schorr had asked to read his report on Sirhan written in December. He had spent days going over his test results for the jury but hadn't had the chance to present his synthesis. Thinking that Schorr wanted only to read it to himself for reference, Howard produced the report. Once he began reading in open court, Fitts objected: "I thought the purpose of this was to refresh the witness's recollection."

"Yes," agreed Judge Walker, "you are not to read it."

Later Schorr would bring up the subject again: "I have to read the report in its entirety in order for the jury or for you to see—"

"I read it," said Howard, cutting him off.

"Well, the jury hasn't heard it," Schorr countered.

"Fine. Can we do it my way?"

"Well, you're asking the questions."

"Fine. Would you like to read the report?"

"If you would like me to, yes."

"I don't want—"

"I would like to, yes."

"Would you? Fine."

At that point Grant Cooper jumped in: "I don't understand. Do you mean read it to himself or read it aloud?"

"I meant aloud," Schorr said, not waiting for Howard to answer. "I meant read it aloud."

"I'm not going to object," Cooper sighed, "if he wants to do it."

Howard then handed Schorr the report and asked him to read two paragraphs from page 3. Perhaps Howard sensed that this was the part Schorr was most eager to read, but when he handed Schorr the report, those paragraphs had already been bracketed. Something was up. Schorr read the paragraphs.

"By killing Kennedy, Sirhan kills his father, takes his father's place as the heir to his mother. The process of acting out this problem can only be achieved in a psychotic, insane state of mind. Essentially the more he railed and stormed, the more he withdrew into her protection.

"He hated his father and feared him. He would never consciously entertain the idea of doing away with him, but somewhere along the line the protecting mother fails her son. The mother finally lets down the son. She whom he loved never kept her pledge, and now his pain has to be repaid with pain. Since the unconscious always demands maximum penalties, the pain has to be death. Sirhan's prime problem becomes a conflict between instinctual demand for his father's death and the realization through his conscience that killing his father is not socially acceptable. The only real solution is to look for a compromise. He does. He finds the symbolic replica of his father in the form of Kennedy, kills him and also removes the relationship that stands between him and his most precious possession, his mother's love."

As soon as Schorr finished, Howard approached and asked, "Who wrote that?"

"I did," Schorr replied.

The characterization of Sirhan's Oedipal manifestations was just the kind of thing the press was hungry for. At recess reporters crowded around Robert Kaiser. Hearing Kaiser give the text of the statement to the reporters, Mary Sirhan, who had been publicly humiliated by the language, approached the defense investigator. "I don't want that. I don't want that," she said. "It's all right if the prosecution gives that to the press, but I don't want you to do it."[1] The prosecution, as it turned out, was only too happy for the press to possess the wording of Schorr's report.

On Monday morning Dr. Schorr was again on the witness stand, and John Howard sought to have the defense psychologist's December 16 report entered into evidence for the prosecution. Before there was time for Schorr to wonder what he was up to, Howard made another offering.

"Your Honor, here we have a book, *Casebook of a Crime Psychiatrist* by James A. Brussel, M.D., and may it be marked People's, next in order, 101."

Brussel's book was not a scholarly text about mental illness, but rather a recently published popular account of gruesome crimes committed by disturbed people. Howard had Dr. Schorr read out loud a passage from Brussel's book taken from a chapter called "The Christmas Eve Killer":

And the more he stormed, the more the mother protected her boy and the more he withdrew into her protecting arms. The boy hated his father, yes—and more important feared him. Therefore, he would never entertain the idea of doing away with the man. . . . Then, somewhere along the line, the protecting mother may have "failed" her boy. She whom he loved never kept her pledge and he began to feel that she really didn't love him. Pain had to be repaid with pain, and since the unconscious always demands the maximum, the pain had to be death.

Now his prime problem was the conflict between instinctual demand for her death and the realization, through his conscience, that killing one's mother is not socially acceptable. The only solution was to look for a compromise. He did. He found a symbolic replica of his mother, killed her, and took valuables that stood for her most precious possession—the thing she denied him, her love.[2]

The similarities of this passage to the one Dr. Schorr had read the previous week from his report were undeniable.

"At the time you prepared your report," questioned John Howard, "were you aware of a book called *Casebook of a Crime Psychiatrist* by James A. Brussel?"

"Oh, yes," replied Schorr. "I read it."

"Doctor, you copied right out of this book, didn't you?"

"I took materials from this book that applied to the paranoid mechanism and I redesigned it to fit in with what I had already said."

Later Grant Cooper would say of this moment that he "could have crawled under a table."[3] Dr. Schorr was beyond help. He now had to play mouse to Howard's cat for as long as the prosecutor wanted the game to go on. And Howard was in no hurry. He had Schorr read other parts of his report and then had him read to the jury the corresponding sections from "The Christmas Eve Killer" or another chapter, "The Mad Bomber." Most of these were virtual matches.

Schorr was forced to admit over and over that he had "borrowed language" from Brussel, and that he had done so to extract the "psychological valuables."

"Doctor," Howard asked, "by the time you graduated from college, did you know how to put quotation marks around or use footnotes to indicate that you had taken from another source?"

Schorr was left with no good answers. "I wanted to make a statement that one would not disbelieve," he said.

It was now March 18; Dr Schorr had taken the stand on March 10 only to numb the jury with a lengthy and pedantic presentation. After that, Howard had skillfully challenged the doctor's methodology. And now, Dr. Martin Schorr's summation of the defendant was shown to be plagiarized.

Bob Greene in *Newsday* described Schorr's last moments at court:

Dr. Martin M. Schorr had the sick look of a man who has just taken a hard right to the belly yesterday when he stepped off the elevator on the first floor of the Hall of Justice at exactly 12:07 P.M. He is just getting used to contact lenses and had to tilt his head backwards to focus correctly before he started walking. A mob of interviewers tried to hold him back. But he kept shaking his head and broke into an awkward trot toward the street door.[4]

Throughout the trial the defense had offered little resistance to the prosecution's case. The promise was that they would fight on ground of their own choosing. This was the first engagement on that ground, and it was a rout.

The unenviable task of following Dr. Schorr onto the witness stand fell to Dr. Orville Roderick Richardson. Like Schorr, Richardson was a clinical psychologist, and like Schorr, Richardson had conducted a number of tests upon Sirhan, including the Rorschach. After he was sworn in, Richardson asked Grant Cooper if he could begin by reading his report.

"It was made by you?" asked Cooper, posing a question that would have seemed silly a few days earlier.

"Yes, it was."

"It is your work product?"

"Yes."

Richardson's report described "a very severe emotional and mental disturbance in a man of bright-normal to superior intellectual potential. He is well informed, shows a good vocabulary, and is capable under conditions of minimal stress of presenting himself in a logical, plausible fashion; however his personality is highly fragile . . . subject to episodes of acute and rapid deterioration." Richardson concluded that Sirhan "could not 'know' the difference between right and wrong, as nondisturbed individuals in this culture would judge this difference."

In presenting the results of his tests, Richardson explained in half an afternoon what it took Dr. Schorr three times as long to cover. From his Wechsler test, Richardson reported a knowledgeable Sirhan, apparently in good contact with reality. "He says that yeast causes dough to rise by fermentation; he gives the population of the United States as two hundred fourteen million; he knows that there are one hundred senators; he says the main theme of the Book of Genesis is Creation; he knows that Homer wrote *The Iliad* . . . and so on."

In the "test of similarities," however, Richardson thought he detected a problem. To the question of how a banana and an orange are alike, Sirhan said, "You have to peel them before you eat them" instead of "They are fruit." He said, "A coat and a dress are alike because they are both worn," instead of "They are clothing." He said, "An ax and a saw . . . cut wood" rather than "They are tools."

To Richardson these responses were "indicative of impairment, some fracture in his intellectual process." But to a member of the jury it may have seemed as though Dr. Richardson was reaching, for Sirhan's answers might well have been considered superior. That a saw and an ax both cut wood is a more distinguishing similarity than the fact that they are both tools. The same would be true of Sirhan's answer concerning the orange and the banana.

David Fitts directed the cross-examination of Richardson, and he began by asking the doctor whether he had an early opinion about Sirhan's psychological makeup, one that was formed before he had examined the defendant.

"Yes," said Richardson, without the equivocation that was present in so many of Dr. Schorr's answers. "I think that there is no denying that the first thing that would pop to mind is a paranoid personality—to a psychologist. Since we know that assassins far back in the United States history are *people* who tend to be paranoid people, and this is what we read in our textbooks, and so the assumption is paranoid."

"Well, given that, it was impossible for you to give a blind test to Mr. Sirhan, isn't that true?"

Fitts then ran Richardson through his Rorschach Examination, exploiting the many differences between his conclusions and those of Dr. Schorr. Fitts pointed to the card where Sirhan saw a dove, and from which Dr. Schorr drew a "violent" inference, but Richardson did not. "He might be talking about some kind of total energy concept," explained Richardson, trying not to dispute the finding of a fellow clinician, ". . . what Klopfer called unmodified relative unsocialized intentional strive personality."

"Well most of the time doves symbolize peace," said Fitts; "isn't that what we are taught?"

"It means different things at different times in different contexts," said Richardson, referring to the test scoring in general. "This is what we mean by the global integration of the Rorschach."

"Doctor, for the sake of brevity, will you agree with me that the psychogram you have illustrated for us . . . doesn't seem to bear any superficial resemblance to the psychogram presented by Dr. Schorr?"

"I would say there are some differences," Richardson conceded, "and those differences may be clinically significant."

Fitts's contention was that many of Sirhan's "abnormal" test responses might be completely normal if cross-cultural considerations were given weight. For example, seeing "a mosque" in one inkblot or a high number of "food responses" might be quite normal for one brought up in Jerusalem in a time of war and food shortage. Fitts also argued that many of Sirhan's "paranoid" responses might be quite reasonable given his present circumstance—incarceration with the knowledge that a great many people harbored malice toward him.

"Now, you have said that based on your diagnosis of him he was, among other things, suspicious, distrustful, felt hostile forces were working against him. . . . Now when you start giving these tests, how do you make allowances for the truth of some of these things which might otherwise be considered, let us say, paranoid characteristics?"

Fitts's question might have been applied to another set of strange responses recorded on Richardson's MMPI test. Sirhan answered "Yes" to the following assertions:

"Evil spirits possess me at times."
"I have had very peculiar and strange experiences."
"When I am with people, I am bothered by hearing very queer things."
"I believe I am being plotted against."

"I have strange and peculiar thoughts."

"I often feel as though things are not real."

"I have periods in which I carry on activities without knowing later what I have been doing."

Just as significantly, Sirhan gave no answer at all (that is, he did not answer "No") to the following:

"I see things or animals or people around me that others do not see."

"Someone has been trying to influence my mind."

"At one or more times in my life, I felt that someone was making me do things by hypnotizing me."

According to Richardson and standard MMPI analysis, these answers all indicate paranoia, yet never did Richardson or any other trial doctor consider a possible literal interpretation. Following the logic proposed by prosecutor David Fitts, if someone really had tried to manipulate Sirhan's mind, these responses wouldn't represent paranoia at all.

Fitts, of course, was not suggesting esoteric explanations, certainly not ones that pointed toward conspiracy. Over and over he offered commonsense rationales for Sirhan's test responses that Richardson had rated as abnormal. Richardson would acknowledge the logic in Fitts's scenarios, but then, like Schorr, he would take refuge in the strictures of the Rorschach scoring.

"Well, I have difficulty sometimes with you, Doctor," Fitts said, finally losing patience. "I mean you admit that something I say is reasonable and logical, but then you go back to the books and the books tell you that . . . it is not right in this case. Is that right?"

"That's correct," replied Richardson. "Training in clinical psychology brings about a certain set of mind toward psychological data. . . . I think that your statements are quite reasonable from the layman's point of view, but not from the clinical psychologist's point of view."

Richardson had not been destroyed as a witness, but throughout the cross-examination Fitts had scored heavily. He made Richardson confess that he tended toward a diagnosis of paranoia before he ever saw Sirhan. Then he made Richardson concede significant differences in his test results from those of Dr. Schorr. Finally, he had gotten the doctor to separate psychology and common sense. In doing this, Fitts had begun to frame in the mind of the jurors, in terms favorable to the prosecution, the choice they would ultimately have to make.

Following Richardson to the witness stand was psychiatrist Dr. Eric H. Marcus, who had been practicing medicine since 1960. Dr. Marcus had been appointed by Judge Alarcon several weeks after the murder to prepare a report on Sirhan's mental state for the defendant's court-appointed attorneys. Marcus had examined Sirhan four times between June and October; he had brought Dr. Richardson into the case, specifically to run tests upon Sirhan.

Dr. Marcus was familiar with the medical/legal intersection. In the year before the Sirhan trial, he had examined ninety accused criminals for the California Superior Court, making recommendations on insanity, diminished capacity, and competency to stand trial. He belonged to all the usual professional fraternities and was the past president of the Southern California Society for Psychiatry and Law and the president-elect of the Medical-Legal Society of Southern California.

Under questioning by Grant Cooper, Marcus was quite willing to say that he had relied heavily on the tests and opinions of others in coming to his own diagnosis. On his extensive list of preparatory reading were two articles, one titled "Presidential Assassination Syndrome" and the other "The Psychiatry of Presidential Assassination." Marcus also told the court that he was present at the February 2 meeting in Cooper's office, attended by Drs. Schorr, Richardson, Diamond, and Pollack. "We reviewed each other's notes," he revealed; "we looked at each other's reports; I think we looked at some case law."

In gathering all of this information Dr. Marcus formed a picture of an emotionally troubled, politically motivated assassin.

"In my opinion," he told the court, ". . . [Sirhan] was mentally disturbed and became increasingly more disturbed during the spring of last year. That is also noted in the psychological tests and I feel that his mental disturbances were relevant and directly related to his political views and his feelings about Robert Kennedy; I feel therefore that he could not meaningfully and maturely think and deliberate on his actions."

"Well now, Doctor," said Cooper, "let me ask you this. A person who is mentally ill, can he not plan?"

"Oh, yes," replied Dr. Marcus.

Cooper here appeared to be setting up to make the primary point for the defense—that a person can form an intent to murder (that is, he can plan the event in advance), but that does not, in itself, under California law, constitute premeditation. Premeditation has to include the capacity for mature and meaningful deliberation.

"And being a person who is mentally ill," Cooper continued, "can he form an intent to kill?"

"Yes."

"And being a person who is mentally ill, can he also entertain malice aforethought?"

"Yes."

"Now will you explain, Doctor, what you mean when you say that in your opinion the defendant could not?"

Could not what? Plan? Form intent? Entertain malice? Premeditate? The prosecution had taken every opportunity to argue that Sirhan had demonstrated some thought process before the murder. Thus, it was crucial for Cooper to separate the legal meaning of premeditation from the more popular concept of premeditation as thinking about something beforehand. He didn't.

In response, Dr. Marcus tried to maintain momentum: "In my opinion Sirhan thought that he was more or less the savior of society. He was going to reorganize or at least destroy the current political leaders. . . . I don't feel he really was competent or capable of having malice within that technical sense."

"All right, now," said Cooper, seemingly still in a fog and unable to formulate a clear question, "was his ability to plan and deliberate and the like?"

"I thought I covered that already," said Marcus, no longer able to keep the ball in the air.

"You covered that in the first answer," Cooper conceded.

The moment was gone. Cooper had managed to throw around the terms "plan," "deliberate," "malice," and "premeditate" in a careless fashion, and in so doing had muddied the very issue that it was crucial for him to make clear.

That Dr. Marcus had relied so heavily on outside opinion in making his diagnosis of Sirhan might have made him vulnerable to cross-examination by David Fitts, but Marcus turned out to be a strong witness when under attack. He was not embarrassed to express an opinion, and he was quite willing to trade sarcastic remarks with the sharp-witted prosecutor. The energy of these exchanges was occasionally reinforced by the sound of thunder, as several fierce storms moved through downtown Los Angeles while Marcus testified. Three times the courtroom darkened, to become momentarily illuminated by the eerie glow of emergency lights.

Under Fitts's questioning, Marcus described to the jury his vision of Sirhan's schizophrenia: "It is as if two people or two personalities exist in him at the same time; a sick personality and a healthy personality. These are not watertight compartments. Sometimes one part, the sick part, may take over; sometimes the healthy part takes over; sometimes they are both doing something at the same time."

Fitts tried to argue that this process might well describe any normal person under stress. He offered himself as an example of "an individual who generally tries to set the image in his household of a kind father, for instance. He puts up with the importunities of his children; he is vexed with them at times; he tries to be tolerant of them; and yet given a sort of a stress situation, such as perhaps having to work on a long trial, he blows up at the kids and does things for which he may be sorry later."

"No, that's not what schizophrenia means," answered Marcus. "What you are describing is sort of a middle-class neurotic phenomenon. 'Schizophrenic' . . . means there is something wrong with the way your brain operates. It's as if—using an analogy—you are using a telephone switchboard and the plugs are crisscrossed."

Fitts asked Dr. Marcus whether Sirhan could premeditate. Marcus replied that he could premeditate about some things but not about things concerning Sirhan's "mistaken political . . . aberrant beliefs."

"What was mistaken about Mr. Sirhan's political beliefs during this time?"

"Well, I think one of his mistakes was assuming that he could start World War Three. That was one mistake.

"He made some other mistakes," continued Marcus. "His mistake was that if he could assassinate President Johnson and the vice president and on down, that somehow he would make a new order of being in the world."

Dr. Marcus might have included in his list of Sirhan's delusions the idea that murdering Robert Kennedy (whose views on the Arab-Israeli confrontation were hardly different from Johnson's, Humphrey's, or Nixon's) would benefit the Palestinian cause.

Fitts was looking to demonstrate that Sirhan was in a rational state before the murder took place, and he had selected a passage from Sirhan's notebook to help him make his point.

"This particular page of the notebook that I am now about to show you"—Fitts held up a piece of paper and advanced toward the witness stand—"can I read it again to you? And ask you questions about it?" Fitts began to read the passage: "'For a person to put his thoughts into words is a difficult task, if you remember that that person is a troglodyte who is therefore more physically inclined than his more urban contemporaries.'

"That's pretty highfalutin language, isn't it, sir?" said Fitts after only one sentence.

"Well, what does 'highfalutin' mean?" replied Marcus. "It sounds crazy to me."

"It sounds crazy to you?" Fitts read on: "'This American politician leads his people to any course that he wants them to—this is possible because the people lack the initiative or are indifferent to the actions of their leaders.'

"Do I make sense?" asked the prosecutor, talking about the cohesion of Sirhan's prose.

"You make face-value sense, I'd say yes."

"There's nothing particularly psychotic or disturbed about that kind of statement, is there?"

"Well, statements aren't psychotic or disturbed," replied Marcus; "only the people who make them."

Fitts continued to read:

" 'Their leaders say, "You have the right to speak against your government and support its changeover—but remember through democratic means only—if otherwise we will blast the hell out of you and besides, you wouldn't want to do anything like that, it is stupid. Just let us run the country, hire our relatives to work for us and earn fat checks. We know what we are doing in Vietnam—we are keeping the economy going through our war spendings. We will keep busy here working on picayunish matters. To impress you all what we really want to do is" [excuse me] "fuck you up, get fat and then quit." '

"Well, that's a criticism of our war policy in Vietnam, isn't it?" crowed Fitts.

"If you want to interpret it that way," replied Marcus.

"Well, that's the way to interpret it, isn't it?"

"Well, that's one way."

"Would you interpret it another way, necessarily?"

"Yes. My interpretation is that this is the ramblings of an angry sick man."

"Why do you say this is rambling?"

"The grammar is off; it varies from rather erudite language to vulgarity; this isn't the type of thing you turn in in a political science course."

Fitts continued: " 'My solution to this type of government, that is to do away with its leaders and declare anarchy the best form of government or no government.'

"—another way of saying anarchy, I take it," said Fitts. "There is some material crossed out here. 'The President-elect is your best friend until he gets in power, then he'—some of this is a little difficult—'then he'—there's something crossed out." Fitts was apparently unfamiliar with how the quotation ended.

"It's interesting," said Marcus, taking over: " 'is your most exploring fucker.' "

Fitts didn't like being pushed aside and began reading from the passage with a deliberate cadence that served only to emphasize the strange language: " 'Suck every drop of blood out of you, and if he doesn't like you, you're dead.'

"Well, now I will agree with you, sir," said David Fitts, no doubt wishing that he had never started with the notebook; "this is not the average composition that might be turned in to a high school English class. At the

same time, the ideas expressed here are expressed by lots of people in criti-
cizing government, are they not?"

" 'The President' . . . sucks 'every drop of blood out' until 'you're dead'?"
said Marcus. "These aren't political views."

Marcus and Fitts sparred for an afternoon, and Marcus parried well. Then
Fitz commenced with his endgame. "Now Sirhan told you, did he not,
that at this time he didn't remember anything more until he was pinned
to a table, is that right?"

"Yes, he told me that."

"You don't believe it, do you?"

"Yes, I believe it."

But if Sirhan were really suffering from amnesia, Fitts asked, why didn't
he show more concern or ask more questions of the police when he was
in custody? Marcus had no answer. A series of skillfully constructed questions by Fitts then forced the doctor to admit that he could not explain
Sirhan's amnesia by way of schizophrenia because the two don't usually
go together, and that he could offer no good explanation for Sirhan's failure to inquire about his arrest.

"Then to go back to the question that I asked you earlier, when
Mr. Sirhan claimed this amnesia in his interview with you, he was lying?"

"That's quite possible," conceded Marcus.

"I think that's all," concluded Fitts.

Marcus's concession was another stunning setback for the defense. The
trial of Sirhan, never a contest of facts, had become a contest of credibility. Were the doctors believable? Was Sirhan? Now one of Sirhan's chief
defenders admitted that it was quite possible Sirhan was lying.

TWELVE

Hypnotic Dreams

�֍ ✖ ✖

WHEN DR. BERNARD Diamond arrived from San Francisco, he was not pleased to learn that Dr. Eric Marcus had admitted in court that Sirhan might be lying about his loss of memory. Marcus felt bad about it and apologized, because it was Diamond who had spent time probing this issue.

Emile Berman called Dr. Diamond to the witness stand the following day, and Berman opened by having the doctor recite his academic credentials. Diamond had graduated from the University of California Medical School in 1939. He had served as a psychiatrist in the army in World War II. He had studied at the Neuropsychiatric Institute of the University of Michigan and at the San Francisco Psychoanalytic Institute. Most noteworthy, since 1964 Dr. Diamond had served on the faculty of the University of California, where he was a full professor in the law school, the medical school, and the school of criminology.

Bernard Diamond was at the very top of his profession. He had served in leadership positions in prestigious psychiatric associations, he had won awards for his achievements in psychiatry and law, and he had served on the California Special Commission on Insanity and Criminal Offenders. The members of the jury might have been impressed by all this, but they weren't given the opportunity. Berman forgot to ask Diamond about his professional credentials.

"Now, then," said the attorney, unaware that he had already lost a wheel, "just tell us where your first examination [of Sirhan] was made and what it consisted of and what, if you are ready to state, what views you had at the time of your first examination."

It was a broad question and Dr. Diamond took advantage. He launched himself into a remarkable monologue that stretched over several days, rarely interrupted by Berman, during which Diamond told the rather extraordinary story of his encounters with Sirhan Sirhan.

Diamond's initial interview with Sirhan took place on December 23. He described Sirhan at that time as being "superficially cooperative."

"It seemed to me that he was more than willing to communicate to me that he had shot and killed Senator Kennedy; that he regarded Senator

Kennedy as an enemy of his people, the Arab people; and that he committed this assassination because he felt it was necessary to prevent Kennedy from fulfilling a promise that Sirhan had heard, or thought that Kennedy had made over television in the previous month."

There was one part of Sirhan's story, however, that Diamond found most peculiar. "I readily observed that he did not describe to me spontaneously either the shooting or the notebook, and I questioned him about these, and he protested to me that he had no memory of the actual shooting and had no memory of the notebook itself."

Sirhan was able to relate to Diamond the chain of events that brought him to the Ambassador Hotel, but his memory stopped with his having coffee with a pretty girl. His recollections began again with his being choked after the shooting. Sirhan could remember being taken away in the police car and being in a room in the police station with various officers talking to him. "Most of all he remembers," Diamond told the court, "the warning of the police officers that he didn't have to say anything, and anything he said would be held against him. . . . He described his state of mind at that time as being one of intense suspicion and that he was confused and he didn't know why he was there."

Besides Sirhan's strange lack of memory of the shooting itself, the other paramount mystery to Dr. Diamond was Sirhan's notebooks. "We talked about the notebooks on many occasions and at no time when he was awake and conscious did he say he had any inconsistent or different attitude about the notebooks, always the same, admitting they were his, but he has no memory of it."

Using photocopies, Diamond and Sirhan would go over the notebooks page by page. "Some of the pages were dated and he would say, 'I can see the date, but I don't remember it; I know this is my writing.' But then he would point to some of the letters that were strange. . . . 'That's not the way I make that letter.' Then he would say, 'Do you think they have had a handwriting expert forge this for me?' And I did respond and say, 'No, I don't think they did.' And then he would say, 'Well, I must have written it.'"

Sirhan's lack of memory of the shooting and the notebooks was disturbing to Diamond. The explanation offered by the prosecution, that Sirhan was lying about this memory loss as some sort of defense ploy, made little sense given that he had admitted to the murder, offered a reason for committing it, and accepted the writing in the notebooks as his own. At that point there was no advantage to claiming a lack of memory. This paradox led Diamond to attempt to probe Sirhan's mind in an effort to discover another answer. The method he used was hypnosis.

Diamond was somewhat apologetic in court about using hypnosis. "I don't go around hypnotizing people every time I see them in my private practice," he offered, "but under special circumstances . . . you have to utilize some kind of shortcut."

Diamond told the court that he decided against using a lie detector because he had little faith in it. His favored tool would have been a "truth serum," like sodium amytal, but because of the slight medical risks involved, that had been ruled out.

Diamond was particularly anxious to make clear that hypnosis is useful in overcoming unintentional mental blocks but that it does not guarantee the truth or accuracy of what a person is saying. "Can a person tell lies under hypnosis?" Diamond asked for the benefit of the jury. "The answer is yes, they can. Hypnosis is especially valuable in overcoming unconscious resistance and unconscious evasions. It is more valuable in doing this than it is in overcoming conscious intentional evasions and intentional lies."

Dr. Diamond hypnotized Sirhan by holding a coin about eight inches from his eyes and giving him repeated suggestions to go to sleep. To the doctor's surprise Sirhan went under quite quickly.

"Sirhan went into a sort of convulsive rage response in which his fists clenched, arms tightened up, and he got a most dramatic contorted rage expression on his face and sobbed. The tears poured down his face. For the first time I had a glimpse or image of a completely different Sirhan than I had previously observed. Never before had Sirhan shown any sign of what I would consider real emotional depth. Everything was a certain superciliousness, a certain superficiality; every other word was 'fuck' or 'shit' and it was a very coarse kind of clever, supercilious, smart-alecky type of approach without any depth to it."

Diamond decided to bring Sirhan back almost right away. "He wakes up kind of startled," he reported. "He looks around and is quite bewildered, obviously quite confused. It takes him a portion of a minute almost to reorient himself. He is immediately suspicious that somebody has done something to him, but he doesn't know what. . . . He would visibly shiver and complain of being cold."

The report of Sirhan's being cold after hypnosis had its parallel during Sirhan's interview by the LAPD's Dr. Marcus Crahan the morning after the postmidnight assassination:

SIRHAN: It's chilly.
CRAHAN: You're cold?
SIRHAN: Not cold.
CRAHAN: Not cold, what do you mean?
SIRHAN: No comment.
CRAHAN: You mean you're having a chill?
SIRHAN: I have a very mild one, yes.[1]

If Diamond had made this connection, he didn't share it with the jury. What was significant to the doctor was Sirhan's posthypnotic attitude.

"He has no recollection of the hypnosis," Diamond told the court. "It is quite totally amnesic; and he denies that the hypnosis has worked. And each and every time that I have ever hypnotized Sirhan, no matter how long he has been asleep, he has denied that I have been successful and feels in some way that he has tricked me. . . . Now I was, of course, impressed with the similarity of his attitude about the hypnosis, hypnotic experience and his loss of memory as far as the shooting was concerned and his repudiation, shall we say, of the notebook."

On January 11 Diamond hypnotized Sirhan and questioned him about the murder of Robert Kennedy. He recounted this conversation for the benefit of the jury:

"Sirhan, did anyone pay you to shoot Kennedy . . . ?

"And he says, 'No,' so I asked, 'Did the Arab government have anything to do with it, Sirhan?'

"And he says, 'No' and I said, 'Did you think this up all by yourself?'

"And he paused for about four seconds and then he said, 'Yes,' and it was clear and unequivocal. . . .

"Are you the only person involved in the Kennedy shooting?

"And he pauses a second or two and he says, 'Yes.'

"I repeat the 'Yes.'

"There was nobody involved at all; why did you shoot Kennedy?

"And he pauses, no answer, and I said, 'Why did you shoot him, Sirhan?'

"And he says, 'The bombers.'

"I said, 'What are the bombers, you mean the bombers to Israel?'

"And he says 'Yes.'

"I said, 'Why did you decide to shoot Kennedy?' And I repeated that several times because there was no response and finally he said, 'I don't know.' "

The pauses that Dr. Diamond noted before some of Sirhan's answers are sometimes referred to as "blocking." This is an indication that the hypnotized subject may be giving a false response. Either by intention of the subject or through hypnotic instruction, the true answer is "blocked" and a substitute answer is offered in its place. The hesitation represents the time taken by this mental process.

Though Diamond drew no conclusions from these pauses, the prosecution, a little while later, referred to this blocking as evidence of Sirhan's insincerity. What the prosecution failed to mention was that this blocking occurred on questions where Sirhan was asked whether anyone else was involved in the crime. If these hesitations were blocking, then the implication is that Sirhan was lying about acting alone or was hypnotically influenced to say that he acted alone. The prosecution was surely not advocating either of these possibilities.

On January 26, Dr. Diamond, working with Dr. Pollack, attempted to take a hypnotized Sirhan, step-by-step, through the tragic events at the Ambassador Hotel. By any measure the taped session was bizarre. As the doctors attempted to move a hypnotized Sirhan toward a simulation of murder, Dr. Pollack tried to provoke his subject. "He can't send the bombers," he said. "You're not going to let him, are you, Sirhan?" Sirhan just groaned and breathed heavily. The session continued:

> DIAMOND: Can you see Kennedy coming? . . . Now what do you see, Sirhan, you're back in the kitchen, now what do you see?
> SIRHAN [under hypnosis, breathing heavily, whispers]: You son of a bitch!
> DIAMOND [ellipsis points indicate short pauses]: You're talking to Kennedy now, huh? . . . He's coming. . . . Reach for your gun, Sirhan. Where is your gun? . . . Where is your gun? Reach for it. [Lots of heavy breathing by Sirhan]. Reach for your gun . . . Sirhan! . . . Take your gun out and shoot it. . . . Who are you shooting, Sirhan? . . . Who are you shooting? . . . You're shooting Kennedy now, huh?[2]

In their efforts to get Sirhan to remember the murder, Diamond and Pollack became positively clumsy in their use of hypnosis. The session was not a skillful search for recollection; it bordered on being a memory implant.

> POLLACK [speaking very slowly; ellipsis points indicate short pauses]: Sirhan, you have wanted to remember the shooting of Kennedy. . . . You wanted to remember your shooting him. . . . Now you'll remember shooting him. . . . You'll remember taking the gun out, pulling the trigger again . . . and again . . . and again. . . . You'll remember all of it. . . . All of this will get clearer and clearer and you'll remember it all? . . . You'll remember it all.

But as the tape of the session reveals, the forces against Sirhan's remembering were so strong as to resist even this hypnotic suggestion. Diamond asked the now-awake Sirhan where he kept his gun. A distressed Sirhan said that he couldn't remember.

> DIAMOND [getting annoyed]: Five minutes ago, Sirhan, you showed me where the gun was. The gun was right here in your belt. . . . You showed us how, you reached for the gun and you showed us how you pulled the trigger. Try to remember.[3]

Sirhan's performance in this hypnosis session was not illuminating. He had mostly sweated and groaned. But the doctors had seen him pull his trigger finger when they told him to shoot, and he had reached into his pants when they told him to reach for his gun. This was, at least, some new information. But Dr. Diamond was still troubled.

"A problem which still was unresolved as far as I was concerned," he told the jury, "was an explanation of the notebook. I felt very dissatisfied with Sirhan's explanations, which were essentially no explanation at all. He denied the notebook in a very odd, peculiar kind of way. He admitted the notebook was his, he admitted most of the time that the writing must be his, but he had no recollection about how it happened and couldn't give me an explanation as to how any part of the notebook came about . . . so it occurred to me that it was possible that at least parts of the notebook might have been written during one of those Rosicrucian correspondence exercises in front of the mirrors, and I decided to experiment with this."

On February 1, Bernard Diamond once again hypnotized Sirhan. Again, he invited Seymour Pollack to sit in on the session. As Diamond explained to the court, his primary problem in hypnotizing Sirhan was that Sirhan would go under too deeply, making it difficult to gain information from him. It was Diamond's idea to try to induce a light trance. To do this he counted backward from five rapidly, while trying to keep Sirhan alert. This seemed to have the effect of not hypnotizing Sirhan at all. As the exercise began, Dr. Diamond concluded that Sirhan was "quite awake." He then provided Sirhan with a pencil and a piece of paper and commanded him to write his name.

"So he proceeded to write his name at the top of the page here, 'Sirhan B. Sirhan,' and then started to write it again, 'Sirhan B. Sirhan,' and by the time he finished the first line . . . it was quite evident that Sirhan had now sort of flipped automatically into a hypnotic trance.

"He continued to write his name, 'Sirhan B. Sirhan, Sirhan B. Sirhan,' and this sort of astonished me and I decided to just allow him to write. He wrote like a robot writes, in a stiff mechanical way, his eyes fixed to the paper, and writing mechanically, taking about thirty seconds to complete a line."

Diamond then told the jury how he asked Sirhan a series of questions concerning the murder:

"Is Kennedy dead?
"And he stared and he wrote 'No, no, no.'
"Is Kennedy alive?
"And I repeated that and he wrote 'Yes, yes, yes,' and that is an example, I might say, of the hypnosis that people, well, they sometimes don't say the truth, but they say what they feel inside of them. . . .
"Does Kennedy talk to you?
"And he writes 'No, no, no.'
"Did anyone tell you to shoot Kennedy?
"And he writes 'No, no, no.'
"Did anyone give you money to shoot Kennedy?
"And he writes 'No, no, no.'
"Was anybody with you when you shot Kennedy?
"And he writes 'No, no, no.'
"And then I say, 'Who was with you when you shot Kennedy?' Sometimes we ask them identical questions, but just in a little different form. . . .
"He writes 'Girl, the girl, the girl.'
"Do you know the girl's name? and he sort of groans and I say, 'Write out the name of the girl.' And there is no response and he just groans."

When Sirhan was asked to write about Robert Kennedy, his response was very similar to some of the entries found in his notebook: "Robert F. Kennedy, Robert F. Kennedy, RFK, RFK, RFK, RFK must die, RFK must die, RFK must die, RFK must die, RFK must die, RFK must die, RFK must die, RFK must die, RFK must die."
In response to Diamond's questions, Sirhan told very much the same story he had told when conscious: he didn't intend to shoot Robert Kennedy; he had gone to the Ambassador Hotel by chance; no one had put him up to the job or helped him along the way. But when it came to the subject of the writing in his notebook, Sirhan appeared to confirm the very thing Diamond had suspected. The questions and answers went as follows:

"Is this crazy writing?"
"Yes, yes, yes, yes, yes, yes, yes, yes."
"Are you crazy?"
"No, no, no, no."
"Why are you writing crazy?"
"Practice, practice, practice, practice, practice."

"Practice for what?"

"Mind control, mind control, mind control, mind control."

"Who wrote your notebooks?"

"I, I, I, I, I."

"Were you hypnotized when you wrote the notebook?"

"Yes, yes, yes."

"Who hypnotized you when you wrote the notebook?"

"Mirror, mirror, my mirror, my mirror, my mirror, my mirror, my mirror."

The next experiment was to wake Sirhan up and see his reactions. Shown what he had written, Sirhan claimed it to be a foreign document.

"This is not Sirhan," he claimed.

When Diamond pointed out that maybe the passages in his notebook were written the same way, he replied, "Are you bugging me?"

"This is what made him feel crazy," Dr. Diamond told the court.

Though the doctor may have proved to his own satisfaction how the notebook pages came into being, he still had questions. "It is customary to simplify the hypnotic procedure to give a posthypnotic suggestion as to how they will be hypnotized the next time," Diamond testified. "Later developments showed that he learned this very well, which made me suspicious, because usually in my experience it is the exception rather than the rule that people pick this up so readily. It requires a certain kind of training period."

During Sirhan's next hypnotic session on February 8, Dr. Diamond ran another test on Sirhan.

"While he was asleep," Diamond told the court in late March, "I told him that when he woke up, in a short while after he woke up, that I will take my handkerchief out of my pocket, which I did, and wipe my forehead, and that when I do that, that would be a signal for him to go over and ask the deputy sheriff what the weather is like outside.

"So then I woke him up and again he had no recollection of having been asleep, but after a few minutes of conversation I took out my handkerchief and he sort of looked around and he walked over and asked the sheriff about the weather.

"He wanted to know if it was raining so I told him, 'Sirhan, who told you to do that?' And he looked around and startled, said, 'No one.'

"I said, 'Well, I told you to do that just five minutes ago when you were hypnotized. . . .'

"He said, I forgot his exact words but, 'You are bugging me; I thought up the question about the weather.'"

Sirhan continued to disbelieve Diamond, so the doctor offered to do another demonstration and tape-record the session for Sirhan's enlightenment.

Robert Kaiser was in the room watching and gave the authors this description of what happened:

"Diamond put Sirhan under hypnosis and gave him a suggestion: 'Sirhan, when you awake you will feel normal, but when I take out my handkerchief you will climb the bars of your cell.' Ten minutes later Sirhan is climbing the bars like a monkey, and we look over and Diamond is blowing his nose. And he says, 'Sirhan, watcha doin' up there?' 'Oh, I'm just getting some exercise.' Anyone in that situation will give a plausible explanation, but it won't be the right one; we all knew he'd been programmed."

This demonstration impressed Kaiser, who already had suspicions that perhaps Sirhan had been hypnotized by a third party and put up to the crime. Kaiser discussed this possibility with Diamond, but Diamond dismissed the whole idea as "a crackpot theory."[4] Diamond believed that Sirhan had performed the murder while in a trance all right; the trance explained so many of the outstanding questions of the case. But Diamond believed that the trance was self-induced, and as he delivered his summation in court, he tried to explain this concept to the jury.

"With absolutely no knowledge or awareness of what was actually happening in his Rosicrucian and occult experiments, [Sirhan] was gradually programming himself, exactly like a computer is programmed by its magnetic tape, programming himself for the coming assassination. In his unconscious mind there existed a plan for the total fulfillment of his sick, paranoid hatred of Kennedy and all who might want to help the Jews. In his conscious mind there was no awareness of such a plan or that he, Sirhan, was to be the instrument of assassination.

"But he was confused, bewildered, and partially intoxicated. The mirrors in the hotel lobby, the flashing lights, the general confusion—this was like pressing the button which starts the computer. He was back in his trances, his violent convulsive rages, the automatic writing, the pouring out of incoherent hatred, violence and assassination. Only this time it was for real and this time there was no pencil in his hand, this time there was only the loaded gun.

"I agree that this is an absurd and preposterous story, unlikely and incredible. I doubt Sirhan himself agrees with me as to how everything happened. Sirhan prefers to deny his mental illness, his psychological disintegration, his trances, his automatic writing and his automatic shooting. . . . Sirhan would rather believe that he is the fanatical martyr who by his noble act of self-sacrifice has saved his people and become a great hero. He claims to be ready to die in the gas chamber for the glory of the Arab people.

"However, I see Sirhan as small and helpless, pitifully ill, with a demented, psychotic rage, out of control of his own consciousness and his own actions, subject to bizarre dissociated trances in some of which he programmed himself to be the instrument of assassination, and then in an almost accidentally induced twilight state he actually executed the crime, knowing next to nothing as to what was happening. . . . I am satisfied that this is how Sirhan Bishara Sirhan came to kill Senator Robert F. Kennedy on June 5, 1968."

Dr. Diamond had taken the witness stand on Friday, March 21. It was Wednesday the 26th when prosecutor David Fitts began his cross-examination. Fitts wanted to dent Dr. Diamond's conclusion that Sirhan's mental problems began with his traumatic childhood in Jerusalem. To do so he challenged the testimony of Sirhan's mother, Mary.

"Don't you suppose," said the prosecutor to Diamond, "that Mrs. Sirhan, having her son in trouble, has some disposition to magnify the horrors of war and the effect on her son in hopes that they will have some impact on this jury and on your psychiatric opinion?"

"Sir," replied Diamond, "I don't think it is possible to magnify the fact of the horrors of war on children."

"Well, it depends, of course, on what they actually were, isn't that true?"

"I think I am familiar with war," said Dr. Diamond, "what the war conditions were. I went through five years of a world war and I have a family—for example, my daughter and granddaughter live in Israel and my son lives there, and I am fully aware of what conditions are. I don't feel they were exaggerated."

David Fitts, however, was most interested in attacking Sirhan's credibility. "The story that he gave you was obviously a structured one," he asserted to Dr. Diamond. ". . . Sirhan had access to newspapers, talked with his lawyers, talked with investigators, knew what he was accused of doing, knew that he was facing a trial for a capital offense. . . . He had adopted an attitude of what he was going to say and what he was not going to say."

"Well, no, that was the difficulty," replied Diamond, not giving ground. "He was talking in ways which to me seemed very strange. He was admitting information which certainly would not help him, and was concealing information which might help him; so there seems to be no logical rhyme or reason to his stories."

Undaunted, Fitts tried again. "Well, isn't it rather usual for, let us say, just a sociopathic personality, a man who commits a crime and gets himself in jail, to concoct a story that might not please everybody, because he thinks it's the only way to help himself?"

"Sirhan had done just the opposite of that," Diamond protested. "He had concocted a story which couldn't possibly help him."

"In view of what? How couldn't it help him?"

"Because Sirhan was quite prepared to admit to me or anybody who would ask him that he killed Senator Kennedy; that he hated Senator Kennedy; and that he had done this to prevent Senator Kennedy from getting elected to the presidency and sending fifty bombers to Israel. This he would tell to anyone who would listen. This did not impress me as a sociopath who is inclined to help himself by concealing his crime. These are the things that he would talk about. What he wouldn't talk about were all these things which were related to his psychological state, and what I regarded as mental illness."

This was a pattern that Dr. Diamond recognized. In 1956 he had written an article on the subject titled "The Simulation of Sanity."[5] "Though most laypeople worry about whether a legal defendant is faking insanity," he said, summarizing his article, "it is my point that it is infinitely more often common that legal defendants fake sanity than they fake insanity."

This was not a concept that David Fitts was going to accept. He still wanted to show that Sirhan was covering up for a crime that he had planned in advance. "Did you know," he asked the witness, "that at some time after the death of Martin Luther King on a Wednesday, that Sirhan in a political discussion with a trash collector named Alvin Clark had said in substance, 'Why are you going to vote for him? I am going to kill that SOB,' or words to that effect? Was that Sirhan in a dissociative state speaking or was that the usual Sirhan speaking?"

"I don't believe he said that, sir," Diamond answered.

"Well, the witness testified to it from the stand," said Fitts, as though this would be the final proof.

"I think the witness was incorrect."

"Is that a polite word for saying that the witness was lying?"

"No," said Diamond, although Fitts had accurately characterized his response. "I prefer to believe Sirhan."

"Why do you prefer to believe Sirhan?"

"Because Sirhan's information is consistent with a large number of other things that he told me. This particular witness's story is not consistent. I think it is quite possible that the witness was not correct."

Fitts wasn't done with this point. "All right. You tell us, then, that he wanted to have himself pictured as a political assassin, that he is one who had consciously decided to do it. Well, why do you suppose Sirhan would have quarreled with the testimony of Alvin Clark? Wouldn't that be right up his street?"

What Fitts seemed to be willing to overlook was that, up his street or not, perhaps Sirhan was angry at Clark, because he hadn't made any such threat in his presence. The police had been very quick to ascribe desire for attention to anyone who had testimony that they didn't agree with. They may have been less discriminating with Alvin Clark.

On June 5, the afternoon after the murder, the *Los Angeles Herald Examiner* published excerpts from an interview with Alvin Clark. In it the trash collector said that Sirhan was "very prejudiced against white people." Clark also said that Sirhan did not drink, never talked about girls, and "once told me he hated Kennedy." But, oddly, it was not reported that Clark said Sirhan had threatened to kill Kennedy.[6] Since Clark was apparently not shy about talking, the absent murder threat in his first rendition is reason to suspect that it was added afterward.

Even with Clark's tarnished testimony, the prosecution was severely lacking when it came to evidence of Sirhan's mature and meaningful deliberation, something they needed if Sirhan was to be convicted of first-degree murder. As a result the prosecutors focused on Sirhan's lack of memory: make the jury believe this is the central question; get them to disbelieve Sirhan, and the case is won.

"Did Sirhan have true amnesia at the time he shot Kennedy?" Fitts asked Dr. Diamond.

"Yes, I think this was a true amnesia at the time he shot Kennedy."

"If Sirhan was truly forgetful of the incidents relative to the immediate killing of Senator Kennedy, should he not have inquired of the police why he was in custody and what he had done?"

This was a question that the prosecution asked over and over again. They seemed to be offering it to the jury as the key to understanding Sirhan's trickery. It was the question that Fitts had used to bully Dr. Marcus, but Dr. Diamond had some expertise in this area, and he wasn't about to be pushed around.

"That's not how dissociative states respond to police apprehension," he answered. "I have some familiarity with dissociative states as they are arrested and what happens to them, and they do not, like in the Hollywood movies, look around with a blank expression on their faces and say, 'Where am I?'

"I have never seen an authentic case of amnesia or dissociation or hysteria or schizophrenia behave that way. That's Hollywood stuff. The typical kind of behavior is a sort of on-guard, cautious attitude of looking around, being very reserved; kind of looking around to see what people's reactions are; to kind of figure it out, being evasive, and sometimes very gradually, over a period of hours and hours and hours, a slow restoration to memory of kind of what is going on. From my study of Sirhan's behavior following his being taken to jail, I think it is very characteristic of this type of slow emergence from a state of dissociation."

Dr. Diamond was unlike the doctors who had testified before him. He had not tried to penetrate the mysteries of Sirhan with inkblots or personality exams. He focused instead on the facts of the case. He overcame his initial disbelief of Sirhan's claims of not remembering the shooting or the notebooks and began to search for explanations. He had hypnotized Sirhan on eight occasions and made some interesting discoveries.

He discovered, first of all, that Sirhan was very easy to hypnotize. He discovered signs that Sirhan had been hypnotized before, perhaps many times. While Sirhan was under hypnosis, Dr. Diamond had gotten him to write in a manner that was strangely similar to some of the writing in his notebook, and when he was awakened, Sirhan denied any familiarity with the work that he had just produced.

Diamond had also demonstrated that Sirhan was very susceptible to posthypnotic suggestion. He had Sirhan do things in his normal awake state that he had been instructed to perform while under hypnosis, with no awareness that he had been programmed. He also noted that Sirhan, after he had been brought out of his trance, would shiver and complain of being cold. At the same time Sirhan would be confused and suspicious, with no memory of what had taken place and a strong inclination not to believe that he had been asleep at all.

The prosecution maintained Sirhan's story was "concocted." Dr. Diamond's reasoning was the clearest response yet to that charge. It made no sense for Sirhan to be lying about his lack of memory, Diamond asserted, since he had already, very willingly, admitted all that could be damaging to him.

Dr. Diamond also presented a logical explanation for Sirhan's conduct in police custody. According to the doctor, the first thing Sirhan heard as he began to emerge from his trance was the police warning that anything he said would be used against him. From his professional experience, Diamond also offered a more realistic view of how a person in such a situation would be likely to act, as opposed to the "Where am I?" stereotype being pushed forward by the prosecution.

All of this led Diamond to conclude that Sirhan had been in a hypnotic trance when he had murdered Robert Kennedy. But how did he get into that trance? Was there some outside direction? Diamond had repeatedly asked Sirhan this very question when he was under hypnosis. The answer was always negative. Diamond apparently attributed little significance to the "blocking" which seemed to occur whenever Sirhan was asked questions of this nature. As Robert Kaiser noted, Diamond did not seem inclined to favor conspiracy in any case.

But what would Dr. Diamond have concluded if he had known that there was a significant body of evidence that more than one gun was fired in the hotel pantry the night of the murder? What would he have thought if it were demonstrated to him that the wounds inflicted on Robert Kennedy appeared to come from a direction, range, and angle inconsistent with Sirhan's position relative to Kennedy? Or if he had known that over two dozen apparently reliable witnesses had seen Sirhan with a mysterious woman before the murder, a woman who was then seen running from the hotel laughing and bragging that she and another had killed Kennedy, and that the police had used unsavory tactics to hide, isolate, ignore, frighten, or discredit these witnesses?

Dr. Diamond may well have reconsidered his conclusions had he known about this hidden information. Sirhan's apparent lack of memory and evidence of hypnotic trance are open to more sinister interpretation when laid beside evidence suggesting other participants. But Diamond was not aware of this evidence due to the overzealous or criminal actions of some members of the police and the lack of diligence on the part of Sirhan's defense attorneys.

Unlike the attorneys at Sirhan's table, Dr. Diamond was not embarrassed by Sirhan's lack of memory. He sought to explain it, and in the end did so quite rationally by concluding that Sirhan had been in a trance. But without all the facts, and lacking the proper support from the defense attorneys, Diamond concluded that Sirhan unknowingly programmed himself to murder Robert Kennedy and unknowingly programmed himself to forget his crime—a feat regarded as next to impossible by leading experts in the field of hypnosis. His entire testimony teetered on this precarious point. Fitts was well aware of this, and although Diamond had probably bested the smart prosecutor in their major points of dispute, Fitts knew how to tip the wagon over with a carefully chosen last question.

"Doctor, in your summation which you read aloud you said, with reference now to the whole diagnosis I believe of Sirhan, you said, 'I agree that this is an absurd and preposterous story, unlikely and incredible.' You said that, didn't you?"

"Yes, I did say it."

"Who were you agreeing with?"

"I agreed with the world."

"I think that's all I have."

The defense attorneys understood that Dr. Diamond's choice of words in his summation was damaging to his own conclusions. After recess that afternoon, it was decided that Diamond would prepare a statement in an effort to clarify to the jury what he meant by these words. He would read the statement in response to a question posed by Emile Berman the next day on redirect examination.

Although Dr. Diamond invested time in formulating his answer, Emile Berman apparently did little to construct what should have been a simple question. It was said that Berman often drank heavily in the evening when he retired back at the Ambassador Hotel, and if he did so that night, it would go a long way to explaining his utterly incompetent performance the next day.

The following morning, with Dr. Diamond on the witness stand, Emile Berman didn't ask his prepared question, because he hadn't prepared one. Instead he read aloud Diamond's *entire* summation. When he was done, he asked, "Now in that context, that is what you really referred to when you were on the witness stand?"

"Well, I am sorry, Mr. Berman," Diamond replied. "I'm not quite clear as to your question."

"What I am talking about is the sentence that says, 'I agree this is an absurd and preposterous story, unlikely and incredible.' That is what I am referring to."

Berman still hadn't asked a proper question. Diamond had no choice but to try to make sense out of it for him. He read his prepared statement, in which he admitted that the Sirhan case raised serious problems of clinical proof and credibility:

"When I first had personal contact with Sirhan I was prepared for the usual case of a paranoid fanatic who dreams of grand delusions. . . . I was not, however, prepared for what I discovered, these stirring instances of hypnosis, dissociate trances, and mystical occultism . . . and that type of psychological thinking that could have resulted in the death of Senator Kennedy and affected the destinies of the entire world."

Following Diamond's statement Berman fumbled about. He began to read a very long passage from the court transcript that appeared to have no bearing on what was being talked about and no point of its own. When he finished he said, "I don't know whether I have discussed this with you," and he began once again to read Dr. Diamond's entire summation. Once again the jury heard the words "I agree that this is an absurd and preposterous story." They then heard all the rest that had been read to them by Berman only a short time ago. Finally, in frustration, Fitts broke in. "If the Court please—"

"I am coming to my question," said Berman before Judge Walker could intervene. "What I want to know is when you started that to the extent I have read it, 'I would agree that this is an absurd and preposterous story, unlikely and incredible,' what were you referring to?"

Diamond was stunned. Clearly Berman had gotten lost in his notes and had somehow forgotten, just like Cooper had done with Dr. Marcus, that he had just asked that very question. Confusion prevailed.

"Objection," said Mr. Howard. "That has been asked and answered."

"What?" said Berman.

"It was asked and answered by the prosecution," said Judge Walker.

"I thought he started out this morning with a question from the same page," Howard corrected, "and an answer read that was prepared last night."

"I didn't know that the objection 'asked and answered' was a proper objection on cross-examination," offered Cooper.

"I don't think this is cross," said Howard.

"I mean redirect. Pardon me."

"Overruled!" said Walker.

Berman then asked Dr. Diamond a third time to explain why he characterized his explanation of the crime as "absurd and preposterous."

"Its unlikely nature, Mr. Berman," Diamond replied coolly, clearly not pleased by this latest gaffe by the defense attorney. "To me this is a script which would never be acceptable in a class B motion picture; and yet these are, I think, the realities of the psychiatric findings."

"If Your Honor please," said Berman. "We have concluded our redirect."

Bernard Diamond climbed down from the stand. He had been brought back to make a final impression on the jury, but whatever enlightenment the doctor was to impart was certainly overshadowed by Emile Berman's inept performance. This was not a good ending, particularly for someone who had been the defendant's most important witness.

THIRTEEN

Betrayal

✴ ✴ ✴

O<small>N</small> F<small>RIDAY</small>, M<small>ARCH</small> 28, the prosecution began its rebuttal. "With the Court's permission," announced John Howard, "the first order of business would center around bringing into this court, and asking permission to show, an approximately twelve-minute film taken at the speech of Senator Kennedy immediately preceding the assassination." Howard told the court that the purpose for showing the film would be to illustrate that nothing in Robert Kennedy's victory address could have triggered Sirhan's supposed dissociate state.

Grant Cooper frowned. Realizing that the film would only rekindle in the minds of the jurors the horror of the murder, he objected. The defense, he said, had not asserted that Sirhan had even heard Robert Kennedy's speech. Judge Walker quickly ruled in Cooper's favor, holding that the film's probative value was well exceeded by its inflammatory possibilities.

After Walker's denial, the prosecution called several witnesses. Adolph Melendres and Frank Patchett were both sergeants in the LAPD; George Murphy was an investigator for the district attorney's office. All three had spent time with Sirhan the morning after the murder, and they gave support to the prosecution's contention that Sirhan was in possession of all his faculties by variously describing their prisoner as intelligent, calm, coherent, lucid, and completely sober.

Later in the morning, Judge Walker interrupted the proceedings: "Ladies and gentlemen of the jury, I have the sad news to tell you—I have the sad news to tell you that President Eisenhower has died. . . . I am going to ask everybody to observe at this moment one minute of silence."

Dwight Eisenhower, in his retirement, had become a personification of the 1950s. He had led the nation in a world of new and fearsome perils—ICBMs, Quemoy and Matsu, the hydrogen bomb—but Eisenhower's America, with some exceptions, was confident and unified. In the decade since the general left office, however, deep divisions had developed along lines of generation and race. Images of this fracturing were present in the news every day, and they would soon appear at the Sirhan trial in the text of the final arguments.

The war in Vietnam was paramount, and the previous month had not been a good one. On March 7, it was reported that 453 Americans had lost their lives in the first week of a new push by the enemy. This exceeded American losses in the first week of the Tet Offensive a year earlier.

Several weeks later tens of thousands of antiwar protestors marched up New York's Sixth Avenue. Many wore armbands that read "33,000," signifying the number of Americans already killed in the war. The actual figure that week was *33,641,* which, for the first time, exceeded the American war dead in Korea.

Coalescing around war and race issues, disobedience was spreading across the nation, the host venues often being universities. In Boston four hundred police had to be called in to expel three hundred student protestors occupying administration buildings at Harvard. At Columbia, radical students seized university buildings, causing trapped professors to flee out windows. At Cornell, one hundred members of the university's Afro-American Society took control of the student-union building, where fighting broke out between the blacks and members of a prominent university fraternity.

In New Orleans a conflict of another sort was being fought. As Jim Garrison's prosecution of Clay Shaw for the murder of President Kennedy neared conclusion, attorney Dean Andrews was called to the stand. Andrews had originally claimed that a Clay Bertrand, a purported Shaw alias, had called after the assassination and asked him to defend Lee Harvey Oswald. Now on the witness stand, he maintained that no such thing had ever happened. Andrews claimed that he had made up the story while he was under sedation and the influence of drugs in a New Orleans hospital.

"So you deliberately lied to the Warren Commission?" challenged assistant district attorney James Alcock.

"I didn't deliberately lie," the short and overweight Andrews replied, to the mirth of some onlookers. "My mouth got ahead of my brain. You can call it a lie if you want to, I call it huffin' and puffin'."[1]

In the end, the jury believed DA Jim Garrison was the one "huffin' and puffin'." In less than an hour they acquitted Clay Shaw. Garrison responded quickly by filing perjury charges against Shaw and Andrews, claims that were ultimately dismissed as being "frivolous" and "vindictive." The district attorney also publicly charged that the case had been sabotaged and that a member of the prosecution had been secretly slipping information to the opposition. In response to these new charges, the American Bar Association hinted that they might want to investigate Garrison's "motives."

One week after Clay Shaw's acquittal, another tangled case was brought to an adjudicated resolution. In Memphis, Tennessee, James Earl Ray pleaded guilty to the murder of Dr. Martin Luther King, Jr.

During the proceedings, both the prosecutor, P. M. Canale, and Ray's flamboyant lawyer, Percy Foreman, told the court that they possessed no evidence of conspiracy: "There have been rumors going around that Mr. James Earl Ray was a dupe, a fall guy, or a member of a conspiracy," said Mr. Canale. "We have no proof other than Dr. Martin Luther King was killed by James Earl Ray and James Earl Ray alone."[2]

In a stunning repudiation of this assertion, however, the confessed assassin stood up in court and declared that his plea of guilty did not mean that there was no conspiracy. Judge W. Preston Battle then asked Ray if he still wanted to plead guilty. Ray said yes. The proceedings ended with the judge sentencing Ray, as had been arranged, to ninety-nine years in prison.

In an interview after Ray's sentencing, Judge Battle admitted that he had been "puzzled" about many aspects of the case, but he defended his decision to accept Ray's plea. "I was convinced then and I am convinced now," he said, "that the trial would have muddied our understanding of the substantial evidence which established Ray as the killer."[3]

A week later the case took another strange turn. James Earl Ray wrote to Judge Battle from his prison cell in Nashville asking to have his plea bargain overturned. Ray had retained a new lawyer, J. B. Stoner, who quickly issued a statement saying that his client was innocent and was "pressured into a guilty plea."[4]

Battle would not have time to act on Ray's request. On Monday, March 31, he was found at his desk in Shelby County Criminal Court, dead of an apparent heart attack. The case was not reopened.

Those close to Dr. King also made statements pointing to conspiracy. Ralph Abernathy, King's successor at the Southern Christian Leadership Conference, asked for continued pressure upon the government "until justice is meted out to all of the perpetrators."[5] The victim's widow, Coretta Scott King, agreed. "This plea of guilty," she said, "cannot be allowed to close the case or to end the search for the many fingers which helped pull the trigger."[6]

The day Judge Battle died in his Memphis office, Dr. Seymour Pollack took the stand as the prosecution's principal rebuttal witness against Sirhan. Dr. Pollack had been brought into the case by the district attorney's office a few weeks after Robert Kennedy's murder, when it became apparent that Sirhan's defense options were mainly psychiatric. Pollack seemed an excellent choice. A forensic psychiatrist who headed the Division of Psychiatry and Law at the Los Angeles County–University of Southern California Medical Center, he was also a consultant for a number of state and county courts.

Recall that as part of Grant Cooper's strategy to gain a plea bargain, Pollack had been given unprecedented access to the defendant and had interviewed Sirhan on eight occasions the last two weeks of January. Pollack had also attended the February 2 meeting in Grant Cooper's office. During that session Pollack maintained that he hadn't come to any conclusions on Sirhan's condition, but several days later he wrote a memo to District Attorney Younger filled with conclusions. In the letter to Younger, Pollack seemed to play both sides of the fence, but in the end he favored the idea that Sirhan was mentally ill and that this illness played a role in the assassination.

When the plea bargain failed, the district attorney's office was not altogether sure how much benefit Pollack would be as a prosecution witness. Would he be called to testify? On March 21, in open court, Grant Cooper asked John Howard what his intentions were.

"Are you going to call Dr. Pollack?"

"Yes," answered Howard.

"You are going to call him definitely?"

"Yes."

"The only reason I ask the question is that if you are not going to call him, we would call him."

Dr. Seymour Pollack, however, took the stand as a witness for the prosecution on March 28. A short man with a round, florid face, Pollack began, as he had done in the past, by seeming to argue both sides of the case.

"I consider Sirhan mentally disturbed," he told the court under Mr. Howard's direction, "but in summation I believe the assassination of Senator Robert Kennedy was triggered by political reasons."

A month earlier Emile Berman had entertained his colleagues with a parody of Pollack's two-faced diagnosis. "He can think pretty good about killing," chirped Berman, pretending to be Pollack, "but, generally speaking, he's a nut!"[7]

Now, on the witness stand, Pollack appeared to earn this derision once again. Much of what he said sounded contradictory. For example, Pollack said that Sirhan "has clinical signs and symptoms of psychosis. He has, for example, many delusions," but "there was nothing whatever that . . . indicated at any time that Sirhan was clinically psychotic," and "it's my belief that Sirhan's ideas, attitudes . . . were not evidence of psychotic delusional thinking."

According to Pollack, Sirhan committed murder for political reasons. "I believe that Sirhan focused on Senator Robert Kennedy as an individual who should die," he said in court, "not only because of the Kennedy promise to give Israel the jet bombers that would cause the death to thousands of Arabs, in Sirhan's opinion, but also because Sirhan wanted the world to see, he wanted the world to see how strongly our United States policy was in the pro-Israel–anti-Arab movement, in spite of our government's professed interest for the underdog, and world justice."

As reviewed in chapter 9, during his eight sessions with Sirhan, Dr. Pollack engaged in a great deal of gratuitous coaching of the defendant regarding his motive. ("Apparently what was eating at you was these elections and how strongly you felt about the American political figures letting the Arab world down"; or "you really want . . . the world to see the Arab suffering . . . to see that American policy has helped [cause] that suffering"; or "The trial is a trial in which you are sort of accusing America of . . . burying a million Arabs.") Dr. Pollack's courtroom explanation of Sirhan's motives resembled, strangely, not so much what Sirhan had said to Dr. Pollack, but what Dr. Pollack had said to Sirhan.

Although the initial phase of Pollack's testimony about Sirhan's diagnosis was, as expected, ambiguous, what followed was a surprising set of assertions about factual matters that were very unfavorable to the defendant.

Under Howard's questioning Pollack asserted that Sirhan had "little or no remorse" about killing Kennedy. He said he didn't believe Sirhan expected to be caught. He interpreted the struggle after the shooting as an attempt by Sirhan "to escape." He said that Sirhan had demonstrated reasonable foresight and planning before the murder, and that there was no evidence that Sirhan was in an "altered state" during the shooting. Pollack stated that the tapes of Sirhan in police custody demonstrated that Sirhan knew "what was going on." He asserted that he believed Sirhan was lying when he said he could not remember writing the notebooks and that he was lying when he said he could not remember the crime itself.

Seymour Pollack was entitled to any diagnosis he had honestly arrived at. Whatever favors the defense had done for him wouldn't change that. One might quarrel with him, as Grant Cooper would, but the diagnosis was his to make. But Pollack's assertions went well beyond the issue of whether Sirhan was mentally ill. They were inferences the doctor had made about matters of fact. Many of them not only contradicted the evidence of the case but contradicted what Dr. Pollack knew or should have known from his own inquiry. In exchange for his hours and hours of sitting and talking to Sirhan in a confidential way, Pollack owed him care and honesty. And in this regard his testimony at Sirhan's trial represented a monumental betrayal of trust.

Concerning remorse, Sirhan had on numerous occasions expressed his distress over his alleged actions, to Dr. Pollack as well as to others. His taped confession to Pollack that the murder went against his conscience, that it violated the teachings of his childhood, family, and church, was a stunning personal moment.

"Where would you be if you didn't have life?" Sirhan had inquired rhetorically. "And here I go and splatter this guy's brains. It's just not me."

Shortly thereafter Pollack mentioned to Sirhan that a number of other people were wounded during the shooting. "What did they do to me," Sirhan had asked, "that they had to be hurt?"

Apparently, to Dr. Pollack, none of this counted as evidence of remorse.

Dr. Pollack also testified that he believed that Sirhan didn't expect to be caught. The doctor offered little to back up this idea, but if it were true, why would it be so? Perhaps Sirhan, contrary to Pollack's assertion of reasonable foresight and planning, was so deluded that he thought he could murder Kennedy in a crowded hotel and walk away, or perhaps he didn't expect to be murdering anyone. In any case, Dr. Pollack's assertion that Sirhan was "trying to escape" is unwarranted by the facts. Sirhan stepped forward and began firing. There was a struggle for his gun. There is no record of an attempt to escape.

Most damaging was Dr. Pollack's contention that Sirhan was faking his memory loss regarding the writing in his notebooks and the murder. "Sirhan's denial of recall of his written notes . . . ," said Pollack, "I interpret as an attempt to avoid some serious condition that would be attributed to his writings, that would be interpreted as evidence of planning, premeditation of killing Kennedy." Pollack saw the writings in Sirhan's notebooks as "attempts to strengthen his intention, to strengthen his courage, to strengthen his capability . . . ," the bizarre repetitions being, presumably, no more than additional evidence of Sirhan's reasonable foresight and planning.

At Pollack's suggestion that he was lying about his notebooks, Sirhan stood up.

"Your Honor, sir—"

"You sit down or I will do what I told you I was going to do," ordered Judge Walker, referring to his threat to have Sirhan put in arm straps and a face mask. Walker called a recess, and Sirhan was escorted toward the holding pen, where Russell Parsons would try to calm him. Dave Smith of the *Los Angeles Times* was near the courtroom door as the group approached. "I don't like him calling me a fuckin' liar," he heard Sirhan say. Then Sirhan turned suddenly to face Pollack: "That son of a bitch."[8]

In the holding pen, Parsons rubbed water on Sirhan's forehead and neck. "That's the way you have to treat these agitated people," he told reporters.[9]

When court resumed a short time later, Pollack continued his deconstruction of the defendant. This time there was no reaction from Sirhan, who was calm to the point of being oblivious, alternately trying on a pair of sunglasses and staring at the ceiling.

For the benefit of the jury Dr. Pollack labeled Sirhan's lack of memory as "conscious denial, . . . a particular method to avoid full legal repercussions." He said he found no evidence of any trance. "Had he been in an altered state of consciousness," the doctor testified, "he would have been perplexed when he awakened, . . . [and] he would have raised questions about where he was, what he was there for." This view mirrored the movie stereotype that Dr. Diamond had warned against and ignored Diamond's point that upon coming out of his trance Sirhan's first admonition from the police was to remain silent.

When Grant Cooper began his cross-examination of Seymour Pollack, he sought to exploit what seemed to be the weakest part of the doctor's testimony—his diagnosis.

"Now isn't it true," Cooper asked the witness, "that in your confidential report to Evelle Younger, the district attorney, on February 5, you diagnosed Sirhan Sirhan as suffering from a borderline schizophrenia, with paranoid and hysterical features? . . . Then you went further and said that you do believe he was clinically psychotic, isn't that right?"

"That is correct."

"Did you also believe he had been growing more disturbed for the last few years?"

"Yes."

"Now, was Sirhan Sirhan a psychotically disturbed individual?"

"I think that Sirhan Sirhan was a borderline psychotically disturbed individual."

"Borderline?"

"Borderline."

Cooper then read several paragraphs from Pollack's memorandum to Younger in which he described Sirhan as psychotic.

"Now was Sirhan a psychotic person?"

"Yes."

"This morning you told us he was not a psychotic person, didn't you?"

"I said he was not clinically psychotic."

Pollack was caught in a web of his own words, and the more he struggled, the more tangled he became. His confident manner gave way to a frightened look. He nervously sipped water and tried to answer Grant Cooper.

"I said that Sirhan clinically had a paranoid personality; that he had, he was underneath, a psychotic personality."

"Underneath?"

"Underneath."

Cooper then began to cautiously chip away at Pollack's assertions about Sirhan. He asked Pollack if Sirhan's reputed hope of "a couple of years for killing a senator" represented mature and meaningful thinking.

"Not as mature or as meaningful as it should have been; as it could have been; yes, I would agree very definitely it is immature thinking to a considerable degree."

But Pollack would go on to maintain that Sirhan did maturely deliberate.

"I said that mature deliberation in the sense that in contemplating the act of killing Senator Kennedy that Sirhan weighed in his mind, he considered it, he examined it, he evaluated it, the reasons for and against it, he considered it, he pondered it, he weighed the facts and arguments. . . . I am saying that Sirhan's decision was not hasty or rash, that the probable consequences of the degree and act were considered by him."

Recall that when Dr. Pollack was trying to convince Sirhan of his political motive during a jail-cell interview, he accounted for the defendant's irrational and apparently nonpolitical actions by saying, "I don't really think you thought the whole thing out." Now up on the witness stand, Dr. Pollack was saying just the opposite. Sirhan not only thought the whole thing out, he carefully weighed the pros and cons as he planned the murder.

Grant Cooper should have never let Pollack get away with such a statement. This was the very crux of the case as Cooper had framed it. The defense attorney should have challenged the doctor to produce the evidence upon which he based his conclusion that Sirhan weighed, considered, examined, evaluated, and pondered the reasons for and against killing Robert Kennedy. What evidence did the doctor possess that such a rational process had taken place? But Cooper, seeming to follow a preset script, let the moment pass, as he had so many others.

He asked Pollack if Sirhan's odd behavior during the police interrogation wasn't "out of keeping with the fact that he understood that he had shot a presidential candidate?"

"No, no. It was not out of keeping with that. He understood fully, I believe, and completely what he had done. . . . He was fully aware of where he was, what was going on and the circumstances. Even in our interview subsequently he made me fully aware—he made me to understand that he was aware of what was going on there."

"What did he say?"

"What did he say? He recalled his conversations with these people."

Pollack's assertion that Sirhan had revealed to him that he "was aware of what was going on" seemed to imply that Sirhan had revealed that he did indeed remember the shooting, yet Pollack's conclusion is merely his own inference. Sirhan had never claimed that he didn't remember the police interrogation—only that he couldn't remember the shooting. Cooper, however, once again failed to follow up and make this point clear to the jury. Instead he asked Pollack whether Sirhan's strange laughing was in keeping with the knowledge of having committed a great crime. This simply led to yet another of Pollack's unsupported assertions.

"His laughing? He was laughing in a very sardonic way about what he had done and how it was possible for him to have carried off this coup and to have killed a very important man." Again, nowhere in the police interrogation tapes does it appear that Sirhan is laughing about having killed a very important man.

Cooper wrestled Pollack for two full days. There were moments when it appeared the defense attorney was getting the best of the psychiatrist. He aptly demonstrated that Pollack was perfectly willing to play with words to the point of medical meaninglessness. But Cooper was never able to get the pin. He could not string together his winning points in a way that the jury might comprehend. The majority of Pollack's unsupported assertions went unchallenged, as the defense attorney attacked instead the doctor's diagnosis.

Pollack's gift to the prosecution was his commonsense view of Sirhan as a deceitful, clever, and scheming political assassin, who faked a memory loss as the foundation for his legal defense. The beauty of this model for a juror was its simplicity: "he's faking it, 'cause he wants to get off."

Looked at more closely, this vision of Sirhan makes little sense. If Sirhan were knowledgeable and clever enough to understand the legal ramifications of the "diminished capacity" defense in California and was already creating a false record, starting with his police interrogation, why wouldn't he have done a better job? Why wouldn't he have faked waking up, or tried to fake insanity, a defense with the possibility of acquittal, rather than "diminished capacity," which would still most certainly mean life imprisonment? Every doctor who examined Sirhan agreed that he tried very hard to convince them that he was not crazy or mentally impaired. In the end Dr. Pollack seems to have succumbed to his frustration and prejudice in the case, and the defense attorneys simply did not have the energy or the vision to expose that prejudice.

Following Dr. Pollack, the prosecution continued its rebuttal by calling to the stand Dr. Leonard B. Olinger. Olinger was a private-practice psychologist who taught abnormal clinical psychology at USC.

In his classes at USC, Dr. Olinger instructed his students on "the ten precautions" that every clinician should observe in administering and evaluating psychological tests. Olinger brought these commandments to court in the form of an oversize chart, which was set up for the jury to see. Under John Howard's direction the doctor described the precautions; most were designed to inhibit the prejudice or preconceived notions of the tester from influencing the test results. Howard asked Olinger if he thought Dr. Schorr and Dr. Richardson had followed these precautions with Sirhan.

"Well, it seems to me," answered Olinger, "there's a great deal read into the data which really is not present in the data."

Attorney and witness then went step-by-step over all the tests administered by Drs. Schorr and Richardson. Olinger made a good case that the doctors found Sirhan to be sick because that is what they were looking to find. He offered numerous examples of test answers that the defense doctors scored as abnormal, but that, according to Olinger, were really just "commonsense responses."

As Dr. Olinger continued to ridicule the doctors who had testified for the defense, Sirhan smiled. He leaned over and told Russell Parsons he liked these guys the prosecution was bringing in. Sirhan liked having it said that his test responses were common sense. He liked it when the prosecution doctors said he was not sick, even though the testimony of these men might cost him his life.

Olinger's critique of Richardson and Schorr lasted almost the entire day. Douglas Robinson of *The New York Times* described the jury in the afternoon as "dazed as bees in smoke." Robinson reported, "By now, no one on the jury should be unfamiliar with each and every ink blot in the Rorschach test or the enigmatic pictures in the Thematic Apperception Test."[10] Dave Smith of the *Los Angeles Times* made a similar observation:

> For more than a month, they have listened to such psychiatric verbal shorthand as C-prime response, small animal movement, inanimate movement, large human response, pure form response, large M and small fm, large F and little c and TH column. It is debatable how efficiently the jurors have been able to translate such arbitrary terms into their meaningful emotional equivalents. But the mere effort has extracted a toll that was apparent Monday as they listened to still more of the same with faces that ranged a gamut of expression from boredom to stupefaction.[11]

When it was time to cross-examine, Grant Cooper went right to work.

"Dr. Olinger, when were you engaged to make this evaluation?"

"I believe it was about a month or so ago."

"Who contacted you, Mr. Compton or Mr. Howard? Do you know who suggested your name to them?"

"I suggested my name to them."

"What?"

"I suggested my name to them."

"You suggested your name to them?"

"Yes."

Cooper then had Olinger review his charted precautions. He had the doctor repeat his belief that Drs. Schorr and Richardson had not been objective, that they had entered the case with preconceived notions. Then he brought the point full circle.

"Doctor, yesterday you were telling us what you taught your students in psychology, and see if I have this correct; maybe I don't use your exact words; but a psychologist should be objective in his approach?"

"Yes, sir."

"And he shouldn't have preconceived ideas or notions about the test materials or protocol . . . he should not consciously or unconsciously be swayed by knowledge of the patient or, in this case, knowledge that the subject was Sirhan?"

"That's correct."

"Now you have told us, Doctor, that you volunteered your services as consultant to the district attorney's office in this case?"

"Yes, sir."

"And I think, am I correct, that you heard some of Dr. Schorr's testimony and you didn't like what you heard, so you called the district attorney and told him you didn't like it?"

"That's not quite, exactly correct, sir."

"Well, you tell me."

"Some of the testimony that was reported to be given sounded as if it were unwarranted by the material that was being presented in support of it."

"All right. Had you ever seen any of the material?"

"No, sir, I had not."

"What had you read about the testimony of Dr. Schorr? Do you remember what? Was it a newspaper you read it in?"

"I don't believe I can recall where I read it."

"Did you hear it on the radio?"

"Probably."

"On television?"

"Probably."

"That was only a small part of his testimony, wasn't it?"

"Yes, sir."

"And from that small part that you read in the newspapers you felt that his testimony was—would you say unreliable?"

"Yes, sir."

"So feeling that it was unreliable, you called the district attorney's office and volunteered your services?"

"Not quite."

"Well, you volunteered to help them?"

"Sort of."

"Is that right?"

"Sort of."

"Well, you volunteered to give them some advice?"

"Information."

"Information. All right. But you don't remember what you read. Do you remember what you read?"

"Not precisely."

"Do you remember the substance of what you read?"

"Only in a general way."

"Well, you had some preconceived ideas and notions, didn't you, before you called the district attorney?"

"Yes."

"Now isn't it a fact, Doctor, that you violated your ten commandments that you gave to your pupils?"

Grant Cooper was in rare form. He forced Dr. Olinger into a series of equivocations. He then made Olinger admit that his description of Sirhan as a "pseudoneurotic schizophrenic" was a diagnosis that was not in any of the psychological manuals. But as well as Cooper was performing, the chief defense attorney was unwittingly doing the prosecution's chores.

As Cooper dismantled Olinger, the message to the jury was simple: here is yet another practitioner of mind medicine, and he is just as wordy and vain as the others. The prosecution could have introduced a dozen Olingers; Cooper could have butchered them all, and it still would have been to the prosecution's advantage.

In arguing "diminished capacity" Sirhan's lawyers forgot the basic elements of the defense. In a sense, they had set the clock back a hundred years and were operating in the old framework of the M'Naghten insanity rule: Was Sirhan crazy or was he not? Did he understand right from wrong? This was not the issue. The issue, under the defense of diminished capacity, was whether or not Sirhan was capable of mature and meaningful reflection upon the gravity of his alleged act.

The evidence on this point was clearly in Sirhan's favor. There were only fuzzy bits and pieces to suggest that Sirhan had thought about the murder beforehand, and no evidence at all that he had gone through any process of reflection. The principal evidence of Sirhan's prior intent appeared in his notebooks; but this, if anything, was evidence that he was not in a normal state of mind.

The primary strategy of Grant Cooper was to place the case in the hands of doctors who looked at Sirhan through the lens of psychological tests. On its face, this was a good plan. The professional qualifications of the doctors were impressive, and their opinions, even those brought in by the prosecution, were united on the fact that Sirhan was mentally ill. But when the psychological tests underlying the medical conclusions were successfully challenged, the doctors appeared foolish and fallible, and the case supporting Sirhan began to crumble.

Since there was little doubt in the public mind as to Sirhan's guilt, the most common characterization of the proceedings at this point was that psychiatry itself was on trial. "In the trial of Sirhan Sirhan there are two defendants," declared *Newsweek*. "The first, of course, is the 25-year-old Jordanian immigrant accused of murdering Sen. Robert Kennedy. The second is the clinical psychologist and his ability to diagnose diseases of the mind."[12]

The *National Review* took a similar but more critical position: "What was on trial in Los Angeles was not the defendant but the testimony of psychiatrists and psychologists, who would have us believe that every criminal is so sick as to deserve society's pity and succor rather than its punishment."[13]

But the most stunning indictment of the medical testimony would come after the trial from an unexpected source—a California prison psychologist. At the time he had encountered Sirhan on death row in San Quentin State Prison, Dr. Eduard Simson had been a practicing clinical psychologist for thirteen years. Simson had earned a B.A. at Stanford and an M.A. at New York University. He then received a postgraduate psychology degree from the University of Louisville and a Ph.D. (magna cum laude) from Heidelberg University.

During the summer of 1969 Simson examined the incarcerated Sirhan on twenty occasions as part of his duties as senior psychologist at San Quentin, a position he had held for six years. He became suspicious when his diagnosis differed greatly from those of the trial doctors. Simson claimed:

Nowhere in Sirhan's test responses was I able to find evidence that he is a "paranoid schizophrenic" or "psychotic" as testified by the doctors at the trial. . . . [I] did not see any evidence of "mental illness" in Sirhan in my extensive psychological testing, nor in his spontaneous behavior during the numerous hours we spent together.

Simson observed that Sirhan was highly intelligent, well oriented, and "an unusually good hypnotic subject." This was significant because, according to Simson, "psychotics . . . are among the poorest subjects for hypnosis" and "paranoid schizophrenics are almost impossible to hypnotize."[14]

Simson came to believe that there was a mysterious truth to this case "which probably still lies very much concealed and unknown to the general public." To discover this truth, Simson believed, one would have to "unlock" Sirhan's mind. Dr. Simson thought he was on his way to accomplishing this task, but his visits with Sirhan were abruptly terminated in the autumn of 1969 by prison authorities, who did not approve of the psychologist's protracted interest in the convicted assassin. Four years later Simson felt compelled to sign a twenty-three-page affidavit explaining the conclusions he had reached during his sessions with Sirhan.

In the affidavit, Simson said that the medical testimony at Sirhan's trial was shameful, "discrediting and embarrassing psychology and psychiatry as a profession."

The doctor wrote:

I am appalled at the conduct of the mental health professionals involved in this case. . . . Assuming that Sirhan killed Robert F. Kennedy, an assumption the validity of which apparently no one seriously questioned, the mental health specialists saw their role primarily in proving what to them was a known fact, rather than discovering the truth.

Simson claimed that the doctors merely worked backward from the assumed fact of political assassination to the "Freudian fantasies" of mental illness.

Simson was not afraid to say that many important questions about the case remained unanswered. He made note of the fact that the handwriting in Sirhan's notebooks differed, "often drastically," from the handwriting he observed in San Quentin.

Whether someone else wrote the notebooks or whether they were written under some special influence, such as hypnosis, is entirely unsolved. If someone hypnotized him when the notebooks were written, who was it? . . . Was [Sirhan] merely a double, a stand-in, sent there to draw attention? Was he at the scene to replace someone else? Did he actually kill Robert Kennedy? Whatever the full truth . . . might be, it still remains locked in Sirhan's mind and in other, still anonymous minds.

The last sentence in Simson's affidavit was blunt: "Sirhan's trial was, and will be remembered as the psychiatric blunder of the century."[15]

FOURTEEN

Life or Death

✳ ✳ ✳

D R. LEONARD OLINGER was the last rebuttal witness to testify for the prosecution. After he stepped down, Judge Walker and the attorneys retired to discuss the instructions the judge would give to the jury after the prosecution and the defense had made their final arguments. Walker asked how long the summations would run.

"Mr. Fitts says 'two,' and I don't believe him," said John Howard, making mischief. "I hold with four hours."

"I tell you this," responded Walker, "I have no faith in estimates of attorneys on how long they are going to argue, because I did it myself and I got up there and fell in love with my own voice."

John Howard was right. David Fitts would speak the next day for more than four hours. He opened by describing how Sirhan approached Kennedy, drew his pistol, and fired eight shots.

> "In this case the People suggest to you that this cold and calculated decision to take the life of Robert F. Kennedy had been arrived at substantially in advance of the defendant's appearance at the Ambassador Hotel, and that the actual act of assassination was simply the culmination of a series of preparatory events, mental processes on the part of this defendant, which had been at work over a substantial period of time."

According to the prosecutor, a string of "uncontroverted facts" illustrated the defendant's nefarious intentions. Sirhan's "clandestine" purchase of his pistol from a friend was a "surreptitious transaction." In attending the June 2 Kennedy reception, Sirhan was "casing the joint." Fitts also drew meaning from the fact that Sirhan left his wallet and identification in his car.

> "I understand that burglars are in the habit of leaving their identification someplace else. Some of those who are caught unwittingly have had a wallet or something drop out of their pocket in places

where they are not supposed to be. It's the sort of precaution which a reasonable assassin might take."

Fitts's argument here probably scored points with the jury, but the logic was tortured. Keeping a wallet away from a crime scene might be rational behavior for a clandestine burglar; it hardly makes sense for one about to commit a murder for which apprehension is near certain.

At the suggestion that he had purposely hidden his wallet, Sirhan became agitated. "He's lying, he's lying, he's lying," he said to Russell Parsons, who was sitting next to him. Sirhan had not shouted these words, but Judge Walker was not going to risk another outburst. Walker called a recess, and two security men escorted Sirhan from the court to a holding pen, where Russell Parsons tried to calm him down.

When court resumed, with Sirhan again present, David Fitts tried to make a connection between the Kennedy murder and the current unrest in the nation.

"Mr. Sirhan, twenty-five years old, isn't the only young protestor in this country. A protest of the youth of this nation seems to be something that has been on the rise. I don't know, maybe it is just me and my time and my generation, but I view it with alarm. Maybe it was always that bad and I didn't know it, but things have happened in the last few years—they are alarming to me and I don't know what is going to happen if these people don't in time change some of their views which they have when they begin to take our places and run the affairs of this country. Just what kind of nation are we going to have? Well, obviously, Mr. Sirhan shares some of these views. They are not delusions."

Although the jury had been instructed to avoid news of the trial, they had not been sealed off from all outside information. They were well aware that there had been riots on several California university campuses. Much of this turmoil centered on the war in Vietnam, race issues, or what was called the "free speech movement." Dirty words spoken into public-address systems, college students wearing cartridge belts—this was a rich emotional vein, and the prosecution was intent on tapping it.

The most recurrent theme for the prosecution was Sirhan's alleged play-acting. "Sirhan lied to us all," asserted Fitts, "and lied with a very logical reason and that is to avoid the full consequences of his act." Fitts described Sirhan's recollections as "pure rubbish" or "pure Sirhan," cleverly making the defendant's very name synonymous with prevarication. "You will have observed that anything in this case which would appear to indicate that this was a deliberate premeditated murder is denied by the defendant, regardless of what it is or who said it."

Fitts's assertion here simply isn't true. Sirhan readily admitted to things that didn't help his case. He admitted that he shot Robert Kennedy. He said he did so for political reasons. He admitted that the notebooks and writing were his, though he claimed to have no memory of making the entries. And even though the foundation of his defense was mental illness, Sirhan continually vexed his doctors and lawyers by vehemently maintaining that he was not mentally ill. But the prosecution would continue to insist that Sirhan lied at every opportunity and was doing so for reasons of self-interest. In the continuing effort to discredit Sirhan, Fitts, incredibly, even attacked the defendant's professed motive.

"It is a rather common occurrence," he told the jury, "the more heinous the crime, the more likely it is that . . . one will fall back upon the defense that he did it for his country, which is, after all, all that is left. This is the entire Sirhan position."

Fitts, here, appears to be trying to tar Sirhan with Samuel Johnson's observation that "Patriotism is the last refuge of a scoundrel." He offers Sirhan's political explanation, which the prosecution was all too happy to accept on other occasions, as evidence of the defendant's perfidy—professed love of country masking an even uglier truth. But what could that truth be? If Sirhan didn't do it for his country, then why did he do it? For personal gain? Because he was crazy? Because he was put up to it? Certainly the prosecution was not embracing any of these explanations.

When it came time to review "the abstruse art" of clinical psychology, Fitts engaged in a little playacting of his own. Defense investigator Robert Kaiser in *"RFK Must Die!"* made the following observation:

> Fitts had expressed himself with great erudition—he seemed to have an encyclopedic knowledge of classical music, Moorish architecture, modern linguistics, the history of art and Middle Eastern diplomacy, among other things—until the psychologists and psychiatrists appeared for the defense. Then Fitts was a dunderhead who had never heard of Mesmer, Freud or Rorschach, or, indeed, the defense of diminished responsibility in California.[1]

Remaining in character for his summation, Fitts termed the medical testimony a "quagmire." He savaged Dr. Schorr for his plagiarism and for his highly interpretive Rorschach exam. He also faulted Schorr on the selection of cards offered for Sirhan's Thematic Apperception Test. "Not a single one of those cards is the kind which would appear to elicit a happy tale," he said, preparing once again to champion the cause of common sense.

Fitts reviewed the cards one by one: "There's the slumped figure in an uncomfortable position with the back turned. Make a happy story out of that, if you will."

Or the woman on the bed: "I look at that bed and it's only big enough for one person; that's one of those little ambiguities; but there she is with her breasts uncovered, a fully clad gentleman with his hands covering his eyes. Make a happy story about that, if you can."

The prosecutor's most caustic remarks were reserved for Dr. Diamond. He ridiculed the idea that the lights and mirrors at the Ambassador Hotel put Sirhan into an unintentional trance that led to the killing of Robert Kennedy. To Fitts, the evidence for "this dissociate thing" was "flimsy," and he had a better explanation: Sirhan had been in custody a full six months and had "structured some sort of story which he hoped would in some measure exonerate him for the crime he knew full well he committed." This point of view conveniently ignores the fact that Sirhan's story remained virtually unchanged during his incarceration, something his attorneys would fail to bring up when it was their turn to speak.

Fitts referred to Dr. Diamond's hypnotic sessions with Sirhan as "séances." He asked the jury, "What is the moral involved? What did we learn from it all?" And Fitts once again read Dr. Diamond's "absurd and preposterous" statement. "Well, I can't improve on Dr. Diamond," he said, although he had just spent a half an hour trying. "If that is what he thinks of this story and that's what he said about it, why need I say anything more?"

Without the assistance of notes, and demonstrating an uncommon ability to put words and thoughts together in a compelling fashion, David Fitts had spoken for the entire morning and most of the afternoon. By any measure, his argument was a stunning success. Using logic, wit, and sarcasm, the prosecutor had taken the thin evidence of Sirhan's premeditation and made a convincing case that Sirhan had planned Robert Kennedy's murder in advance and was lying when he said he hadn't. David Fitts had given the jury strong moral and emotional reasons to convict Sirhan Sirhan of first-degree murder. It was now up to Sirhan's lawyers to give them reasons to convict the defendant on a lesser charge.

The following morning Russell Parsons rose for the defense and made what might be the worst closing argument in modern legal history. "If Your Honor please," he said, "I might make a peculiar start here, but I think you will forgive me under the circumstances." Parsons had decided to open with a review of the Sirhan family history.

"The Sirhans were living in a nice home; she described it; no one has told you differently. There have been men in this courtroom from

Palestine. She told you that they had a lovely home, the best of furniture; her husband was employed by the British with a good job. . . .

"All right, what happens? All of a sudden they had to give up their home, their home that had been their home for years. That is bound to have an effect on people, when you have to just pack up and leave."

Parsons had told the jury that he was not going to plead for sympathy—that he just wanted them to know the facts. But the defense attorney was appealing for sympathy. Worse still, this appeal was repellent in content and tone.

"She told you about the toilets, the little holes in the pavement in this building; and it was borne out by the young Arab whom we brought here from Chicago. Fortunately, we were able to find him, and he came here and told about how the toilet conditions were such—I don't like to stress this—but it paints the picture of how these people lived; and when the toilets overflowed out into the street. . . .

"She told you about the food; the Arab boy told you that the food they had, he told you about the margarine and someone suggested was it liquid, was it like Mazola?"

Russell Parsons spoke as though the jury couldn't help but make a meaningful connection between the Sirhan family's toilet conditions or margarine in Palestine and the shooting death of Robert Kennedy in Los Angeles. He continued:

"He came to this country and he did pretty well. He did pretty well in school . . . but he had a sister lying there with an incurable disease. And he played hooky from school that he might tend the wants of the poor dying sister. You can't be very bad when you do that. . . .

"Have you ever seen the Sun and Fun Candy Store in Palm Springs? She ran that, and so he loved her. Is he to be condemned?"

For loving his dying sister? Certainly not. But Sirhan was on trial for murdering Robert Kennedy, and Parsons, as the defense attorneys had been doing all along, was not dealing with the facts of the case: he was instead running frantically around the periphery.

Parsons did, however, take one stab at discussing the circumstances of the murder.

"I think it has been said he fired the revolver eight times. Well, when a fellow who is as small as he is has got two great big burly ex–football players—one a champion of the world—admirable characters, but powerful—are lying on you trying to grab your hand and the gun is going back and forth, how can you say he shot it eight times? Nobody knows who pulled the trigger. Tell me—think it over—he's lying there and they are on top of him. Who pulled it? Are you sure? Some of you fellows when you're shaving all alone some morning, think that over."

In view of the substantial open issues of fact in this case—evidence of more bullets than Sirhan could have fired, wounds in Robert Kennedy inconsistent with his position relative to Sirhan, trajectory diagrams that defied the laws of Newton, all issues that the defense attorneys could have explored if they had the will—it is pathetic to read this attempt to inject the idea that maybe Rafer Johnson really killed Robert Kennedy. It is hard to imagine anyone taking a word of it seriously, before the shaving mirror or anywhere else. Its effect for Sirhan in the minds of the jurors must have been negative.

Parsons followed this absurdity with another as he engaged in an odd moment of breast-beating. "The responsibility is clearly in the hands of we lawyers. If there was anything we didn't do, honest, I don't know what it was. We tried every way we could; we have sought advice; we have had it; we have had numerous lawyers. And to the credit of my profession, I thank God I am a lawyer."

Parsons here laid bare his self-absorption. To whom was he speaking? The press? Historians? Those were words that one might utter after the case is lost. They were certainly not ideas that would inspire a jury to believe that the defense attorneys had confidence in their own presentation.

In another statement, Parsons contended, incredibly, that there was "not one word" of evidence offered at the trial to refute the medical testimony of the defense witnesses. "I thought we did pretty well," he said, congratulating himself. "We brought these men from all over."

Douglas Robinson of *The New York Times* called Parsons's summation "impassioned, old-fashioned rhetoric."[2] This was a generous characterization for an argument that was incompetent, sloppy, and crude. There was an edge of vulgarity in Parsons's speech, evident as he reviewed the list of doctors. Of Dr. Schorr: "It only takes a seventy-cent phone call to find out whether anything he said was untrue." Of Dr. Georgene Seward, who had made a brief appearance for the defense: "Weren't you impressed with her, or am I some kind of sap?" Of Dr. Marcus: "Now here is a man appointed by the Court and is the Court powerless, do they have to appoint some nincompoop to guide the defense in one of the most important cases ever tried in the world?"

Parsons continued: "Who else did we bring here? We brought the doctor from the University of California, one of the great institutions in

America. It's had some rough days lately, but it's still a great institution. And he came here. . . . We picked the best men that we could find. Blame me if they weren't good enough."

In an odd effort to cultivate the sympathy of the jury, Parsons made mention of the multiple tragedies that had befallen the Kennedy family. "There isn't a man in America," he intoned gravely, "who shouldn't say a prayer for the remainder of that family—every night." Perhaps it was the defense attorney's overdramatic presentation that struck Sirhan, but at that delicate moment he let out a small laugh. Sirhan quickly covered his mouth with his hand, but he had been noticed.

Sirhan's dismal sense of occasion would be matched by that of his attorney, as Parsons finished his summation with a vision that could hardly be expected to warm the hearts of the jurors.

> "I would like your verdict to spell in every hamlet on every desert in the Arab Republic; in Europe; that a man can get justice in America and that is neither life imprisonment or the death penalty, because this case doesn't warrant it—not for this sick wretch. No matter what he did. Think that over. . . .
>
> "It's going to take a little courage to return a proper verdict in this case; a little courage to see that justice is done; but it should and must be done. It will go down in the history books.
>
> "Thank you."

The court took a short recess; then Emile Berman stood up. "I do not intend to repeat any of the matters that were so broadly touched upon by Mr. Parsons," he assured the jury, "but I do want to talk to you specifically about a thing called trauma." For emphasis, Berman spelled the word for the jury.

Berman then outlined what he called Sirhan's six major traumas, beginning with his abandonment by "dear, old ever-loving dad," to his humiliation at the Arab defeat in the Six-Day War of 1967. Contradicting his stated intentions, the defense attorney from New York covered much the same ground as his predecessor, and in the end he concluded that Sirhan "was just a sick little boy."

At the lunch recess Grant Cooper paid a visit to Sirhan. "Trust me," he said to his client. "You won't like what I say. But I'm trying to get second degree. Trust me."[3]

Back in court and standing before the jury, Cooper began by praising David Fitts for "one of the finest closing arguments for the prosecution that I have heard in my forty-one years at the bar." Then, as though he were trying to loosen the mood at a Rotary luncheon, he told a story of a boy who fell into a barrel of molasses. Mimicking the words of the sugar-coated youngster, Cooper invoked divine assistance: "Oh, Lord, make my tongue equal to this opportunity."

Grant Cooper's tongue had been equal to the task many times in the past. His defense of Dr. Bernard Finch and his mistress, Carole Tregoff, for murder was regarded as classic courtroom melodrama, as Cooper hung the jury with his stirring reenactment of Finch's supposed struggle to wrest the gun from his wife's hand before—as the story went—she shot herself. But here Cooper made it clear one last time that there was to be no contest of fact.

"We are not here to free a guilty man," he told the jury. "We tell you, as we always have, that he is guilty of having killed Senator Kennedy. . . . Whether Mr. Sirhan likes it or not, under the facts of this case he deserves to spend the rest of his life in the penitentiary." To this there was a barely audible moan of protest from Mary Sirhan sitting in the second row.

Cooper then engaged in a little pop psychology.

"There is a good Sirhan and a bad Sirhan and the bad Sirhan is very nasty . . . but I have learned to like him just as Mr. Parsons said he has learned to love him, and so I have learned to love him, the good Sirhan but not withstanding that we as lawyers owe the obligation to do what we think is right . . . and I, for one, am not going to ask you to do otherwise than bring in a verdict of guilty of murder in the second degree."

Cooper then launched himself into an elongated discussion of the concepts of law at play in the case and the instructions they would be getting shortly from Judge Walker. "Now what I am telling you is legalese," he said to the jury, "that's why I'm trying to explain it to you."

In the role of erudite uncle, Cooper reviewed the elements of murder, the difference between direct and circumstantial evidence, levels of culpability. He offered definitions of premeditation, malice, diminished capacity, and transferred intent, but he provided no insights or clever ways to think about these concepts. Instead he droned on, the molasses now clearly sticking to his tongue.

"The instructions with respect to harboring malice, there are two elements, ladies and gentlemen. First, if you find that he had diminished capacity to a substantial degree where it would affect his ability to premeditate and deliberate and reflect upon the gravity of the event or, second, you don't have to be satisfied with that; if you entertain a reasonable doubt as to whether he has substantially reduced mental capacity to the extent that it affected his ability to maturely and meaningfully deliberate and premeditate and reflect upon the gravity of the event, you could find him guilty of first-degree murder."

The mind-numbing legal lessons went on for the entire afternoon and a good portion of the next morning. Eventually Cooper began to talk about the case. He reviewed Sirhan's threats to Kennedy in his notebooks. "Is that mature thinking?" he asked. "Is that meaningful thinking?"

Cooper was eager for the jury to understand that first-degree murder was reserved for especially heinous crimes. He had one in mind.

"By a bad man I am talking about the kind of man who, we will say, just by way of example, who is married, married a long time and he meets some cute little chick younger than his wife and he falls for her and decides that he wants to go to Tahiti or someplace with this young girlfriend of his but he doesn't have enough money, so he takes out a life insurance policy on the wife for one hundred thousand dollars. That has happened. Then he and his girlfriend plan to kill and do away with his wife so that he can not only get her out of the way but get the one hundred thousand dollars and then live in luxury with his girlfriend of younger years.

". . . This is a bad individual."

Cooper then asked the jury to compare the wife killer with Sirhan.

"What was the motive? It wasn't for gain for him; political motive, yes; but something in his immature mind, because of illness that the psychiatrists and psychologists told you that he had, he believed that it was right; how stupid. He believed that he shouldn't be punished for it; how stupid. How immature."

Grant Cooper's instincts told him that Dr. Bernard Diamond had not endeared himself to the jury with his testimony. He understood that the jury was not likely to embrace the doctor's idea that Sirhan was in a trance, and he also realized that the prosecution had done a good job at casting Sirhan as a fake and a liar. Thus, as he concluded his four-hour argument, Cooper tried to put distance between himself and Dr. Diamond by attempting to refocus the jury onto a single point.

"I don't care whether he was in a hypnotic state at the time he fired the shot, or whether he was in a trance as Dr. Diamond said; this is beside the point. The question that you are here to determine is not what his condition was at the time he fired the shot, but whether he could maturely and meaningfully premeditate . . . whether or not the defendant had diminished capacity. That is the only issue you have before you. . . . I will now pass from our shoulders to yours the responsibility and the proper and intelligent fate of Sirhan Sirhan."

The following morning Lynn Compton would make the final argument on behalf of the prosecution. For only the second time in sixty days, Mary Sirhan was not in court. Her son Adel explained that she did not want to hear what Mr. Compton was going to say.

"I will guarantee you this is not going to be a long or very profound dissertation on the principles of psychiatry or of the law," Compton began, to the probable relief of the jury.

"I am simply going to appeal to your common sense. . . . Now again, as I say, I'm not the most profound or articulate guy and I'm a little bit—oh—embarrassed, I guess it is, to stand up here and follow a Stanford man like Mr. Fitts, with his great command of the language and his great literary knowledge, and talk about a lot of things that I don't know about."

As if to emphasize his humble bloodline, Compton declined to stand at the podium as his predecessors had, but instead unbuttoned his suit jacket, sat down on the end of the prosecution table, and looked directly at the jury. With folksy charm, thick hands, and a large nose visibly off-center from a football injury, Compton, at least to some in the press, very effectively played the role of Spencer Tracy.

He was quick to compliment the efforts of the defense team. "They have done an outstanding, workmanlike job in seeing that the system works," he said in a slow drawl. "And the system has worked." The prosecutor's regard for the opposing attorneys was, most likely, genuine, but his words were also cleverly designed to take what respect they had earned with the jury and divert it from their client to his—the legal system itself.

Compton was also vocal in his approval for the police and the prosecution.

"There were no secrets, no surprises, no sandbagging on our part. A public trial, so that the world, through the media of the people who came here as observers, could see and report to anyone who was interested in everything that went on—no Star Chambers, no secrets—wide open for everybody to look at and criticize if they want; but there were no secrets."

Having praised both the prosecution and the defense, Compton turned his sights on the real villains of the trial, the men "whose profession is based on finding something wrong with people."

"I can't for the life of me believe anyone can go back to June 5 and crawl inside his head and tell you what he was thinking about when he put that bullet in Senator Kennedy's head by showing him pictures of a kid with a violin or a man standing with his hands up to his face or a woman in a bed. . . .

"I think it would be a frightening thing for the administration of criminal justice in this state if the decision of the magnitude of this case turned on whether or not he saw clowns playing pattycake or whether they were kicking each other in the shins when he is shown some inkblot."

There were no outbursts from Sirhan as Compton spoke. Martin Kasindorf of *Newsweek* described the defendant as looking "unutterably sad, lonely and downcast, his pallid face cradled in his left hand, gazing at Compton like a bereft child."[4] The prosecutor turned to meet Sirhan's eyes. "They like him, they say," he said with contempt, referring to Sirhan's lawyers. "I don't like him. I think he is a cunning vicious man."

After lunch Judge Walker began his instructions to the jury. "In determining the guilt or innocence of the defendant you are to be governed solely by the evidence introduced in this trial and the law as stated to you by me. The law forbids you to be governed by mere sentiment, conjecture, sympathy, passion, prejudice, or public opinion." By three o'clock Walker was finished, and the jury of seven men and five women was sent to the dingy, beige-colored conference room on the ninth floor of the Hall of Justice, just a floor above the small courtroom where, for the previous two months, they had listened to the testimony of ninety witnesses.

The jury had been instructed to deliberate only during normal court hours. In the time they had left on Monday afternoon, they elected as foreman their best-educated member—Bruce D. Elliott, a computer analyst who held a Ph.D. degree.

The following day there was no word at all from the jury room, but on the second full day of deliberations the jurors sent a note to Judge Walker asking for clarification on the definition of second-degree murder.[5] That same afternoon Russell Parsons managed to push himself back onto center stage when he told newsmen that Sirhan was expecting to be exchanged for some prisoner in an Arab country. Parsons said that a State Department "official" had discussed the idea with him a few months back. With nothing else to report, some newsmen began to write stories about the rumored exchange. Bob Greene of *Newsday* was one. Parsons told Greene that Issa Nakhleh, the Arab lawyer associated with the defense team, had gone to New York to discuss the possibility of this exchange with visiting King Hussein of Jordan.

"Why do you think he has been out there?" Parsons asked. "He hasn't been there for fun, you know. I was going to go to Jordan myself, but then we decided that this would be better." Greene asked who the United States would want in an exchange. Parsons shrugged. "I'm sure they have a lot of people we want."

Later it was discovered that Nakhleh never met with Hussein, and the government "official" who had supposedly started the whole thing was merely a translator, a former low-level employee of the State Department, who was accompanying a Lebanese businessman on a visit to Los Angeles. His comment to Parsons was that "such exchanges happen oftener than you think."[6]

The next morning at 10:47 A.M., three buzzes were heard on the signal system, indicating that a verdict had been reached. In less than half an hour all the principals were in court. Judge Walker asked jury foreman Bruce Elliott whether the jurors had reached a verdict.

"We have, Your Honor," replied Mr. Elliott.

The judge took six white forms from Elliott. He looked at them briefly and then glanced at the defendant as he handed them to the court clerk.

"We, the jury, find the defendant, Sirhan Bishara Sirhan," said Alice Nishikawa in a clear voice, "guilty of murder in the first degree."

Sirhan, dressed in a light-blue shirt with gray slacks, remained impassive as the verdict was read. The wire-service reporters, on the other hand, moved quickly for the doors. Under California law the jury would now, in a separate hearing, have to decide between a sentence of life in prison or death. Judge Walker ordered the penalty trial to begin the following Monday, April 21.

The jury had deliberated for almost seventeen hours, delivering their verdict on the sixty-third day of the trial. When the panel was polled for the first time on Tuesday, eight jurors voted for first-degree murder, two for second-degree, and two were undecided. Several hours later the vote was ten first-degree, two undecided. On Wednesday one of the undecideds, former alternate juror Ruth Stillman, twenty-six, an insurance adjuster, joined the majority. That left Susan J. Brumm, sixty-two, as the last holdout. During deliberations Brumm repeatedly referred to Sirhan as "that young kid," but Ms. Brumm changed her vote the following morning. Oddly, it was the fact that Sirhan had never been in trouble before that led her to conclude that he must have had the capacity to control himself.

Court was again in session the afternoon after the verdict (without the jury), as preparations were made for the penalty hearing. Grant Cooper put forth several "offers of proof" for Judge Walker's approval. The first was that Mr. Issa Nakhleh, the Palestinian UN representative, be permitted to give historical background to the Arab-Israeli conflict so that the jury might better understand Sirhan's mind. The second was that Evelle

Younger, the district attorney, be called as a witness for the defense to testify that during the plea bargain he was in favor of recommending life in prison for Sirhan.

Cooper's third proposal was that the defense be permitted to introduce witnesses who would argue against the efficacy of the death penalty. Judge Walker didn't hesitate to deny this and the two preceding motions, holding that background on the Arab-Israeli conflict was irrelevant, that the negotiations during plea bargain were privileged, and that the death penalty was a debate topic more appropriate for the legislature.

At the penalty hearing on Monday morning Mary Sirhan was once again called as a witness. Robert Kaiser described the scene in *"RFK Must Die!"*:

> She rose from her seat in the second row, from which she had watched and wept through most of the trial, and marched bravely to the stand with dignity, a diminutive homely woman in a light blue skirt and matching jacket, climbed into the jury box, adjusted the microphone on her bosom and moistened her lips. She frowned and blinked at Cooper from a face ravaged by tears enough for ten. She had buried eight of her thirteen children, lived through two wars, been abandoned by her husband. Now she was asked to testify at the death penalty hearing of her son, the assassin.[7]

"Mrs. Sirhan," asked Grant Cooper. "In his entire life, before the shooting, was Sirhan Sirhan ever at any time in any trouble with the law?"

"He has never been," she replied. "And that is not from me or from him. That is because I raised him up to the law of God and his love."

"Thank you, Mrs. Sirhan; I have no further questions."

It was the shortest penalty hearing in California history. In less than a minute it was time for final arguments to determine whether Sirhan would be sentenced to life in prison or death in the gas chamber at San Quentin. Assistant district attorney John Howard spoke first.

"The only question now is the proper punishment for a political assassin in the United States," he began. ". . . If death is to be the reward for political aspiration, you will know your candidates as two-dimensional images on the television screen or as disembodied voices over the radio."

In the preceding weeks it had been reported widely in the newspapers that the prosecution was not going to seek the death penalty. Two weeks earlier, Buck Compton had told the press that very thing. "I think the public would be satisfied with a sentence of life," the deputy DA had said. But now, with the verdict of guilty in hand, John Howard seemed to be taking a hard line against Sirhan:

"In resolving the question of this defendant's guilt you have found him lacking in honesty, in integrity, and even in the courage of his convictions. At the same time he obviously enjoyed the star status and the opportunity to engage in dramatic theatrics. . . . Perhaps you observed his reaction when Mr. Russell Parsons, in his address to you, urged in all sincerity that America pray for the ill-starred Kennedy family. . . .

"This defendant will regard permission to live as a further triumph of imprisonment, for life imprisonment is an entry into a form of custodial society that can only suffer by the inclusion of this defendant. You may not be obliged to hear this defendant boast that he committed the crime of the century. Others will."

John Howard's speech was genuine old-fashioned rhetoric, permitted in the final argument, and very effective. The prosecutor described a newspaper article he had read a few days earlier about the war in Vietnam. "Apparently it was a good week. Only two hundred and two Americans killed. The Sirhan trial dominated the paper and the front page. We have lavishly expended our resources for the sake of a cold-blooded political assassin, while content to send patriotic Americans to Vietnam with a seventy-dollar rifle and our best wishes."

In making his final appeal to the jury, the word "death" never passed John Howard's lips, but the meaning of his words was unmistakable. "Sirhan Sirhan was entitled to a fair trial, which each of you has now given to him. He has no special claim to further preservation. I would ask on behalf of the prosecution that each of you in your hearts have the courage of your conviction to write an end to this trial, and to apply the only proper penalty for political assassination in the United States of America."

Grant Cooper was stunned. He believed that the prosecution would not push for the death penalty, but John Howard had just done so, and in very harsh terms. It was now up to Cooper to raise the last voice in Sirhan's behalf.

"Shortly after midnight on the morning of June the fifth a young vigorous senator fresh from his victory in the California primaries . . . met his untimely death . . . a victim of hate, hate generated in the bowels of war, a hate engendered at an early age in the child Sirhan, hate that consumed a once healthy mind, hate that had reduced that mind to one described by the evidence as a substantial mental illness."

Cooper reminded the jury that they were gathered to decide the ultimate issue, "an issue which should be God's alone." The choice, said

Cooper, was "whether Sirhan Sirhan end the rest of his natural life behind the bars of a penitentiary or shall he forfeit his life by inhaling the deadly fumes of cyanide gas . . . in the gruesome green room at San Quentin.

"Do you realize that yours is the power of discretion of a king?" Cooper continued, trying to increase the pressure. "A benevolent monarch or a despotic dictator? This is your awful power."

Cooper had never argued at a penalty hearing. He had built his reputation on hanging juries, and he knew now that he was looking for just a few jurors who would hold out against putting Sirhan to death. Most of his arguments were generic, many of his references were biblical, and hardly any of it seemed genuine.

> "Remember—the taking of human life by the law also begets violence. 'Vengeance is mine, saith the Lord.'
>
> ". . . The Bible teaches us that love is reflected in love, but how many of us heed this biblical teaching? Instead it is hate, hate, hate; violence, violence, more violence; wars, wars, and more wars. When will we ever learn that love is truly reflected in love? In the name of God, whence cometh all understanding, I appeal to your judgment; . . . let this circle of violence end here in this courtroom."

Cooper suggested that sparing Sirhan's life would be a "posthumous tribute to Senator Kennedy." He quoted Robert Kennedy on the night Martin Luther King, Jr., was slain: "'Whenever any American's life is taken by another unnecessarily—whether it is done in the name of the law or in defiance of the law . . . the whole nation is degraded.'"

Then in dramatic fashion Cooper turned toward the defendant.

> "And now, Sirhan Sirhan—I have done all that I could do to the very best of my ability, for you and for the American system of justice, which I serve and revere.
>
> "And to you, Mary Sirhan, his mother, I say . . . 'May your prayers be answered.'"

Sirhan returned Grant Cooper's gaze without emotion. Mary Sirhan wept.

Almost exactly a week after they had retired to consider the verdict, members of the Sirhan jury found themselves back in the ninth-floor conference room to decide the penalty. The first vote appeared to show a jury evenly divided—five jurors voted for death, three for life, with four undecided. But the jurors arguing for death were more tenacious and persuasive. By the next day the vote was nine for death, one for life, with two undecided. Soon only one juror, Alfonso Galindo, a Roman Catholic Mexican American, stood in the way of a unanimous verdict.

"What crime deserves capital punishment if not this one?" other jurors asked Galindo. Finally, Wednesday morning, after almost twelve hours of deliberation, Galindo changed his mind. "You've convinced me," he said. "Let's all go home."[8]

As the courtroom filled, Grant Cooper walked about in an agitated state. "I don't like it," he said to *Newsday* reporter Bob Greene. "I can feel a chill in my bones." Cooper then offered his analysis, "The weak ones crumbled, just like they did the first time around. They couldn't stand the pressure."[9]

It was 11:30. Sirhan calmly stared at the jurors as they filed into the courtroom. Some looked back; most avoided his gaze. Alice Nishikawa was handed the verdict. "We the jury," she read, "having found the defendant Sirhan Bishara Sirhan guilty of murder in the first degree, as charged in count one of the indictment, now fix the penalty at death."

After the jury was polled, Grant Cooper followed Sirhan out of the courtroom to the holding pen, where Cooper expressed his regret. "We did the best we could," he said, tears flowing from his eyes.

Moved by the emotion, Sirhan, in a momentary reversal of roles, sought to console his attorney. "Even Jesus Christ couldn't have saved me."[10]

After court adjourned, the jurors returned to the Biltmore Hotel, where they had been sequestered since they were chosen in mid-February. Douglas Robinson of *The New York Times* described the scene as they arrived at the hotel.

> As the jurors walked off a sheriff department bus, looking haggard and exhausted, a crowd of newsmen and spectators pressed around the security men guarding them. A number of persons in the throng applauded.
>
> The jurors, their heads down, ignored the applause.[11]

Once Sirhan's fate was cast, many of those who had hailed the jury's verdict the week before now felt uneasy. Writing in *The New York Times,* Tom Wicker voiced his distress: "This supposedly civilized nation is deliberately going to take the life of a distraught, displaced Arab boy who in some tortured shadow world of his own shot down Robert Kennedy."[12] Former Supreme Court justice Arthur J. Goldberg wrote a letter to Ronald Reagan asking the governor to commute Sirhan's sentence. Senator Edward Kennedy wrote a letter on behalf of Sirhan to District Attorney Evelle J. Younger.

Not all the reactions were negative. William F. Buckley, Jr., in the *National Review,* folded all the legal assistance and attention Sirhan had commanded into his newly promulgated "Law of Inverse Hazard for the Killing of Important People."[13]

Reaction in the Middle East was also strangely sanguine. The semi-official Egyptian newspaper *Al-Ahram* noted that if Sirhan had been acquitted, "it would have meant the assassination was a rash act committed by an unbalanced person, therefore any political significance would have to be discounted." But as it was, the paper noted with apparent satisfaction, "murder in the first degree proved Sirhan was fully aware of his act."[14]

In an editorial, *The New York Times* expressed revulsion for the sentence passed upon Sirhan, calling it "a retreat to the law of the jungle." Nevertheless, like other journals, the newspaper's overall expressions about the trial were congratulatory:

> Justice was on trial with Sirhan B. Sirhan. Now . . . after a long and careful trial, it can be said that justice has been served. . . . The public at home and abroad may never know what goes on inside the twisted mind of an assassin. But at least, it has been able to see an open trial fairly conducted.[15]

FIFTEEN

The Hidden Files

✷ ✷ ✷

A BOOK TITLED *Special Unit Senator: The Investigation of the Assassination of Senator Robert F. Kennedy* was published in 1970 by Random House. The author was Robert A. Houghton, chief of detectives, LAPD. Special Unit Senator was also the name of the elite task force set up by Chief Houghton in June 1968 to investigate the Kennedy murder. Houghton's book was coauthored by professional writer Theodore Taylor.

In the foreword, dated August 1, 1969, just three months after Sirhan's trial, Houghton claimed that "the book . . . was written for the sole purpose of acquainting the American public with the facts of the investigation, and with the evidence, or lack of evidence, as it exists, of conspiracy in association with Senator Kennedy's assassination. *The material herein was drawn from the files of the Los Angeles Police Department* [emphasis added]."

As a detective thriller, Houghton's book is in a class by itself—a genre in which the police don't go out and catch the killers, but rather go out and find there are no killers. Its most dramatic moment occurs when Sergeant Enrique Hernandez, using his polygraph machine, breaks witness Sandra Serrano, freeing the police from the obligation to find an accomplice to the murder, the girl in the polka-dot dress.

Though Houghton's book praised the police investigation, confirmed Sirhan's guilt, and discounted any notions of conspiracy, the office of the district attorney was not pleased with the prospect of its publication. In a memorandum to assistant DA Joseph P. Busch, dated a month after Houghton had written his foreword, Sirhan prosecutor John Howard informed Busch that he had reviewed Houghton's book for certain legalities, most specifically to determine if its publication would adversely affect the pending Sirhan appeal. Howard told Busch:

1. The publication will not affect the appeal.
2. Legal position of Chief Houghton in publishing same is questionable. . . .
3. It is ethically improper for Chief Houghton to benefit financially from the efforts and work product produced and paid for by LAPD.[1]

Despite Howard's unofficial conclusions, no injunctive or disciplinary action was ever taken against Chief Houghton. Not addressed by Howard's memo was the issue of whether it was appropriate for Houghton and his coauthor, Theodore Taylor, to have access to the secret police files for the purpose of writing a book when these files were being denied to the public. This question would form the basis for a court battle in 1975.

In the summer of 1973, Allard K. Lowenstein, a former New York congressman and a friend of Robert Kennedy's, attended a meeting of people interested in the circumstances of Kennedy's death. Lowenstein had led the successful "Dump Johnson" movement in 1968, but in 1970, he had been gerrymandered out of his House seat. Even so, the former congressman was outspoken enough to merit inclusion on President Richard Nixon's secret enemies list.

At the meeting, which took place in the Los Angeles home of actor Robert Vaughn, Lowenstein was confronted with evidence that Robert Kennedy had not been murdered by Sirhan Sirhan acting alone. He was skeptical. "Nothing seemed clearer to me at the time," he recalled, "than the absurdity of this notion. Everyone had seen Sirhan shooting at Senator Kennedy."[2] Nevertheless, after examining the evidence, Lowenstein became convinced that there were serious outstanding questions, and that the refusal on the part of the Los Angeles police to open their files was a breach of public trust.

Lowenstein then fashioned an informal coalition to work for public disclosure. Among those who would soon join this effort were Robert Joling, president of the American Academy of Forensic Sciences; former Los Angeles deputy DA Vincent Bugliosi, who prosecuted Charles Manson; and Paul Schrade, the Kennedy friend and campaign aide wounded in the head at the Ambassador Hotel the night Kennedy was shot.

As part of his inquiry Lowenstein submitted a list of questions about the murder investigation to the LAPD chief, Edward Davis. Among other items, he inquired about the ceiling tiles and the doorframes taken from the Ambassador Hotel kitchen by the police. Though Davis promised to get back to Lowenstein, a reply never came. "The official response to my questions was as peculiar as the contradictions in the evidence," recalled Lowenstein. "Every official I saw at the DA's office was polite and talked about cooperation, but nobody did anything. . . . When a question was answered at all, the answer often turned out to be untrue—not marginally untrue, but enthusiastically, aggressively, and sometimes quite imaginatively untrue."[3]

In December 1974, Allard Lowenstein and Paul Schrade held a press conference at the Statler Hilton Hotel in New York, seeking to put pressure upon those holding the secret files. "I reject conspiracy theories until the evidence is in," said Schrade, "but we're asking questions and we want answers."[4]

Lowenstein was less cautious in his pronouncements. "I do not believe on the basis of the evidence in its present state," he said, "that Sirhan Sirhan is the murderer of Robert Kennedy." Lowenstein said that he had spoken recently with Sirhan's chief defense attorney, Grant Cooper, and that Cooper had made the stunning admission "that had he known during the trial what he has since learned, he would have conducted a different defense."[5]★

Just five days after the Schrade-Lowenstein press conference, a secret seventy-six-page response to Lowenstein's inquiry was submitted to assistant chief of police Daryl F. Gates. The cover sheet of the memo read:

> This separate addenda [sic] contains confidential information relative to the questions submitted by Allard Lowenstein. The information has not been revealed prior to this report and may conflict with previous statements made by the Chief of Police and other officials.
>
> Serious consideration should be given to the release of this information.[6]

Gates heeded the warning; the information was not released. But although Daryl Gates could stonewall Allard Lowenstein, there were others to whom he had to answer. On August 21, 1975, the assistant chief of police was called before the Los Angeles City Council to explain the alleged disappearance of evidence from the Robert Kennedy case file. The issue had been raised by Councilman Zev Yaroslavsky, who had been disturbed by rumors that the doorframes and the ceiling tiles taken from the Ambassador Hotel were now either missing or destroyed.

"One would have thought," said Yaroslavsky to Gates before the meeting, "that after all of the problems with the John F. Kennedy assassination, the police department would be a little more sensitive to the preservation of evidence."[7]

When questioned about the missing ceiling panels at the hearing, Gates replied:

> "They have absolutely no value whatsoever. All of the testing, the real important testing, as far as trajectory and the line of fire and the number of bullet holes, that was done prior to their removal [from the pantry]. . . . We made those tests and they showed absolutely nothing. They proved absolutely nothing. They did nothing so far

---

★Grant Cooper died in 1990. His widow, Phyllis, also an attorney, in an interview with the authors, maintained that her husband never had any second thoughts about the defense he provided for Sirhan. This leaves open the question of whether Cooper was patronizing Lowenstein or was reluctant to share his doubts with his wife.

as supporting the investigation or supporting the guilt or innocence of anyone."[8]

Gates went on to say that X-rays of the ceiling panels had been made but that "the records of the X-rays and the X-rays themselves are not in existence." In addition Gates asserted that spectrographic analysis was also probably done by LAPD criminalist DeWayne Wolfer. "He [Wolfer] believes he did make a spectrographic analysis. Ordinarily he would not have conducted a spectrographic analysis, but because we were being so thorough, I think he did."[9]

Gates told the councilmen that the missing doorframes and the ceiling tiles were destroyed by the LAPD on June 27, 1969. If true, the destruction occurred only one month after the *Los Angeles Free Press* article by Lillian Castellano and Floyd Nelson citing evidence of extra bullets in the doorframes—and just three weeks after District Attorney Evelle Younger publicly promised full release of police files.

A week after Gates's revelations, Allard Lowenstein pointed out some contradictions in the police position regarding the missing items. In a letter to Samuel L. Williams, president of the Board of Police Commissioners, Lowenstein asserted:

Assistant Police Chief Daryl Gates says that the ceiling panels were destroyed in June, 1969. Yet on October 11, 1971, a Police Department Board of Inquiry, in a report . . . described as a "reevaluation of the evidence," stated that "an inspection of the ceiling tiles removed from the pantry and a study of the schematic diagram showing the trajectory of the bullets fired by Sirhan refute the contention advanced by Mr. Harper [concerning a second gun]."

How were panels destroyed in June 1969, "reevaluated" in October, 1971? Did the . . . Board of Inquiry announce a "reevaluation" that had not in fact taken place? Mr. Gates now says that these panels "did nothing so far as supporting the investigation or supporting the guilt or innocence of anyone." But in October 1971, an inspection of these same panels was said to "refute" a challenge to the official version of the murder.

Speaking about the police commission's continued refusal to grant access to the investigation file, Lowenstein wrote: "Confidence will not be restored by invoking slogans about civil liberties to refuse reasonable requests designed to answer serious questions, while information leaks out piecemeal about the destruction of crucial evidence."[10]

Lowenstein had little confidence in the abilities of the police commission. Later he would publicly characterize its role in the disclosure process.

"Whatever its motives," he wrote, "the commission has lent a kind of respectability to the cover-up, and it has done so with a clumsy arrogance that leads one to wonder if it took lessons from the Hapsburgs, who are said to have ruled Austria by tyranny tempered only by incompetence."[11]

While the controversy over the missing evidence continued to boil, several legal initiatives were begun in the California Superior Court. In one, Paul Schrade, as a victim of the crime, petitioned the court under the California Public Records Act to open the files. Schrade was joined in this suit by CBS News. One of the petitioners' main arguments was that when Chief Robert Houghton wrote his book *Special Unit Senator*, his civilian coauthor, Theodore Taylor, had utilized the police files, which amounted to prior public disclosure. Thus, the petitioners asserted, they, too, should be granted access.

City attorneys weighed in with an impressive series of sworn affidavits from police officials, rebutting the petitioners' claims. Retired chief Edward Davis and acting chief Jack G. Collins provided statements, as did Houghton himself. To their knowledge, they said, the Robert Kennedy case file had been locked up at headquarters, with access provided only on a strict "need-to-know" basis.

As Houghton stated:

I did write a book with the assistance of Theodore Taylor. I had no recollection, of having shown the ten-volume *Summary* [*Report*] to Taylor, but I did show Taylor some items and some material from LAPD files. Much of the material I showed Taylor was material used in the trial of Sirhan, or held by the district attorney. . . . At no time did Taylor ever come to Parker Center and go into the police investigative files.[12]

On this part of the lawsuit Schrade and CBS lost. Presiding judge Robert A. Wenke held that Taylor's access to the information did not constitute prior disclosure. The LAPD was permitted to keep the files secret.

A decade later Philip Melanson would interview writer Theodore Taylor, who, strangely, had not been called to testify in the 1975 court action. Taylor described to Melanson how he had come into possession of the police files. He related how he had picked up tapes and documents and transported them to his home while the investigation was still ongoing: "My car was parked outside of Parker Center and I kept loading this crap in there. I don't know, the guy helped me with a cart; he had a big cart. And I thought, Jesus Christ, what really do I have here?"

Taylor related that he drove the files to his home and stored them in an office in his garage because there wasn't room in his study. Melanson asked Taylor how complete was the material turned over to him:

TAYLOR: I had access to some papers that I shouldn't have had access to. . . .

MELANSON: In what sense, since they were giving you most everything? What do you mean you "shouldn't have"?

TAYLOR: Well now, these papers were not involved, did not come from LAPD. They were FBI . . . Central Intelligence [CIA]. He [Houghton] said, "For Chrissakes, you know, you're looking at 'em and I'll give 'em to you for forty-eight hours and then you get 'em back up here and don't copy anything down from 'em."

MELANSON: That's an example of how much he turned over?

TAYLOR: He just turned over everything he had.[13]

The combined pressure of hearings before the police commission, the city council, and the California Superior Court prodded the district attorney's office to initiate a reinvestigation of their own. Acting district attorney John E. Howard appointed private attorney Thomas F. Kranz on August 14, 1975, as special counsel to "independently review all the previous evidence, transcripts, interviews, and documents relating to the Sirhan case, and make his own independent investigation into the assassination of Robert Kennedy."[14]

A year and a half later a 135-page document titled *The Report of Thomas F. Kranz on the Assassination of Senator Robert F. Kennedy* (*Kranz Report*) was released to the public. In his opening remarks Kranz made it clear that the motivating force behind this new investigation was "not the validity of the verdict in the Sirhan case, but the erosion of public confidence in the system of justice in Los Angeles County due to the many questions that were continually being raised in the Sirhan matter."[15] What seemed to escape Kranz was that this erosion of public confidence and the many questions being raised concerned the most fundamental conclusions of the police investigation. In characterizing these questions as "the orchestration of controversy," Kranz revealed a mind-set that was neither incisive nor open-minded. Though Kranz did briefly criticize criminalist DeWayne Wolfer for "sloppy" work, the report turned out to be an elaborate apology for the police.

In July 1977, Allard Lowenstein forwarded to the Los Angeles County Board of Supervisors a list of corrections to the *Kranz Report*. Lowenstein and his colleague, political scientist Gregory Stone, addressed seventy-five significant misrepresentations and errors contained in the report, inaccuracies that served to obscure important issues of fact.

According to the Lowenstein–Stone review, Kranz misrepresented key evidence regarding Kennedy's position in the pantry, the observed bullet holes in the pantry doorframe, the testimony of witness Sandra Serrano, and, on numerous occasions, the conclusions of the 1975 firearms panel, which refuted DeWayne Wolfer's trial testimony that victim bullets could be conclusively matched to Sirhan's gun. "A scientific ballistics hearing subsequently linked all the bullets to only one weapon,"[16] claimed Kranz in his report. This, as Lowenstein and Stone pointed out, was grossly inaccurate and represented either a failure to grasp the most elemental facts of the case or a serious disregard for the truth.

In concluding their review, Lowenstein and Stone asserted:

> Whatever Mr. Kranz found or didn't find, his findings have not changed these facts:
>
> Law enforcement agencies violated for eight years their own promises that the investigation "work product" would be made available. They "lost" or destroyed key evidence and documentation, and suppressed the fact of this destruction. They opposed the firearms testing, which, when finally conducted, further discredited the official handling of physical evidence. They concealed the identities of police officers, misrepresented their observations, and then obstructed the effort to obtain statements or testimony from them. They have continually misstated basic facts and stonewalled legitimate inquiries.[17]

In the foreword to his report Thomas Kranz asserted, "This report is my product and no changes in either content or substance have been made by any other persons." This may be an overstatement. Recently released documents from the district attorney's office, provided to the authors by Los Angeles attorney Marilyn Barrett, reveal that Kranz's vaunted independence as a special counsel was limited. In making the report, Kranz used the district attorney's top RFK case investigator, William R. Burnett. An undated memo from Kranz to Burnett states:

> What I'd like to have you do is just take a look at this rough draft, it's pretty lengthy actually it's 19 tapes (sides). Give me your ideas when you have a chance. . . . Anyone in Tom McDonald's office can tell you where the rough draft copy is—I will talk to you next week. Thank you, Tom.[18]

In the report, Thomas Kranz made particular efforts to dismiss speculation that there were bullets or bullet holes in the destroyed doorframes. He claimed to have interviewed "FBI investigators" who confirmed the fact that there were no such holes. But how thorough was his search?

In 1976 former FBI agent William Bailey, who had been at the Ambassador Hotel shortly after the shooting, swore an affidavit to former prosecutor Vincent Bugliosi that he had seen two bullet holes in the center divider between the pantry doors. In 1977 (the month is unclear), DA investigator William Burnett spoke to Bailey by telephone (an audiotape of this conversation was found in a closet of the DA's office in 1986). During the conversation Bailey made the same assertion to Burnett.

> BAILEY: There were at least two bullet holes in the center post, between the two swinging doors.
>
> BURNETT: You say at least two bullet holes. Now how do you base your determination that these were bullet holes?
>
> BAILEY: Let's put it this way, Bill. Short of actually taking the wood off myself and examining it, I would say that I'm reasonably certain they were bullet holes. I've seen bullet holes in wood before. I looked into these holes, they were definitely not nail holes. There appeared to be objects inside, imbedded inside. They were not nails.[19]

Despite this conversation and despite the fact that Bailey had gone on record with this information the previous year and provided the name of another agent who could corroborate his observations, there is no mention of William Bailey in the supposedly comprehensive *Kranz Report.*

Also unanswered by the *Kranz Report* is an obvious question: Why was it necessary to spend public money and a year and a half to reinvestigate the Robert Kennedy murder, when the police had already produced, at considerable public expense, a more comprehensive fifteen-hundred-page *Summary Report,* which they were refusing to open for inspection? What was the purpose of such a report if it was not to be released? Knowing the controversy it was causing, why did the police department fight so hard to keep it secret?

Allard Lowenstein speculated on possible motives for the suppression of evidence in a 1977 article in *The Saturday Review:*

> I do not know whether Sirhan acting alone murdered Robert Kennedy. I do know what happened when we tried to find out. Eventually, reluctantly, against all my instinct and wishes, I arrived at the melancholy thought that people who have nothing to hide do not lie, cheat, and smear to hide it.
>
> It is possible that the small number of people in key places who have worked to head off inquiries and cover up facts have done so simply because their reputations or careers are at stake; but the fact that this is a possibility does not make it acceptable to allow the situation to rest as it is, for there are other possibilities, too.[20]

Three years later, on March 14, 1980, fifty-one-year-old Allard Lowenstein was murdered. Dennis Sweeney, a deranged former colleague in the civil rights movement of the 1960s, entered Lowenstein's law office in New York and shot him five times with a handgun. Some writers and researchers have suggested that Lowenstein's energetic efforts in the Robert Kennedy case were the reason behind the murder. Lowenstein's closest associate, Gregory Stone, remained unsure. "It's clear that Dennis Sweeney was a nut," he said some years later. "The only question is whether he was a handled nut."[21]

In 1983 Gregory Stone edited and published a book about his former colleague, titled *Lowenstein: Acts of Courage and Belief.* That same year, Stone met Philip Melanson, a professor of political science at the University of Massachusetts. Melanson had studied and written about political violence in the United States, and the two soon decided to continue the probe begun by Lowenstein. A year later, a formal request for release of the case files was made to the Los Angeles Police Commission by the newly endowed University of Massachusetts RFK Assassination Archives, of which Melanson was director. A group of nineteen journalists, academics, and political officials wrote letters supporting disclosure. These included RFK biographer and adviser Arthur Schlesinger, Jr.; Massachusetts congressman Barney Frank; forensic scientist Dr. Cyril Wecht; and Kennedy Library archivist Henry Gwiazda. Several film industry people also wrote letters. Said historian Schlesinger: "There would seem no reason why, seventeen years after this tragic event, this information should still be withheld. The material is of indisputable historic significance. . . . Every consideration of scholarly and national interest calls for disclosure of all information related to Robert Kennedy's death."[22]

The publicly stated rationale for keeping the files secret had always been murky. During hearings before the police commission in 1985, Chief Daryl Gates claimed that release of the files would jeopardize rights to privacy. "There are still people who are living that I think would be harmed, seriously harmed," said Gates.[23] But whom was he referring to? If Sirhan alone had shot Robert Kennedy and the police had conducted an honest investigation, who could be harmed by release of the investigation files?

During another police commission hearing in 1985, Commissioner Samuel Williams questioned Professor Melanson about the privacy issue.

"Can you tell me," he said, "that if someone was staying as a guest in the [Ambassador] hotel that night, and no one knew they were there, that information would not come out?"[24]

So this was it? The investigation files in one of the most important political murders of the century were being withheld (at that point for seventeen years) because some political figures or private citizens might have been staying at the hotel with women who were not their wives?

In the end public pressure helped the commission overcome its concerns about secret hotel visits. At a highly charged hearing on July 30, 1985, it voted to release the LAPD's *Summary Report* first, then the main file. The commission's formal motion, however, left room for extreme censorship by promulgating the following "standard": ". . . remove items that are prohibited by law from being released, and those items which were to be held in confidence per agreements with other public agencies and information from informants; with due respect to issues of privacy and national security *and any other privileges not enumerated above* [emphasis added]."

The motion carried no timetable. The petitioners were puzzled by the emphasis on national security in a domestic assassination that officially had no conspiracy dimension, foreign or domestic.

Chief Daryl Gates made a final pitch to the commission: release the file at a "future date certain" when no one could be harmed, but not now. Later in the hallway a reporter asked Gates what date he had in mind. "In the 1990s," he replied.[25]

Despite his history of fierce resistance to opening the files, Daryl Gates, in a remarkable passage in his 1992 book *Chief: My Life in the LAPD,* credited himself with disclosure:

> By now, everyone was demanding to see our files. Personally, I had no objection to opening them up. The problem was, the files contained information given to us on a confidential basis. We had all kinds of information from people who were around the senator, what they were doing, who they were with, *private* information. I didn't think we had any right to disregard a confidential relationship. This only added more fuel to the conspiracy theories. "If the police weren't hiding something, they'd let us into that file. So they're hiding something, they know there's a conspiracy, and that's why they won't give us that file."
>
> Finally, I got so sick of this, I recommended the files be placed in the hands of our archivist, pointed out what we thought was confidential and let him worry what to do about it.[26]

After a year of foot-dragging and broken promises, the *Summary Report* was released by the police commission with great fanfare. Despite reminders from the pro-disclosure group that the report was merely a secondhand summary of the primary case record and should have been released seventeen years earlier, the media bought the spin generated by the LAPD and the commission: that this was a landmark in public disclosure and would satisfactorily answer any reasonable questions regarding the case.

Despite the positive reviews, the value of the *Summary Report* had been greatly reduced by those who processed it for release. Taking full advantage of the police commission's guidelines, the report had been "redacted" (a favorite term among the commissioners) to the point where the name of almost every witness and investigating officer was deleted. Numerous paragraphs and pages were also blacked out. Researchers who wanted to know who said what to what investigator were completely stymied. Hope for any real revelations, and for holding the LAPD accountable, then rested in the release of the primary file. But how and when would that happen?

In 1986, in response to continued public pressure, Los Angeles mayor Tom Bradley appointed a distinguished committee of archivists, jurists, and professors to find a suitable repository for the LAPD files. Though not yet in the public domain, the investigation file—at least what remained of it—was out of the department's hands for the first time since it resided in writer Theodore Taylor's garage.

While the battle to open the LAPD files was being waged before the police commission in 1985, a separate attempt was launched to secure the case files of the FBI. A decade earlier Bernard Fensterwald, Washington attorney and assassination researcher, had used the Freedom of Information Act (FOIA) to obtain three thousand pages of RFK assassination documents and photos from the FBI, including the crucial photos of the holes in the pantry doorframe, which the Bureau labeled "bullet holes."

While the documents pried free by Fensterwald provided important insights into the case, researchers were quite sure that the complete FBI file was many times larger. The difficulty in formulating any FOIA request resides in asking for files using the code names they are actually stored under. For example, a person might petition the FBI for its "Sirhan" file without knowing that the FBI's main file was stored under the name "KENSALT" (assault on Senator Kennedy). Without clues to a broader search the petitioner would get only what was in the requested file.

Under the direction of attorney Jim Lesar of Washington and cocounsel Lawrence Teeter of Los Angeles, Gregory Stone and Philip Melanson filed a seven-page request letter. It asked for headquarters and field-office files and asked that searches be conducted for a strange list of acronyms and rubrics. The outcome of this carefully designed, broad-spectrum search was thirty-two thousand pages of previously unreleased documents—a tenfold increase on the 1975 release to Fensterwald.

Documents were processed in Washington, D.C., and shipped to the Robert F. Kennedy Assassination Archives in Massachusetts in batches of fifteen hundred to twenty-five hundred pages. Some were heavily deleted. But the censorship of selected sentences, paragraphs, and pages was accompanied by a far more troublesome problem: the name of every agent who worked on the case was blacked out. Lesar and Teeter immediately wrote to the Bureau requesting that the practice be halted and the names restored. They pointed out that in similar releases on the assassinations of President Kennedy and Dr. King, agents' names were not expunged. Why do so in the RFK case?

The Bureau refused the request, arguing that the agents' privacy outweighed the value of historical research. The FBI did, however, offer to restore the name of any agent within the precise context in which it may have been previously disclosed. Thus, if the petitioners could provide documentation that an agent had conducted a particular interview, the Bureau would restore that agent's name to the released interview.

Stone and Melanson rejected this offer to give them what they already had and instead responded with a list of over one hundred agents who had worked on the case, garnered from books, newspapers, and previously released documents. They argued that it was not a matter of privacy, since the identities of most agents were in the public record. The real issue was which agents did what, when, and how in this controversial investigation.

Five congressmen wrote FBI director William Webster and asked that the names not be deleted. In a written response Webster said, "The identities of remaining FBI and other law enforcement personnel are being withheld as disclosure would constitute an unwarranted invasion of their privacy. . . . Public identification could conceivably subject them to harassment or annoyance in the conduct of their official duties and in their private lives."[27]

The dispute was taken to federal court.[28] The case for disclosure seemed to the plaintiffs to be clear. Witnesses' names were not deleted. How could public servants accountable for their conduct have a more elevated right to privacy than witnesses? Lesar and Teeter argued that deletion of the names effectively insulated the Bureau from scrutiny of its performance in the case and all but precluded meaningful research by scholars and journalists.

The plaintiffs mustered nineteen supporting affidavits testifying to the importance of the names, the precedents for disclosing them, and the absence of any problems in previous releases of agents' names. These came from professors, reporters, authors who had written books about the Bureau, a former agent, and a former director of the Bureau's Freedom of Information office.

Government lawyers produced no supporting affidavits. Although the FBI's major claim was that agents would be harassed, there was not a single statement documenting that this had ever occurred.

But in January 1989, federal judge Charles Richey issued a decision in favor of the FBI. He ruled that the agents involved "have a legitimate interest in preserving the secrecy of matters that conceivably could subject them to annoyance or harassment in either their official or private lives."[29]

On April 19, 1988, twenty years after the assassination, public disclosure of the primary case file was finally achieved. The panel appointed by Mayor Bradley had decided upon the California State Archives in Sacramento as the proper repository for the files. The archives were under the direction of state archivist John Burns, who oversaw the sorting and cataloging of the fifty thousand pages of material.

Under Burns's direction there was virtually no censorship. The names and most of the deleted passages were restored to the *Summary Report*. However, Burns and his staff could disclose only what they were given by the LAPD. During two decades of secrecy, key evidence and materials had been lost or destroyed. In a public report, archivist Burns made note of these items:

> Police admitted the destruction of the door jambs and ceiling tiles, removed from the crime scene. A .22 caliber projectile taken from Sirhan pocket (evidence item #6) is also missing. 2410 photographs collected in the case were destroyed approximately 2½ months after the shooting. Archives photo indexes note that photos related to bullet fragments and shell casings, comparison tests, Kennedy clothing, gun firing tests, witness re-enactment of shooting, and tracing and location of bullets are absent from the file.[30]

The press, which had been overly kind to the police two years earlier when the heavily edited *Summary Report* was released, now ran critical reports on the missing items. On *World News Tonight*, ABC's Peter Jennings spoke about the newly opened files, saying they provided "some answers, and some more questions." A segment followed, reported by ABC correspondent Ken Kashiwahara:

> KASHIWAHARA: They are reminders of a national tragedy and controversy: 50,000 documents collected by the Los Angeles police after the murder of Robert Kennedy. . . . But the public release of the murder evidence has failed to answer questions about whether there was a *second* gunman because of evidence that is missing. State Archives officials say that a bullet taken from Sirhan's pocket is missing and that the police destroyed more than 2,400 photographs. Did Sirhan act alone?
>
> JOHN BURNS (CALIFORNIA STATE ARCHIVIST): I have gone through this material extensively but I can say that I *cannot* draw a firm conclusion.[31]

Although the doorframes and the ceiling tiles had been on record as being destroyed for over a decade, for many people this was the first notice. The police, on the other hand, were ready with their justifications. During an interview on Los Angeles television, retired chief of detectives Robert Houghton tried to explain the missing doorframes:

"After the trial was over and I can't remember who it was came to me and asked me ah—whether or not it would be proper to destroy or get rid of those doorjambs. . . . And I presume they asked that the tile, about the tiles at the same time, to store them for . . . as we intended to do . . . in perpetuity, without taking up a lot of space. . . . So I told them if they had the adequate, ah, ah, evidence . . . from those doors . . . er, the doorjambs . . . ah, then go ahead and destroy them, as long as that evidence maintained in, was maintained in file; if anybody is, ah, curious about that they should go to the actual record where people, experts were testifying under oath, in my opinion."[32]

In a newspaper interview Houghton said that the idea that police had destroyed important evidence was "just crap." Speaking again about the possibility of bullet holes, he remarked, "There were holes all over the place, but not bullet holes. . . . Look, all you have to do is go to the trial testimony. . . . All this came out at the trial."[33] Houghton, of course, was incorrect: there was no testimony at the trial concerning any holes in the hotel pantry.

In a statement to UPI, former Los Angeles chief of police Edward Davis characterized the disclosure process. "It's like opening up a collection of pornography to a bunch of sex-hungry pornography addicts," he said. "They're going to fondle the gun, touch the wood, stick their fingers in the bullet holes."[34]

As colorful as Davis's statement was, the former chief of police had apparently forgotten several facts: (1) "the wood," presumably the doorframes, had been secretly destroyed by the police twenty years earlier, and (2) according to the police, there were no bullet holes.

Although the "missing items" grabbed the headlines, the true significance of the file release was that for the first time it was possible to see if the official version of the crime was borne out by the physical evidence and the surviving interview transcripts. The reason for keeping the *Summary Report* secret quickly became clear. Now, for the first time, witnesses could be shown what it is the police asserted they had said. Some would forcefully deny making the statements. In other cases where the *Summary Report* asserted that a witness had admitted fabricating a story, all that could be found in the interview transcripts was the admission that the witness lacked an absolute certainty. In other instances where witnesses had changed their story, transcripts and tapes of those sessions revealed the extreme pressure to which these witnesses were subjected by police interrogators.

Over the next several years, as researchers sifted through the thousands of pages of documents and hundreds of audiotapes, it became clear that there had been many instances of misconduct by the police. As a result of these discoveries a working committee was formed under the banner of the Truth and Accountability Foundation, an organization founded by Gregory Stone. The committee (including Stone, Floyd Nelson, Marilyn Barrett, Paul Schrade, journalist Dan Moldea, and Philip Melanson) began to collate its research into the newly opened files.

But then tragedy struck. On a sunny afternoon in late January 1991, Gregory Stone drove to a local park, sat under a tree, and took his own life with a pistol. Unknown to most of those around him, Stone had been engaged in a losing battle against depression. The news of his death stunned his colleagues on the Robert Kennedy case. After a period of shock and reflection, a decision was made by the group to continue the work and proceed with a new legal initiative. A year later, on April 2, 1992, a petition, officially referred to as a "Request," was presented to the Los Angeles County Grand Jury by Paul Schrade, who had been wounded the night Kennedy was murdered, twenty-four years earlier.

The Request was a fifty-page document, supported by eight hundred pages of exhibits. It began:

> This Request to the Los Angeles County Grand Jury is being submitted because newly discovered evidence indicates that the Los Angeles Police Department ("LAPD") engaged in "willful and corrupt misconduct" in its investigation of the assassination of Senator Robert Kennedy. . . . This evidence shows that the LAPD was on notice of substantial evidence that at least one more gun was being fired at the same time that Sirhan was firing his gun, which evidence the LAPD decided to ignore. In addition, the evidence shows that the LAPD ignored material evidentiary leads, engaged in a concerted cover-up of its failures, and otherwise failed to conduct a thorough investigation of the crime.[35]

The Request asserted that the LAPD's acts of misconduct included the destruction of evidence, the falsification of evidence, and the coercion of witnesses, which it described in its subsequent pages. The Request then asked the grand jury to appoint a special prosecutor to investigate the alleged acts of misconduct and to take action against those it found guilty of "obstruction of justice." It was signed by over fifty individuals and organizations, including the Southern California ACLU, actors Edward Asner and Martin Sheen, United Farm Workers president Cesar Chavez, former presidents of the American Academy of Forensic Sciences Dr. Robert Joling and Dr. Cyril Wecht, filmmaker Oliver Stone, former Senate Watergate Committee chief counsel Samuel Dash, author Norman Mailer, former RFK press secretary Frank Mankiewicz, historian Arthur Schlesinger, Jr., and Harvard law professor Gary Bellow.

In asserting its legal foundation, the petition cited section 919c of the California Penal Code: "The grand jury shall inquire into the willful or corrupt misconduct in office of public officers of every description within the county." The petition maintained that its cause was timely under the rules of discovery because "decisive new evidence has been discovered in the LAPD's files on this case, which were released for public inspection only as recently as April 1988."

Official reaction to the Request was carefully muted. "This has been looked at a number of times before, and it hasn't resulted in anything different," said chief of police Daryl Gates, "so I am not going to comment on it."[36]

The timing of the submission was awkward. The sitting grand jury had only two months' tenure, not enough time to consider the document placed before them. Without recommendation it was passed on to the incoming jury. In the spring of the following year four members of the Criminal Justice Committee met with Paul Schrade and Marilyn Barrett, attorney for the petitioners. Both Schrade and Barrett left the meeting with the impression that the committee was interested in "doing something." What followed were several months of silence. Finally on June 22, 1993, more than a year after the submission of the petition, Marilyn Barrett received a letter of one sentence:

> With regard to your concerns about the Los Angeles Police Department's policies and procedures governing the safeguarding of evidence, the Criminal Justice Committee of the 1992–93 Los Angeles County Grand Jury has looked into the matter and has discussed it with the Los Angeles Police Department.
>
>   John A. Grande, Foreperson[37]

"Discussed it?" said Paul Schrade in an incredulous moment. "We asked the grand jury to investigate the LAPD, not go have lunch with them."[38]

Attempting to stimulate the grand jury into meeting its responsibilities, Barrett wrote back, thanking the jurors for their attention. She then asked if the jury would be good enough to answer several questions. Who were the LAPD officers the Criminal Justice Committee had met with? What actions did the grand jury or the LAPD take against officers accused of misconduct? If no action was taken, what was the reason? Did the grand jury analyze evidence that more than one gun was fired during the murder? If so, what were its findings? And so forth. "Responses to the foregoing questions," wrote Barrett, "will greatly help to assure the public that its very legitimate concerns have not been disregarded."[39]

In a telephone call following her letter, Marilyn Barrett was advised by John Grande that the 1992–1993 grand jury would not have time to respond to her letter but would forward it along with the Request to the incoming jury for action. Later in the summer Barrett discovered that the Request had not been forwarded, but had been logged as "closed." In September she resubmitted the Request, reminding the grand jury that "the public's right to demand accountability is indisputable. Nevertheless [they have] yet to get a full accounting from the LAPD concerning its destruction of evidence (much of which was destroyed even before Sirhan Sirhan's criminal trial began or appeals from his conviction were heard)."[40]

In February, Barrett received a letter stating that the material she had submitted had been already "thoroughly analyzed." The letter invited her to submit anything new she might have, but requested that she refrain from "reargument or reiteration." It was signed "Terry L. White, Grand Jury Legal Advisor." White was an employee of the district attorney's office.[41]

In her reply a month later Barrett asserted, "There is simply no justification for the conclusion that the previously submitted information has already been appropriately handled. The obligation of the Grand Jury . . . remains unfulfilled." Barrett then questioned the involvement of Terry White. "In view of Mr. White's employment in the DA's office, any participation whatsoever by him in your deliberations on this case would be a clear violation of the conflict of interest rules."[42]

Barrett then accepted the invitation to submit new material. Over the preceding months she had gained access to files in the district attorney's office concerning the Robert Kennedy case, files that had not been made public previously. "In reviewing the DA's files," she wrote, "I found a number of documents that suggest the DA's office itself was involved in covering up an inadequate investigation by the LAPD and its own office." What followed were nine single-spaced, typed pages summarizing additional evidence of official wrongdoing.[43]

In early May, Barrett got a phone call from the chairperson of what was now called the Criminal Justice Information Systems Committee, inviting her and Paul Schrade to meet with the committee in private. The meeting took place on May 10 at the county courthouse. Both Barrett and Schrade were immediately impressed with the caliber of jurors and their apparent interest in the subject. Then the bad news. The jurors informed the petitioners that they had no power to investigate any action without prior approval of the district attorney.

Schrade and Barrett were shocked. "That, of course, is not our reading of the statute," Barrett commented later. "I believe they were being honest with us. I just think that's what they were told."[44] The remaining discussion centered upon recommendations the grand jury could make to safeguard evidence in the future. Schrade and Barrett left. After more than two years, the effort to hold the LAPD accountable for its actions by going through proper legal channels was finished.

The sting of this final setback had barely had time to sink in when, the next morning in the *Los Angeles Times,* a column by Bill Boyarsky attacked outright the grand jury system.

The Los Angeles County Grand Jury is supposed to be the people's watchdog, exposing corruption and inefficiency in government. . . . As anyone familiar with the process knows, that isn't the way it works. . . . Smart politicians have long been aware of the situation. So when reporters uncover waste or dirty dealings, the pols [politicians] immediately turn the matter over to the grand jury. They do this knowing the panel will never have the time to investigate. It's like dumping a potential scandal into a bottomless pit.[45]

Boyarsky, it turns out, had been approached by two jurors from the 1992–1993 grand jury, Don Dodd and Richard Mankiewicz, who a year earlier had been on the committee that met with Schrade and Barrett. Their complaints were now printed in Boyarsky's column. "It is our view that it is a mistake for anyone to serve on the Los Angeles County Grand Jury," the two reported. "One cannot escape the conclusion that grand juries are merely meant to give the appearance of citizen watchdogs, but are prevented from acting as such."[46]

In a telephone interview with the authors, Mankiewicz explained why he thought the grand jury system was so ineffective. "Because you are all twenty-three virgins," he explained; "it takes you months to figure out what you are supposed to be doing." Mankiewicz remembered the Request and the presentation made by Schrade and Barrett, but he indicated that there simply was not the time or the resources for the jury to act independently. "If powerful people want something covered up, it will be covered up," he said. "And the grand jury can't do anything about it. By the end of our term we realized that the grand jury as now constituted is useless except as a flunky for the district attorney."[47]

SIXTEEN

Prison and Parole

✳ ✳ ✳

On November 13, 1970, while Sirhan Sirhan was occupying a cell on San Quentin's death row, a legal appeal on his behalf by attorney Luke McKissack was filed with the Supreme Court of California. Two years earlier Grant Cooper had considered McKissack, then in his mid-twenties, for the position of interim attorney in the original trial but had decided instead upon the more tread-worn Russell Parsons. After the trial, with Cooper, Berman, and Parsons no longer actively involved, McKissack had assumed the position of lead attorney.

The appeal brief, eight hundred pages in length, contained eighteen formal arguments questioning the adequacy of Sirhan's trial. Many of the points had been argued by the trial attorneys. There were objections to the court's rejection of the original plea-bargain agreement, objections to the legality of the seizure of evidence from Sirhan's home, objections concerning the makeup of the grand jury and the trial jury, and an assertion that Sirhan didn't have the capacity to maturely and meaningfully reflect upon the gravity of his crime.

Prior to his assumption of the Sirhan appeal, McKissack's most well-known clients were Black Panthers Angela Davis and Elmer Pratt. Davis had been accused of providing guns for a deadly courtroom-escape attempt in San Rafael. Pratt had been accused of murder in Los Angeles. (Davis would be subsequently acquitted, Pratt convicted.) With Sirhan Sirhan added to this list, McKissack became the object of abnormal scrutiny by Los Angeles authorities, and a number of unflattering memos about him circulated. One, written to Los Angeles district attorney Joe Busch on June 3, 1971, stamped CONFIDENTIAL, asserted that

> according to a confidential source (so far proven, to be reliable), McKissack and friends are actively participating in various Panther (Pratt faction) criminal plots. . . . Over the past four months we have received information from several sources which describe criminal conduct on the part of Luke McKissack.[1]

The following month another memo written to DA Busch by Richard Hecht, head of the Organized Crime and Pornography Division, alleged that "a Black Panther working in the Clerk's Office had assisted another person in switching bullets which were part of the Sirhan evidence" and that this person "still has a friend in the Clerk's Office involved in altering and/or changing the Sirhan exhibits."[2] The motive for the Black Panthers to alter evidence in the Sirhan case now had a rationale, however strange: McKissack represented both.

Another document in the files of the DA's office was a bizarre, unsigned spiderweb diagram. It showed the purported nefarious interlocking relationships of people involved in either the Sirhan appeal or the challenge to the competency and integrity of LAPD criminalist DeWayne Wolfer. In this diagram McKissack was identified as a "communist" who had "past felony involvement, including conspiracy murders + cocaine to panther in court."[3] McKissack's coattorney in the appeal, George Shibley, was also designated "communist." So was attorney Barbara Blehr, who had mounted the public challenge to DeWayne Wolfer's promotion to chief forensic chemist.

The claims of criminal misconduct on the part of Luke McKissack were baseless, as were the claims against Shibley and Blehr. They are perhaps best understood as representative of the siege mentality then rampant in Los Angeles law enforcement, part of a general strategy to discredit anyone involved in left-wing politics or who questioned the official version of the Robert Kennedy murder. Although a grand jury was convened to hear complaints against the county clerk's office for mismanaging access to the Sirhan exhibits, no charges were ever filed.

On February 18, 1972, the California Supreme Court ruled by a vote of 6 to 1 that the death penalty as practiced in California violated the state constitution's prohibition against cruel and unusual punishment. "We have concluded that capital punishment is impermissibly cruel," said the court. "It degrades and dehumanizes all who participate in its process." In its decision the court held that the cruelty of the punishment "lies not only in the execution itself and the pain incident thereto, but also in the dehumanizing effects of the lengthy imprisonment prior to execution."

The day the court's decision was announced, a picture of a broadly smiling Mary Sirhan dominated the front page of the *Los Angeles Times*. Out of the 104 persons on death row in California, Sirhan Sirhan had become the poster boy for the abolition of the death penalty.

"This is the happiest day of my life," Mrs. Sirhan was quoted as saying. "I just knelt on my knees and prayed and thanked God for what He did and the mercy He had."[4] The *Los Angeles Times* praised the new ruling as "a decision of persuasive clarity and wisdom."[5]

Reaction by public officials was less enthusiastic. Sirhan's prosecutor, Evelle J. Younger, now attorney general of the state of California, called the new ruling "ill-advised" and suggested several remedies, including a state constitutional amendment. The attorney general argued that the court was applying its own definition of cruelty and not that of society. He also voiced contempt for the court's ruling that long delays in carrying out the death sentence were a determining factor, citing "the procrastination which this court has built into our system of criminal justice."[6]

Four months later, on June 16, the California Supreme Court denied Sirhan's appeal, filed two years earlier by Luke McKissack, and upheld his conviction for the murder of Robert Kennedy. At the same time, in accordance with their ruling in February, the court reduced Sirhan's sentence to life in prison. This action was reinforced two weeks later when the United States Supreme Court, by a ruling of 5 to 4, struck down as "cruel and unusual" the death-penalty laws as then written in most states.

In December of 1974 former congressman Allard Lowenstein, a friend of Robert Kennedy's who had begun his own investigation into the murder, petitioned Los Angeles district attorney Joseph Busch to reopen the Sirhan case. Lowenstein cited three reasons to reopen the investigation.

Evidence which indicates that at least nine bullets were fired during the assassination, and Sirhan's gun held only eight.

Evidence which showed the gun to have been fired inches from Senator Kennedy's head, and witnesses said Sirhan never got that close.

Ballistics which indicated a television news producer wounded during the shooting was shot by a gun other than the one which killed Senator Kennedy.[7]

Joseph Busch rejected Lowenstein's plea, saying that these questions were answered during the original investigation conducted by the police. He added that he would be more inclined to open the case if the request came directly from Sirhan's attorney.

Four weeks later such a request came, not to DA Busch, but to the California Supreme Court. It came in the form of a writ of error coram nobis. The writ differed from the appeal filed previously on Sirhan's behalf because, as the appeal was unable to do, the writ requested the high court to consider evidence in the Sirhan case beyond the trial record. Attorney Godfrey Isaac, who had drawn up the fifty-five-page document, claimed to newsmen that the new evidence "tended to show that Senator Robert Kennedy was not killed by bullets from Sirhan's gun." He went on to assert that this evidence had been "deliberately, intentionally and willingly suppressed by the prosecution and their agents."[8]

The following month, the California high court turned down, without comment, Isaac's attempt to reopen the case. In reaction to the decision, Sirhan's attorney said he believed that the evidence presented in the writ "showed scientifically that Sirhan could not have committed this act. . . . It is difficult to accept, as final, a determination made without a court hearing."[9]

Despite the failure of Isaac's writ, the winds of change continued to blow favorably for Sirhan in 1975. As a result of a quickly growing prison population and the increased practice of sentencing criminals to open-ended and widely varying prison terms, a movement developed in California to institute more uniformity and certainty into the sentencing and parole policies. A motion was introduced into the state legislature to end indeterminate sentencing; several lawsuits challenged the prolonged incarceration of inmates. Thus, in March 1975, in response to this pressure, the nine-member California Department of Corrections Adult Authority instituted a new set of guidelines, establishing a fixed range of sentences for each type of crime. These guidelines were also to be applied to men already in prison serving indeterminate sentences, giving them "a date certain" when they could expect to be released. Among the reasons stated for this new policy was the tendency of the system to hold men who had committed highly publicized crimes much longer than those who had committed more egregious but less noted ones.

Pursuant to this new policy, on May 20, 1975, a three-member panel of the Adult Authority interviewed Sirhan over a two-day period. They then granted him a parole date of February 23, 1986. Questioned by the press, the chairman of the Adult Authority, Ray K. Procunier, praised the decision of the panel. "I'm proud as hell that [they] didn't search for some bogus reason to deny him [Sirhan] or refer it to someone else," he said. "It would have been simple to rationalize, to do the popular thing and avoid the issue. . . . This should prove we don't have any political prisoners."[10]

Citing figures that showed that men convicted of first-degree murder "have been going out, on the average, in about 11 years," state prison official Philip Guthrie also defended the 1986 date, which would have given Sirhan almost eighteen years of time served. "He's at the top of the range for most inmates," Guthrie said. "The Adult Authority didn't choose to deny him or go beyond the range because they figured the guy had been well-behaved and it would be difficult to say that because of who he killed he was going to do more time."[11]

In the same way that he had played a symbolic role when the death penalty was abolished, it was inevitable that Sirhan would become the focus for the debate on the new parole policy. News of his parole date, still a decade away, made front-page headlines. The *Los Angeles Times* published a cartoon showing a smiling Sirhan sitting in his cell marking off the days till his release.[12]

There was also published in the *Times* an impassioned protest of Sirhan's parole date by state treasurer Jesse Unruh, who had helped rescue Sirhan from a violent crowd the night of the murder:

> Sirhan did not commit "just another murder." The record clearly indicates he planned and carried out a political assassination. The .22 caliber bullets which he fired into Robert Kennedy did far more than kill Rose Kennedy's third son; they wiped out the votes of 1.4 million Californians cast just hours before. These shots also destroyed the hopes of millions of other Americans, let alone of other peoples around the world.
>
> The act was treason—and its perpetrator should be treated as a traitor as well as a murderer.[13]

Unruh's missive brought a flood of letters. Most were outspoken in their desire to have Sirhan's parole date revoked. Some, however, took issue with Unruh's logic:

> Unruh notes Kennedy's 1.4 million votes; suppose he'd only received half as many? Twice as many? Does the value of Kennedy's life or the length of Sirhan's term go up or down accordingly? Suppose the personal loss to me of my girlfriend . . . would be greater than the loss of a local politician. Yes, we must protect our politicians, but who are they? Is Bob Dylan included?[14]

Following his receipt of a parole date, Sirhan was transferred from San Quentin, where he had been residing on death row, to the Correctional Training Facility at Soledad. There, though still in a special protected unit, he would have more contact with other prisoners. Shortly thereafter the Los Angeles district attorney's office began to hear from prisoners who claimed to have exclusive information about Sirhan.

One of these was Daniel T. Estrada, who was in San Quentin with Sirhan from 1972 to 1973. In his audiotaped interview with the DA's chief investigator on the RFK case, William Burnett, Estrada claimed to have occupied the cell next to the convicted assassin for seven months. Estrada told Burnett that he had information that Sirhan had been behind the prison murder of an inmate named Ronald Woods. The reason? According to Estrada, Sirhan had told Woods that "there were more people involved" in the Kennedy assassination. Thus Woods had to be silenced.[15]

In 1977 Carmen Falzone, a recently released inmate who had been with Sirhan in Soledad, also approached investigator Burnett with a story. Falzone claimed that he was recruited by Sirhan to help in a plan with Sirhan's brothers to steal plutonium and smuggle it to Libyan leader Muammar al-Qaddhafi. During the taped session with Burnett, Falzone reported that Sirhan told him, "I did it by myself," referring to the murder of Robert Kennedy. Then, according to Falzone, Sirhan reenacted the crime. "Oh, he showed me how he brought the gun up with his left hand, 'cause I stopped him. I goes, 'Whoa—you're left-handed?' He says, 'I can shoot with either hand.' That's a direct quote."

Falzone then described how worked up Sirhan got over this piece of theater. "He was enraged," says Falzone. "Always obscenities. The word Kennedy and fuck were synonymous."[16]

Daniel Estrada had miscalculated. The DA's office wasn't interested in stories about a conspiracy to murder Robert Kennedy. But Carmen Falzone's tale had allure. Here, Sirhan is both a lone assassin and a dangerous terrorist.

As the tape of his meeting with the DA's investigator reveals, Falzone finds a willing ear for his story. The former inmate agrees to follow additional leads in the Libyan plot, so long as he is compensated "for expenses." He then comes up with another condition: "I do not want to be under the jurisdiction of a parole office," he says, "where somebody can pull a couple of strings and find out where the fuck I live."

"If you come forward," Burnett responds, "you wanna pull a vanishing act on us and disappear out of sight?"

"After it's over; yes, I do."[17]

In 1978 *Playboy* magazine would run the story of the Libyan plutonium plot in an article titled "Inside Sirhan." The article was written by James McKinley, whom *Playboy* would describe as their "assassinations expert." A full-page drawing of Sirhan's face accompanied the story, with a keyhole drawn in place of the mouth, implying that *Playboy* had finally been able to unlock the hidden thoughts of "America's most secretive assassin." The article claimed that while at Soledad, Sirhan had formed "an intimate bond of trust with a cellmate who, for the first time, reveals the twisted mind of Robert Kennedy's killer."

The "cellmate" who had sold the story to *Playboy* was Carmen Falzone, who might better have been described as a fellow inmate, since Sirhan did not share his cell with anyone. In the article, Falzone was described as a "master criminal" who specialized in "sophisticated con jobs." It didn't seem to occur to McKinley or *Playboy* that they might be helping to promote one of Falzone's con jobs. Falzone said of his relationship with Sirhan,

The first couple of months, I thought he was kinda neat, and he thought I was kinda neat. He knew who I was—the superburglar on the tier—and I knew who he was. I was attracted to him, sure: He has an aura of power around him. . . . I was curious; I wanted to get into his pants. It was a challenge.

Falzone described Sirhan to *Playboy* as "the perfect terrorist," who, with "hate oozing out of him," had confessed to Falzone that he made up his "psycho act" and "all that trance and hypnosis stuff." (For the record, Sirhan has always denied that he was psychotic and has never claimed that he was hypnotized.) Falzone intimated that Sirhan was receiving messages from Muammar al-Qaddhafi through Sirhan's brother Adel.

Falzone then went on to describe the Libyan plot: First, Falzone would make parole. Then, once on the outside, he would smuggle a saw, some amphetamines, and a radio transmitter to Sirhan concealed in a canned ham at Christmas. Finally, the day of the escape would come. Sirhan would ingest the pills, saw the bars on his windows, climb down to a roof below, then radio Falzone, who would appear in a helicopter, which, using a cargo net, would pluck Sirhan off the roof.

Where would they go? According to Falzone he would stash Sirhan in a specially equipped tractor-trailer rig and then hide him on the nation's interstate highway system: "I'd have a radio scanner, TV monitors, living space, the works in the truck."

Falzone claimed that Sirhan wanted "50 tactical nuclear weapons" for Qaddhafi. How would he get them? "I could probably go onto a SAC base," said Falzone, seeming to forget that this was supposed to be Sirhan's plot, "meet some people, force some favors, then fly in a cargo plane or roll in the right vehicle, all with the right looking people, and hand them some dummy papers, then drink a cup of coffee while they load what I want for me."

As reported by *Playboy,* Falzone was so disturbed by this plan that he decided to go to the DA, because he was hoping they would "do something about the potential danger." *Playboy* then quoted a "spokesman" for the district attorney's office, who said, "We asked Mr. Falzone to take a polygraph examination and he passed the polygraph on the stories Sirhan supposedly told him."[18]

As bizarre and patently unlikely as it was, the Libyan plutonium story would surface again three years later, this time in a petition submitted to the Board of Prison Terms (the new name for the California Adult Authority) by Los Angeles County district attorney John Van de Kamp. His petition sought a hearing to rescind Sirhan's scheduled parole. Among the witnesses Van de Kamp proposed to bring before the board was Carmen Falzone.

The petition apparently had great meaning to Van de Kamp, because he delivered it in person to Sacramento, whereupon he held a press conference. He held another the same day when he returned to Los Angeles. The *Los Angeles Times,* which supported Van de Kamp's position editorially, had the good sense to describe the district attorney as "an unannounced candidate for state attorney general."

Van de Kamp's petition alleged that Carmen Falzone had revealed to authorities "some rather startling facts about Sirhan." It then reviewed the plot to steal nuclear material and send it to Qaddhafi. The story, as it was intended, made headlines in the California newspapers. The *Los Angeles Times* reported that Van de Kamp said that Falzone passed a lie detector test regarding his statements.[19]

In addition to Falzone, Van de Kamp had several other witnesses with stories to tell about Sirhan. One was Philip C. Clark, a former inmate at San Quentin, who was prepared to say that Sirhan had told him he was a member of the Black September breakaway faction of the Palestine Liberation Organization, and had been assigned to murder Edward Kennedy, Ronald Reagan, and former secretary of defense Robert McNamara. A third story revealed in Van de Kamp's petition was from an inmate named Lawrence Eugene Wilson, who had been convicted of murdering a man while committing a robbery at a motel. Wilson told authorities that he had had a conversation with Sirhan the previous year. The alleged conversation was printed in the newspapers:

> WILSON: I wonder, if Ted Kennedy were to become President, if he would be assassinated, because of what happened to his two brothers?
> SIRHAN: I know he would be. If I get out of here in 1984 and he's still President, I'll do it myself.
> WILSON: Haven't you done enough time?
> SIRHAN: Well, I've got a commitment to certain things and my commitment is that I've got to take care of business.[20]

Several days after John Van de Kamp's petition was filed, the California Board of Prison Terms released documents which disputed the district attorney's portrayal of Sirhan as a self-proclaimed terrorist. In these documents prison officer J. V. Billman was quoted as saying, "I believe Lawrence Wilson's account to be a malicious fabrication. I have never known Sirhan to discuss any aspect of this case with anyone."[21]

Van de Kamp's campaign against parole spurred a flurry of local comment on his petition, most of it favorable. A few letters to the *Times* protested the district attorney's motives and logic. One writer asked, "Does our esteemed DA feel that the punishment should fit the victim rather than the crime?"[22]

Another commented:

> Van de Kamp said, "My position is that a political assassination should not be compared with an average murder because it tears at the very fabric of a democratic society." Average murder? What is the definition of an average murder? Each and every murder, regardless of a victim's name or reputation, tears at the very fabric of a democratic society.[23]

Van de Kamp's initiative resulted in a hearing before the Board of Prison Terms in late April 1982. About a week before the hearing, an article by staff writer Bill Farr appeared in the *Los Angeles Times* alleging that Lawrence Eugene Wilson was now suspected of forging the name of author Joseph Wambaugh on a letter to the parole board urging his release. The very next day another article written by Farr appeared with the headline FBI HUNTING WITNESS IN SIRHAN CASE. The story read:

> Carmen Falzone, a former prison inmate scheduled to be a key witness in Dist. Atty. John Van de Kamp's effort to keep Sirhan Sirhan behind bars, is now a fugitive being sought by the FBI.
>
> The FBI confirmed Thursday that a warrant charging Falzone with interstate transportation of stolen property has been issued by the bureau's Salt Lake City office.
>
> The charge stems from the theft of a $750,000 coin collection from safe deposit boxes in a Salt Lake City bank.[24]

The Farr story then quoted state Board of Prison Terms chairman Raymond C. Brown. "Falzone is still on the list of witnesses for the Sirhan hearing later this month," he said, "but under the circumstances, it is unlikely that he will show up." Five years after his negotiations with deputy DA Bill Burnett, Carmen Falzone had finally pulled off his vanishing act.

Neither Carmen Falzone nor Philip Clark testified at Sirhan's parole hearing. James Park, a former associate warden at San Quentin, testified that he doubted very much whether Clark, who was not on death row, could have possibly penetrated that area to talk with Sirhan about Black September assassination plots, as he had claimed.

Lawrence Wilson did attend the hearing, despite the bad press regarding his veracity. He took the stand and, with Sirhan glaring at him, retold the story of Sirhan threatening the life of Senator Edward Kennedy. Sirhan's attorney, Luke McKissack, pressed Wilson on several fronts. He asked Wilson about another case in which he had come forward with information on a fellow prisoner and then flunked a lie detector test. He asked Wilson about the letter with the forged signature of author Joseph Wambaugh.

Wilson denied writing or forging the letter but refused to answer any further questions, saying, "I don't wish to discuss that at great length because there is a possible criminal action and a civil matter involved."[25]

McKissack subsequently called several fellow inmates from Soledad. Robert William Bell, who was in prison serving a sentence for burglary, testified that he had been solicited by Lawrence Wilson to corroborate Wilson's claim that Sirhan had threatened the life of Senator Edward Kennedy.

"I went along at first," said Bell, "and agreed that I would say I overheard Sirhan make that Kennedy death threat to Larry Wilson. But I always intended to come here to tell the truth, that it didn't really happen. . . . It's all through the system that Larry Wilson is lying about the [Sirhan] matter."[26]

Thomas Nicochea, another resident of Soledad, testified that Wilson approached him with a proposal to lie about the supposed Sirhan conversation, but that he turned Wilson down immediately. Another prisoner, William Kogan, also testified against Wilson, calling him "an opportunist."[27]

Wilson's credibility was further damaged when the parole board's chief investigator, Richard Washington, Jr., testified to a series of incidents on record that demonstrated "the pattern of deceit Wilson has employed to gain his ends, including trying to blame his own father for the murder he committed."[28]

With three of John Van de Kamp's principal witnesses discredited, the hearings went forward with great emphasis now placed on two threatening letters Sirhan had written while in prison. In one, Sirhan had threatened Soledad correctional officer Vern Smith in 1975 for failing to provide him with medical attention to a painful dental problem. The other was written from San Quentin in 1971 to Sirhan's attorney, Grant Cooper, and began "Hey Punk!" In it Sirhan threatened the life of defense investigator Robert Kaiser "if he continues to talk about me like he's been doing on radio and TV. . . ." It ended: "Don't forget [Cooper], you son-of-a-bitch, you are the one who cost me my life."[29]

After thirty-two witnesses over a two-week period, deputy district attorney Larry Trapp rose to offer a summation for his boss, John Van de Kamp. "Mr. Sirhan will boldly tell you he has been punished enough and suggest to you that he has paid his debt to society," said Trapp. "But Sirhan, who took it upon himself to rewrite history, is like a debtor who is bankrupt. He can never repay the debt."

Trapp argued that to let the parole date stand "means we in California will risk sending a message to every misfit, fanatic and political crusader that assassination in this state is worth only 13 years."[30]

When Luke McKissack rose for Sirhan, he pointed out that if paroled on schedule in 1984 (the date advanced two years for good behavior), Sirhan would have served sixteen years, more time than many murderers who had committed more egregious and aggravated crimes. McKissack then reminded the board that Sirhan's treatment should not depend upon "who the victim was and his stature in society."[31]

Following these summations Sirhan rose and read a statement in which he expressed remorse for the death of Robert Kennedy, denied having made any death threats against Edward Kennedy, and characterized the threatening letters he wrote in the early 1970s as "regrettable" expressions of frustration.

Three weeks later the three-member hearing panel revoked Sirhan's scheduled parole date, saying that in the fourteen years since he assassinated Senator Kennedy he had demonstrated "a pattern of threatening behavior." In making its determination the panel requested a psychiatric evaluation of Sirhan, expressing concern with his "loner status," a concern that appeared to ignore the repeated attempts by unscrupulous inmates to use their contact with Sirhan to fabricate incriminating stories about him, often with what appeared to be official encouragement. The decision stated that "this panel is not impressed with the apologies offered by Sirhan. . . . [His] threats and conduct do not indicate the prisoner has made a substantial change for the better."[32]

At a press conference after the decision, DA Van de Kamp told reporters, "We are pleased with the decision because it is the right decision. The people of this country and, indeed, the people of the world, can collectively heave a sigh of relief that Sirhan will remain in prison."[33]

Five months later John Van de Kamp would be elected attorney general of California.

In 1982, the same year Sirhan's parole date was revoked, Princeton University Press published *American Assassins,* a book by Professor James W. Clarke. The book was a study of this nation's best-known political assassins (not all of whom succeeded in killing their intended victims).

Clarke began his section on Sirhan by asserting that of the sixteen assassins studied, Sirhan "stands out as possibly the shrewdest, most devious and remorseless of the lot . . . no other assassin, with the possible exceptions of John Wilkes Booth and Carl Weiss, hated his victim more."

Clarke claimed to see in Sirhan's notebooks "the efforts of a determined assassin to prepare himself psychologically for the assassination as well as for his anticipated capture and defense." He cited the Carmen Falzone article in *Playboy* magazine to show that Sirhan was still hopeful that "Arab terrorists would be successful in arranging the circumstances for his release." He compared Sirhan to the Black September terrorists who murdered the Israeli Olympic athletes in Munich in 1972.

Clarke's portrait of Sirhan was harsh, but also conventional. It did not take into account great bodies of information not consonant with its conclusions. For example, a review of Sirhan's interviews with his doctors and lawyers reveals that he is noteworthy for his *lack* of hatred for his victim. His notebooks hardly constitute a shrewd posture for his legal defense, and other than his Arab origins and his having voiced anti-Israeli sentiments, he has remarkably little in common with Black September. Nevertheless, Clarke's book would become the unofficial manifesto for those opposing parole for Sirhan.

When Sirhan returned before the Board of Prison Terms in 1985, he was accompanied by the psychiatric report that the board had asked for when it revoked his parole. In the report, prepared by prison staff psychiatrist Dr. Philip S. Hicks, Sirhan was described as "an exemplary inmate . . . a man who is in good contact with reality . . . a pleasant, cooperative person [who] demonstrates maturity and good judgment concerning his situation."

Hicks found Sirhan to be "of above average intelligence, intellectually curious [with] a remarkably good memory for detail." He concluded, "There appears to be no psychiatric contraindication to parole consideration. He has no demonstrable predilection toward violence at this time."[34]

The report was presented to a three-member panel of the Board of Prison Terms, consisting of Raymond Jaurequi, Joseph Aceto, and chairman Rudolph Castro. Because the previous parole hearing in 1982 had generated so much public interest, the hearing in 1985 was also well covered by the press. While not allowed into the hearing room itself, the newsmen were allowed to view the proceedings from a separate room via closed-circuit TV. After hearing appeals for justice from Sirhan's attorney, Luke McKissack, who maintained that Sirhan had already paid his debt and was no longer a threat to society, and from deputy DA Larry Trapp, who maintained that a message had to be sent that political assassination would not be tolerated in California, the board asked that the hearing room be cleared so they could deliberate. The closed-circuit TV monitor was turned off.

After an hour or so, panel chairman Rudolph Castro appeared in person before the newsmen to announce that Sirhan was once again to be denied parole.

"How long did you deliberate?" asked one of the newsmen.

"About forty-five minutes," replied Castro.

The newsmen then informed Castro that they knew this to be a lie, because while the TV monitor had been turned off, the sound monitor had not. The newsmen asserted that the board had deliberated no more than three minutes and that much of that was horseplay and dirty jokes.

At that point Castro announced, "On the advice of counsel I am curtailing further discussion on this."

An edited transcript of what the newsmen heard was printed in the *Los Angeles Times*:

> CASTRO: For the record the time is 2:40. Prisoner will leave first. *(Pause, footsteps, papers being shuffled.)*
> JAUREQUI: Is it all right if I kiss you on the forehead? *(Interrupted at the end by someone.)*
> VOICE: *(Spanish vulgarity for sexual intercourse.)*
> VOICE: *(Inaudible words)* . . . somebody kissing him in the bucket.
> VOICE: He kissed you, why can't I?
> CASTRO: *(Spanish vulgarity.)*
> JAUREQUI: *(Spanish vulgarity.)* Get the bum to do it.
> CASTRO: *(Spanish vulgarity.)*
> JAUREQUI: *(Spanish vulgarity.)* He kissed you in the elevator.[35]

After what Luke McKissack estimated was one minute and forty seconds of discussion, Rudolph Castro then enumerated the reasons why Sirhan would be denied parole: "the lack of sufficient programming, the crime itself, the need for in-depth diagnostic evaluation. Agree?"

Moments later, speaking about transferring Sirhan to another prison, one of the board members said, "We'll send his ass down there for as long as possible."

Then a few minutes later a panel member said, "Let's make sure the sound is off."

"Oh, hey," replied Castro, "that is very important."

"Terrific," said another panelist to general laughter. "The whole world will know."[36]

Sirhan's attorney, Luke McKissack, quickly criticized "the atmosphere of frivolity" in the deliberations as heard by the attending press, saying that "American justice is now on trial."[37]

In Sacramento, William Elliott, head of the state Board of Prison Terms, responded, "At this point, we don't perceive what happened in the deliberations to be a fatal flaw to the hearing. They may have come quickly to a decision, but then they really took quite a bit of time to deal with all of the ramifications and the setting up of Sirhan's future programming."[38]

Parole hearings for Sirhan Sirhan would take place in 1986, 1987, 1989, and 1990. The transcripts of these proceedings are very similar. Luke McKissack would point to evidence that Sirhan was suitable for parole. Sirhan would express remorse. Deputy DA Larry Trapp would speak of the heinous nature of the murder. And the hearing panel, in denying parole, would utter words about crimes against democracy.

In 1992 Sirhan was scheduled for another hearing at his new home at California State Prison at Corcoran. In a chamber outside the hearing room the escorting prison officials told Sirhan that he could enter the hearing room only if he were wearing chains and manacles. Sirhan refused. The hearing went on without him or his attorney. He was again denied parole.

Although Sirhan's refusal to attend his 1992 parole hearing in chains was not reported in the news, another hearing that same year did make big headlines. This was a reversal hearing in Los Angeles Superior Court on behalf of Clarence Chance and Benny Powell. Both men had been convicted of the 1973 murder of a Los Angeles County sheriff's deputy. They had been in prison for more than seventeen years but had consistently maintained their innocence.

At the hearing before Judge Florence Cooper, the attorneys for Chance and Powell introduced statements by the two witnesses at the original murder trial, teenage girls at the time, that they had been intimidated and coerced by the police to change their statements to implicate Chance and Powell. The attorneys were also able to demonstrate that Chance was in custody at the time of the shooting and could not possibly have committed the murder.

At the original 1975 murder trial, both girls had given their now-admitted false testimony against Chance and Powell. But the case against the defendants was still weak, so the prosecutors introduced another witness, who testified that Benny Powell had bragged to him in prison that he had indeed murdered the sheriff's deputy. The witness swore that he was telling the truth and had received no incentives to make these statements. This witness was Lawrence Eugene Wilson, the same man whom authorities would bring forward at Sirhan's 1982 parole hearing to swear that Sirhan intended to murder Senator Edward Kennedy if Sirhan were released on parole.

At the 1992 reversal hearing, Sandra Smith, the attorney representing Benny Powell, would say that Eugene Wilson "lied with the knowledge of the officers who investigated the case." The attorneys then introduced evidence that the police had concealed the fact that Wilson had earlier implicated two other men in the crime, concealed evidence that Wilson had failed two polygraph tests concerning his statements about Powell, and that in return for his testimony Wilson had received a three-room prison "suite," where he was allowed private conjugal visits.[39]

The Los Angeles DA's office did not oppose the release of Chance and Powell, saying that Wilson's testimony at the original murder trial was tainted, although that fact was, as the story went, unknown to the prosecutors at the time. At the conclusion of the hearing, Judge Florence Cooper released both Chance and Powell, saying that the police conduct in the case was "reprehensible." LAPD chief Daryl Gates, however, continued to defend the actions of the officers involved. "No one was framed at any time," he said. "The detectives were persistent in seeking the truth." Gates attributed any shortcomings in the case to "procedural error."[40]

By December 1994, when Sirhan was scheduled for his next hearing, the rules at Corcoran prison had changed. Sirhan was escorted into the hearing room without chains and seated at a table before the three-man Board of Prison Terms panel. Also at the table was Lawrence Teeter, a criminal defense lawyer who also specializes in environmental and civil rights litigation. Teeter had recently replaced Luke McKissack as Sirhan's attorney of record.

The proceedings, which were televised live by Court TV, began with Board of Prison Terms commissioner Steve Baker reading a short history of the crime. The commissioners then reviewed Sirhan's conduct in prison. It was noted that Sirhan had been discipline-free for twenty years. It was also revealed that Sirhan had maintained a 4.0 average in his academic studies, which had been discontinued. A letter was read in which Sirhan was offered a job by family friend Rose Lynn Mangan if he were to be released on parole.

When the commissioners were finished, deputy district attorney Lawrence Trapp was introduced. Trapp, as he had done since 1980, spoke on behalf of the Los Angeles district attorney's office. He cited "three major factors" in support of the DA's position that Sirhan should not be given parole.

"The first factor is the extraordinary degree of violence associated with this criminal event. The second factor was the extraordinary degree of planning over an extended period of time, as well as Sirhan's relative calmness immediately following the criminal activity. And finally and the factor most interesting to me is the almost unparalleled degree of heartlessness and remorselessness towards the inmate's victim, this, again, over a long period of time."

In offering other examples of Sirhan's nefarious intent, Trapp recited to the parole board Sirhan's "rapid fire" at the shooting range, his failure to carry a wallet to the scene of the crime, and his calm demeanor during the shooting. Trapp asserted:

"Finally, in case any doubt remains as to Sirhan's intent all along, during the course of the trial Sirhan asserted, 'I killed Robert Kennedy, willfully, premeditatively, with twenty years of malice aforethought.' Nevertheless, despite his courtroom assertion, Sirhan through the years has continued to attempt to mitigate his responsibility for his crime by claiming diminished capacity and even amnesia for the events surrounding the assassination."

"The issue before us today," answered Lawrence Teeter, when it was his turn to speak, "is the question of whether Mr. Sirhan's release would present an unreasonable risk to society. That's the issue and that's the only issue." Teeter went on to quote excerpts from various psychological reports done on Sirhan within the past decade.

1986 report by Dr. Philip S. Hicks: "This individual appears to be genuinely rehabilitated since incarceration, and demonstrates no evidence of current fanaticism or proneness towards violence. He appears to be an excellent candidate for parole."

1986 report by Dr. Robert Dry: "I believe this man has made a considerable personal change. . . . His potential for violence is very low. . . . I would recommend that Mr. Sirhan continue in his present program but with an early discharge being seriously considered."

1989 report by Dr. Clyde Martin: "During observation in the institution the inmate has psychiatrically improved moderately and in a less controlled setting such as a return to the community the inmate is likely to hold any present gains. . . . At this time his potential for violence is less than that of the average inmate."

1990 report by Dr. Douglas A. Farr: "If he is paroled he should be able to maintain his maturation in terms of his personality. He appears to have considerable family support and should be able to parole in the United States without undue difficulty."

After he had read the excerpts from the medical reports, Teeter changed tactics. "Mr. Trapp remarks that Mr. Sirhan shot Robert Kennedy from nearly point-blank range," he asserted. "Now . . . the problem is that no witnesses have testified that he ever got that close—"

"Excuse me, Counselor," interrupted Commissioner Baker. "Are you going to readjudicate this case? I'm not going to allow you to do that."

"No, but I think I am entitled—"

"No, you're entitled to speak to the suitability of parole of Mr. Sirhan. If you want to retry the case, file an appeal and go through the courts."

Despite Baker's objections, Teeter was determined to go on record that there were major evidentiary questions still open in the case.

"No, I understand," he replied. "I was simply trying to direct myself to what I consider an important factual inaccuracy in the board's file about the circumstances under which the crime took place. This is a telling inaccuracy because if the witnesses place the gun as far away as they did, then it would be physically impossible for Mr. Sirhan to have fired the shots that killed Robert Kennedy."

"It's not relevant to this hearing."

"I understand your position. But I did want to address that one comment in the board's file." Teeter went on to question Trapp's use of the Sirhan "twenty years of malice aforethought" comment, slipping in that Sirhan's trial attorney Grant Cooper never contested the fact of whether or not Sirhan actually committed the murder. Teeter next attacked the parole board's repeated allusions to Sirhan's inability to remember the crime as evidence of his lack of remorse. "Lack of recollection of what he is supposed to have done does not equate with lack of remorse," Teeter said. "He has again and again at hearings over the years spoken in very moving terms about how tragic these events were and about how he wishes they hadn't happened and how sorry he is that they did happen."

Teeter then reviewed Sirhan's suitability for parole. "Is this man a danger to the community? Well, the psychiatric reports say he's not. His behavior says that he is not. His plans for the future say that he is not. His lack of any criminal history except for this offense says that he is not. His expressions of remorse say that he is not. And again I would like to emphasize the question of whether Mr. Sirhan actually killed Robert Kennedy was never proven. . . . It was not proven by the district attorney's office because they didn't have to. Mr. Sirhan's lawyers just gave it away and rested upon a mental defense."

In concluding his remarks Teeter deftly held off censure while taking one more swipe at the conduct of Sirhan's trial. "You're absolutely correct," he asserted. "This board is not authorized to set aside someone's conviction because of constitutional violations, because of the ineffective assistance of counsel, because of newly discovered evidence, because the police destroyed evidence that would demonstrate his innocence; you are not authorized to grant any of that relief. But I think it is very clear you are authorized to grant one form of relief, which is to authorize his release on parole, and I would ask you to do that at this time. . . . Thank you."

After a thirty-minute break the members of the parole board returned to the room. Commissioner Steve Baker read a statement "concluding that the prisoner is not suitable for parole and would pose an unreasonable risk of danger to society and a threat to public safety if released from prison. Offense was carried out in an especially atrocious, cruel, and callous manner. . . . The prisoner has progressed in a limited manner while incarcerated, and has failed to develop a marketable skill that can be put to use upon release."

Several hours after the parole hearing, Lawrence Teeter, unfettered by any rules of discourse, spoke freely to the authors:

"At every parole hearing, the same words are spoken. 'Sirhan cannot be let go because we have to send a message that assassins are dealt with severely in California.' The truth is that in this case, the police covered the tracks of the real assassins. Evidence was destroyed, witnesses were intimidated, and files were kept secret. Because of this, they must demonize Sirhan. If Sirhan is not the monster they make him out to be, then they will have to answer real questions about this case.

"I have no doubt Sirhan is an innocent man. The evidence shows that he was unconscious at the time of the shooting, and I believe that this unconsciousness was the result of sophisticated hypnosis. If this is so, then Sirhan is a victim of this crime and not a perpetrator."

The next day in *The New York Times* there was a story on the difficulties encountered by televangelist Jim Bakker in expelling newsmen from his front lawn following his release from prison. There was another story concerning Paula Jones, who had accused President Bill Clinton of sexual misconduct. Jones, it was reported, was having legal difficulties with *Penthouse* magazine. Despite the fact that the day before, for the first time in twenty years, an attorney for Sirhan Sirhan had asserted in a legal forum that important evidence in the Robert Kennedy murder had been suppressed, there was no story on the Sirhan parole hearing.

SEVENTEEN

The Phantom Photographs

✳ ✳ ✳

O N THE MORNING of July 2, 1996, attorney Christine Harwell stood up in Los Angeles County Superior Court to deliver her opening statement in a lawsuit that had its beginnings the night Robert Kennedy was murdered. Ms. Harwell represented Jamie Scott Enyart, who was suing the city of Los Angeles for not returning photographs he took at the Ambassador Hotel the evening of the assassination.

Scott Enyart was fifteen years old in 1968. He had gone to the primary-night celebration at the Ambassador with several friends, equipped with a camera and an unauthorized press pass. As Robert Kennedy spoke to his supporters in the Embassy Room, Enyart took photographs from in front of the stage. What happened next is in dispute, but Enyart claims that after the speech, he followed Kennedy into the hotel pantry.

"The evidence from the police department's own records will show," said Ms. Harwell to the jury, "that Mr. Enyart stood on a steam table above the crowd immediately behind the senator taking pictures of the assassination in progress, that he was the *only* photographer to take pictures at that time. We will prove that had Mr. Enyart's negatives been available for use in the investigation and trial of Sirhan B. Sirhan . . . many questions that plague us today would have been answered about whether or not someone else may have shot off guns at the same time."[1]

In 1968 Christine Harwell had worked for the Los Angeles Police Department as a clerk, hoping that their regulations barring women from becoming police officers would change. They didn't, and Harwell left the department to study law.* In 1996, at age forty-seven, she would castigate her former employer in front of the jury, saying that the most crucial pictures taken by her client were either lost or "destroyed to hide what they showed . . . to keep the LAPD from being embarrassed for doing a

---

*Harwell would go on to become a U.S. District Court staff attorney for nine years before joining the law firm headed by Alvin Greenwald, a successful and respected business attorney, who was also Scott Enyart's father-in-law.

one-sided job and hiding evidence in one of the three major political assassinations of the century."

On May 26, 1988, just a month after the LAPD's files on the Robert Kennedy assassination had been made public, thirty-five-year-old Scott Enyart had written to Los Angeles chief of police Daryl Gates.

> Dear Chief Gates, My name is Jamie Scott Enyart and I was present the tragic evening Senator Robert Kennedy was assassinated. I was 15 years old and taking photographs for a school assignment when this tragedy occurred. After your men arrived I was taken as a witness to Rampart Station where I described what happened and volunteered my film for use in the investigation. Now, twenty years later, I understand the files are open and I had hoped, by writing to you, I could now have my film returned to me.[2]

Enyart said he was enclosing "Xeroxes of my pictures your detectives gave me years ago" to help in locating his film. He told Gates that he wished to express his appreciation for his efforts "to rid our city of violent crime, drugs and gang activity." He enclosed an envelope so that Gates might return autographed photos of himself for Enyart's two children who "consider officers of your department as friends and role models."

A month later Enyart received back a letter from Chief Gates saying that "everything that was in possession of the Los Angeles Police Department concerning the Kennedy investigation has been delivered to the custody of the State of California." He provided Enyart with the name and telephone number of deputy state archivist Laren Metzer, who had already agreed to help Enyart look for his film. Gates thanked Enyart for his "assistance and cooperation in the Kennedy investigation"[3] and enclosed two autographed photographs of himself.

Enyart then wrote to the state archives, enclosing the same photocopies he had sent to Gates and requesting that, if possible, his film be located. On October 11, Laren Metzer replied on behalf of chief archivist John Burns that they had been unable to locate any photographs or film that matched the photocopies sent by Enyart. "I can only conclude," wrote Metzer, "that your photographs were among the 2,400 images destroyed by LAPD in August 1968."[4]

That photographic prints were burned by the LAPD is not in question. A property report dated August 21, 1968, says that two police officers took "2410 S.U.S. Unit photographs without code numbers to County General Hospital and deposited these photos in the hospital incinerator and witnessed their destruction."[5] The police maintain that all photos burned were duplicates, however, no records were kept of what was destroyed.* At the same time, there is no evidence that Scott Enyart's photographs were among those burned. Nevertheless, the failure of his photographs to appear once the files were opened angered Enyart.

A year later, in August 1989, Scott Enyart filed suit against the City of Los Angeles seeking two million dollars in damages for the loss or destruction of his photographs.[7] Enyart claimed that the night of the assassination he had shot three 36-exposure rolls of film, which he said had been taken from him by the police. He claimed that several months after the murder he was able to recover from the police only eighteen prints and no negatives.

The city responded by claiming that Enyart's suit was not timely and was barred by the statute of limitations. The court agreed and the case was dismissed. Enyart appealed. In December 1993, the California Court of Appeal overturned the lower court's decision, saying, "The [LAPD's] own actions for over 20 years prevented [Enyart] from obtaining his property or any information about its status or existence."

With the case back on the calendar, the city began to organize for the fight. Although his office had 358 attorneys on staff, city attorney James Hahn retained Louis "Skip" Miller of the law firm Christensen, White, Miller, et al. to handle the Enyart case.

Christensen, White, Miller, et al. had been one of the law firms hired by Los Angeles the previous year to defend councilman Nate Holden against charges of sexual harassment. The firm received a reported eight hundred thousand dollars for its successful defense, and the money spent on Holden's defense became a page-one story in the *Los Angeles Times*. The Christensen partner who had defended the Holden lawsuit was Skip Miller. His assumption of the Enyart case stimulated another protest in the *Los Angeles Times*. "Why," asked columnist Bill Boyarsky, "is Los Angeles paying . . . Miller, a Century City courtroom star, instead of letting a deputy city attorney do the job for about a quarter of the cost? Is it because the city is trying to cover up failures in the Kennedy investigation, as Enyart charges?"[8]

With the outside law firm in place, trial preparations moved forward. Motions for discovery were filed, depositions taken, and a new search for

---

*An August 20, 1968, memo from Captain Hugh Brown, second in command at SUS, to Chief Robert Houghton described the extensive search for five lost photographs. It then set forth procedures for cataloging all case photos, even those of "no value," procedures designed to "prevent incidents of this nature in the future." The burning of the unrecorded twenty-four hundred photos occurred the day after the date on this memo.[6]

Scott Enyart's missing photographs begun. Then an unexpected discovery. In August 1995, attorneys for the city found photos and negatives in the state archives that seemed to match those that Scott Enyart had received back from the police in 1968. The pictures had been booked and filed under the name of George Ross Clayton, and there was only one set of negatives with thirty images. Clayton could not be located, but from what could be deduced from the original 1968 police reports, there appeared to be a legitimate question as to whether Clayton had been the source of the film.

Scott Enyart and his attorney Christine Harwell traveled to Sacramento to inspect the new discovery. Although the images there appeared to match the photographs he had received back from the police, Enyart claimed that there was some mistake. The film found at the archives was Ilford brand, 125 ASA, but Enyart said that on the night of the California primary he had been using Kodak Tri-X, 400 ASA.

Enyart suggested that if the images were indeed his, then some sort of forgery must have taken place. He would testify at his trial that he noticed enhanced contrast in the images, which suggested to him a generational copying from the original negatives. He also noted that the single roll of film in the archives appeared to include images from all three of the rolls he said he had shot. He said that some of the photographs appeared to be out of sequence. And there were no photographs at all from inside the pantry.

The discovery of film that appeared to match the photographs that Scott Enyart had accepted as his in 1968 changed everything. If this was Enyart's missing film, then there wasn't much left to his lawsuit or his story. And Enyart's suggestion of forgery didn't seem to make sense: while a reworked replica of Enyart's original negatives onto old film stock might not be beyond the powers of the most sophisticated conspirators one could imagine, as a choice it would seem a poor substitute for simply not finding the film.

With the authenticity of the discovered film now challenged, superior court judge Emilie Elias* ordered the negatives delivered from Sacramento to the court in Los Angeles, where they could be used as evidence in the trial and be examined by photographic experts for both the plaintiff and the defense. On January 12, 1996, just a month before the scheduled start of the trial, courier George Phillip Gebhardt flew from Sacramento to Los Angeles. In his locked briefcase was a folder containing the negatives.

When he arrived in Los Angeles. Gebhardt went to the Midway

---

*Emilie Elias is a court-appointed jurist, empowered to preside at trials. Her official title is commissioner. She has the powers of a judge and will be referred to as a judge in these pages.

Senator Kennedy addresses his followers at the Ambassador Hotel after winning the California primary.

(UPI/Bettman/Getty Images)

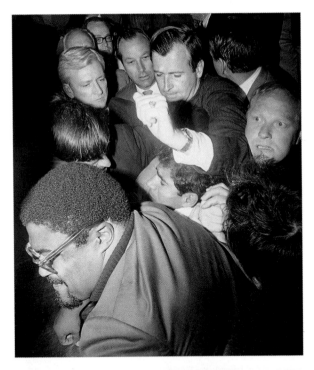

The struggle to disarm Sirhan (profile visible in the center of the melee): In the foreground is former Los Angeles Rams tackle Roosevelt Grier, who recovered the revolver; on the extreme right (with only half his face showing) is hotel maître d' Karl Uecker, who has Sirhan in a headlock; and visible just behind Grier's head, looking directly at Sirhan, is writer George Plimpton.

(UPI/Bettman/Getty Images)

Clutching rosary beads given to him by busboy Juan Romero, Robert Kennedy lies wounded on the floor of the hotel pantry. His wife, Ethel, is at lower left.

(UPI/Bettman/Getty Images)

Sirhan Sirhan is taken into custody immediately after the shooting.

(UPI/Bettman/Getty Images)

L.A. coroner Thomas Noguchi points to two holes in the doorframe of the pantry doorway. *(University of Massachusetts, Dartmouth, Robert F. Kennedy Assassination Archives [UMDRFK])*

FBI photo close-up (released in 1975) of the two holes to which Noguchi was pointing. FBI caption reads: "Close up view of two bullet holes which is [sic] located in the center doorframe inside kitchen serving area and looking towards direction of back of stage." *(UMDRFK Archives)*

LAPD officers Charles Wright and Sergeant Robert Rozzi examine what appears to be a bullet in a pantry hallway doorframe. Years later, when asked how sure he was that the object in the hole was a bullet (on a scale of one to ten, with ten being a certainty), Wright responded, "as close to a ten as I'd ever want to go without pulling it out." *(UMDRFK Archives)*

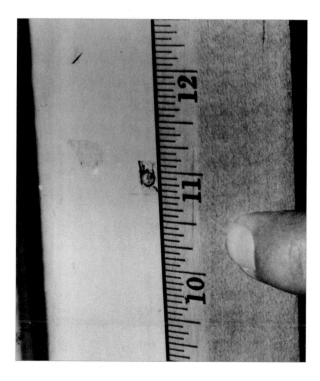

Close-up of what officers Wright and Rozzi were examining.
(Castellano-Nelson Collection, UMDRFK Archives)

LAPD photograph of police criminalist DeWayne Wolfer pointing to an apparent bullet ricochet mark on pantry door hinge.
(UMDRFK Archives)

FBI photograph (released in 1975) of this same hinge. FBI caption to photo describes "reported location of another bullet mark which struck hinge."
(UMDRFK Archives)

L.A. coroner Thomas Noguchi standing behind LAPD detective wearing Senator Kennedy's suit coat. Metal rod penetrating suit coat simulates the flight path of a bullet. According to the report of police criminalist DeWayne Wolfer, this bullet "passed through the right shoulder pad of Senator Kennedy's suit coat (never entered his body) and traveled upward striking victim Schrade in the forehead."

(Castellano-Nelson Collection, UMDRFK Archives)

Shooting victim Paul Schrade.
(California State Archives)

Muzzle distance test conducted by LAPD. This comparison test demonstrated that shots that hit Robert Kennedy were fired at point-blank range. *(UMDRFK Archives)*

Photo of Ambassador Hotel pantry where Robert Kennedy was shot.
(Castellano-Nelson Collection, UMDRFK Archives)

Sirhan family in Palestine, 1946. *Standing, left to right:* Saidalla, Ayda, and Shariff. *Sitting:* Mary Sirhan holding nine-month-old Sirhan B. Sirhan, Munir (the first child to be named Munir, who would be killed during fighting in Jerusalem), Adel, and Bishara Sirhan. *(Rose Lynn Mangan Collection)*

Sirhan Sirhan during interview with Grant Cooper before his trial.
(Robert Blair Kaiser Collection, UMDRFK Archives)

L.A. District Attorney Evelle Younger seated *(center)*, and flanked by Chief of Detectives Robert Houghton *(left)*, and U.S. Attorney Matthew Byrne *(right)*, introducing the team to prosecute Sirhan: *(standing, from left to right)* Lynn D. Compton, John E. Howard, and David N. Fitts. *(UPI/Bettman/Getty Images)*

Sirhan attorneys arrive at the Hall of Justice: *(left to right)* Russell Parsons, Grant B. Cooper, and Emile Zola Berman. *(UPI/Bettman/Getty Images)*

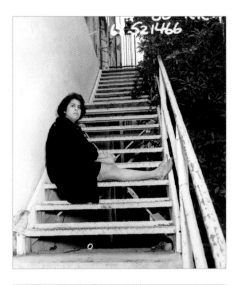

Sandra Serrano on the back stairway of the Ambassador Hotel where she claimed to have encountered the woman in the polka-dot dress. *(California State Archives)*

LAPD photo of one of the polka-dot dresses used by police for comparison in questioning witnesses Sandra Serrano and Vincent DiPierro. (California State Archives)

Kennedy campaign worker Valerie Shulte modeling the green dress with yellow shapes that she wore the night of the shooting. Both the defense and the prosecution would accept Shulte as the missing polka-dot-dress woman. (California State Archives)

Page from Sirhan's notebook dated May 18, 1968, where the writer speaks of his increasing "obsession" to eliminate Robert Kennedy. Passage repeats phrase "Robert Kennedy must be assassinated" fourteen times then ends with the sentence "I have never heard please pay to the order of of of of of of of of of of of this or that." *(California State Archives)*

Two pages from Sirhan's notebook.

[Right] Page written by Sirhan while in prison under hypnosis, bearing controversial date "Friday 31, January 689." Sirhan writes "RFK must die" a dozen times, then writes that he doesn't know who killed Kennedy. When asked who he was with when Kennedy was killed he writes "girl the girl the girl."

Gregory Stone, protégé of Allard Lowenstein, re-
searched and analyzed Robert Kennedy case for almost
two decades. *(Jenny Stone)*

Paul Schrade and former congressman Allard Lowenstein at a New York press conference in 1974, where they publicly challenged the official version of the Robert Kennedy case. Lowenstein would be murdered in 1980.

Sirhan Sirhan speaking at his parole hearing in 1986.
(UPI/Bettman/Getty Images)

Rent-A-Car, where he picked up a white Mazda sedan. On Century Boulevard just outside the airport, the courier stopped for a red light. According to his videotaped testimony in court (Gebhardt had suffered a heart attack shortly after this incident and testified from his hospital bed), a red car pulled up next to him and a Hispanic man got out and began to bang on his own car for no apparent reason. A block later the white Mazda was making a dull thumping noise. Gebhardt pulled over, got out to inspect, and found that his right rear tire was slashed. When he got back into his car, the briefcase with the negatives was gone.

With the most important piece of evidence now stolen, the trial was postponed. The rising intrigue, however, found a forum in the media. In a story printed in the *Los Angeles Times,* Enyart's attorney Alvin Greenwald hinted at conspiracy. "Somebody, for some reason," he said, "is making sure those photos do not reach public view."[9]

"What happened here," said attorney Skip Miller in the same story, "is just a petty theft. A run of bad luck."[10]

The television show *Unsolved Mysteries* was quick to broadcast a story on the Enyart case. During that program a photograph was displayed that was said to be new evidence. It was from *Robert Kennedy: The Last Campaign,* a book by Bill Eppridge and Hays Gorey, documenting Robert Kennedy's 1968 quest for the presidential nomination. The book included ten photographs Eppridge had shot in the chaotic hotel pantry after the attack upon Robert Kennedy. In the selected print, a young man with a camera could be seen in the background, standing on a table, taking photographs. The young man was said to be Scott Enyart.[11]

Court TV, which was hoping to televise the upcoming trial, then ran a story of its own. In the nationally televised segment, assistant city attorney Edmund Fimbres commented on Enyart's claim that he took photographs of Kennedy being shot. "It's just a fish story," he said. "Over the years, the fish has gotten bigger."

The Scott Enyart story first came to public attention with the advent of Ted Charach's 1973 film documentary, *The Second Gun,* in which Charach claimed that Kennedy was shot not by Sirhan's gun, but by a gun held by someone behind the senator. Charach's principal suspect was security guard Thane Eugene Cesar, who was standing behind Kennedy and who admittedly had his gun drawn that night but denies he fired it. In his documentary, Charach interviews a teenage Scott Enyart, who tells his story of being at the Ambassador Hotel and of having his film taken by the police, who later returned only twenty-six prints but not the negatives. "I definitely feel that there are some missing," says Enyart.[12]

Charach then displays Enyart's photos of a victorious Kennedy at the podium while the senator's speech plays behind. Then Kennedy leaves the stage and the screen flashes blank ten times, representing Enyart's supposed unreturned photos, while the soundtrack is the ensuing chaos in the pantry. It was a cinematic device, and a good one, to represent what is not known about what happened when Robert Kennedy was shot. But in Charach's video Enyart did not say he was in the pantry or saw Kennedy "fall from the frame," as he would later on. Perhaps he said these things and Charach cut them from the video, but why would Charach do that? In any case, in the public mind, and perhaps in Scott Enyart's mind, the young high school photographer became the person who photographed the murder of Robert Kennedy and whose photos were taken by the police and never returned.

From that time forward, the story of Scott Enyart's missing photos became standard fare for anyone reviewing the anomalies and police misconduct surrounding the murder of Robert Kennedy. In books and TV documentaries it was told and retold, like the story of the Three Wise Men trotted out each December. Thirty witnesses could come forward and claim that the police had bullied them or altered their statements, but Scott Enyart's narrative just seemed to illustrate the whole thing in color. Articulate and clear-eyed, Enyart told a story where the details flowed easily, and it sure seemed like he had witnessed the murder. But now Scott Enyart had brought his story to court.

In the last week of June 1996, jury selection for the Enyart trial got under way. The jury pool was a varied mix of mostly working-class Angelenos. Attorney Skip Miller, intent on finding out which panelists believed that President John Kennedy had been murdered by conspiracy, repeatedly screened the candidates by asking, "Did you enjoy Oliver Stone's movie *JFK,* or did you find it long and tedious?" Panelists who enjoyed the movie were not likely to become jurors.

Not to be outdone, and understanding this to be a case about the value of photographs, the plaintiffs had their own cinematic litmus test: "What did you think about *The Bridges of Madison County?*"

As the jury was being selected, Judge Emilie Elias denied Court TV's request to televise the trial. The decision was made without comment, but it was understood that the judge was concerned that the presence of television cameras would serve to sensationalize the trial and distract the jury.

In his opening statement to the jury, Skip Miller likened the case to a "Sherlock Holmes mystery." He said, "This is an interesting case. I think you'll enjoy it. Contrary to all the discussion, it really isn't about the assassination, it isn't about willful and intentional manipulation of evidence. For Pete's sake, who would want to do that?"

According to Skip Miller, Scott Enyart's claim that he took important photographs in the hotel pantry was just "wishful thinking." He said that the reason Enyart had no access to the investigation files for twenty years was that the police had to "protect confidential informants." He told the jurors that they would have to decide for themselves whether or not the recent theft of the negatives was "part of the Evil Empire's twenty-eight-year plot."

During his statement Miller only occasionally glanced at his notes for reference. He spoke with confidence and moved easily about the courtroom in something that resembled a prowl. He was smartly dressed and looked younger than his forty-nine years.

Miller told the jury that there were two key questions. Did Scott Enyart take three rolls of film as he claimed or just one roll? Was Scott Enyart in the hotel pantry when the shots were fired, or was he still in the Embassy Room? Miller promised to prove that Enyart took only one roll of film and was not in the pantry. He offered Enyart's own words as proof. "In his own statement to police that night there's no mention of pantry. I read that statement over a dozen times. . . . There's not a word in there that's spelled P-A-N-T-R-Y."

After Miller finished speaking, the plaintiffs called their first witness, Jamie Scott Enyart. Dressed in a rumpled linen suit, the tall, attractive, slightly gaunt Enyart took the witness stand. In answer to his attorneys' questions, Enyart began to tell his story. He related how at a young age he had become interested in photography. Later he would tell the jury about Scott Enyart Studios, the professional photography business he had run for almost twenty years. This was important, because his lawyers wanted to demonstrate that at the time of the murder, Enyart had the skills to take good photographs under difficult circumstances and would be using the proper camera and film to do so.

Enyart would go on to relate events the night Robert Kennedy was shot. He told how he had brought his camera to the Ambassador Hotel so that he could take pictures for his high school newspaper. He said he was in the company of two friends and that they all had arrived at the hotel at around six in the evening.

Enyart told the court how later in the evening he had managed to get to within five feet of the podium, from which point he was able to take pictures of Kennedy's victory address. After the speech, Enyart said, he anticipated Kennedy's move to the Colonial Room and, using a side exit in the Embassy Room, managed to intercept Kennedy as he walked down the narrow hallway behind the stage. Enyart said he stepped in behind Kennedy and followed him into the pantry, hoping to get some candid shots.

"As I got into the pantry I was about ten feet behind him," Enyart told the authors in 1992, "continuing to take pictures as he began to shake hands with people. All of a sudden I saw him drop from the frame. He fell. And I continued taking pictures. I backed up, jumped up on a table. Everyone in front of me had been shot and fell and I jumped up to get out of the way."

Enyart said he continued to take photos for a brief time. Then he stopped.

"Once I realized what happened, particularly when Ethel Kennedy came into the room five months pregnant, kneels down next to her husband and says, 'Please, leave us alone,' I couldn't take pictures anymore. The rest of the press behaved like animals. They just crawled all over the place. They blocked the doors—the ambulance attendants couldn't get in—so they could bring in more lights and get more footage of this poor man dying on the floor with his wife next to him."[13]

Enyart said he made his way back out into the Embassy Room. When he tried to leave the hotel about a half an hour later, however, he said he was surrounded by police officers who took his film. In Enyart's deposition, Skip Miller asked the witness about this exchange.

"When you say the film was confiscated, in other words, it was demanded and seized?"

"It was taken at gunpoint."

"Gunpoint?"

"That's correct."

"Was the gun pointed at you?"

"That's correct."

"Did you resist? Is that why the gun was pointed at you?"

"I was running away from what I thought were evil people which turned out to be two detectives in suits. . . ."

"And how did the guns get drawn?"

"At the main entrance to the Ambassador Hotel there are two glass electric doors. I waited until the doors were closing and I ran out as they were closing which put some distance between myself and these two gentlemen. At that point I was grabbed and put down on my face on the red carpet. My camera was taken, my wallet was taken, my pockets were emptied. . . . I looked up and saw guns pointed at me, at which point they basically saw that they had a kid and didn't abuse me."

Enyart said he was then placed in a squad car and was questioned by two detectives who sat on either side of him. Miller asked what the detectives wanted to know. Enyart responded that they wanted to know whether or not he had seen the shooter.

"What did you say in response to the question?"

"I said, I don't know. I said I was taking pictures at the time and maybe—I said I couldn't tell without looking at the pictures."

"So you didn't have a view of the shooter . . . ?"

"At the time I would not have known who the shooter was. I saw Robert

Kennedy and I saw a number of people through the viewfinder as I was taking these pictures. I saw Robert Kennedy fall as he was shot. Whether or not in those photographs you would see Sirhan who was in front of him because I was behind him, I cannot tell without seeing those photographs. . . ."

"Would you agree with me that since you weren't called as a witness that the police and the prosecutor concluded that you could not give eyewitness testimony as to the Kennedy shooter?"

"Objection!" said Christine Harwell. "The witness cannot testify as to what others conclude."

"I'll rephrase. Will you agree with me that you were not an eyewitness to the Kennedy shooting?"

"I will not."

"Did you actually see Sirhan shoot Robert Kennedy?"

"Objection! It assumes facts not in evidence."

After his film and camera had been taken from him, Enyart said he was driven to the back of the hotel, where he was put into a holding room. Later he was transferred to Rampart Station by jail bus. There at around six in the morning he was briefly interviewed by the police.

On the second day of the trial, in a hushed courtroom, an audiotape of Scott Enyart's police interview was played for the jury.

"I'm Sergeant McGann from Homicide Division, Scott. I understand you took some pictures, did you?"

"Yes."

"—of the shooter—of the suspect doing the shooting?"

"I'm not exactly sure. I was about four feet from the stage while Mr. Kennedy was speaking, and after he stopped speaking and began to walk off the stage, the crowd started to clear; so I immediately headed for the door. . . ."

"Were you in the Embassy Room?"

"Embassy Room. . . . Right about here," said Enyart, apparently pointing to a small layout of the hotel the interviewing officers had for this purpose.

"Okay, and he left this way?"

"Yes, he left this way and I left this way. I got to about here, and the crowd was going toward him, like they always do, to shake his hand and everything; so I figured I can catch some good pictures. So there was a table here about three and a half feet tall, I'd say, so I got up on it so I was above everyone, and I was going to—and then the shots started to be fired, and I took pictures and kept taking pictures."

"While all the shots were being fired?"

"While the shots were being fired, maybe a little afterward. I'm not exactly sure. I couldn't tell. I can only tell by the pictures."

"This was down a hallway, more or less, you were shooting?"

"No. Can I—I'll show you."

"Uh-huh [yes]. Let's use this one here [apparently referring to a sketch of the hotel floor plan]."

The next exchange contained pauses, as Enyart could be heard drawing upon the floor plan.

"Here was a bar and here was this table. I was right here, and I headed over to here, got to about here. And Mr. Kennedy walked off the stage and got to about here. I got up on the table and was above, and I took pictures down at it—and a friend of mine was there, too, taking pictures, and I'm sure he has some pictures. I can get in touch with him."

"What is his name?"

"Brent Gold."

"Okay. So that's about all you can tell us, then, about this thing. Did you see the suspect that did the shooting?"

"Couldn't exactly say, 'cause, no, I don't believe I saw the suspect."

"You were just taking pictures of everything and everybody?"

"Yeah. And I took a picture of a boy come running back. His face was bleeding rather bad, and he came running back. I got a picture of that. There are miscellaneous pictures on the roll. . . . Do you want a description of the film so you'll know how to process it?"

"No, they'll send it down to the lab and take care of it."

"Will I get the film back?"

"Might get the prints or the negatives. I don't know. We—"

"Because it was kind of important to me."

The officers then gave Enyart a card. "Give us a call and we'll let you know."[14]

As Skip Miller had said in his opening remarks, whether or not Scott Enyart was in the pantry when the shooting occurred was the pivotal issue. And what Enyart told the police the night of the murder about his whereabouts would have to be considered strong evidence of where he had actually been. The frustrating reality for both sides was that Enyart's murder-night interview can bear either interpretation: that he was in the pantry or that he wasn't.

Miller's assertion to the jury, that the word "pantry" does not occur in the interview, is correct. But this has little meaning because the night of the shooting, few people besides hotel personnel were referring to the narrow room next to the kitchen as the pantry. Most intriguing is that as the tape plays, one can hear Enyart drawing a map of his movements for the detectives. "I was right here, and I headed over to here, got to about here. And Mr. Kennedy walked off the stage and got to about here."[15] The map that Enyart drew was not found in the LAPD's released files.

Thus, the question remains, what map did Enyart draw? He was asked whether he had seen the suspect who did the shooting. That would tend to support his claim that he had drawn a route into the pantry. More important, the police reports of Enyart's interview also tend to support his claim. A file card describing the taped interview bearing the names "Calkin/McGann" states about Enyart: "Was in kitchen when Kennedy came in, climbed on table to take pictures, heard shots, kept taking pictures. Did not see suspect."[16] An interview report written out by officer T. J. Miller reads: "Was in Embassy Rm taking pictures of speech. Kennedy left podium subj went to hallway outside kitchen. Got up on table to take pictures. Subj believe[s] at that time he may have gotten pictures of shooting. Subj turned undeveloped pictures over to police."[17]

Scott Enyart claims that in the months following Robert Kennedy's murder he tried a number of times to recover his photographs from the police. Finally, on one visit to police headquarters, he was brought to a room where photographs were locked away. The young man watched as several envelopes were removed from a steel cabinet.

"I was not allowed to look at my photographs," Enyart recalled to the authors. "They took this stack of prints, and one of the detectives shuffled through them and separated them into two piles. He gave me the photographs from one roll of film—everything leading up to the assassination—and then some pictures I had taken after the assassination. What he didn't give me were the pictures that I took in the pantry."[18]

Under direct examination, Scott Enyart was a compelling witness. He spoke with confidence and certainty about his missing photos. He demonstrated an advanced knowledge of photography. He spoke in great detail about the night of the assassination.

Enyart also identified himself in two photographs taken in the hotel pantry after the shooting. One was the Bill Eppridge photo that had appeared on *Unsolved Mysteries*. That photo had been taken perhaps several minutes after the shooting. Another photograph, by amateur photographer Richard Harrison, taken during the struggle for Sirhan's gun (and thus less than a minute after the shooting), recorded a shadowy figure apparently standing on the table where Enyart said he was. Identification was impossible, but Enyart claimed that the figure was wearing a sport jacket like the one he had worn and appeared to be in a stance consistent with the taking of photographs.

After a week of direct testimony, Skip Miller began his cross-examination of Scott Enyart. He showed disdain for the witness, and his questions were often tinged with sarcasm. Miller attacked on all fronts, and he paid particular attention to Enyart's detailed description of the events in the pantry.

"Has your memory improved over the years?" asked Miller.

Enyart responded that certain things leave a strong imprint in the mind. "My first child was born nineteen years ago," he said, "and I can remember that as though it happened yesterday."

Miller then took portions of Enyart's story and found passages in books and articles that described them in a similar way, suggesting that Enyart's memories had been pasted together after the fact, from secondary sources. Enyart had in court told of Robert Kennedy lying on the floor with a "halo of blood" spreading from his head. Miller read a description of the murder which used that very image. Enyart claimed he had not read the passage.

"So the word 'halo' occurred to you?" challenged Miller. "Came out of your head?"

"I was raised Roman Catholic," Enyart responded. "The word 'halo' was very familiar to me."

Miller asked Scott Enyart about his attempt to market a book titled *A Witness to History* and a proposed screenplay with the same title. Both were to feature Scott Enyart's story and his photographs. Miller read a portion of a letter Enyart had written to his agent in June of 1991, in which Enyart referred to the ongoing lawsuit against the city as enhancing the value of the proposed project by providing a focus for public interest in his story. "Isn't it a fact," asked Miller, "that you were marketing this story as part of an effort to advance this lawsuit?" Miller probably had it backward. A more realistic reading of Enyart's letter would be that the lawsuit was being used to enhance the value of the screenplay.

On Thursday, July 11, Miller would interrupt his cross-examination of Enyart to introduce a witness for the defense, photographer Bill Eppridge. Still a working photojournalist, Eppridge was on his way to Atlanta to photograph the Olympic Games for *Sports Illustrated*. From the witness stand he told the jury of the events the night of the murder, when he had been taking photographs for *Life* magazine. The courtroom became still as he recounted how he entered the pantry moments after the shooting to find first Paul Schrade and then Robert Kennedy lying on the floor.

Miller then showed Eppridge an enlarged version of his photo with the young man on the table in the background.

"Do you recognize this photograph?" asked Miller.

"Yes," answered Eppridge. "I took that photograph."

"Do you know who this person is up on the table?"

"Yes. That's Harry Benson."

Harry Benson was a photojournalist from Great Britain. He had been Bill Eppridge's friend and rival, and Eppridge made it clear that there was no question in his mind that the young man in the photograph was Benson. Upon resuming the witness stand, Scott Enyart would tell the jury that after hearing Bill Eppridge's testimony, he had changed his mind and was now willing to accept that the young man in the photo was not Scott Enyart. Later Harry Benson would appear in court. Even after twenty-eight years, the image of the young man, which had borne only a generic likeness to Scott Enyart, bore an undeniable resemblance to Benson.

After Bill Eppridge, Miller resumed his examination of Enyart. He introduced into evidence a portion of Theodore Charach's 1973 film documentary *The Second Gun,* in which Charach spoke to a young Scott Enyart in 1970. Over the objections of Enyart's attorneys, Judge Elias refused to allow the jury to see other portions of the documentary that explored allegations of conspiracy in the Robert Kennedy murder. A video monitor was wheeled into place, and the Enyart segment was shown.

In the interview Scott Enyart talked about going to the Ambassador Hotel with his friends and then taking photographs. "I shot a thirty-six exposure roll of film," Enyart said on camera, "and I got twenty-six prints back. I definitely feel there are some missing."[19] The video went on to display the Enyart prints.

"Now Mr. Enyart," said Miller when the video was done. "Last year in deposition you said you received back from the police eighteen prints, is that not so?"

"Yes."

"And in court a few days ago you said you got back twenty prints?"

"Yes.

"Can you tell me, Mr. Enyart, why in the video we just saw you say you received back twenty-six prints?"

Enyart was forced to say that over the years he must have "misplaced" some of the pictures given back to him by the police.

It was a devastating day for Scott Enyart. Bill Eppridge's repudiation of his claim to be the young man on the table wasn't fatal to his case, because the picture had been taken some minutes after the shooting, at a time when Enyart may have already been off the table. But the Eppridge testimony had been dramatic, and the best interpretation for the plaintiff was that Scott Enyart had been mistaken or perhaps reckless with the evidence.

The Charach video was also damaging. While the camera was rolling, Enyart told Charach that there were twenty-six prints provided to him by the police. Where were they now? If the photos were so important to Enyart, how were they lost? Enyart said that they had been kept in different envelopes over the years and "shuffled" around. It wasn't much of an answer from a plaintiff whose trademark until this day had been care and precision. Now either Enyart had misstated the evidence or he had lost some of the very pictures he was accusing the LAPD of losing.

There were other problems. Skip Miller was quick to point out that during the video Enyart had not mentioned being in the pantry or seeing

Kennedy fall. Enyart responded that he had told Charach those things and that he had no say in what appeared on the documentary. Miller asserted that during the video Enyart had not said anything about taking three rolls of film. Enyart answered that he had been speaking only about the crucial second roll of film, which had been shot in the pantry.

As the trial progressed Judge Elias made it clear that she intended to limit the scope of the case. "We are not trying conspiracy or retrying Sirhan Sirhan," she said. "We are not here to try whether there were two gunmen." But the Enyart lawsuit and the Kennedy murder shared a common border, one that was not easy to fence or patrol. Despite efforts to assure otherwise, the haunting underlying theme of the two-month trial became the assassination of Robert Kennedy.

The defense attorneys, understandably, did not want the assassination to enter the case for fear it would prejudice the jury against the city and the police. The plaintiff's attorneys wanted certain questions about the murder brought into evidence because they felt it demonstrated possible motive for the loss or destruction of Scott Enyart's photographs. The sharpest battles were fought on this terrain.

When the plaintiffs called former L.A. county coroner Thomas Noguchi, Skip Miller objected.

"I don't have an understanding as to what he could possibly testify to."

"Yes, you do," replied Judge Elias.

"I don't. I'm not just saying that. I don't."

"We went through this." The judge sighed. "It's a question of, if Mr. Enyart shot photographs of Mr. Kennedy as he was falling, what would have, from Dr. Noguchi's analysis, what would have been in the view."

Dr. Noguchi would go on to testify, as he had twenty-eight years earlier at Sirhan's trial, that the gun that killed Robert Kennedy had been fired from within a few inches of Kennedy's head.

Although there are no known photographs of the shooting in the pantry as it was taking place, the belief that the event was captured on film has endured in the public mind. Stories in the press and statements by various officials have helped perpetuate this myth. One story in the *Los Angeles Times* stated, "The shooting of Kennedy, recorded on television film and by still cameras, occurred in the pantry just off the Ambassador's main ballroom floor."[20] In 1975 a police spokesman defended the police investigation by saying, "We think that Sirhan Sirhan killed this guy because we got it on TV."[21]

But no pictures of the murder of Robert Kennedy have ever emerged. Thus, if Scott Enyart's alleged pantry photos actually captured Robert Kennedy at the time he was assaulted, their commercial and forensic value would be considerable: Robert Kennedy was shot at point-blank range, and photographs taken at that moment might very well have captured the gun or the gunman or both. Such a circumstance might also represent a motive for their disappearance. These were considerations that the plaintiff's lawyers were eager to impress upon the jury.

The care, or lack thereof, demonstrated by the police concerning the evidence was also an issue that the plaintiffs wished to bring out. Toward this end, they subpoenaed Philip Melanson, who, as director of the RFK Assassination Archives at the University of Massachusetts, was granted the status of expert witness. Melanson testified that he had found "glaring inaccuracies" in the LAPD *Summary Report,* and that in the report there was little "that threatened anyone's privacy," or that justified the twenty years of secrecy. He also spoke about a "pattern whereby some of the least important, most trivial material seems to have been carefully preserved without problem, whereas other categories . . . some of the most central and most controversial—were missing."

Paul Schrade, the campaign aide who was wounded at the Ambassador Hotel, was also called to testify. Under the direction of Christine Harwell, Schrade spoke about the efforts to get the police to open their files. Harwell asked Schrade about a meeting that he and former congressman Allard Lowenstein had with police chief Ed Davis in 1974.

"Did you make a request of Chief Davis to give you further access to the LAPD records and photographs?"

"Yes. He said that we should submit questions to him in writing and to Sam Williams, president of the police commission, which we did."

"And did you get an answer to your questions?"

"Never."

Following Schrade, journalist Theodore Charach was called. Like Schrade, Charach had also been present at the Ambassador Hotel the night of the murder. It was Charach's documentary that the defense had used the week before to cast doubt upon Scott Enyart's story. Now, however, Charach bolstered the plaintiff's case by testifying that he had seen Scott Enyart up on the table in the pantry when he entered the room shortly after the shooting. Then, in an embarrassing moment for the plaintiffs, Charach also asserted he recognized Scott Enyart in the Eppridge photograph, which had previously been shown to be a picture of Harry Benson.

Another alumnus of the Sirhan trial, retired police officer Frank Patchett, was called as a witness by the plaintiffs. In charge of case preparation for Special Unit Senator, Patchett was the liaison between the police and the district attorney's office. In this capacity, he had the primary responsibility for determining who was placed upon the official list of witnesses in the pantry at the time of the shooting.

Patchett's testimony was consistent and believable, but the former police sergeant could not explain why Scott Enyart had not been reinterviewed in light of the police reports that he had possibly taken photographs of the murder. Under Christine Harwell's questioning, Patchett admitted that he had no recollection of seeing any police reports about Scott Enyart or any memory of eliminating him from the pantry list. "Why Mr. Enyart does not appear on the list of people in the pantry, I cannot tell you," said Patchett. "But I can guarantee you that at the time there was a good reason, and what that was I don't know."

As Scott Enyart had testified, he had gone to the Ambassador Hotel on primary night with a friend named Brent Gold. Both young men had brought cameras and they had spent much of the evening in each other's company. But Brent Gold was not called as a witness by the attorneys for Scott Enyart; he was called by the city.

Gold, a psychotherapist by profession, testified that Enyart and he had been "best of friends" while they had been in junior high school and had shared an interest in photography. Gold said that he had no knowledge of what kind of film Enyart shot the night of the murder, nor how many rolls of film Enyart had brought with him, but he also said that both of them frequently used the inexpensive Ilford brand hand-loaded film. This was significant because the negatives found at the California State Archives were Ilford, but Enyart was claiming that he had used Kodak film the night Robert Kennedy was shot.

As photographs taken that night reveal, both Brent Gold and Scott Enyart were in front of the stage, close to each other, when Robert Kennedy was speaking. Defense attorney Skip Miller asked Gold to describe where he went after Kennedy's speech had ended.

"I simply walked out to the front," said Gold, "to the lobby."

"Which way did Scott Enyart go?"

"We were together."

"Did you walk together?"

"Yes."

"Did either you or Mr. Enyart attempt to fight against the crowd and go in the direction of the podium?"

"No."

Gold testified that both he and Enyart were in the hotel lobby just outside of the Embassy Room when they heard the first screams and commotion indicating something was wrong inside. According to Gold, both of them went back into the Embassy Room to see what had happened and became separated.

Miller then asked Gold if they had ever subsequently talked about what had happened at the hotel. Gold said they had.

"Until the lawsuit was filed, did Mr. Enyart ever tell you that he had been in the pantry and took the only pictures in the world of Senator Kennedy being shot?"

"No," answered Gold. "He never said that he had taken pictures of Senator Kennedy being shot."

Gold would go on to say that after high school he and Scott Enyart had encountered each other only a few times at social gatherings. Then in 1992 Gold saw Enyart being interviewed on TV, claiming that he had been in the pantry during the murder. Gold said he called Enyart on the telephone because he was "fearful" that he was going to get himself into trouble, "because I knew where we were. I knew we were both outside in the lobby area when Kennedy was shot and he wasn't in the pantry."

"And what did Mr. Enyart say?" asked Miller.

"He said that wasn't his recollection of the event."

Upon cross-examination Scott Enyart's attorneys were able to show that Brent Gold's memory was not crisp, continually chasing Gold back to his notes to refresh his recollection about events in the past. They also elicited from Mr. Gold that he had spent more than twenty hours with police detectives and lawyers for the city.

"Did you enjoy participating with the LAPD," Gold was asked, "the detectives and talking about the events and meeting with them at Parker Center and going out to the hotel? Did you enjoy that?"

"This entire process has been extremely painful and upsetting to me," responded Gold. "I would never want to speak out against a friend, especially a friend of thirty years. No, it has not been fun."

Enyart's lawyers did what they could do, but the problem remained. Scott Enyart had said one thing, and his former friend Brent Gold had said something quite different. Who was telling the truth, and who would the jury believe?

While the movies talked about during jury selection were *JFK* and *The Bridges of Madison County,* the true cinematic antecedent of the Enyart trial was Michelangelo Antonioni's *Blow-Up.* In this 1960s classic, a series of apparently innocent photographs are enlarged and enhanced until the image of a murder weapon emerges from obscure shadows. But murder-scene photographs by Scott Enyart or anyone else were not at the trial, and the negatives found at the state archives were also missing, so they couldn't be analyzed to see if some sort of forgery had taken place. But when certain photographs at the trial were enlarged, the resulting images didn't support Scott Enyart's assertions.

The Bill Eppridge photo, when enlarged, showed a young man who didn't look particularly like Scott Enyart. Moreover, a blow-up of one of the "Clayton" prints solved another mystery. Earlier in the trial Enyart had suggested that the print seemed to be out of sequence because it appeared to be shot before Kennedy had even taken the stage. But the enlarged print produced by the defense attorneys revealed the obscure but unmistakable image of shooting victim Irwin Stroll being carried out into the Embassy Room. Thus, the "Clayton" prints were not out of sequence as Enyart had suggested.

After five weeks of bruising, often acrimonious conflict in court, Christine Harwell, representing Scott Enyart, stood once again in front of the jury. By California law the plaintiffs in a civil lawsuit speak first in final argument, the defendants respond, and then the plaintiffs speak again.

With a stern look on her face, Harwell began by praising the competence of attorney Skip Miller, calling him "a very skilled attorney, a very clever attorney." She then went on to describe ways in which she thought Miller had been clever. She pointed to his representation that Scott Enyart had not spoken the word "pantry" in his police interview, even though few people were using that word the night of the murder. She scorned Miller's attempt to cast Enyart's financial stake in his photographs as a motive for fabrication. She noted Miller's attempt to discredit Enyart's account of the murder by finding other, similar descriptions. She mentioned the "halo" of blood. "Of course, had Scott Enyart described Kennedy's head resting in a 'pool' of blood," she said, "no doubt Mr. Miller could have found another reference somewhere else which used that term."

Harwell went on to speak about Skip Miller's literal reading of the transcript of Enyart's police interview. "Of course, reading the transcript of the interview and listening to the interview are two very different things," said Harwell. "When we listened to the tape we heard a young man drawing a map of where he had been. We hear a police officer asking Mr. Enyart if he had seen or photographed the shooter. Why would the police ask Scott Enyart if he had seen the shooter if Scott Enyart had drawn them a diagram that hadn't even put him in the pantry? Why would the police report of this interview assert that Scott Enyart had said he was in the pantry, if it had been their understanding that Scott had only been in the Embassy Room?"

Harwell then set forth for the jury the list of strange anomalies in the case: Enyart having his film taken from him at gunpoint, his not receiving back his negatives, his not being reinterviewed or included on the list of pantry witnesses, no film being on file under his name, the failure of his interview to appear in the *Summary Report,* and the theft of the newly found negatives. "Are all of these occurrences just coincidence?" asked Harwell. "Innocent mistakes? I don't think so. I think what we see here is a consistent and deliberate attempt to erase Scott Enyart and his photographs from the record of this case."

Harwell told the jury that pressing a civil suit is a very expensive proposition, that the lawsuit against the city had placed a tremendous burden upon the Enyart family. "Do you really think Scott Enyart would have put himself and his family through this terrible ordeal if he were missing just a couple of photos? If he hadn't really been in the pantry at the time of the murder? If he hadn't been outraged at his treatment at the hands of the police?"

As she closed her remarks Harwell wanted the jury to understand that the cost to the Enyart family was not just financial. "The LAPD has put Mr. Enyart through a degrading process and tried to make him out to be a profiteer. You know that is not so. We ask for justice."

Christine Harwell had made a forceful appeal on behalf of her client. The atmosphere in the courtroom was charged. As Skip Miller began his argument, he attempted to reduce the pressure.

"This is a case about Mr. Enyart's photographs," he reminded the jury. "It is not a kick in the door, send a message to the police, kind of thing."

Miller said that Enyart's claim against the city was one fabricated with "smoke and mirrors." He replayed the Enyart segment of the Charach documentary and reminded the jury that on the video Enyart had not claimed to have shot three rolls of film or even to have been in the pantry. He said that Enyart had come forward now because he had a motive.

Miller said that Enyart's motive could be found in a letter to his agent in which he talked about promoting the proposed screenplay of his story. "There's nothing wrong with him trying to break into Hollywood, sell his screenplay. Go for it. All the luck in the world. But don't come into court, spin a yarn, and try to get a jury to conclude that you are a 'witness to history.' That was the title of his proposed story. But he wasn't a witness to anything. And it's not right for him to come to court and ask you to help him sell his property to Hollywood."

Miller then spoke of the police handling of the evidence in the case. "They were doing their job and they did it right." He called the theft of the negatives outside the L.A. airport a "snafu." He said, challenging the jury, "If you believe that we had something to do with that, then you believe in the tooth fairy."

Miller ended his summation to the jury by saying that Scott Enyart had been trying to "pull a fast one." His emotional level rising, the attorney said, "He doesn't deserve a dime. I think he's dishonored the court process. He's dishonored the memory of that night by trying to profit from it. This case is all about profit, personal gain, self-promotion, and greed. Just say no."

Skip Miller sat down; Christine Harwell rose again. The defense attorney's accusations had reddened her face. Abandoning her notes she spoke in an uncharacteristically angry voice.

"Mr. Miller has said that Scott Enyart was not a witness to anything," she said to the jury. "Well, just ask yourself. Why was he apprehended? Why was he interviewed? Why was his film immediately developed? Why is there no diagram? Why is there no receipt? Why is there no logging? Why is there no booking? No follow-up report? No indexing?"

Harwell then made reference to the seven years she had been working on the lawsuit. "I have spent a lot of time on this case," she said in a more measured tone. "I care and believe in my client. I think that you know the truth. That Mr. Enyart took those pictures, he didn't get them back, and they have never been produced to him. It's up to you to determine what that is worth."

The following day Judge Emilie Elias gave her instructions to the jury. She instructed them that in a civil suit a plaintiff does not have to prove his case beyond a reasonable doubt, but only by a preponderance of the evidence. She reminded them that only nine of the twelve jurors had to agree to decide any issue.

Because the trial had taken weeks longer than anticipated, it had been assumed that the jury was fatigued and eager to go home. A quick verdict was expected. It didn't come. Rumors of discord in the deliberations began to leak out, and day after day, no verdict arrived. Soon the rumor spread that the jury was deadlocked eight to four. But which way?

After two weeks of jury deliberations, a crisis developed: jury foreman Robert Pinger, a high school history teacher, announced that he had to leave the jury to ready himself for the coming school year. He then filed with the court a statement outlining his frustrations with the deliberation process and alleging "misconduct" on the part of several jurors. After Pinger's final day with the jury, but before he had been officially released and replaced by an alternate, attorney Skip Miller obtained a detailed statement from him as to what had occurred in the jury room. Upon learning this, Judge Elias exchanged harsh words with the defense attorney.

"Mr. Miller, I can't think of anything more inappropriate than you having talked to a juror in the middle of deliberations. . . . I think it's outrageous."

"I don't agree at all, Your Honor. I think I had an obligation to do it. It was entirely appropriate; this juror was released from jury duty."

"No, he wasn't. If you really want to know, he wasn't. He was told not to speak to anyone and you contacted him. . . ."

"Instead of being angry at me . . . I would think this court would be angry and concerned about what was going on inside the jury room. . . . I did nothing wrong. For this court to get upset with me, I don't understand it. Where are you coming from, Your Honor? Where, I mean, are we talking about justice? Fairness?"

"Mr. Miller, I've heard enough."

"Excuse me, Your Honor, I take this whole thing very seriously."

"Mr. Miller, why don't you wait until more reporters come and you can make your comments then."

"Excuse me, Your Honor? I don't understand that kind of a comment."

"It was inappropriate and I shouldn't have said it—I was outraged that you would do this and—"

"You were outraged? You're not upset about what was going on for the last two weeks in your courtroom, Your Honor?"

"Mr. Miller, I'm very upset about your behavior and if you don't stay quiet I'm going to start a contempt hearing. Okay? That's how upset I am."

The conversation between Miller and Elias returned to normal, and Miller was not cited for contempt. Miller's strident words in this exchange would be a clue to the verdict to come. On Thursday August 22, after three weeks of deliberation, the jury awarded Scott Enyart $450,600* for the loss of his photographs.

The verdict had not been unanimous. The final vote had been nine to three, the minimum necessary for a judgment. And even that was shaded by a cloud. Ex–jury foreman Robert Pinger later would tell the authors that he believed the verdict in the Enyart case had more to do with "anti-civic-authority sentiment" on the part of some jurors than it did with the evidence of the case.

As would be expected, the heavy judgment in Scott Enyart's favor released strong emotions on both sides. Enyart, of course, was elated. In the hall outside of the courtroom he characterized his battle with the police as "David versus Goliath." He told newsmen, "I'm thrilled, but I would much rather have my three rolls of film."[22]

The defense team tried to avoid the newsmen, but their frustration was evident. "Absurd in the extreme"[23] was Skip Miller's comment. He also privately promised the Enyart lawyers that their client would "never see a dime" of the award, alluding to the probability of appeal.

On October 15, attorneys for the City of Los Angeles asked the judge to declare a mistrial. The city charged that a new trial should be granted because Scott Enyart's lawyers were "allowed to present witnesses who misled and inflamed the jury with allegations of a purported conspiracy and cover-up by the LAPD, resulting in a jury poisoned by speculation as to a possible conspiracy to assassinate Senator Robert F. Kennedy." The city also alleged "serious misconduct" on the part of some jurors. "There was talk in the jury room," said assistant city attorney Ed Fimbres,

---

*On September 18 the plaintiffs were awarded an additional $175,000 in interest, which brought the total judgment to $625,600.

"like 'Everybody knows that the man screws over the people. Everybody knows that the LAPD doesn't know how to take care of evidence. Everybody knows that there was a conspiracy that killed the Kennedys.' It was highly improper."

Attorneys for Scott Enyart were less judgmental. "There is conduct here," said Christine Harwell, "that is viewed as improper by some and proper by others, and that's just the nature of the process." Judge Emilie Elias apparently agreed. On November 22 she denied the defense motions for a new trial. After the ruling, assistant city attorney Fimbres seemed perplexed. "We thought we put on a very compelling case," he said. "It was just a very, very strange trial."

Strange indeed. With missing photographs, stolen evidence, and sharply conflicting testimony, the Enyart trial served to rekindle the many frustrations felt by both sides in the smoldering twenty-eight-year debate over Robert Kennedy's murder. What else it accomplished was unclear. For some observers the large verdict in Enyart's favor was the spanking the Los Angeles Police Department deserved for its inadequate and secretive handling of the Robert Kennedy murder investigation. For others, Enyart's suit against the city represented the perfect example of how evidence can be distorted to further the interests of kooks and profiteers.

Both views are parochial. Despite the large verdict in his favor, Enyart's claim to have taken important pictures of Robert Kennedy's murder seemed more in doubt after the trial than before it began. Conversely, even if it could be proven that Enyart didn't take photos of Robert Kennedy as he was murdered, that wouldn't dispel the many other disturbing questions still open in the case.

In the last week of December, the City of Los Angeles brought the Enyart lawsuit to the appellate court of California. Soon after the appeal was filed, the original edition of this book went to print. The following addendum was written by William Klaber in 2017.

I was in attendance every day of the five-week Enyart lawsuit. I had a seat in the gallery that was considered mine. After hours, I spent time with Christine Harwell and Alvin Greenwald, Enyart's attorneys, whom I respected and whose company I enjoyed. I shared with them my knowledge of the case and my observations of the day. I had been sympathetic to the Enyart lawsuit; it fit with everything I knew—the many instances of the LAPD misstating, hiding, or destroying evidence.

But by the end of the trial I wasn't so sure. The jury may have decided in Enyart's favor, but my own verdict, as stated, was that Enyart's story was more in doubt at the end of the trial than it was before it began. Part of that doubt had been created by the thirty prints taken from the Ilford-brand film that had been found in the Cal Archives under another name. Those prints, twenty-six of which Enyart had agreed were his back in 1968, seemed to show Enyart in front of the podium as Kennedy spoke, then a retreat to the back of the hall, and finally more pictures in the Embassy Room showing the distress and chaos following the shooting. The story told by these photos follows what Enyart's friend Brent Gold had testified to, that he and Scott had left the rally together and had been in the hotel lobby when the commotion had drawn them back into the Embassy Room.

I spoke to Brent Gold on the phone as the trial wound down. There was sadness in his voice, sadness at having had to testify against a friend. Gold said he didn't know what kind of film Enyart was using that night, but he did say that he and Scott often used hand-rolled Ilford film in their projects for personal or high school photography projects. It was cheaper, and there was a certain cachet to rolling your own. If the found Ilford negatives were real, and not a forgery, then Scott Enyart was not telling the truth about photographing the murder of Robert Kennedy. But Enyart said at his trial that he had been shooting with Kodak, factory-sealed, thirty-six-print film.

Several years after the publication of the original *Shadow Play,* it came time to box and store the thousands of pages of documents I had reviewed and the hundreds of audiotapes I had listened to for the purpose of writing this book. While doing this, I came across a cassette tape of a Scott Enyart interview recorded by researcher David Cross. The interview took place in 1988, eight years before Enyart's film was either found in the Cal Archives or forged and placed there, so the issue of what kind of film Enyart was using had little meaning at the time. I didn't know what I was looking for, but I played the tape. It was standard fare at first, but then it came. Cross asked how many photos Enyart had taken, and Enyart replied, "There were probably about thirty shots per roll, they run a little short when you roll yourself." There it was. From his own statement it would appear that the Ilford negatives found in the Cal archives were Scott Enyart's after all. And there were no pictures taken in the pantry. My best interpretation is that a young man had fallen in love with a story about himself. He married that story and repeated it so often that perhaps to this day he believes it to be true. But it would seem that it's not. In this particular case, it would appear that it was the Los Angeles police who were telling the truth.

In 1999 the City of Los Angeles won its appeal of the Scott Enyart verdict. A new trial was ordered, but it never took place.

EIGHTEEN

"Trailing Edge Waveforms"

✱ ✱ ✱

IN THE SPRING of 2005, Brad Johnson, a senior writer at CNN, contacted an electrical engineer named Philip Van Praag and asked him to listen to an obscure audiotape that he had found in the California State Archives. The tape had been made on a cassette recorder that belonged to journalist Stanislaw Pruszynski, who had taped Robert Kennedy's final speech and then followed the senator into the pantry, not realizing that his recorder was still on. Johnson hoped that Van Praag, who was an accomplished sound engineer and had written a book on the evolution of recording technology, might use new digital enhancement techniques to discover how many shots had been fired in the hotel pantry that night. Van Praag listened to the Pruszynski tape and was discouraged by the poor quality. "I was not impressed at all," he recalled later to the author, "but, I thought, 'I'll take this back to my lab and see what's there.'"

What was there was enough to set Van Praag into motion. He knew that the audio cassette produced by the California State Archives was a low-quality copy of a low-quality original, so he approached the Cal Archives and asked permission to make a superior reproduction of the reel-to-reel version of the Pruszynski tape that they possessed, itself something like a third- or fourth-generation copy of the original. The librarians at the archives were understandably reluctant to let evidence, however briefly, pass out of their hands, but they finally said yes. Van Praag was allowed to play their tape one time on a high-quality playback machine that he provided, so he recorded that one pass on five different machines, analog and digital, to gain as much perspective as he could. He then brought the resulting tapes back to his workshop in Arizona, hoping to peer into the past by way of digital magic.

Van Praag pursued a multistep audio analysis, attempting first to discover exactly where Pruszynski was when the shooting began and how he was moving during the time the shots were fired. Having established the approximate distance and motion, he then went at the problem from the opposite direction, recording gunshot sounds on a cassette recorder and microphone that were roughly equivalent to the consumer-grade equipment that Pruszynski had used, and onto a magnetic cassette tape that was similar to that which was available in 1968, with the purpose of gaining knowledge of how a .22 caliber gunshot might register on the kind of equipment that Pruszynski had. With that in hand, Van Praag then did what he called a "preliminary testing" of the shooting period, utilizing "analog laboratory active-filtering equipment, along with other tools such as interval elongating computer software and a frequency domain spectrum analyzer."[1]

Van Praag's initial findings were first publicly broadcast in 2007 on Discovery Times Channel's show *Conspiracy Test: The RFK Assassination,* on which Van Praag said that he had found thirteen shot sounds, spread over a little more than five seconds.★

According to Van Praag, two shots were fired at first, then a pause of about 1.33 seconds, and then a flurry of shots. This would support Karl Uecker's claim that he had grabbed Sirhan's gun hand after the second shot and brought it down to the steam table, a scenario that makes it very hard for Sirhan to have put four point-blank shots into Kennedy from behind.

As thirteen shots were more than Sirhan could have fired with his eight-shot revolver, the findings suggested to Van Praag another avenue of inquiry. "If we consider the possibility of two guns being fired," he said to Discovery Times, "then we could say that over the same period of time we would have a random distribution of shots, and the likelihood that we would have a couple of virtually overlapping shots. And when you listen to the tapes, that's exactly what we have."[2] Van Praag identified these "double shots" as shot numbers 3 and 4, and shot numbers 7 and 8. In conjunction with Van Praag's findings, Discovery Times conducted a test with an expert firing an Iver Johnson Cadet 55 as fast as he could. The average gap between these "fast as possible" shots was .366 seconds. But the double shots on the Pruszynski tape had gaps of .122 and .148, meaning that they could not have come from the same gun. It would also explain why so many people described the shooting as sounding like the uneven staccato of firecrackers.

Discovery Times provided its own acoustic experts, Wes Dooley and his assistant Paul Pegas of the California-based Audio Engineer Associates, who were to review and vet Van Praag's work. Those taping *Conspiracy Test* hoped that the review could be done in a day, but after a day, Dooley asked for more time. By the end of the second day Dooley and Pegas were able to say that they had confirmed ten shots and one double shot (the second and, according to Van Praag, the more apparent of the two), each

---

★The words Van Praag used were "approximately thirteen shot sounds," but he later clarified the assertion, saying he had found thirteen shot sounds but couldn't rule out one or two others that might have been concealed by loud screams finding something less than what Van Praag had found in over a year's worth of work, but confirming nonetheless the presence of a second gun, as any gunshots in excess of eight would be proof of a second gun, as would any double shot.

Van Praag was not surprised or put off that Dooley had not discovered every shot that he had found given the short amount of time he had to do it. "If it were as simple as putting on a good set of earphones, you wouldn't need an audio expert," he told the author. Van Praag then went on to describe something that sounded like a high-tech game of *Where's Waldo?* using "computer enhancement techniques to identify genuine gunshot sounds out of a sometimes overwhelming montage of other sounds. It's not something you can do in a day." And Wes Dooley didn't seem to think there was much of a conflict between what he and Van Praag were able to find. "You can't back away from the real stuff," he said, regarding his own finding that a second gun was firing.[3]

While Van Praag and Dooley both found more shots on the Pruszynski tape than Sirhan could have fired, Discovery Times, on the same program, presented a dissenting opinion from Philip Harrison, an English audio expert. Harrison had been brought into the case by anti-conspiracy author Mel Ayton, who arranged for a copy of the Pruszynski tape to be provided to Harrison. Philip Harrison then reported to Discovery Times that he had found evidence of seven shots, with a possible candidate location for Sirhan's assumed eighth shot.

Harrison's audio report was not examined on the *Conspiracy Test* program, but it makes interesting reading. Harrison's report doesn't speak of a single possible location for Sirhan's eighth shot but rather of four locations that are candidates. At one point Harrison candidly admits that the seven shot sounds that he found could not be identified on their own as being shots from a .22 caliber revolver. "However," he states, "taking into account the events of the early hours of June 5, 1968 . . . it is fair to conclude that these are the sounds of Sirhan's gun being fired."[4] To say it another way, knowledge of what you are looking for helps you find things you might otherwise miss. But it could also work the other way: the boundaries of what you are looking for could restrict what you are able to find. Ayton's instructions to Harrison, or what he was told about the case, are not public knowledge. For example, was Harrison aware of the purported bullet holes in the doorframes, which would represent shots in excess of Sirhan's limit? But whatever he was told, whatever his commission, Harrison appears to be searching for evidence of Sirhan's *eight* shots, and this may have caused him to overlook some things. For example, Harrison apparently finds evidence of Van Praag's double shots. He finds a possible shot at .19 seconds after shot 7, but he dismisses it because "the higher frequency content is different [yes] and the auditory quality is not consistent with the other shots [yes]. Also, it would require the trigger to be pulled in a very short space of time following shot 7 [yes]."[5] So Harrison decides that this second sound is not a shot sound, because it has different sound characteristics than his other shots and would require the gun to be fired at an impossibly short interval. He is not considering a second gun.

Harrison had the same objections about the suspicious sound he found at 0.14 seconds after shot 3, but added another objection, that is, the sound was categorically not "the sound of a .38 revolver being fired in the room."[6] But why did it have to be a .38 caliber revolver? And if it is definitely not the sound of a .38 caliber revolver, does that mean it cannot be a gunshot sound?

As Discovery Times reported, Phil Van Praag found thirteen shots on the Pruszynski tape, Wes Dooley found ten, and Philip Harrison found seven. But Van Praag was the one who by far put in the most time and the most effort. And he wasn't finished with his investigation.

On February 21, 2008, Phil Van Praag stepped to the dais to present his scientific findings to the Sixtieth Annual Scientific Meeting of the American Academy of Forensic Sciences in Washington, D.C. The five-day event was held at the sumptuous Marriott Marquis Hotel, and the keynote speakers were Senator Jeff Sessions of Alabama and Senator Joe Biden of Delaware. During the prior year, a call had gone out for people to submit summaries of work that they wished to present at this meeting. Van Praag's submission was titled "Acoustic Analysis of Gunshot Recordings Utilizing Frequency Selective Integrated Loudness Envelope Evaluation," and it concerned the application of new audio techniques to an old audiotape of the Robert Kennedy murder. Van Praag's application was reviewed and accepted, and he was invited to present his findings.

Standing at the head of the hall, Van Praag told those assembled the story of how the Pruszynski audiotape had come to him by way of CNN senior news writer Brad Johnson, and how with Johnson's help he had gotten the California State Archives' permission to make a best possible copy of the reel-to-reel tape that they had. He then explained in detail all the steps he had taken to best discover what was on the Pruszynski tape, and how he had found, to a reasonable degree of certainty, thirteen shot sounds, though he didn't rule out the possibility of one or two others masked by screams as those nearby came to realize what was happening.

He then explained how he had found two double shots, numbers 3 and 4, and numbers 7 and 8, and how an expert had test-fired the Iver Johnson Cadet as fast as he could, proving the discovered double shots were too close together to have been fired by a single gun.

Then the new discovery. "One distinguishing characteristic of gunshots," he said, "is the presence of a trailing edge waveform envelope.

This is what makes gunshots identifiable from other sounds like balloons popping or firecrackers that might be mistaken for gunshots."

Van Praag then described how he began to look closely at those waveform envelopes, what might be thought of as gunshot fingerprints. "As I examined the frequency content of those trailing waveform envelopes, I discovered an anomaly in five of them. This anomaly presented as a single frequency component, at 1600 hertz, a level not found in the other shot sound waveforms." According to Van Praag this anomaly "was present in one, and only one, of each double shot pair."[7]

Curious about what could be causing this anomaly, Van Praag arranged and recorded an independent firing-range test using two different .22 caliber guns, an Iver Johnson Cadet 55 and a Harrington & Richardson 922. The Cadet 55 was the model Sirhan had fired the night of the murder, and the H&R 922 was the only make and model .22 caliber handgun that had the identical class characteristics as the Cadet 55, with six riflings, a right-hand twist, and a 0.054-inch land-width mark, which meant that a bullet fired from that gun could easily be mistaken for a bullet fired from the Cadet 55. It was also the gun that security guard Thane Eugene Cesar admitted that he owned, though Cesar said he was carrying a .38 caliber pistol that night.

Van Praag placed his microphones forty feet away from the guns, both in front and behind their direction of fire, to mimic the approximate distance Pruszynski was from the shooting. What he discovered was that the Iver Johnson Cadet matched the frequency print of the eight shots. But with the H&R 922, "a frequency anomaly was found when analyzing recording from the rear of the gun, but not from the front, the same 1600 hertz as that discovered within the five anomalous Pruszynski shot sounds." As everyone agrees, Sirhan was firing in an east-to-west direction. According to Van Praag, his field tests placed the second gun firing in a direction away from the microphone, "which means that gun was firing in a west to east direction, opposite to that of Sirhan's direction of fire."[8]

Phil Van Praag had laid out his methods and observations to the American Academy of Forensic Sciences. And by these scientific observations he had, forty years after the murder, identified thirteen shot sounds on the Pruszinski audiotape—eight shots matching Sirhan's gun firing westward, and five other shots, matching another gun, firing in the opposite direction. At the end of Van Praag's presentation there was a round of polite, mostly technical, questions. Following that, Paul Schrade, who had come to the event with Van Praag, was asked to stand. As a friend of Robert Kennedy who had been wounded the night of the murder and as someone who had fought for years to have the police files opened, he received an extended, vigorous ovation.

If an H&R 922 really was the gun that fired the bullets that killed Kennedy, as Van Praag's tests seem to suggest, there is nothing to say this revolver had to be in the hand of security guard Thane Eugene Cesar and not in the hand of the mysterious taller dark man who was seen with Sirhan earlier and seen again in the pantry with a gun and running out of the pantry with that gun. But Thane Cesar did own an H&R 922 at the time, though he has always denied that he carried it the night of the murder, or that he fired any gun that night. Phil Van Praag's test results call into question, yet again, the LAPD's failure to adequately question Cesar the night of the shooting, their failure to examine his gun to see if it had been fired or even what caliber it was, and their failure to investigate his false claim that he had sold his .22 caliber handgun months before the assassination, when, as it was discovered, he sold it some months after. And it might explain the strange, gentle escort off the stage that Cesar received, not asked any difficult questions, and more oddly still, not called as a witness to a capital crime in which he had a security obligation and a front-row seat.

The finding of thirteen shots from two separate sources also confirms Nina Rhodes's account given publicly that she had heard ten to fourteen shots fired, some from the vicinity of Sirhan and others from the vicinity of Senator Kennedy. Recall that, in place of the usual tape recording or interview transcript, the FBI produced a convenient "interview summary," which strangely stated that Nina Rhodes had reported hearing "eight distinct shots." And if five shots came from the second gun, we would expect to find in addition to the two bullets found in the senator, three bullets penetrating the ceiling tiles in the area above Kennedy, Uecker, and Sirhan. And if this were so, it would explain why the ceiling tiles were also secretly destroyed, because, like the doorframes, there were more bullet holes in them than the police were willing to account for.

Van Praag's findings, as reported to the American Academy of Forensic Sciences, scientifically supported what criminalist William Harper had laid out forty years earlier, that the evidence in the case demonstrated two firing positions, one being Sirhan's, who fired eight shots wounding five witnesses and putting three bullets in the wood doorframes as shown by the police and FBI photographs, and that of a gunman behind Robert Kennedy, putting four bullets into him or his clothing, and perhaps firing a fifth bullet that missed altogether.

In 2005 Sirhan's attorney Larry Teeter died. He had represented Sirhan Sirhan for ten years, bravely taking his client through several frustrating parole board hearings. In search of a replacement, the Sirhan family approached human rights attorney William Pepper, who initially declined. But Pepper reviewed the facts of the case and over time became convinced that Sirhan was an innocent man. So in 2007, along with attorney Laurie Dusek, William Pepper became Sirhan Sirhan's attorney of record.

As a young man in 1964, Bill Pepper was the citizens campaign chair in Westchester County for Robert Kennedy's successful run in New York for the Senate. During that time he got to know Robert Kennedy and the Kennedy family. In 1966 Pepper went to Vietnam as a photographer, and in January 1967 *Ramparts* magazine ran Pepper's photo essay "The Children of Vietnam," which depicted children maimed by the U.S. Army's use of napalm. Martin Luther King, Jr., saw the *Ramparts* essay and asked to meet with Pepper. Dr. King was already thinking that the war was immoral, and not unrelated to civil rights, but his meeting with Pepper helped to solidify his opinions. He was said to have openly wept when Pepper showed him the photos in his files that had not been published. The two men became friends, and Pepper was present at Riverside Church in New York on April 4, 1967, when King made big headlines by coming out against the war. A year later Martin Luther King and Robert Kennedy would be dead.

In 1977 Bill Pepper was admitted to the bar, having gotten his law degree at Boston College. Later that year he received a phone call from Ralph Abernathy, who had been Dr. King's right hand at the Southern Christian Leadership Conference. Abernathy said he was having doubts about the official version of how Dr. King had died, and wondered if Pepper would go with him to talk to James Earl Ray, the confessed and convicted assassin. Pepper agreed, but the project was put off because Pepper had other obligations and wanted to research and prepare his questions for Ray. Finally, in August 1978, Pepper, Abernathy, and two others went to Brushy Mountain State Penitentiary and spent five hours with James Earl Ray. Both Abernathy and Pepper came away with the belief that, whatever his role, Ray had not shot Martin Luther King. This new opinion weighed on Pepper's mind, but it was not until ten years later, when he became convinced that Ray had no knowing involvement in the assassination, that William Pepper decided to become the attorney of record for James Earl Ray.

Piece by piece, witness by witness, William Pepper began to reconstruct the murder of Dr. Martin Luther King, and the puzzle he was putting together looked nothing like the official version of the crime. Any attempt to summarize the many stunning discoveries made by Pepper and the testimony of the witnesses he found would be a disservice to his courageous work on a very complex story. Anyone interested would do well to read Pepper's excellent book *The Plot to Kill King*.

During the time he represented Ray, Pepper had become close to the remaining family of Martin Luther King. In 1997, King's son Dexter met with James Earl Ray in prison and came out saying that he believed Ray to be innocent. Pepper's efforts to get James Earl Ray a trial ultimately failed, and Ray died in prison in 1998.

After Ray's death, Bill Pepper became the King family attorney, and on their behalf he filed a civil lawsuit in Memphis in 1999 titled *Coretta Scott King et. al. v. Loyd Jowers and Other Unknown Co-conspirators,* wherein the King family sued for the wrongful death of Dr. Martin Luther King as a means to get the discovered evidence and witness testimony recorded in a legal forum. As Pepper reports, the "unknown co-conspirators" consisted of "agents of the City of Memphis, the State of Tennessee, and the government of the United States,"[9] and despite the lawsuit title, the actual identities of many of these men were known and spoken at the trial. Seventy witnesses testified at the trial, which lasted three weeks, and they told a very different story than the one told thirty years earlier. A repentant Jowers, who testified by deposition, said that James Earl Ray was a scapegoat and that a Memphis police sharpshooter had been recruited to fire the fatal shot from the bushes behind Jowers's bar/restaurant, with Jowers taking and hiding the rifle while the shooter and his spotter got away. The jury took less than an hour to come back with a judgment for the King family.

That a jury in a court of law had found other people and not James Earl Ray responsible for the murder of Martin Luther King should have been big news, but most American newspapers failed to properly report on or follow up on this story. Anti-conspiracy op-ed pieces did appear, all written by men who had not been at the trial and who attacked not the evidence presented but the motives of those bringing it forward. The King family, however, was grateful that the truth (incomplete as it was) had come out. They would say that this trial represented closure for them and they would no longer speak to the media about the murder but merely refer anyone inquiring to examine the trial transcript. Not very much to ask of a nation that once a year gushes about what a great man Dr. Martin Luther King was, but on every other day is reluctant to pose even the most simple questions about how he died. And, of course, the same could be said for Robert Kennedy. And so it was that in 2007, the attorney who had represented the accused and convicted assassin of Dr. Martin Luther King now signed on to represent the accused and convicted assassin of Robert F. Kennedy.

Having reviewed the tape recordings of Sirhan in police custody the night and morning after the murder, and the tape recordings of Sirhan under hypnosis in his jail cell awaiting trial, Bill Pepper became convinced that

Sirhan's lack of memory of the crime was real and not feigned. But what did it mean?

To try to answer that question Pepper approached Dr. Daniel P. Brown, a professor in Psychology at Harvard Medical School. In his professional career Brown had been qualified as an expert witness on psychological assessment, trauma, and the effects of suggestive influence. Brown was the senior author of the textbook, *Memory, Trauma Treatment and the Law*. He had also served as a consultant for the prosecution at the International War Crimes Tribunal in the Netherlands, had written four books on hypnosis, as well as guidelines on forensic interviewing with hypnosis, which appeared in *The Comprehensive Textbook of Psychiatry*.

Pepper asked Brown to interview Sirhan to search for a memory of events leading up to the murder of Robert Kennedy, and to make an evaluation of Sirhan's mental status. "The central question Bill asked me," Brown reported to the author, "is whether or not Sirhan was a subject of coercive influence that rendered his behavior involuntary."[10]

Over the next five years Dr. Brown interviewed and tested Sirhan on sixteen occasions, totaling more than 90 hours. Attorney Laurie Dusek was in attendance for each of those sessions. In addition, Brown spent many more hours reviewing the existing psychological record on Sirhan as well as all the tapes of Sirhan's sessions with the defense and prosecution doctors while awaiting trial, including those in which Sirhan was hypnotized and prodded to reenact the murder. Brown was himself an expert in the use of hypnosis in forensic inquiries and on occasion he put Sirhan under hypnosis in search of answers. "I've hypnotized thousands of individuals over a 40-year professional career," he said as we sat in his office in eastern Massachusetts. "Mr. Sirhan is one of the most hypnotizable individuals I've ever met. He is also exactly the type of person who could have been induced by others to engage in uncharacteristic action for which he would subsequently become amnesic."[11]

Brown was never able to completely penetrate Sirhan's lack of memory about the murder but he did uncover bits and pieces. He discovered what he termed a "distinctly different alter personality state, a personality state that responds in a robot-like fashion upon cue."[12] In this altered state Sirhan would adopt a gun firing posture and then act as though firing a gun at a firing range. This altered state never appeared when Sirhan was not hypnotized, and he would have no memory of his actions once awakened from his hypnosis. Dr. Brown also found a memory in Sirhan of being in some sort of hospital during a two-week period when he had gone missing, and a memory of being brought to a gun firing range and taught to fire upon command. Brown spent considerable time trying to pry loose more memories of the woman Sirhan said he had coffee with and who then led him into the pantry. "I think this woman was his handler," he said, "and that it was her cue, a pinch on the arm, that sent Sirhan forward with his gun to shoot at Robert Kennedy." All of this is fantastical, the stuff of movie plots, except for the fact that at least two dozen witnesses saw the woman with Sirhan, and Vincent DiPierro said of the moments just before the shooting, "It looked like she was almost holding him."

And what to make of Sirhan's apparent genuine lack of memory? "The tapes of his police interviews the night of the murder and the morning after appear to show a calm, reflective person with no knowledge that he had done something horrific," said Brown. "He had never done a violent thing is his life. Had no political or religious affiliations that might have led him to kill. If he had shot Bobby on behalf of the Arab people, why wouldn't have said so? In my opinion, Sirhan was trained through coercive persuasion to serve as a distractor, so that a second shooter could render the fatal shot."[13]

On March 2, 2011, William Pepper, accompanied by cocounsel Laurie Dusek, attended Sirhan's parole hearing—Pepper's first, Sirhan's fourteenth.[14] The presiding commissioner was Mike Prizmich. As things were set to get under way, Sirhan's breathing was audible. Commissioner Prizmich asked if he were okay. Sirhan said that he had been down with "Valley Fever" for several months. Asked if he were getting medication, Sirhan said that he had been given Diflucan, but that he did not improve, so the dose had been doubled. Prizmich said he was sorry to hear this.

The first hour was the standard recap of the crime and then a review of Sirhan's prison record, which was mostly excellent. But there were the occasional incidents, sometimes with inmates and sometimes with guards. The ones with guards were most troubling to the parole board, and Sirhan tried to explain that sometimes a guard would take a dislike to him for no explainable reason and then try to provoke Sirhan into a response after which he then could be punished. The parole board found it hard to believe that a guard might do such a thing, and of course if he did, there were always the in-house avenues of recourse. Sirhan did not try to explain what risks might accompany an in-house avenue of recourse; rather he replied that he dealt with these provocations by reporting the incidents to his attorney, who would then write to the warden.

Then, in response to a question, Sirhan told a strange story of something that had happened to him immediately following the attack on 9/11. "Those two towers hadn't crumbled yet," said Sirhan, "before I was placed in [solitary] at Corcoran with the accusation that I ordered the attack." Sirhan had just showered and had a towel on his head and was watching the television coverage of the event, and a particular guard saw him and took the towel to signify some Muslim something and accused Sirhan of being in on the plot to attack New York. And as absurd as this claim was, it caused Sirhan to be placed in solitary confinement. A week later a story about the incident appeared in *The Washington Post,* which said that the FBI was now looking into Sirhan's correspondence to see if there was any connection between him and the 9/11 terrorists. As punishment for his supposed role in the attack, Sirhan was said by his family to have been kept shackled in solitary for a year.[15]

When it was his turn, deputy DA David Dahle spoke, as he had twice before, on behalf of the district attorney of Los Angeles, who "vehemently" opposed parole for Sirhan, first of all because the crimes for which Sirhan was convicted "stand out as some of the most despicable heinous crimes" on record in California. According to Dahle, not only did Sirhan kill a human being, but he canceled the votes of all the millions of people who had voted for Kennedy. It was, in short, "a crime against democracy."

When Bill Pepper spoke at the hearing, he was in a bit of a box. In any normal interview he would be off and running with the evidence that showed a second gun or evidence that showed that Sirhan had been programmed in some way. But the parole board had made it clear that they were not going to consider case evidence. But Bill Pepper did talk about Dan Brown's report on his many hours of work with Sirhan. Pepper said that Dr. Brown was absolutely certain that Sirhan was not faking his lack of memory. In the past, parole boards had chosen to disbelieve this lack of memory, and they used Sirhan's supposed lie about not remembering as proof that Sirhan did not have remorse and would not take responsibility for his actions.

Bill Pepper's point this day was that by every criteria that was supposed to guide the parole board, Sirhan was deserving of parole regardless of who was murdered. "For 43 years he's had good behavior. He's had education, AA attendance, participation in a program that we brought to him, and reports that he is low risk for violence. He has shown remorse. He has a place to live. . . . And if you look at your own list of criteria, you will see that he fulfilled every requirement. . . . This man is 67 years of age. He is not a threat to anyone. I ask you to give him a date and let him return to his family."

There was a recess, and when the hearing resumed, Commissioner Prizmich announced that Sirhan posed "an unreasonable risk to society" and was not ready for parole. Then, in the tone of a high school disciplinarian, he launched into a litany of concerns about "deep-seated issues" and Sirhan's "many failures." Perhaps Sirhan's eyes glazed over at having to hear it all again. "You've got to listen here, guy," demanded Prizmich, who then went on to talk about the tragedy that the Kennedy family suffered and that they had already suffered a great tragedy [in Dallas], to which Sirhan responded, "But that wasn't my doing."

Prizmich was incensed. "You're not going to talk in the middle of my—you're going backwards, partner." He then went on to say that Sirhan should have done more self-help programs and needed to stop his attitude of being the victim "even to the point of making a comment that the CO's were alleging the twin towers might have been directed by you—you made that comment here today."

"But they did, sir," said Sirhan, who had suffered in solitary because of it.

"You're not going to interrupt me again. That was an immature comment to make." A minute or two later Prizmich was in the middle of a long, convoluted sentence that was hard to understand, and Sirhan strained to follow.

"You're looking quizzical," said Prizmich, and then a pause.

"I don't understand," said Sirhan.

"I didn't invite you to talk," snapped Prizmich, although it seemed he had. And so it went, with Commissioner Prizmich going on about how Sirhan should have taken classes in anger management, and if none were offered he should have gotten a book about it. And because, at age sixty-seven, Sirhan was still such a great threat to society, parole would be denied for another five years, when he would be seventy-two.

On October 25, 2012, an official FBI memo titled "RFK Tape Review" was sent to the FBI laboratories in Quantico, Virginia.

> On October 9, 2012, FBI Los Angeles was advised of a request to re-examine evidence in the assassination of Robert F. Kennedy by [name blanked out]. The basis of the request was a claim by Forensic Scientist and Electrical Engineer Philip Van Praag that his examination of an audio recording of the event revealed thirteen shots, not eight, were fired during Senator Kennedy's assassination. If true, this would necessitate a second gunman as convicted assassin Sirhan Sirhan used an eight-shot .22 caliber Iver Johnson revolver.[15]

The FBI memo ordered the lab to examine the Pruszynski tape to see if Van Praag's findings could be corroborated. But whose name was blanked out? Who could have made such a request? Turns out the request was made by Robert F. Kennedy, Jr., the fallen senator's son, in a September 25 letter to the U.S. attorney general Eric Holder, written after Kennedy Jr. had consulted with Paul Schrade about the new acoustic evidence pointing to a second gun. "Paul was a close friend of my father," said Kennedy in his letter.

> He was standing beside my father when Daddy was killed, and Paul was himself wounded by a bullet. With boundless energy and a clear mind, Paul continues to pursue my father's ideas, an endeavor to which he has devoted his life. He organized with the support of my mother and my family the building of the new Robert F. Kennedy Community Schools on the former Ambassador Hotel site. Paul and his team . . . strongly support this new evidence which is conclusive and requires a new investigation.[16]

In response to Robert Kennedy, Jr.,'s letter, Eric Holder requested that the FBI examine the Pruszynski tape. They did and on May 13, 2013 quietly reported that "The designated area recorded on the specimen [tape] was of insufficient quality to definitely classify the impulse events as gunshots, confirm the number of gunshots, or determine the identification of specific weapon(s)."[17] The analysis and tests that led to these conclusions were not released, but when they finally emerged by way of the Freedom of Information Act, they revealed what researcher Shane O'Sullivan termed "outdated methodologies."

> The analyst describes searching for videos of Van Praag's work on YouTube and working from low resolution grabs of my film [*RFK Must Die* documentary] on Van Praag's discoveries in an effort to find out precisely where to look, how to look, and what to look for. These are details he could have discovered by simply picking up the phone and calling Van Praag or inviting him to the FBI's Quantico laboratory for a briefing.[18]

The FBI certainly did not have to agree to Van Praag's findings, but it seems strange that they would not have consulted him on how he found what he found. And, of course, there must have been a huge incentive for the FBI to find nothing at all. A conclusion like Van Praag's, that thirteen shots were fired in the pantry from two different directions, would have called into question the official version of everything from Dealey Plaza on forward. And such a finding would have not only pointed the finger at the LAPD for a failed and dishonest investigation, it would have pointed the finger back at the FBI for its part in it. So the FBI report simply said that its examination of the Pruszynski tape could not confirm that the "impulse events" were even gunshots, much less give an accounting of them. It is a statement that is difficult to contradict and one which might be best thought of as the safest way out—a punt.

. . .

When William Pepper and Laurie Dusek took over the defense of Sirhan Sirhan, they inherited the ongoing petition for a writ of habeas corpus first filed by Sirhan's former attorney Larry Teeter. Teeter was searching for a way to overturn the Sirhan conviction and gain a new trial. His petition was based upon fourteen grounds, including that the prosecution suppressed evidence that more than one gun was fired in the hotel pantry and that Sirhan was denied his right to have an effective assistance of counsel. In 2002 Teeter's petition was followed by a second that added new grounds, including his assertion that one of Sirhan's investigators, Michael McCowan, was acting as a spy for the police, which McCowan to this day denies.

In various forms Teeter's and then Pepper and Dusek's petitions regarding the writ bounced around in the courts, being denied here on a technicality, only to pop up again on appeal or a move to another venue. Between 2010 and 2015 there were no fewer than thirty-four petitions, responses, corrected objections, sur-replies, orders, motions, rulings, and appeals. In a 2013 radio interview Pepper tried to put the mishmash into some perspective. "Courts generally don't look kindly on petitions such as ours," he said; "it's much easier for them to rule on technicalities or procedural issues than to deal with the actual facts of the case." Anticipating another defeat in state court, Pepper spoke about bringing the Sirhan petition before the U.S. Court of Appeals for the Ninth Circuit, "which has ruled that 'actual innocence' must take precedence over a procedural defect of the case."[19]

Pepper and Dusek next got their petition before U.S. district court judge Beverly Reid O'Connell. They argued for a new trial, or at least for an evidentiary hearing where Pepper could present the evidence in support of Sirhan's "actual innocence." The respondent was the State of California, which submitted a brief, signed by the state's Attorney General Kamala Harris, in support of the state's contention that Sirhan did not deserve an evidentiary hearing.

The ground being fought over greatly favored California—the bar is set very high when attempting to prove "actual innocence." The state did not have to disprove any of Pepper's assertions; it only had to cast doubt upon them. Thus in regard to Philip Van Praag's research that showed thirteen bullets fired in the pantry from two different guns, the state merely said that two other men had found only seven shots. It didn't matter that Van Praag's work was backed up by recorded scientific observations; doubt had been created, and doubt was something that did not go well with "actual innocence."

The physical evidence that would tend to confirm Van Praag's thirteen shots were the doorframes and the ceiling tiles and the purported bullet holes found in them. The secret burning of the doorframes and the ceiling tiles was an indefensible action and very likely a serious crime. That it happened with no notice just three weeks after the issue was raised in the *Los Angeles Free Press* carries with it the heavy presumption that the story told by the doorframes was one that the police didn't like. If there were no bullet holes, one would think that the LAPD would be happy to preserve the wood to challenge the notion that a second gun was firing.

The brief filed by the state could have left this alone and easily won the day. But the state of California, forty-five years after the fact, still felt the need to defend the police destruction of this important evidence. It sought to discredit the notion that there were any bullet holes in the frames. According to the brief, the witnesses and police officers who had seen them were mistaken, and the wire-service and FBI photos of those holes were mislabeled, and FBI agent William Bailey, who had stated that he had seen the bullet holes, could hardly be considered evidence withheld by the LAPD, because Bailey was not in the possession of the LAPD. This conveniently slid over the fact that while Bailey was not in the possession of the LAPD, the doorframes were. And they were withheld from the defense team of Sirhan, and they were destroyed without notice by the LAPD, and all the records of the tests supposedly done on those doorframes and ceiling tiles also vanished.

In the face of all that apparent malfeasance, the state of California chose to write history this way: "Officer Wolfer testified . . . that the door jamb was examined thoroughly (including the use of X-rays) that there were many holes in both sides of the door jamb, but that there were no bullet holes."[20] The reader may recall that in 1971, after the doorframes were destroyed but before anyone knew that they had been, Wolfer said that there were holes in the doorframes but none caused by bullets. "They were caused by some object poking the wood—a ramrod, a tray, a dish tray. . . . That could have certainly caused it."[21] This was Wolfer's "thorough" examination—holes maybe caused by dish trays, holes so closely resembling those caused by bullets that they fooled police investigators, FBI investigators, and Wolfer himself, who was photographed the night of the murder proudly pointing to them, before he had the doorframes taken down and brought to the police station and booked as evidence.

The great burden Pepper and Dusek had to bear was that even if one accepted Phil Van Praag's findings that a second gun was firing, that still wouldn't prove "actual innocence" on the part of Sirhan, who was there shooting as well. To find "actual innocence," one would have to believe that Sirhan's actions were involuntary. The work of Dr. Dan Brown went a good distance toward showing that to be the case, and Dr. Brown's work will probably be the closest anyone will ever get to unlocking the mystery in Sirhan's mind. But how do you prove that someone was hypnotized? What constitutes proof of that?

The reader may recall that at the shooting, writer George Plimpton had remarked on Sirhan's "enormously peaceful eyes." According to Plimpton, "In the middle of a hurricane of sound and feeling, he seemed peaceful." Patrolman Adair had rushed into the pantry and made a similar observation. "He had a blank, glassed-over look on his face—like he wasn't in complete control of his mind." Patrolman Placencia had thought the dazed man in his patrol car "was under the influence of something." Down at the police station deputy DA Howard had repeatedly asked the prisoner if he knew where he was. Later Sirhan made cheery small talk about children, *To Kill a Mockingbird,* and the teachings of Jesus, with no seeming idea of what has happened. And later still were the agonizing sessions of Sirhan under hypnosis with doctors Diamond and Pollack searching for a memory of the crime. These circumstances don't prove that Sirhan was hypnoprogrammed, but they do indicate that something highly unusual was going on. Nevertheless, in its brief asking Judge O'Connell to deny Sirhan a hearing on the evidence, the state of California found it perfectly appropriate to say of Sirhan, "He was highly alert, conscious, and not surprised at all about what he had done and about his predicament immediately after the shooting."[22]

On January 5, 2015, district court judge Beverly Reid O'Connell dismissed the petition for the writ of habeas corpus on the grounds that it was "untimely." Procedure and technicalities won again. Pepper and Dusek filed an appeal with the Court of Appeals for the Ninth Circuit.

At 9 A.M. on February 10, 2016, at the Donovan Correctional Facility in San Diego, Sirhan Sirhan's fifteenth parole hearing would be called to order by presiding commissioner Brian Roberts. Next to him was deputy commissioner Keith Stanton. Seated at a table across were Sirhan Sirhan, William Pepper and Laurie Dusek, Sirhan's attorneys, and Paul Schrade, a ninety-one-year-old victim of what would be called in this hearing "the life crime." Unlike the parole hearing in 2011, there were no television cameras in the room.[23]

The first hour or so was spent going over ground that had been gone over at all the other Sirhan hearings. There were reports that Sirhan had been a model prisoner, and other reports of incidents. There were reports from multiple prison psychologists that said that Sirhan was a low risk for violent behavior, and reports from other authorities that expressed reservations. And like other parole commissioners before them Roberts and

Stanton were eager to know if Sirhan had now come to have a memory of the murder, and if he hadn't, why he had admitted to the crime.

"I was told that I had shot him," answered Sirhan. "Grant Cooper, my attorney, told me that."

Bill Pepper tried to come to his defense. "Dr. Brown spent over 90 hours with him and did everything possible, both hypnotically and otherwise to bring out the recollections. And he found out he was not feigning. He simply literally could not remember those things."

When deputy commissioner Stanton took over the questioning, he reached back into the past and dug up a conversation that Sirhan supposedly had in Soledad prison in the 1970s. The conversation was with a Mr. Carmen Falzone, and in it Sirhan supposedly told Falzone that he remembered the crime perfectly and simply made up the "mind blank thing." Falzone, the reader may recall, was the jailhouse snitch who had claimed in a story sold to *Playboy* magazine that Sirhan tried to recruit him into a plot to steal fifty tactical nuclear weapons from a Strategic Air Command base and ship them to Muammar al-Qaddafi. Since his story supposedly showed what a serious threat Sirhan could be if he were ever released, Falzone was invited to speak at Sirhan's parole hearing in 1982. Falzone failed to show because he was suddenly wanted by the FBI for another crime. But as ridiculous as Falzone's story was shown to be, Carmen Falzone made an appearance at Sirhan's 2016 parole hearing by way of Commissioner Stanton's question as to whether Sirhan had ever told Falzone that he remembered the murder in detail. Sirhan calmly replied that he had never said such a thing to Carmen Falzone. Stanton then brought up the statement of Alvin Clark, the Pasadena trash collector who'd said at Sirhan's trial that Sirhan had bragged to him that he would murder Robert Kennedy. The reader may recall that later it came out that Clark said during his FBI interview that he was willing to say anything to get Sirhan convicted. Sirhan calmly replied that he hadn't said those words to Alvin Clark. Then Stanton brought up something that Sirhan actually *had* said. It was during his trial in a moment of extreme frustration, when Sirhan was trying to rid himself of his attorneys so they wouldn't embarrass him by calling two particular young ladies to the witness stand. Stanton spoke these words like they pretty much answered all the questions: "I killed Robert Kennedy willfully, premeditatively, with twenty years of malice aforethought."

Bill Pepper jumped in: "Twenty years? What?"

"That's the quote," said Stanton.

"And how old would he be at that time? Come on, four?"

"I'm just saying."

"Four years old?"

But however dubious the quotes that Stanton threw at Sirhan, the commissioner would show that he had done his homework, that he had actually read the affidavit prepared by Dr. Brown of Harvard on his ninety hours of mind-probing, hypnotic explorations with Sirhan. And once the issue was brought to the floor, Pepper was happy to explore it.

> STANTON: I believe . . . there is a theory at this point, I guess I would call it, that Mr. Sirhan was basically being used as a distraction and was hypnotized. . . .
>
> PEPPER: Yes.
>
> STANTON: And the girl actually played a part in this.
>
> PEPPER: Yes.
>
> STANTON: But when she tapped him on the shoulder that was the hypnotic cue for him to start to go . . . that's the theory at this point?
>
> PEPPER: Yes, that became Dan Brown's view. And to put it into a factual picture, when he talks about being choked he had—he had gotten off two shots. His arm was then pinned to the steam table and he was being choked. Bob Kennedy was hit in the rear at powder burn range. At the time he had gotten off two shots and couldn't—had no control over his gun.
>
> ROBERTS: But these facts are not supported by the—
>
> PEPPER: Oh, they are supported. . . . [H]is hand was pinned to the table and the bullets went all over the place while Bob was being hit with four bullets in the back at powder burn range.
>
> ROBERTS: Stop, stop, stop. I'm not interested in that whole—you're asking us to retry the case.

When it was his turn, deputy DA David Dahle stood, as he had three times before, and spoke about "the heinous nature of the crime," that somehow Sirhan's murder of Robert Kennedy was more overtly cruel and vicious than other murders for which a man of seventy-two might expect parole. Then the deputy DA gave the crime a facelift—something that people today might better understand. Sirhan's murder of Robert Kennedy was now, according to Dahle, "a terrorist act."

Bill Pepper followed Dahle and immediately protested what he termed "the worst rank kind of hearsay" thrown at Sirhan by both deputy commissioner Stanton and deputy DA Dahle. He then went for his main point. "You had three clinical opinions . . . and all of them have provided a picture of this man which is contrary to everything the State counsel [Dahle] would have you believe. Sirhan has a low potential for violence and a low potential danger to the community. This panel can assert its own judgment, substitute it for Dr. Carrera, Dr. Sani, and Dr. Brown, but I suggest that you seriously consider not doing that."

Pepper went on to say that he had been a friend of the Kennedy family

and had known Robert Kennedy and had worked for him in his successful Senate run in 1964. "I dare say Bob Kennedy would urge this panel to
grant this man, finally grant this man parole."

After Pepper, the parole board had one more person to hear. Paul Schrade
had not been in Sirhan's presence since he testified at Sirhan's trial, some
forty-seven years earlier. But he was at the hearing this day. According to
California law, any victim of a crime has a right to speak at a parole hearing. And unlike the attorney for the convicted defendant, a victim of the
crime is not restricted as to what they may talk about or how long they
may speak. And Paul Schrade intended to speak his mind.

"I'm from Los Angeles and I am 91," he began. "I was among six persons who were shot at the old Ambassador Hotel just after midnight. I
know that [Sirhan] did not kill Robert Kennedy. And I'm here because of
that. And I wouldn't be here if I wasn't sure of that. I loved Robert Kennedy and I would not defend somebody who killed him. Kennedy was a
man of justice. Justice so far has not been served in this case."

Schrade then turned and broke the rules by addressing Sirhan directly.
"Sirhan, I want to forgive you. You've been charged with shooting me,
Robert Kennedy, and four others. I don't believe the charges against you
for shooting Robert Kennedy are true. And I don't hold it against you,
because I don't think you knew what you were doing. . . . There is clear
evidence of a second gunman in that kitchen pantry who shot Robert
Kennedy. One of the bullets, the fatal bullet, struck Bob in the back of the
head. You were never in the position to do that. The evidence clearly shows
you were not the gunman who shot Robert Kennedy."

Turning back to the parole board, Schrade continued. "What I am saying is that Sirhan himself was a victim and still is a victim. . . . While Sirhan
was standing in front of Bob Kennedy and the shots were creating a dis-
traction, the other person, the other shooter, secretly fired at the Senator
from behind and fatally wounded him."

Schrade supported this assertion by referring to Philip Van Praag's declaration to the parole board in which he described what he found when he
investigated the Pruszinski tape. "Van Praag found a total of 13 shots," said
Schrade. "Sirhan's gun held no more than eight bullets." Schrade then
spoke of Van Praag's "double shots," shots that could not both have come
from Sirhan's revolver, and Van Praag's discovery that five of the thirteen
shots featured a unique audio-resonance characteristic. "Those five shots
were fired in an eastward direction into the back of Robert Kennedy, opposite to the westward direction in which Sirhan is known to have fired."

Paul Schrade spoke for nearly twenty minutes. As he brought things to a
close, he looked at the commissioners. "I hope you will consider all of the

accurate details of this crime that I have presented. . . . [I]f you do this in the right way and the just way, I believe you will come to the conclusion that Sirhan should be released. . . . I know and you should know that Sirhan did not shoot Robert Kennedy, did not kill him."

And then, as if to counter the Dahle allegation that Sirhan was now a terrorist, Schrade offered his own view. "The terrible truth is that he is a political prisoner."

The parole board took a recess of about an hour, and when they returned Commissioner Roberts informed all present that "Mr. Sirhan continues to pose an unreasonable risk of danger to society and is therefore not suitable for parole today."

After a consoling hand to the shoulder from his attorney, Sirhan stood and tried to shake hands with Paul Schrade, but he was blocked by two corrections officers. As Sirhan was turned and being led away, Schrade was overcome. "I'm sorry, Sirhan. It's my fault," he said, his voice cracking as it tried to follow Sirhan out of the room. "I should have come sooner. I didn't know. I'm sorry, Sirhan."

And thus it was that a friend of Robert Kennedy who had proudly looked on as Kennedy spoke at the Ambassador Hotel, a man who had been struck down by a bullet most surely fired by the man being led from the room, apologized to that man, forty-seven years after the fact, for taking so long to come to his aid, for taking so long to realize that he, too, was a victim of the crime. It was, by any measure, a remarkable moment.

Two months later Sirhan's petition before the Court of Appeals for the Ninth Circuit was denied.

Epilogue

✶ ✶ ✶

In the autumn of 1993, William Klaber visited Sirhan Sirhan in prison. The following is a brief portrait of Sirhan based on that visit.

AN HOUR NORTH of Bakersfield, amid endless acres of cotton, California State Prison at Corcoran rises from the dusty plains like a fortress from the future. Steel poles housing high-powered lights rise like spines of a sea urchin, and on the perimeter, cyclone fences topped with stainless-steel razor wire straddle a twenty-foot alleyway guarded by gun towers at regular intervals. This is where California keeps its high-profile security risks. Juan Corona and Charles Manson are here. So is Sirhan Bishara Sirhan.

Upon entering the prison one must surrender all possessions—wallet, keys, coins, belt—but once you are scanned and frisked, the walk to the visiting room is undramatic. There are no echoing footsteps, no reverberations from closing steel doors. The visiting room itself, with painted cement-block walls and asphalt tiles, resembles a nicely kept truck-stop cafeteria, complete with microwave for heating single-serving cans of what is normally thought of as children's lunch food. In one corner a thin man in blue prison fatigues lightly strokes the head of a heavy woman with a tired look on her face. In another, a Hispanic prisoner with tattoos on his biceps sits with his wife and three children.

Dressed in jeans, sneakers, and a blue work shirt, Sirhan Sirhan enters the room. An awkward smile betrays his initial discomfort. He greets his visitors, then embraces his brother Adel. Sirhan asks about the fires that have been raging in the hills near the family's home in Pasadena. Adel replies that there has been damage in nearby Altadena, but only drifting smoke in their neighborhood, except that the wind that preceded the fires brought down the large eucalyptus tree near the house.

"The whole thing?" asks Sirhan.

"No, about half. But it landed right on the fence in the side yard."

Sirhan shakes his head, but despite the sad nature of the story, news of a tree that he has not seen for twenty-five years seems to give him fresh energy.

Corcoran has been Sirhan's home since 1992. He says it is more pleasant than Soledad or San Quentin, where he had spent the majority of his years without freedom. To the uninitiated, however, the prison's galvanized perimeter would seem to fence a bleak emotional landscape.

"The worst part is the monotony," says Sirhan, trying to describe life at Corcoran. "A bell rings, you get up. Another rings, you eat. And every day is exactly the same."

While extended imprisonment can smother a man's soul, it can also, in a perverse way, be kind to his body. In some manner this may be true of Sirhan. Though he is nearly fifty, Sirhan has no age lines on his face. There are just the slightest traces of gray in his hair. If he were wearing it differently, were his hair standing up on his head, he would look remarkably like the Sirhan who was on the front page of every daily newspaper in the country the day after Robert Kennedy was shot.

But despite this resemblance to a known villain, it is difficult to escape the feeling that, as the most enigmatic man behind bars in America today, Sirhan Sirhan has been miscast. He is bright-eyed, considerate, well-spoken, and has the sly little smile of everybody's kid brother. His manners and conversation appear to lack calculation, and there is a charming boyishness about him, though he is intellectually inclined and conversant in world affairs. Yet dark mysteries, undiminished by the passage of time, still cling to this man, the most immediate being that he has been in jail for almost his entire adult life for a crime he says he has no memory of committing.

To visit Sirhan as a journalist is difficult. One needs the prisoner's cooperation, his family's cooperation, and the often complicated approval of the prison authorities, who are strict, perhaps obstructionist, when it comes to granting access to high-profile prisoners. Over the last twenty-five years, only a handful of people have been able to see Sirhan in this manner.

To gain access to Sirhan as a visitor, as we were doing, is less complicated.* Sirhan's cooperation and that of his family are still needed, but the prison requirements are merely generic. In addition, a visitor can spend the whole day with the prisoner, while a journalist is usually restricted to a one-hour interview.

A visitor, however, can bring nothing into the prison, including any kind of recording device. No video cameras, tape recorders, pens, pencils, or writing pads. Once inside, pencils, about two inches in length, are available, as well as scraps of paper. But the pencils, dull to begin with, quickly become unusable. Employing the lip of an opened soda can, Adel does his best to sharpen them as the conversations proceed.

A handsome man at age fifty-seven, Adel Sirhan is the third oldest of

---

*During this visit I was accompanied by Adel Sirhan, case researcher and family friend Rose Lynn Mangan, and journalist Dan Moldea.

the five Sirhan brothers. Living in the same house that the family owned when Robert Kennedy was murdered, Adel takes care of his mother, Mary, and manages what there is of Sirhan's affairs. In years gone by, Adel sang and played the oud at the Ali Baba and other Arabic nightclubs, and around his eyes are the crinkled vestiges of good times and late nights. These days, however, Adel works evenings in a bookstore, and there is little in the way of time or money to devote to pursuits beyond the necessary. He survives, he tells me, "with a faith in God and a sense of the absurd."

Over the next six hours there is, of course, mixed in with the serious talk, a great deal of casual conversation—sports, gossip, current events. The other opportunity for needed breaks is provided by the vending machines in the corner. Snack-food wrappers soon litter our table. Sirhan pays particular attention to a Mounds bar, eating it one small piece at a time. "It's a delicacy," he says in subtle mockery of his situation, explaining that inside at the commissary, which he can visit twice a month, there is available without variation only Snickers and PayDay.

On a normal day Sirhan is awakened at 5:30, and after breakfast he begins his duties cleaning in the prison, for which he is paid eighteen dollars a month. Sirhan's cell, which he occupies by himself, is about eight by ten feet in dimension, with floors, walls, and ceilings of unpainted cement, and a five-inch slit for a window. This cell is part of what is called a Protective Housing Unit, which Sirhan shares with just thirty-seven other inmates, who are presumed to require special security either because of the nature of the crimes they committed, or, more usually, because they have something to fear from other prisoners.

During our conversations Sirhan describes the staff at Corcoran as "professional," and their relationship with the inmates as "symbiotic." How many other prisoners in his block would make that observation is unclear, but Sirhan is the only prisoner in the unit to opt for a radio instead of a television in his cell. "TV is pretty boring," he says. "It's just the same stupid jokes and phony laughter." Sirhan mostly tunes his radio to KVPR, the National Public Radio affiliate out of Fresno. He enjoys listening to ethnic music and the evening news program *All Things Considered*. He regards the news of the Palestinian/Israeli peace accord as stunning. "Really, I never thought I'd live to see this," he says. It's his brightest and most animated comment of the day.

In his off-hours Sirhan likes to jog and lift weights. Though he stands five feet four and weighs one hundred and forty, he claims he can bench press three hundred pounds, though he is at first reluctant to tell me this for fear people will think he is a brute. Sirhan says he gets along "well enough" with the other prisoners, but he has no friends. Sirhan must keep his distance. Because of who he is, some prisoner is always willing to sell stories or make deals with authorities based on new information they say Sirhan has told them in confidence.

Even though the event is decades old, when the conversation turns to his trial, Sirhan's emotions begin to surface. "All this talk about killing my father and marrying my mother," he says, "—it was ridiculous. It was insulting. I protested."

During his trial Sirhan did frequently object to Grant Cooper's handling of his defense. In response, Sirhan claims that Cooper would remind him how much per hour his time was worth on the open market. "I had the best criminal lawyer in California," Sirhan says. "He knew all the tricks of the trade. Unfortunately, he used them all on me."

This view on Sirhan's part is perhaps a bit self-serving. As is documented, Grant Cooper and Sirhan Sirhan did not relate well to each other. Cooper openly admitted that he didn't understand Sirhan. Sirhan tried several times to have Cooper dismissed. But Sirhan could hardly be said to have offered Cooper constructive assistance. At the time of the trial, Sirhan's dissatisfactions had little to do with his attorney's failure to explore the physical facts of the case. Sirhan was as blind in this direction as Cooper. Nevertheless, as Sirhan sits in prison several decades later, his resentment, justified or not, is still apparent.

As we begin a reconstruction of his movements on the day of the assassination, Sirhan offers his own version of unkind fate. "If the horses had been running that night," he says, "I would have been down at the track." In place of playing the horses, Sirhan claims he went downtown to observe a parade celebrating the one-year anniversary of the Israeli victory in the Six-Day War.

"I'm not sure if I was just going to watch or heckle or what, but I wasn't going down there to shoot anybody, I know that."

But Sirhan had misread the advertisement, and the parade was to be held the following night, so, as the story goes, he found his way to the Ambassador Hotel, where several election-night parties were under way. While there he consumed four Tom Collinses, which, he says, "I drank like lemonade." The drinks made him sleepy, so Sirhan says he left the Ambassador and went to his two-tone DeSoto parked on New Hampshire Street. Sirhan has stated in the past that he must have picked up his gun during this visit to his car.

"Do you have a memory of actually getting your gun?" I ask.

"Well, no. I must have. Pollack [the prosecution psychiatrist] told me that."

"Do you remember being in your car?"

Sirhan scrunches his face, trying. "Well, I remember walking up a hill."

Sirhan says he was too drunk to drive home, so he returned to the

Ambassador, where he became intrigued by a teletype machine. "It didn't seem real, a typewriter, that was typing with nobody there."

After that Sirhan remembers having coffee with a pretty girl, bright lights, mirrors, and then . . . nothing . . . until he is being beaten and choked by an enraged mob.

"Do you have any vague recollections at all of the event?" I ask. "Anything, even dreamlike?"

"I'm sorry," Sirhan says. "I just don't have any mental images of shooting Robert Kennedy. Clearly, I was there. I just can't remember."

A major purpose of the prison interview was to come to some judgment as to Sirhan's sincerity. A tour of duty in the Bronx criminal courts had taught me never to confuse mild manners or good elocution with innocence.[1] I had reviewed the audiotapes of Sirhan's police interviews and the recorded conversations with his attorneys and psychiatrists. I had found nothing to indicate that Sirhan's lack of memory had been fabricated, but now I was looking for anything that might indicate deception. During our time together I found nothing false in Sirhan's words, mannerisms, or demeanor.

But the things Sirhan does recall are open to question. His recollections are a little like an old family story, remembered more from its retelling than from the actual event. In attempting to recall things that took place twenty-five years ago, Sirhan is covering ground that has been walked on so many times that no original footprints remain. Nevertheless, it is hard for me to resist the temptation to probe further.

"What about the girl?"

"She was very pretty," Sirhan says, "with brown hair."

"What was she wearing?"

"Forget about polka dots," he says, smiling, aware of the controversy, but unwilling to add to it. "I don't remember anything about what she was wearing."

When we begin to talk about his parole situation, Sirhan becomes agitated. His anger is apparent, yet he struggles to control himself. He knows that any ill-considered comment will be used against him in his next hearing and all those that follow.

Sirhan tells me the story of his first parole hearing at Corcoran in 1992. Moments before he was to be led into the hearing room he was approached by an escort officer, who told him he could go in only if he was wearing manacles and chains. Sirhan refused and was led away, his next parole hearing to be in two years. There is no doubt in Sirhan's mind that he did the right thing. "What board," he asks, "is going to believe that I'm ready for the outside if I'm brought in tied up like an animal?"

Sirhan has come to expect disappointment at his parole hearings. "I come before the board, I have done well in school, my record is good, but they say I need more psychological tests. Two years later I have the tests, the tests say I'm fine, but then the board wants me to go through an AA program. I haven't had a drink in twenty-five years, but I go through the AA program and I come back two years later, but now they say they want to see my job offers. Job offers? Just what's supposed to be on my résumé?"

Sirhan believes that he has not received impartial treatment from the parole board. "There are many people who have committed worse crimes, whom I have seen come and go," he says. "The whole thing has just become political." He pauses and then tags on a strange afterthought. "It's like we're still living under George the Third."

The discussion then returns to the assassination and the discovery of Sirhan's notebook, surely one of the most bizarre pieces of evidence ever introduced at a trial to prove the requisite state of mind for first-degree murder. What is Sirhan's explanation?

"I believe the notebook is mine," he says. "I just don't remember writing those things."

Does he have any memory of being angry at Robert Kennedy?

"I had a lot of affection for Bobby Kennedy," he answers, "but I felt ambivalent. I saw him as a caring, gentle person who stood up for the downtrodden, the blacks, the Latinos, but it hurt that he wouldn't stand up for everybody."

Of course, talk of motive by Sirhan must be viewed with great caution. If he is telling the truth that he has no memory of planning to shoot Robert Kennedy, then discussion of motive on his part must be after-the-fact rationalization. I point this out to him.

"I'm aware of that," Sirhan replies. "I'm just trying to explain what must have been propelling me forward. But, honestly, I don't know. Clearly, I was there, but still it's a mystery, because I really don't have it in me to kill anyone—drunk or not. That's what I don't understand."

A little while later he would say, "I must have known about the jets," referring to the Johnson/Eshkol agreement, but his words lack conviction.

In the space of twenty minutes Sirhan has just demonstrated the strange duality of mind that he has consistently maintained for twenty-five years. On the one hand, he doesn't remember planning to kill Robert Kennedy and can't imagine performing the act; on the other, he believes that he murdered Robert Kennedy because he was a threat to the Palestinians. Which is the real Sirhan?

For most people this has not been a difficult question. When I had posed it to Manuel Pena, the former police lieutenant who helped prepare the Sirhan case for trial, he didn't hesitate. "If they ever parole Sirhan," he said, "I'll make you a bet right now that within months he's gonna jump and he'll be over there with Abu Nidal and he will be a prize, prize terrorist. He'll be doing Allah's work, which is 'Kill more whities.'"

When I reminded Pena that Sirhan is a Christian, he replied, "Yeah, but it's still the same."[2]

Pena's view, sincerely held, is similar to that of many law enforcement officers and parole board members. It runs counter to the police investigation, which found no ties between Sirhan and any terrorist group. Sirhan barely had what could be described as a passive political life, much less an active or violent one.

In our conversations Sirhan is remarkably nonassertive. Although he knows I am a journalist, at no time does he ever argue or hint that he might be innocent. Though he is aware that such ideas have been advanced, Sirhan never promotes the notion that perhaps he had been manipulated by others. His recounting of events, the ones he can remember, seems straightforward.

Through the involvement of researcher Rose Lynn Mangan, Sirhan has become aware in recent years of some of the evidentiary conundrums in his case. But unlike other prisoners convicted of capital crimes, he is hardly an expert. At one point when we begin a discussion about the ballistic evidence, he stops the talk with a gesture. "You must understand," he says apologetically, "you know much more about this than I do. I don't spend my time thinking about these things. If I did, I would go crazy."

Although he seems grateful for the company, it is becoming apparent that, for Sirhan, having visitors is stressful. He is being forced to think about things that happened many years ago, things he doesn't normally think about, things he can't change.

"I wish I had just gone up and shook his hand," he says, speaking of Robert Kennedy. "If I could bring him back to life, of course, I would do it. If I could go back and trade my life for his, I would do that, too—he was the father of eleven children. But none of us have that power."

I ask Sirhan what he would like to do if he were released.

"Live a quiet life somewhere," he answers. "Help people if I could."

What kinds of things would he find enjoyable?

"I'd like to walk down a street," he says, "say hello to someone, go into a store, buy a quart of milk."

As we prepare to leave the prison, the pencils are returned, the candy wrappers gathered. Sirhan and Adel embrace once more. There is a weary look on Adel's face not apparent before. Sirhan, in contrast, seems more lively.

"So, am I the great devil you were expecting to meet?" he asks.

"All that and worse," I answer to his mirth. But the jest, as intended, avoids the question. What Sirhan is really seeking is a new verdict, and, in truth, it is hard to know what to think. Evidence suggests the presence of a second gun, but there are no accomplices in Sirhan's memory. Reliable witnesses saw Sirhan with a woman, but he says he was alone the night of the murder. Sirhan claims not to have planned to shoot Robert Kennedy, yet he offers a motive for doing so. At times it's as though his mind is a hall of mirrors in which every image is a reflection of another, making him a most awkward protagonist. Nothing in Sirhan's youth appears to lead to the most pivotal moment of his life. Nothing of significance happens to him after that moment. And the moment itself is invisible to him.

Sirhan's public persona is a blank sheet upon which investigators, prosecutors, psychiatrists, con artists, parole officers, assassination buffs, and journalists get to paint a picture. Communist, terrorist, political martyr, psycho killer, innocent dupe, robot assassin—Sirhan's tragedy is that he is exactly whomever we wish him to be: a stand-in for random societal violence, unpunished terrorism, or the dark forces suspected of murdering a generation of this nation's most charismatic leaders. He cannot be let go, because the political cost would be to appear to appease these evils or recognize their existence. Meanwhile, what's left of a human being approaches his fiftieth year in prison, retribution for an act of violence that has never been adequately explained.

Acknowledgments

✳ ✳ ✳

The authors owe a special debt to Jean Klaber and Judith Melanson for their patience, advice, and support throughout this five-year project. We gratefully acknowledge the numerous other persons whose assistance helped bring this endeavor to fruition.

The late congressman Allard K. Lowenstein, in the face of official recalcitrance, courageously pursued unanswered questions about the assassination until his tragic murder in 1980. His associate, the late Gregory Stone, dedicated his life to the continuance of Congressman Lowenstein's work, forming the link between the early researchers and the modern historians of the case.

The late Lillian Castellano was the driving force behind the Los Angeles–based Kennedy Assassination Truth Committee. Her tenacious efforts to bring light into the case record was a model of citizenship. Floyd Nelson, also a founder of the Truth Committee, continued Ms. Castellano's work after her death. His selfless contribution stretches over three decades.

Paul Schrade was a friend of Senator Robert Kennedy's. He was also seriously wounded during the assassination. His vigorous pursuit of the truth regarding Kennedy's death while constantly upholding the senator's living political legacy is a true profile in courage. Attorney Marilyn Barrett played a central role in converting Gregory Stone's research into the 1992 petition to the Los Angeles County Grand Jury.

With her selfless energy, Judith Farrar of the Robert F. Kennedy Assassination Archives at the University of Massachusetts has greatly assisted the research that has gone into this book. Bill Pepper and Laurie Dusek, Sirhan's attorneys, were also very generous with their time and thoughts.

Author and former Sirhan defense investigator Robert Blair Kaiser generously shared his recollections of the Sirhan trial. His brilliant 1971 book *"RFK Must Die!"* remains indispensable to any serious student of the case, and without his insights into the behavior and motivations of Sirhan Sirhan, any attempt to approach this central mystery would be incomplete.

Attorney Phyllis Cooper was kind enough to share her memories of her late husband, Grant Cooper. Through her grace and intelligence the authors gained a fuller understanding of the man who was the lead attorney for the Sirhan defense team.

Sirhan Sirhan granted two rare, extended interviews that greatly enhanced the authors' understanding of the protagonist of this legal drama. Adel Sirhan, brother of Sirhan Sirhan, and researcher Rose Lynn Mangan were instrumental in helping arrange these interviews. They were also most generous with their knowledge of the trial and the case.

Michael Caruso, then of *Vanity Fair,* had the courage to commission this story as a magazine article when others feared to do so. Terry Moran of Court TV had the vision to present material contained in this book during his coverage of Sirhan's previous parole hearing. Gretchen Young of HarperCollins was the first to believe that the story of Sirhan's trial should be a book. Our agent Stuart Krichevsky and editor George Witte of St. Martin's Press showed skill and determination in bringing this project to completion.

Our researchers Doria Alfiero, David DeSousa, and Laura Speanburg spent many hours pursuing the arcane.

The expertise, advice, and assistance of the following people also played an important role in bringing this book into being: Howard Bean, Malcolm Brown, Mike Clark, Dennis Cotton, Michael DeMelo, Terry Dumont, Judy Ferrar, Amity Gaige, Winifred Gallagher, Rick Hornung, Walter Keller, Helen Koss, Mara Lurie, Deborah McDonald, Brett Melanson, Jess Melanson, Betty Popovich, Lisa Porto, Tom Rumpf, Michael Segell, Tina Skerritt, Liz Tucker, Jennifer Walsh, and Eric Weisberg.

While not necessarily sharing the authors' viewpoints or objectives, the following people connected to the Robert Kennedy case were kind enough to share their experiences and insights: Al Albergate, LADA office; William Bailey, former FBI special agent; Andy Boehm, journalist; Sheldon Brown, LADA office; William R. Burnett, LADA office; Frank Burns, Ambassador Hotel witness; John Christian, journalist; William Cowden, L.A. Police Commission; David Cross, attorney, case researcher; Angelo DiPierro, Ambassador Hotel witness; Vincent DiPierro, Ambassador Hotel witness; Steve DuBoss, Ambassador Hotel witness; Scott Enyart, Ambassador Hotel witness; Edmund Fimbres, assistant city attorney, Los Angeles; Evan Freed, Ambassador Hotel witness; Brent Gold, Ambassador Hotel witness; Maria Gomez, Superior Court of Los Angeles; Alvin Greenwald, attorney for Scott Enyart; Brooker Griffin, Ambassador Hotel witness; Margaret Hahn, Ambassador Hotel witness; Christine Harwell, attorney for Scott Enyart; Frank Hendrix, president, Ace Guard Services; Robert Houghton, LAPD, former chief of detectives; Godfrey Isaac, attorney for Sirhan Sirhan; Brad Johnson, researcher; Dr. Robert Joling, forensic expert; Roger LaJeunesse, FBI liaison with LAPD; Betsy Langman, journalist and case researcher; James H. Lesar, attorney, FOIA (FBI) action; Luke McKissack, attorney for Sirhan Sirhan; David Mendelsohn, journalist; Skip Miller, attorney representing the city of Los Angeles; Judy Mitchell,

Ambassador Hotel witness; Dan E. Moldea, journalist; Paul Nellen, journalist; Shane O'Sullivan, journalist; Manuel Pena, LAPD, member of SUS; Robert Pinger, jury foreman, Enyart trial; George Plimpton, journalist, Ambassador Hotel witness; Lt. Robert Priola, California State Prison at Corcoran; Nina Rhodes, Ambassador Hotel witness; Amadee O. Richards, RFK case supervisor, FBI; Paul Sharaga, LAPD, Ambassador Hotel witness; Barbara Schlei, L.A. Police Commission; Dr. Martin Schorr, defense psychologist, Sirhan trial; Steven Sowders, LADA office; Dr. Herbert Spiegel, expert on hypnosis; Robert Talcott, L.A. Police Commission; Theodore Taylor, coauthor of *Special Unit Senator;* Lawrence Teeter, attorney for Sirhan Sirhan; Jack Thomas, journalist; William Turner, journalist; Karl Uecker, Ambassador Hotel witness; Lisa Urso, Ambassador Hotel witness; Phil Van Praag, audio engineer; Dr. Cyril Wecht, forensic expert; Robert Wiedrich, journalist; Nancy Zimmelman, at California State Archives.

Notes

* * *

All quotations from the trial of Sirhan Sirhan, including pre-trial court proceedings such as jury selection and plea bargain negotiations in chambers, are taken from the trial transcript itself, with minor editing for clarity and flow, and are not individually footnoted. Copies of the trial transcript may be found at the California State Archives in Sacramento, the Robert F. Kennedy Assassination Archives at the University of Massachusetts, North Dartmouth, MA, and the Assassination Archives and Research Center on the Mary Ferrell Foundation website. These sources are identified as CSA, RFKAA, and AACR in the notes below to indicate where a particular document or audiotape, not part of the court proceedings, may be found. For additional information one might visit Shane O'Sullivan's excellent website sirhanbsirhan.com and longtime investigator Lynn Mangan's website sirhansresearcher.com.

Chapter 1: The Embassy Room

1. John Doe (Sirhan) interrogation, June 5, 1968, LAPD no. 28918, audiotape K62, CSA.

2. Jesse Unruh, trial testimony, February 14, 1969, trial transcript, p. 3267.

3. Lisa Urso, interview with Philip H. Melanson, October 30, 1987, Phil Melanson collection, Box 5, document 11, RFKAA.

4. George Plimpton, I-1020, LAPD witness interview, June 5, 1968, audiotape K19, CSA.

5. Dan E. Moldea, *The Killing of Robert F. Kennedy* (New York: W. W. Norton, 1995), 47–48.

6. John Doe (Sirhan) interrogation, June 5, 1968, LAPD no. 28976, audiotape K63, CSA.

7. Vincent DiPierro, LAPD witness interview, June 5, 1968, audiotape K5, CSA.

8. John Doe (Sirhan) interrogation, June 5, 1968, LAPD no. 28917, audiotape K64, CSA.

9. This conversation was described by both Sergeant Brandt and Adel Sirhan in court proceedings of October 22, 1968, and again by Adel Sirhan in conversation with author William Klaber in October of 1993.

10. "Transcipt of Johnson Speech Naming Panel on U.S. Violence," *New York Times,* June 6, 1968.

11. "Reagan, Scoring Courts, Links Shooting to Permissive Attitude," *New York Times,* June 6, 1968, p. 29.

12. Ibid.

13. Tom Buckley, "Yorty Defends Disclosure from Suspect's Notes," *New York Times,* June 7, 1968, p. 26.

14. Robert Blair Kaiser, *"RFK Must Die!"* (New York: Dutton, 1970), 97.

15. Buckley, "Yorty Defends Disclosure . . . ," p. 26.

16. James Reston, "World Morality Crisis; Kennedy New Victim of Lawlessness Threatening Modern Public Order," *New York Times,* June 6, 1968, p. 20.

17. John Kenneth Galbraith, "Tufts University: Violence Commission Criticized," *New York Times,* June 10, 1968, p. 52.

18. Jack Gould, "TV: Truman Capote Defines His Concept of Justice," *New York Times,* June 15, 1968, p. 71.

19. "Yevtushenko: 'You Shoot at Yourself, America,'" *New York Times,* June 8, 1968, p. 15.

Chapter 2: Summer of '68

1. Dial Torgerson, "Sirhan Hires New Defense Attorney," *Los Angeles Times,* June 20, 1968, p. 28.

2. Ibid.

3. Robert Kaiser, interview with William Klaber, 1993, audiotape 49, Klaber collection, RFKAA.

4. Summary of the Los Angeles Police Department Investigation of the Senator Robert F. Kennedy Assassination (*Summary Report*), 1968, p. 1422, CSA.

5. Russell Parsons, interview by Betsy Langman, Los Angeles, 1974, audiotape, RFKAA.

6. John W. Finney, "Defeat for Doves Reflects Deep Division in the Party," *New York Times,* August 29, 1968, p. 1.

7. Lacey Fosburgh, "Sirhan Trial Judge," *New York Times,* April 12, 1969, p. 16.

8. "Sirhan Prosecutor Urges Easing of News Restrictions," Associated Press, October 25, 1968, p. 38.

9. David N. Fitts, Deputy District Attorney, "Meeting with Grant Cooper," Memorandum, File No. 100-272, LADA files, document 7, Klaber collection, RFKAA.

10. Kaiser, *"RFK Must Die!",* 327.

Chapter 3: The Friars Club

1. Gene Blake and Howard Hertel, "U.S. Probes Alleged Transcript Bribe in Friars Club Trial," *Los Angeles Times,* December 3, 1968, p. 3.

2. Gene Blake and Howard Hertel, "Cooper Ordered to Answer Friars Transcript Quiz," *Los Angeles Times,* January 8, 1969, p. 1.

3. Gene Blake, "Five Found Guilty in Friars Club Card Cheating Conspiracy," *Los Angeles Times,* December 3, 1968, p. 1.

4. Gene Blake and Howard Hertel, "4 in Friars Club Case Get 4-to-6-Year Terms," *Los Angeles Times,* February 4, 1969, pt. 2, p. 1.

5. Ovid Demaris, *The Last Mafioso* (New York: Bantam, 1981), 252–58.

6. Gene Blake and Howard Hertel, "Cooper Ordered to Court Today Over Friars Transcript," *Los Angeles Times,* January 7, 1969, p. 3.

7. Robert Blair Kaiser, "Conversations in Jail with Sirhan," *Life,* January 17, 1969, pp. 21–25.

8. Dave Smith, "Sirhan Jury Selected," *Los Angeles Times,* January 25, 1969, pt. 2, p. 1.

9. Ibid.

10. William Tuohy, "New Palestine Liberation Chief Vows to Escalate 'Revolution,'" *Los Angeles Times,* February 5, 1969, pt. 1, p. 1.

11. Carl Greenberg, "Reagan Calls Campus Violence Part of Plot to Destroy Nation," *Los Angeles Times,* February 8, 1969, pt. 1, p. 1.

12. John Douglas, "Sirhan Trial Moves Into Crucial New Phase," *Los Angeles Herald Examiner,* February 5, 1969, p. 39.

Chapter 4: The Secret Deal

1. Dr. Orville Richardson and Dr. Eric Marcus had been been appointed by the court. Dr. Martin Schorr and Dr. Bernard Diamond had been retained by the defense. Dr. Seymour Pollack had been retained by the prosecution.

2. Kaiser, *"RFK Must Die!"* 370–72.

3. Seymour Pollack, M.D., *Memorandum to Mr. Lynn Compton, Chief Trial Deputy District Attorney,* February 5, 1969, Series III, LADA collection, RFKAA.

4. Bob Greene, *Newsday*, February 12, 1969.

5. Kaiser, *"RFK Must Die!"*, 309.

6. Ibid., 319.

7. Ibid., 379.

8. Ibid., 380.

9. Ibid., 381.

10. Ibid.

11. Grant Cooper, in taped interview with journalist Betsy Langman, Los Angeles, 1973, audiotape, RFKAA.

Chapter 5: Doorframes and Dish Trays

1. Al Stump, "Daily Drama Unfolds in the Sirhan Trial," *Los Angeles Herald Examiner,* February 16, 1969, p. A7.

2. As recalled to Rose Lynn Mangan by Grant Cooper in 1969; further supported by written report of police telephone interview of Grant Cooper by Lt. Booth on June 8, 1971, in which Cooper summarized to Booth this conversation with Harper.

3. DeWayne Wolfer, in deposition for defamation lawsuit filed by Wolfer against Los Angeles attorney Barbara Blehr, September 1971, RFKAA.

4. Dr. Thomas T. Noguchi, in written statement given to Vincent Bugliosi, Los Angeles, December 1, 1975, Floyd Nelso collection, RFKAA.

5. Robert Rozzi, in written statement given to Vincent Bugliosi, Los Angeles, November 15, 1975, Floyd Nelson collection, RFKAA.

6. Moldea, *The Killing of Robert F. Kennedy,* 240.

7. Statement of John Shirley, given to Lillian Castellano of the Kennedy Assassination Truth Committee, Match 1969, Box 71, item 762, Marilyn Barrett collection, RFKAA.

8. Statement of Dale I. Poore, given to Dinko J. Bozanich of LADA's office, December 16, 1975, item 1, p. 15, LADA files, Klaber collection, RFKAA.

9. Robert Wiedrich, "Felt Him Fire His Gun, Hotel Worker Says," *Chicago Tribune,* June 6, 1968.

10. William Bailey, interview with William Klaber, 1993, audiotape 1, Klaber collection, RFKAA.

11. Moldea, *The Killing of Robert F. Kennedy,* pp. 230–41.

12. Dion Morrow, "Officer Ordered Items Destroyed," *Santa Monica Evening Outlook,* August 21, 1975.

13. Evelle Younger, legal brief in response to Paul Schrade lawsuit before Judge Wenke, Superior Court (December 1975), RFKAA

14. *Summary Report of the Los Angeles Police Department Investigation of the Assassination of Robert F. Kennedy*, Final Report, February 1969, Vol. II, Chap. III, p. 152, CSA.

15. Moldea, *The Killing of Robert F. Kennedy,* 86n.

16. *Summary Report,* Vol. II, Chap. III, p. 152, CSA.

17. Confrontation between Paul Schrade and Chief Daryl Gates at police commission hearing, as related to the authors by Paul Schrade in 1993.

18. Moldea, *The Killing of Robert F. Kennedy,* 245.

19. Ibid., 259–60.

20. Wolfer, Blehr deposition, 1971.

21. Karl Uecker, interviewed by John Burns, California state archivist, taped in Sacramento, April 13, 1990, tape F3901:850, CSA.

22. Report of Joseph Busch, District Attorney of Los Angeles County, June 28, 1971, p. 70, RFKAA.

Chapter 6: The Criminalist

1. Thomas T. Noguchi with Joseph DiMona, *Coroner* (New York: Simon & Schuster, 1983), 104.

2. Written statement of Karl Uecker, given to Allard K. Lowenstein in Dusseldorf, Germany, February 20, 1975, RFKAA.

3. Ralph Blumenfeld, "New Questions: The Death of RFK," *New York Post Magazine,* May 23, 1975.

4. Affidavit of William Harper (1970), Robert F. Kennedy Assassination Archives, Philip Melanson research papers, box 6, No. 12, RFKAA.

5. Martin Patrusky, in affidavit given to Vincent T. Bugliosi, Los Angeles, December 12, 1975.

6. Sir Gerald Burrard, *The Identification of Firearms and Forensic Ballistics* (New York: A. S. Barnes, 1962), 154–55.

7. Lowell Bradford, 1974, cited in *The Report of Thomas F. Kranz on the Assassination of Senator Robert F. Kennedy (Kranz Report),* p. 44, RFKAA.

8. Barbara Blehr, Letter to Los Angeles Civil Service Commission, May 28, 1971, cited in *Report of Joseph Busch,* June 28, 1971, p. 2, RFKAA.

9. DeWayne Wolfer, *Report of Joseph Busch,* June 28, 1971, appendix E, RFKAA.

10. Dave Smith, "Sirhan Case—Was There a 2nd Gunman?" *Los Angeles Times,* August 16, 1971, pt. 1, p. 1.

11. Moldea, *The Killing of Robert F. Kennedy,* p. 137n.

12. *California v. Sirhan, Testimony of DeWayne Wolfer,* September 16, 1975, Superior Court of California, Robert A. Wenke Judge, Godfrey Isaac for Paul Schrade, pp. 121–24, RFKAA.

13. Dinko J. Bozanich, deputy district attorney, *Memorandum to Joseph P. Busch, District Attorney,* July 30, 1974, p. 23, RFKAA.

14. *California v. Sirhan, Testimony of DeWayne Wolfer,* Howard Privett for CBS, pp. 109–12, RFKAA.

15. Ibid., p. 11.

16. Ibid., p. 21.

17. Ibid., p. 39.

18. Charach and Harper have always maintained that they never tampered with Sirhan exhibits.

19. Bozanich, *Memorandum,* p. 4.

20. Gregory Stone, "RFK Manuscript" (unpublished, 1983), chap. 5, "Firearms, Wolfer and the Forensic Panel," p. 39, RFKAA.

21. Ibid.

22. Gene Blake, "Criminalist Gave False Testimony, Court Decides," *Los Angeles Times,* December 5, 1975, pp. 3, 25.

23. *Kranz Report,* March 1977, p. 63, RFKAA.

24. Ibid.

25. Ibid.

26. Myrna Oliver, "LAPD Suspends Forensic Chemist," *Los Angeles Times,* May 31, 1980, pp. 1, 29.

Chapter 7: Missing Persons

1. Theodore Charach, *The Second Gun,* film documentary, 1971.

2. Don Schulman, *On Air Radio Interview with Jeff Brent of Continental News Service,* June 5, 1968, tape No. 38, RFKAA.

3. Dave Smith, "Sirhan Case—Was There a 2nd Gunman?" *Los Angeles Times,* August 16, 1971, pt. 1, p. 1.

4. Ibid.

5. Charach, *Second Gun.*

6. Don Schulman, *Interview at DA's Office,* 1971, tape No. 32, RFKAA.

7. Lt. F. J. Patchett, to Commander G. M. Beck, Intra-Department Correspondence, August 5, 1971, p. 3, RFKAA.

8. Don Schulman, *Interview with Bill Burnett and special counsel Thomas Kranz,* 1976, tape No. 40, RFKAA.

9. Albert LeBeau, I-228, FBI Interview, June 7, 1968, Series II, Witness Interviews, RFKAA.

10. William Schneid, FBI Interview, June 1968, Series II, Witness Interviews, RFKAA.

11. Albert LeBeau, I-228, LAPD Interview, June 26, 1968, AARC.

12. Special Unit Senator, *Summary Report,* February 1969, Albert LeBeau LAPD Interview, I-228, June 26, 1968, RFKAA.

13. Laverne Botting, FBI LAFO 56-156, Sub File X-4, Vol. 15, p. 930, AARC.

14. Laverne Botting, SUS, Microfilm Vol. 84, SUS Final Report, p. 1288, AARC.

15. Ethel Creehan, SUS, Microfilm Vol. 51, I-70–I-134, p. 46, AARC.

16. Ethel Creehan, SUS, Microfilm Vol. 77, SUS Final Report, p. 916, AARC.

17. Nina Rhodes, I-845, FBI LAFO, Vol. 4, sec. 2, p. 3051, RFKAA.

18. Statement of Nina Rhodes, given to Phil Melanson, 1992, RFKAA.

19. Statement of Evan Freed, given to Phil Melanson, 1992, RFKAA.

20. Evan Freed, I-174, LAPD interview, June 14, 1968, audiotape K-16, CSA.

21. Evan Freed, FBI interview, September 11, 1968, Series II, Witness Interviews, RFKAA.

22. Dr. Marcus McBroom, interview with Gregory Stone, March 9, 1986, audiotape and transcript as exhibit 60 in Request to the Los Angles County Grand Jury, RFKAA.

23. George Green, I-613, FBI LAFO, Vol. 4, sec. 1, July 15, 1968, pp. 259–61, CSA.

24. Jack Merritt, I-258, FBI LAFO, Vol. 4, sec. 2, p. 334, CSA.

25. Richard Houston, I-3837, LAPD interview with Officer Sartuche, September 22, 1968, CSA.

26. Darnell Johnson, I-54, FBI LAFO, Vol. 1, sec. 2, June 6, 1968, pp. 407–409, CSA.

27. Booker Griffin, I-76, LAPD interview, July 25, 1968, audiotape K11, CSA.

28. Fernando Faura, *The Polka Dot File* (Trine Day Pub., 2016), pp. 160–61.

29. Kaiser, *"RFK Must Die!"*, p. 129.

30. Jeanette Prudhomme, I-16, LAPD interview with Officer J. Ryan, August 8, 1968, CSA.

31. John Fahey, I-622, LAPD interview, June 14, 1968, audiotape K32, CSA.

32. John Fahey, interview with F. Faura, June 12, 1968, audiotape confiscated by police on June 14, 1968, reappeared in 1988 as K50, CSA.

33. Faura, *The Polka Dot File,* pp. 118–19.

34. John Fahey, polygraph session with Lt. Enrique Hernandez, September 13, 1968, audiotape K165, CSA.

35. Jerry Cohen, "23-Man Task Force Selected to Probe Kennedy Murder," *Los Angeles Times,* June 14, 1968, p. 8.

36. Robert Houghton and Theodore Taylor, *Special Unit Senator* (New York: Random House, 1970), 302.

37. Lacey Fosburgh, "Rumors Dispelled in Trial of Sirhan," *New York Times,* February 28, 1969, p. 14.

38. Grant Cooper, *Declaration to the Los Angeles Superior Court,* May 22, 1969, a copy of which is Exhibit VI in *Writ of Habeas Corpus on Behalf of Sirhan Sirhan, Trial Case no. 233421,* May 6, 1993, filed by Adel Sirhan and Rose Lynn Mangan, RFKAA.

Chapter 8: The Spotted Ghost

1. Discrepancy between court testimony and grand jury testimony brought to the attention of authors by Rose Lynn Mangan.

2. LAPD, Emergency APB, June 5, 1968, SUS Files, Microfilm, Vol. 32 (Broadcasts and Teletypes), p. 126, CSA.

3. Police Calls, June 5, 1968, audiotape K24, CSA.

4. Paul Sharaga, interview with William Klaber, 1993, audiotape 91, Klaber Collection, RFKAA.

5. Paul Sharaga, interview with SUS (disputed), September 26, 1968, document in SUS files at CSA and also copied and submitted with the *Request to the Grand Jury* submitted April 2, 1992, RFKAA.

6. Paul Sharaga, Affidavit alleging that interview of September 26, 1968, never took place, sworn July 14, 1988, included in *Request to the Grand Jury*, RFKAA.

7. Sharaga, interview with William Klaber, RFKAA.

8. John J. Ambrose, *Memorandum to Allan McCurdy, Chief, Branch Area Offices Division*, June 7, 1968, LADA files, RFKAA.

9. Sandra Serrano, LAPD Interview, June 10, 1968, audiotape K4, CSA.

10. Ibid.

11. David T. Lykken, "Science, Lies and Controversy: An Epitaph for the Lie Detector," address to Convention of the America Psychological Association, 1991, Wikipedia.

12. Houghton and Taylor, *Special Unit Senator*, 120.

13. Philip H. Melanson, *The Robert F. Kennedy Assassination* (New York: Shapolsky Publishers, 1991), p. 248.

14. Sandra Serrano, polygraph session with Sgt. Enrique Hernandez, June 20, 1968, audiotape K3, CSA.

15. Jerry Cohen, "Police Halt Hunt for Mystery Girl," *Los Angeles Times*, June 22, 1968, p. 1.

16. Houghton and Taylor, *Special Unit Senator*, 126.

17. Manuel Pena, interview with William Klaber, 1993, audiotapes 18 and 19, Klaber collection, RFKAA.

18. Ibid.

19. Vincent DiPierro, polygraph session with E. Hernandez, July 1, 1968, audiotape K12, CSA.

20. Kaiser, *"RFK Must Die!"*, 255.

21. William Turner and Jonn Christian, *The Assassination of Robert Kennedy* (New York: Thunder's Mouth Press, 1993), 82–83.

22. Sandra Serrano, interview with NPR radio host Jack Thomas, April 22, 1988.

Chapter 9: Malice Aforethought

1. "Notes on Kennedy in Suspect's Home," *New York Times*, June 6, 1969, p. 1.

2. Luke McKissack to Carol Hemingway, broadcast KPFK, Los Angeles, April 22, 1988.

3. Robert Kennedy at Temple Isaiah, May 20, 1968, *Los Angeles Times*, May 21, 1968.

4. Seymour Pollack, interview with Sirhan Sirhan, January 19, 1969, audiotape 125, RFKAA.

5. Kaiser, *"RFK Must Die!"*, 126.

6. Ibid., 188.

7. Ibid., 421.

8. Ibid., 275–76.

9. Ibid., 277.

10. Ibid., 280.

11. Ibid., 288.

12. Ibid., 248–54.

13. Ibid., 324–27.

14. Pollack and Diamond, January 19, 1969, audiotape 128, RFKAA.

15. Seymour Pollack, interview with Sirhan, January 1969, *The RFK Tapes* audio documentary, by William Klaber, 1993, RFKAA.

16. Kaiser, *"RFK Must Die!"*, 257.

17. Ibid., 320.

18. Ibid., 425.

19. Ibid., 422.

20. Dave Smith, "Sirhan Trial Opens," *Los Angeles Times*, January 8, 1969, p. 22.

21. Terrence Smith, "Father of Suspect Sickened by News," *New York Times*, June 6, 1968, p. 1.

22. Kaiser, *"RFK Must Die!"*, 345.

23. Ibid., 230.

24. Ibid., 466.

Chapter 10: Sirhan Bishara Sirhan

1. Kaiser, *"RFK Must Die!"*, 406.

2. Ibid., 562.

3. Ibid., 415–16.

4. Al Stump, "Sirhan Memory 'Failing,'" *Los Angeles Herald Examiner,* March 7, 1969.

5. Kaiser, *"RFK Must Die!"*, 421.

Chapter 11: Rorschach and Freud

1. Kaiser, *"RFK Must Die!"*, 444.

2. James A. Brussell, *Casebook of a Crime Psychiatrist* (New York: Bernard Geis Associates, 1968).

3. John Siegenthaler, *A Search for Justice* (Nashville, TN: Aurora Publishers, 1971), 369.

4. Bob Greene, *Newsday,* March 19, 1969.

Chapter 12: Hypnotic Dreams

1. Kaiser, *"RFK Must Die!"*, 89.

2. Drs. Pollack and Diamond, interview with Sirhan under hypnosis, February 1, 1969, audiotape 226, RFKAA.

3. Ibid.

4. Kaiser, *"RFK Must Die!"*, 536.

5. Bernard Diamond, "The Simulation of Sanity," *Journal of Social Therapy* 2, (1956): 158–65.

6. "Friends Describe Sirhan," *Los Angeles Herald Examiner,* June 5, 1968.

Chapter 13: Betrayal

1. Martin Waldron, "Lawyer Testifies He Made Up Story," *New York Times,* February 26, 1969, p. 16.

2. Martin Waldron, "Ray Admits Guilt," *New York Times,* March 11, 1969, p. 9.

3. "Judge Preston Battle Dies," *New York Times,* April 1, 1969, p. 47.

4. "Ray Changes His Mind," *Newsweek,* March 31, 1969, p. 29.

5. John Herbers, "US Will Continue Its Inquiry on Ray," *New York Times,* March 11, 1969, p. 1.

6. "Ray: 99 Years—and a Victory," *Newsweek,* March 24, 1969, p. 32.

7. Kaiser, *"RFK Must Die!"*, 415.

8. Dave Smith, *Los Angeles Times,* April 2, 1969.

9. Ibid.

10. Douglas Robinson, "Sirhan Jury Told Test Scores Err," *New York Times,* April 8, 1969, p. 7.

11. Dave Smith, "Psychiatrist's Testimony Sends Sirhan into Rage," *Los Angeles Times,* April 9, 1969, pt. 2, p. 1.

12. "Test Case," *Newsweek,* April 7, 1969, p. 94.

13. "Psychiatry on Trial," *National Review,* May 6, 1969, p. 427.

14. Dr. Eduard Simson, interview by Betsy Langman, 1973, audiotape 94, Klaber collection, RFKAA.

15. Affidavit of Dr. Eduard Simson, 1974, Phil Melanson collection, RFKAA.

Chapter 14: Life or Death

1. Kaiser, *"RFK Must Die!"*, 480.

2. Douglas Robinson, "Sirhan Called a 'Little Sick Boy,'" *New York Times,* April 11, 1969, p. 26.

3. Kaiser, *"RFK Must Die!"*, 486.

4. Martin Kasindorf, "Verdict on Sirhan," *Newsweek,* April 28, 1969, p. 41.

5. Douglas Robinson, "Sirhan Jury Asks for Clarification," *New York Times,* April 17, 1969, p. 21.

6. Kaiser, *"RFK Must Die!"*, 496.

7. Kaiser, *"RFK Must Die!"*, 502.

8. Martin Kasindorf, "The Jury vs. Sirhan," *Newsweek,* May 5, 1969, p. 35.

9. Kaiser, *"RFK Must Die!"*, 509.

10. Douglas Robinson, "Sentenced to Die," *New York Times,* April 24, 1969, p. 1.

11. Ibid., p. 29.

12. Tom Wicker, "In the Nation: Sam Yorty and Sirhan B. Sirhan," *New York Times,* June 3, 1969, p. 46.

13. William F. Buckley, "Reflections on the Sirhan Trial," *National Review,* March 11, 1969, 247.

14. "Egyptian Paper Describes Sirhan Case as Political," *New York Times,* April 21, 1969, p. 17.

15. "The Sirhan Verdict," *New York Times,* April 18, 1969, p. 42.

Chapter 15: The Hidden Files

1. John E. Howard, Memorandum to Joseph P. Busch, Assistant District Attorney, RE: *Special Unit Senator* by Robert Houghton, September 12, 1969, LADA files, document 5, Klaber collection, RFKAA.

2. Allard K. Lowenstein, "Suppressed Evidence of More Than One Assassin?", *Saturday Review,* February 19, 1977, p. 6.

3. Ibid., 9.

4. John M. Crewdson, "Lowenstein Says Year's Study of Evidence Shows Sirhan Was Not Assassin of Kennedy," *New York Times,* December 16, 1974, p. 29.

5. Ibid.

6. "Confidential Addenda to the Lowenstein Inquiry," submitted to Assistant Chief Daryl F. Gates, Decmber 20, 1974, exhibit 9, *Request to the LA County Grand Jury,* RFKAA.

7. William Farr, "Some Material on Kennedy Destroyed," *Los Angeles Times,* August 22, 1975, p. 3.

8. Ibid.

9. Ibid.

10. Allard Lowenstein, letter to Samuel L. Williams, August 27, 1975, exhibit 8, *Request to the LA County Grand Jury,* RFKAA.

11. Lowenstein, "Suppressed Evidence," p. 11.

12. Declaration of Dr. Philip H. Melanson, re: Houghton affidavit, p. 4, December 30, 1991, exhibit 19, *Request to the LA County Grand Jury,* RFKAA.

13. Melanson, *The Robert F. Kennedy Assassination,* 90.

14. *The Report of Thomas F. Kranz on the Assassination of Senator Robert F. Kennedy,* March 15, 1977, p. 1, RFKAA.

15. Ibid., 2.

16. Ibid., 65.

17. Gregory Stone and Allard Lowenstein, "List of Corrections to Kranz Report," July 17, 1977, RFKAA.

18. Thomas Kranz, "Memo to DA Investigator Bill Burnett," undated, LADA files, document 25A, Klaber collection, RFKAA.

19. William Burnett, interview with William Bailey, 1977, audiotape 192, RFKAA.

20. Lowenstein, "Suppressed Evidence," 12.

21. Gregory Stone, personal communication to Philip Melanson, 1985.

22. University of Massachusetts RFK Assassination Archives, "Request for Release of Files," to the Los Angeles Police Commission, 1984, Series V, private investigations, RFKAA.

23. David Freed, "Police Told to Disclose Summary of RFK Case," *Los Angeles Times,* July 31, 1985, p. 2.

24. Exchange with Commissioner Samuel Williams at police commission hearing in February 1985 described by Philip Melanson in conversation with William Klaber in 1992.

25. David Freed, "Police Told to Disclose Summary of RFK Case," p. 3.

26. Daryl Gates, *Chief: My Life in the LAPD* (New York: Bantam, 1992), 152.

27. Webster Letters, Philip Melanson collection, Series II, Box 4, No. 4, RFKAA.

28. *Stone and Melanson v. Federal Bureau of Investigation,* No. 90-5065, D.C. Cir., RFKAA.

29. *Stone and Melanson v. FBI.*

30. John Burns, "List of Items Missing," *Request to the LA County Grand Jury,* exhibit 27, RFKAA.

31. *World News Tonight with Peter Jennings,* ABC, April 19, 1988.

32. Robert A. Houghton, remarks broadcast on KTTV, June 6, 1988.

33. Lance Williams, "Prober Insists Purged RFK Evidence Useless," *San Francisco Examiner,* April 1988.

34. Russell Snyder, "RFK Files Raise New Questions on Police Probe," UPI, April 25, 1988.

35. *Request to the LA County Grand Jury,* 1992, RFKAA.

36. Andrea Ford, "Investigation Urged in LAPD's Handling of Kennedy Slaying," *Los Angeles Times,* April 3, 1992, B3.

37. John A. Grande, Foreperson, Letter to Marilyn Barrett, Marilyn Barrett collection, Box 31, Grand Jury—Letters re: Grand Jury Submission, RFKAA.

38. Paul Schrade, Interview with William Klaber, 1993.

39. Marilyn Barrett collection, Box 31, Grand Jury—Letters re: Grand Jury Submission, RFKAA.

40. Ibid.

41. Ibid.

42. Ibid.

43. Ibid.

44. Marilyn Barrett, Interview with William Klaber, 1994.

45. Bill Boyarsky, "Grand Jury," *Los Angeles Times,* May 12, 1994, p. 13.

46. Ibid.

47. Richard Mankiewicz, Interview with Philip Melanson, May 1994.

Chapter 16: *Prison and Parole*

1. Unsigned memo to DA Joseph Busch, June 3, 1971, LADA files, document 6, Klaber collection, RFKAA.

2. Richard Hecht, Memorandum to DA Joseph Busch, July 28, 1971, LADA files, document 1, Klaber collection, RFKAA.

3. Unsigned, undated diagram found in the files of the Los Angeles County District Attorney, LADA files, document 25A, Klaber collection, RFKAA.

4. Gene Blake, "California to Seek Rehearing of Court's Death Penalty Ban," *Los Angeles Times,* February 19, 1972, pt. 1, p. 1.

5. "The Death Penalty Overruled," editorial, *Los Angeles Times,* February 21, 1972, pt. 2, p. 1.

6. Gene Blake, "High Court Gets Younger Petition on Death Penalty," *Los Angeles Times,* March 4, 1972, pt. 2, p. 1.

7. "Sirhan Case Rejected," *Los Angeles Times,* December 17, 1974, pt. 2, p. 4.

8. Robert Kistler, "High Court Rejects Sirhan Plea," *Los Angeles Times,* February 14, 1975, pt. 1, p. 30.

9. Ibid.

10. William Endicott, "Panel Went by Book on Sirhan Parole," *Los Angeles Times,* May 22, 1975, pt. 1, p. 32.

11. Ibid.

12. Paul Conrad cartoon, *Los Angeles Times,* May 22, 1975, pt. 2, p. 7.

13. Jesse Unruh, "Unruh Calls Sirhan a Traitor," *Los Angeles Times,* June 6, 1975, pt. 2, p. 7.

14. Tom Wheeler, letter to editor, *Los Angeles Times,* June 17, 1975, pt. 2, p. 6.

15. Daniel Estrada, Interview with Kranz and Placencia, undated audiotape, box 8, tape 209, Marilyn Barrett collection, RFKAA.

16. Carmen Falzone, Interview with William Burnett, August 11, 1977, audiotape 224, RFKAA.

17. Ibid.

18. James McKinley, "Inside Sirhan," *Playboy,* April 1978, pp. 96–98, 206–14.

19. Bill Farr, "Sirhan Threat to Kill Ted Kennedy Told," *Los Angeles Times,* August 13, 1981, pt. 1, p. 1.

20. Ibid., p. 28.

21. "New Testimony Disputes DA's View of Sirhan," *Los Angeles Times,* November 25, 1981, pt. 1, p. 14.

22. Raul Rodriguez, letter to editor, *Los Angeles Times,* June 8, 1981, pt. 2, p. 8.

23. Kathy McNelis, letter to editor, *Los Angeles Times,* June 8, 1981, pt. 2, p. 8.

24. Bill Farr, "FBI Hunts Witness in Sirhan Case," *Los Angeles Times,* April 16, 1982, pt. 2, p. 1.

25. Bill Farr, "Killer Tells of Sirhan Threat on Ted Kennedy," *Los Angeles Times,* April 27, 1982, pt. 1, p. 23.

26. Bill Farr, "Witness: Hidden Razor Blades Found," *Los Angeles Times,* May 3, 1982, pt. 1, p. 3.

27. Bill Farr, "Testimony on Sirhan Threats Challenged," *Los Angeles Times,* April 28, 1982, pt. 1, p. 3.

28. Ibid.

29. Sirhan Sirhan, letter from prison to Grant Cooper, 1972, box 5, file 6, Sirhan, RFKAA.

30. Bill Farr, "Sirhan Plea for Parole Invokes Kennedy Name," *Los Angeles Times,* May 11, 1982, pt. 1, p. 17.

31. Ibid.

32. Bill Farr, "Sirhan's 1984 Parole Date Revoked; Threats Cited," *Los Angeles Times,* May 22, 1982, pt. 1, p. 1.

33. Ibid., p. 28.

34. Bill Farr, "Psychiatric Test Shows Sirhan as a Model Inmate," *Los Angeles Times,* June 26, 1985, pt. 2, p. 1.

35. John Kendall, "Sirhan Attorney Assails Parole Unit," *Los Angeles Times,* August 21, 1985, pt. 1, p. 3.

36. Ibid., p. 28.

37. Ibid., p. 3.

38. Ibid., p. 28.

39. Elka Warner, "Judge Frees Men Imprisoned 17 Years," UPI, March 25, 1992.

40. Sheryl Stolberg, "Council Seeks Probe in Case of Wrongly Convicted Men," *Los Angeles Times*, April 1, 1992.

Chapter 17: The Phantom Photographs

1. All quotes from the Scott Enyart lawsuit are taken from the trial *Jamie Scott Enyart v. March Fong Eu,* no. C734190, Superior Court of the State of California. A complete set of the audiotapes of the trial can be found in the Klaber collection at the RFKAA.

2. Jamie Scott Enyart, letter to Chief Daryl Gates, May 26, 1988, Scott Enyart file, Klaber collection, RFKAA.

3. Daryl F. Gates, Chief of Police, letter to Scott Enyart, July 1, 1988, Scott Enyart file, Klaber collection, RFKAA.

4. Laren Metzer on behalf of John F. Burns, Chief of Archives, letter to Scott Enyart, October 11, 1988, Scott Enyart file, Klaber collection, RFKAA.

5. Evidence Report, "Burning of S.U.S. Photographs," August 21, 1968, exhibit 14, Request to the Grand Jury, RFKAA.

6. Captain Hugh Brown, "Memorandum to Chief Robert Houghton on Procedures to Preserve Photographs," August 20, 1968, exhibit 13, *Request to the Grand Jury,* RFKAA.

7. *Jamie Scott Enyart v. March Fong Eu,* no. C734190, Superior Court of the State of California.

8. Bill Boyarsky, "The Spin," *Los Angeles Times,* July 9, 1996, p. B1.

9. Emi Endo and Eric Malnic, "Kennedy Photo Mystery Deepens," *Los Angeles Times,* January 18, 1996, p. B1.

10. Ibid.

11. Bill Epperidge and Hays Gorey, *Robert Kennedy: The Last Campaign* (New York: Harcourt, 1968).

12. Theodore Charach, *The Second Gun,* 1971.

13. Scott Enyart, Interview with William Klaber, audiotape 24, Klaber collection, RFKAA.

14. Scott Enyart, Police Interview, June 5, 1968, audiotape K19, CSA.

15. Ibid.

16. LAPD SUS Files, microfilm, Vol. 7, card index, AARC.

17. LAPD SUS files, microfilm, Vol. 52, interview, AARC.

18. Scott Enyart, Interview with William Klaber, audiotape 24, Klaber collection, RFKAA.

19. Theodore Charach, *The Second Gun.*

20. "Had No Choice," *Los Angeles Times,* May 22, 1975, p. 32.

21. Ralph Blumenfeld, "The Death of RFK," *New York Post,* May 23, 1975.

22. David Bloom and Janet Gilmore, "Photographer Awarded $450,600," *Daily News,* August 23, 1996, p. 14.

23. Ibid.

Chapter 18: *"Trailing Edge Waveforms"*

1. Declaration of Philip Van Praag, November 14, 2011, Exhibit C, affidavit in support of Petition for Writ of Habeas Corpus, case 05686 CAS, filed by Sirhan attorney William Pepper, 6a; document can be found on website sirhanbsirhan.com.

2. Discovery Times Channel, *Conspiracy Test: The RFK Assassination,* 2007, available on YouTube.

3. Ibid.

4. Report of Philip Harrison, 2007, provided to the author by Philip Van Praag, William Klaber collection, RFKAA.

5. Ibid.

6. Ibid.

7. Philip Van Praag, "Acoustic Analysis of Gunshot Recordings Utilizing Frequency Selective Integrated Loudness Envelope Evaluation," presentation to the American Academy of Forensic Sciences, February 21, 2008. According to Van Praag, the content and wording of his speech was, in most places, a virtual match to the wording in his "Declaration" given to attorney William Pepper in 2011. Since a copy of the speech could not be located, I have used here the words from the "Declaration."

8. Ibid.

9. Dr. William F. Pepper, *The Plot to Kill King* (New York: Skyhorse Publishing, 2016), xxix.

10. Interview with Daniel Brown, Ph.D., in his office in Newton, MA, November 2017.

11. Ibid.

12. Ibid.

13. Ibid.

14. Life Term Parole Consideration of Sirhan Sirhan, CDC No. B-21014, Pleasant Valley State Prison, March 2, 2011. Quotes from this proceeding are taken from the parole hearing transcript, which can be found on the website of the Mary Ferrell Foundation.

15. FBI Memorandum, "RFK Tape Review," October 25, 2012, Van Praag file, Klaber collection, RFKAA.

16. Robert F. Kennedy, Jr., "Letter to Eric Holder, Attorney General of the United States," September 25, 2012, "The Full Story of Sirhan Parole Hearing," Shane O'Sullivan, whowhatwhy.org.

17. FBI Memorandum, "Report of Examination," May 13, 2013, Van Praag file, Klaber collection, RFKAA.

18. Shane O'Sullivan, "The Full Story of Sirhan Parole Hearing," February 16, 2016, whowhatwhy.org.

19. William Pepper, *Let Them Talk,* with Paul DeRienzo, October 21, 2013, YouTube.

20. Respondent's Supplemental Brief Regarding Actual Innocence, CV-00-5686-CAS-AJW, September 26, 2011, p. 29, from the website of the Mary Ferrell Foundation.

21. Wolfer, Blehr deposition, 1971.

22. Respondent's Supplemental Brief Regarding Actual Innocence, CV-00-5686-CAS-AJW, February 1, 2012, p. 15, from the website of the Mary Ferrell Foundation.

23. Life Term Parole Consideration of Sirhan Sirhan, CDC No. B-21014, R.J. Donovan Correctional Facility, February 10, 2016. Quotes from this proceeding are taken from the parole hearing transcript, from the website of the Mary Ferrell Foundation.

Epilogue

1. In 1969 author William Klaber worked on a sentencing project for the Vera Institute of Justice in the criminal courts of Bronx County, New York.

2. Manuel Pena, Interview with William Klaber, 1992, audiotape 19, Klaber collection, RFKAA.

Index

✳ ✳ ✳